W9-CNU-436

Prayerbook Reform in Europe

Prayerbook Reform in Europe

The Liturgy of European Liberal and Reform Judaism

by JAKOB J. PETUCHOWSKI

Foreword by SOLOMON B. FREEHOF

The World Union for
Progressive Judaism, Ltd. New York

838 FIFTH AVENUE, NEW YORK, N.Y. 10021 U.S.A.

Library of Congress Catalog Card Number: 68-8262

This volume has been published with the assistance of the Cultural Fund of the Conference on Jewish Material Claims Against Germany, Inc. *It is the third of a series of books planned for publication by the* World Union For Progressive Judaism, Ltd. *with the cooperation of the* Claims Conference *and the* Union of American Hebrew Congregations.

PRODUCED IN THE UNITED STATES OF AMERICA

To my sons,

Samuel Judah,
Aaron Mark,
Jonathan Mayer.

Appreciation

It is my privilege and *z'chut* to express the gratitude and appreciation of the World Union for Progressive Judaism to Rabbi Dr. Jakob Petuchowski for his scholarly research and splended compilation of the history of liturgical reforms in the European part of our movement. Ours is the inordinate satisfaction of knowing that this work was undertaken under our aegis, with the enthusiastic and attentive cooperation of our Executive Director, Rabbi William A. Rosenthall, and with the generous support of the Conference on Jewish Material Claims Against Germany. The World Union is happy and proud that it has been able to participate in this program of distinguished publications. It is good to know that we are partners, though admittedly quite junior, in the mitzvah of Torah—the study of our prayers.

But *lo lanu,* not unto us, rather to Professor Petuchowski must go the praise and the thanks. Not only has he perceptively realized the inherent meaning of the *SIDDUR* and given logical order and arrangement to the changes in the liturgy, but he has truly made of it an *Avodat ha-lev*—a service of the heart, ripe in scholarship and warm and loving in consecration. His systematic and scrupulous study of the changes in the past suggest the possibilities of new and creative worship forms, with relevant and poetic texts, for our generation and for future generations of Jewish worshippers. It is my privilege to acknowledge our warm thanks and deep indebtedness to him.

RABBI DR. JACOB K. SHANKMAN
President
World Union for Progressive Judaism

Contents

Introduction

REFORM JUDAISM made its first appearance on the stage of Jewish history as a movement for liturgical reform; and, ever since, Reform Judaism's changing theological emphases and nuances have been reflected by successive editions of the prayerbook. A history of Liberal and Reform liturgy, therefore, particularly as it unfolded on its native European soil, is the history of a not unimportant aspect of Jewish religious liberalism. It is, in a way, surprising that such a history has not been written heretofore. The standard histories of Reform Judaism, by Philipson and by Seligmann, do indeed make frequent references to liturgical developments. The two volumes of source material marking the rise and the growth of Reform Judaism, by W. Gunther Plaut, likewise contain relevant selections; while the histories of Jewish Liturgy, by Elbogen and by Idelsohn, each devote one chapter to the liturgy of Reform Judaism.[1] But, as far as we are aware, never before has the attempt been made to give an exhaustive treatment of this important manifestation of Liberal and Reform Judaism. As far as we know, the prayerbooks of European Liberal and Reform Judaism have never even been catalogued completely. Yet in as multicolored and multifaceted a phenomenon as is represented by Liberal and Reform Judaism every single prayerbook, indeed, every new edition of a single prayerbook, had its own contribution to make, and its own story to tell. To assemble all of that material, for purposes of analysis, has been one of the tasks we have set for ourselves.

Alas, the ravages of time and of catastrophic recent history have been such that it was no longer possible to consult all the prayerbooks which have ever been published by Liberal and Reform Judaism in Europe. Still, the 171 items which we have been able to list in our "Chronological Bibliography," after a search of some five years, undoubtedly represent the majority of Liberal and Reform prayerbooks which were published in Europe. They shed light on the various tendencies which went into the making of Progressive Judaism, on the different stages of the movement's evolution, and on the local conditions and circumstances within which that evolution took place.

But, in compiling this volume, we wanted to do more than just write the liturgical history of European Liberal and Reform Judaism. We also wanted to place into the reader's hands a source book of Liberal and Reform liturgical material. Liberal and Reform congregations now exist in all parts of the world. Some of them have yet to produce their own prayerbooks. Others are thinking of revising the prayerbooks which are currently in use. If Progressive Judaism is to remain faithful to its own inner dynamics, there will never be an end to the process of prayerbook revision. Such a revision will always take into account the needs of time and place, even as it will endeavor to utilize whatever is of abiding value in Judaism's long liturgical tradition. But revisions of the prayerbook could also be greatly aided by the availability of the results of a process of liturgical revision which has now been going on for a century and a half. Some of the past innovations are now deemed by a more mature judgment to have been mistakes, which need not be repeated. Other, more felicitous, innovations of European Liberal and Reform Judaism may well deserve rediscovery, adoption, and adaptation in the future. It is for this reason that we have quoted many passages at length—particularly in Hebrew. Too often the early Reformers receive less than the credit which is their due. We remember them as fighters for the right to introduce prayers in the vernacular. But they have also been liturgically creative in Hebrew; and their efforts in that direction should be preserved for posterity.

Nothing short of reprinting all the prayerbooks we have consulted (and all of them may never be assembled again) would have yielded the kind of "source book" we would have liked to present. But limitations of space compelled us to be selective. We have confined ourselves to major rubrics of the services for Sabbath and weekdays, and to the Seven Benedictions of the Festival Service. While we have listed the High Holy Day prayerbooks in our "Chronological Bibliography," we did not—with two exceptions—deal with the High Holy Days in this volume. Yet the attentive reader, learning from this volume the principles of revision which were operative in the daily and Sabbath liturgy of a given rite, will have no difficulty surmising how the same principles must have been applied to the liturgy of the High Holy Days.

The two exceptions we have made refer to the Memorial Service and to the new versions of the *Kol Nidré* formula. The former, at first confined in several rites to the Day of Atonement, represents one of the original contributions of Liberal and Reform Judaism to the totality of the Synagogue, including many Modern Orthodox rituals. The latter were included here for practical reasons. The finding of appropriate words to fit the cherished (and indispensable) tune of *Kol Nidré* is a problem which has by no means been universally solved in our congregations. Having the new versions of *Kol Nidré,* produced by European Liberal and Reform Judaism, conveniently assembled may, hopefully, be of some value to the present and future liturgists of Reform Judaism—quite apart from the innate interest which those versions have for the historian of the liturgy.

If, throughout this volume, we use the rather cumbersome terminology, "Liberal and Reform Judaism," this is due to the different names by which the various constituents of Progressive Judaism were, and are, known—names, moreover, which have different connotations in different parts of the world, and which also tend to change in meaning as time goes on. Thus, in the Germany of the eighteen-forties, the first strivings for a moderate reform of the liturgy, within an essentially traditional framework, were considered as manifestations of "Reform." However, in twentieth-century Germany, that kind of "Reform" was known as "Liberal Judaism," while it was only the extremely "radical" *Reformgemeinde* of Berlin, far to the left of "Liberal Judaism," which called itself "Reform." In England, on the other hand, "Reform" is the appellation of those congregations which, in spite of some major modifications, have basically remained faithful to the traditional pattern of Jewish worship, while the far more radical variety of Progressive Judaism in England is known as "Liberal Judaism." To add to the confusion, it must be stated that the latter was greatly influenced by American "Reform Judaism," bearing in mind that, in America, the labels are reversed again. Yet, in Switzerland, in France, and in Holland, "Liberal Judaism" has, liturgically, more affinity with German than with English "Liberal Judaism," while, some sixty years ago, French "Liberal Judaism" was probably closer to German and American "Reform Judaism" than to German "Liberal Judaism."

To avoid further confusion, we have found it best to retain each country's self-chosen designation, and to speak, in the aggregate, of "Liberal and Reform Judaism." Moreover, we have included in our consideration the liturgies of congregations which did not claim, in any technical sense, to be either "Liberal" or "Reform." This applies, for example, to the liturgy of the official synagogues of Sweden, which has been revised in accordance with the principles laid down by the German Rabbinical Conferences, and which, in successive editions, has rather closely followed the pattern of German "Liberal" prayerbooks. We have included such liturgies because they met the criteria which distinguish Liberal and Reform prayerbooks from those of the Orthodox rite.

What those criteria are may best be seen from a pamphlet issued in 1850, by the Israelite Supreme Council of Mecklenburg-Schwerin, and signed, among others, by David Einhorn, who was then chief rabbi of Mecklenburg-Schwerin. Entitled, *The Points of Difference Regarding Public Worship Between the Various Religious Parties,*[2] the pamphlet lists the following "points of difference":

> (1) Does Judaism permit, or even compel, its adherents to pray before the divine Throne of Judgment for vengeance, and for the destruction of enemies and heretics?
>
> (2) In the case of prayers which presuppose conditions which

have long since passed, must (or may) we recite them, or not?
(3) Must the Pentateuch be read through within one year, or can it be read in a triennial cycle?
(4) Does the prayer for the restoration of animal sacrifices, so often repeated in the traditional liturgy, have a binding religious character for us, or not?
(5) Are the prayers for a Return to Palestine to be retained or not?
(6) Must the Israelite pray in Hebrew, a language which he frequently does not understand, or may he pray in the intelligible mother tongue?

In each instance, "so-called Orthodoxy" is presented as affirming the first option, while the advocates of Reform are seen to opt for the second.

This 1850 list of criteria clearly shows a combination of practical innovations (e.g., the triennial cycle of Torah readings, prayer in the vernacular) and dogmatic considerations (e.g., omission of prayers for a Return to Palestine and the restoration of the sacrificial cult). For our part, we have decided to include in our treatment any prayerbook published in Europe which would meet two or more of the above criteria.

In addition to the writing of a history and the compilation of a source book, we have had yet a third aim in mind: the editing of a *Sepher Ha-Zikkaron,* a Book of Remembrance, commemorating the liturgical achievements of European Judaism. It was in the flourishing centers of German Jewish life that the liturgy of Liberal and Reform Judaism had its beginnings and its earliest developments. But, while there is today some Progressive Jewish activity in Germany, the major Jewish centers there have been destroyed—together with their Jews. It is only fitting that, in addition to the other German Jewish achievements which we mournfully and proudly remember, we also preserve the memory of German Judaism's liturgical productivity. In our volume, we also deal with the prayerbooks edited in England, France, Holland, Sweden, and Switzerland. Yet by far the greatest number of prayerbooks we describe here had their origin in German Judaism, while even many of the others, directly or indirectly, owe much to their German predecessors.

Some may see in the very multiplicity of German Liberal and Reform prayerbooks the sign of an unfortunate lack of religious unity. We feel, however, that the plethora of prayerbooks should rather be regarded as an eloquent testimony to the liturgical creativity of German Jewry, and to the seriousness with which German Jews approached their liturgical problems. Only the indifferent do not care. Men of conviction will argue even about minutiae. German Liberal and Reform Jews cared. Their struggles and their achievements merit remembrance. They also merit something else. The history of German Liberal and Reform Judaism has often been misunderstood and misrepresented. That history may suggest one kind of evaluation when measured by standards applicable to a different environment. But it may suggest quite a different evaluation when seen in the light of its own background. It has been our endeavor throughout this volume not only to let the sources speak for themselves, but also to provide such contemporary background material as will enable the reader to measure the progress which has been made with due regard to time and to place. May the memory of the pioneers of Liberal and Reform Judaism in Germany bring blessing to the labors of their successors in other lands and in new times!

With the exception of the items designated in the "Acknowledgments," the English translations in this volume are all our own. Where English passages are quoted, the original spelling and punctuation have been retained.

While examining the prayerbooks and the polemical literature to which they gave rise, we noticed, from time to time, that some of the prayerbooks were printed by the Berlin Press and Publishing House of H. Itzkowski. We also noted that H. Itzkowski, with blessed impartiality, likewise printed some of the Orthodox attacks upon the new prayerbooks. Ties of kinship bind us to that famous Berlin printer; and our interest and curiosity were aroused. Of course, it is easier for a printer and publisher to preserve his impartiality and objectivity than it is for an author. Nevertheless, we have endeavored to preserve some of that Itzkowski impartiality within the present volume. We have relegated our personal bias and predilections to the "Epilogue," while trying as much as possible, in the rest of the book, to confine ourselves to an objective presentation of the facts. The reader will have to judge to what degree we have succeeded in this.

J.J.P.

Foreword

THE REFORM movement was the first modernist movement in Jewish life. It came into being only a century and a half ago, but the era which inspired it seems now to be so far back in the past that it appears as outgrown as the medieval times. Reform was the child of the Enlightenment. Its doctrines were simple, clear and confident. It believed that all racial and religious prejudices were due to ignorance, that knowledge would disperse old hatreds, that slavery and oppression were on the way out, that human comradeship was inevitable, with liberty and friendship for all.

There is no need to stress the painful fact that that roseate mood has vanished. History has made mock of the old hopes and psychology has thrown doubt on our absolute faith in reason. We live today in another world of experience and mood.

It is remarkable, therefore, that the Reform movement which was the child of the Enlightenment and was so confident of the power of knowledge and brotherhood and freedom should have managed to outlive the death of its world hopes and continued to endure and, in fact, to flourish. The institutions which it founded, synagogues, union of synagogues, rabbinical seminaries, organizations of rabbis still exist and are growing stronger from year to year. Evidently there is more to the movement than its articulate platform. Like a courageous individual, a movement may outlive the wreck of its hopes and find new strength to live. What, then, are the true elements of strength in the Reform movement which nerved it to outlive its era and to continue to grow? We need new studies in depth of the Reform movement. There have been all too few histories of Reform. The pioneer work was David Philipson's *Reform Movement in Judaism,* Bernfeld's *Toldot Ha-Reformazion hadadit,* then Caesar Seligmann's *Geschichte der Reformbewegung,* and just two years ago the fine history of Reform by Gunther Plaut, *The Rise of Reform Judaism.* But more histories are needed, particularly specialized histories which, confining themselves to a limited part of the field, are able to dig deeper into the soil.

This is the unique value of Petuchowski's work hereby presented on the history of liturgical reform in the European Reform movement. The choice of the changes in prayerbook and worship as the first of the specialized studies is a wise one. Other fields might have been selected, such as the social organization of Reform, its attempts to have synods of laymen and rabbis to legalize the changes adopted. One might discuss the relationship of Reform to the Halacha, the inherited legal system, or its relationship to the modern science of Jewish studies initiated by Leopold Zunz when he was a young Reformer in Berlin, and similar studies. But the liturgy is properly the first theme for special study. The Reform movement began with laymen and their concern was the synagogue and its worship, because of the meaninglessness of the prayerbook, totally in Hebrew and in Aramaic, to the average non-scholarly worshiper, the change in musical taste which made the old cantorial trills less attractive and so forth. These early Reformers believed that if the service could be made more modern and more attractive, more people would come to synagogue worship. Therefore the first great efforts at Reform were the revision of the prayerbook and the reorganization of the synagogue procedure.

From the desire to make the service more attractive which involved the shortening of the service, it was an easy second step to come to the decision as to *which* prayers could well be left out and which must certainly be retained. Thus their sense of the aesthetic soon became involved with questions of belief and changing convictions and thus unconsciously the efforts of Reform deepened in the direction of Jewish theology. Therefore a study of the changes in the prayerbook was actually a study of the changes in mood and mind of the Jews in western Europe. Therefore Dr. Petuchowski moves from the question of what was changed to *why* certain prayers were changed and helps us understand the scale of values of the founders of the movement.

A necessarily limited term of reference has created some difficulty for the author. Dr. Petuchowski deals with the liturgical development of European Reform. This limitation is imposed upon him by the fact that the Conference on Jewish Material Claims Against Germany devotes its grants to those studies which perpetuate the life of European Jewries. The author therefore has to omit a discussion of the various liturgical developments in the United States where Reform Judaism has come to its largest growth. It is not that by restricting himself to Europe the author means to imply that the vast Reform movement in America, with its seven hundred congregations, is of no importance in the history of the development of Reform, but rather that important as it is, it falls beyond the limits of the field mapped out for him. However, by judicious references and comparisons he relates the original pioneering of liturgical reforms in Europe to those developed in the United States of America.

This progressive study in depth is seen in every chapter, but particularly in the chapter which discusses the dispute over the recitation of the blessing before the Hallel Psalms, "Praised be Thou Who hast commanded us to read the Hallel." The dispute particularly was concerned with the Hallel to be recited on Chanukah. The author explained that the basis of the dispute was the fact that Chanukah was post-Biblical and therefore it was difficult to say that God commanded this blessing. I might suggest an additional explanation: They objected to a blessing which declared that *any* text in the liturgy was to be recited because God commanded it; for if they granted in any case that the text of the liturgy is a Divine mandate, then they had no right to change the prayerbook at all, which was exactly what Moses Sofer the great Orthodox authority of Hungary declared. They had to take the point of view that the prayerbook was a human construct and therefore was susceptible to change when human tastes changed.

Be that as it may, the book is of special merit. It is a pioneer of special study of a crucial segment in the development of Reform. It is complete in its field, understanding and enlightening, and is an important chapter in the story of this first modernist movement in Judaism which though it lived to see the tragic failure of the roseate visions of the age in which it was formed, managed to find new strength and thus endure through changes and continue to flourish.

RABBI DR. SOLOMON B. FREEHOF
Hon. Life President, World Union for Progressive Judaism

Acknowledgments

This book could not have been written without the help of those many, in all parts of the world, who volunteered their assistance in response to the author's personal request, and as a result of appeals published by the World Union for Progressive Judaism, and in the New York weekly, *Aufbau*. Sincere thanks are herewith expressed to the following, for important information, and for the gift or loan of prayerbooks:

Mr. Georg Altmann (*Ramat-Gan, Israel*), Mrs. Helene Anker (*Los Angeles, Cal.*), Dr. Abraham Berger (*The New York Public Library*), Mrs. Lilli Dellheim (*Baltimore, Md.*), Dr. Dora Edinger (*Evanston, Ill.*), Mr. Richard A. Ehrlich (*Allston, Mass.*), Mr. John W. Friedmann (*Mercer Island, Washington*), Dr. Eric Friedland (*Brookline, Mass.*), Mrs. Carol Grunewald (*Ventnor, N.J.*), The Hebrew Union College Library (*Cincinnati, Ohio*), Professor Klaus Herrmann (*Montreal, Que.*), Mrs. Fred W. Hoexter (*Youngstown, Ohio*), Rabbi Wolli Kaelter (*Long Beach, Cal.*), Dr. Alfred Karger (*Quito, Ecuador*), Mrs. Ferdinand Kaufmann (*New Rochelle, N.Y.*), Mrs. Hugo Klein (*Union, N.J.*), Mrs. Rosemary Kremnitzer (*Jackson Heights, N.Y.*), Mrs. Kate Lehman (*Los Angeles, Cal.*), The Leo Baeck College (*London, England*), The Leo Baeck Institute (*New York, N.Y.*), Rabbi Dr. N. P. Levinson (*Karlsruhe, Germany*), The Liberal Jewish Synagogue (*London, England*), Mr. Eric Mandell (*Philadelphia, Pa.*), Mrs. Klara Mannheimer (*Stockton, Cal.*), Rabbi Dr. Kurt L. Metzger (*Bradford, Pa.*), Mr. Theodore Pfaelzer (*Pine Beach, N.J.*), Rabbi Dr. A. Phillip (*Jerusalem, Israel*), Mrs. Claire Pollak (*Providence, R.I.*), Mr. Ludwig Ries (*Forest Hills, N.Y.*), Mrs. Vicky Rosden (*New York, N.Y.*), Rabbi Dr. Frank F. Rosenthal (*Olympia Fields, Ill.*), Mrs. Selma S. Rosenthal (*New York, N.Y.*), Mrs. Herbert Sax (*St. Louis, Mo.*), Mr. Max Schnell (*Portland, Oregon*), Mr. Rudy Stahl (*Richmond, Va.*), the late Professor Nathan Stein (*Hempstead, N.Y.*), Mrs. Emma Steiner (*New York, N.Y.*), and The West London Synagogue of British Jews (*London, England*).

Very special help was rendered the author by Rabbi Dr. Leo Baerwald (*New York, N.Y.*), Rabbi Jakob J. Kokotek (*London, England*), Miss Peggy Lang (*London, England*), Rabbi John D. Rayner (*London, England*), Rabbi Dr. Lothar Rothschild (*St. Gallen, Switzerland*), Rabbi Dr. J. Soetendorp (*Amsterdam, Netherlands*), the late Chief Rabbi Dr. Kurt Wilhelm, of blessed memory (*Stock-*

holm, Sweden), and Rabbi André Zaoui (*Paris, France*). To them, the author's indebtedness is profound.

Grateful acknowledgment is also expressed to the Liberal Jewish Synagogue of London, and to the West London Synagogue of British Jews, for permission to quote at length from their prayerbooks, and to the Board of Editors of the *Hebrew Union College Annual* for the permission to reprint here the chapter, "Reform Benedictions for Rabbinic Ordinances," which, in a slightly different form, had first appeared in *HUCA,* Vol. XXXVII (1966).

I am also grateful for the detailed research undertaken, under my direction, by some of my former students: Rabbi Stephen A. Arnold (*Ideas of Immortality in American Reform Ritual,* 1961); Rabbi Edward M. Maline (*Controversies over the Hamburg Temple Prayer Book,* 1963); Dr. Max Selinger (*Samuel Holdheim, Theologian of Early Reform Judaism,* 1962); Dr. Sefton D. Temkin (*The Liturgy of the West London Synagogue of British Jews,* 1963); Dr. Joseph S. Weizenbaum (*An Analysis of Nogah Tsedek,* 1962). Their dissertations are available at the Hebrew Union College Library, in Cincinnati.

My old friend, Lillian Godman (*of San Bernardino, Cal.*), and the Rev. George Liebenow (*of Cincinnati, Ohio*) have rendered me great assistance by providing translations from the Swedish sources which I have used. My student, Mr. Leslie Gutterman, has assisted me in the compilation of the index. I am thankful for their great help.

Above all, however, I must express my gratitude to my dear and devoted helpmeet, Elizabeth R. Petuchowski, for her assistance and advice in many of the finer points relating to the translations from German and French, for her guidance in matters of style, for proofreading the manuscript, and for sharing her husband with this project over some five years.

ONE

Chronological Bibliography of European Liberal and Reform Prayerbooks

IN THE FOLLOWING PAGES WE LIST THE VARIOUS RITUALS WHICH WE have either been able to consult in the writing of this study, or the existence of which we have otherwise been able to ascertain. There has thus far been no complete bibliography of this kind. Nor, alas, can the present bibliography make any claim to completeness. It has taken a number of years merely to assemble the material listed here, and it is to be feared that, by now, some links in the liturgical chain may be altogether lost.

In our bibliography we have restricted ourselves to regular prayerbooks for weekdays, Sabbaths, festivals and holy days. We have excluded mimeographed and experimental service leaflets as well as youth services, memorial services, specially printed confirmation and marriage services, and leaflets containing prayers for patriotic occasions. We have also excluded hymnals and songsters, although, particularly in the early phases of Reform, they played a major role in the reformed worship services. They do, however, merit a separate treatment in their own right, for which this is not the place. But we have made an exception in the case of those hymnals or songsters which also contain prayers the inclusion of which in the worship service marked a pronounced departure from Orthodox liturgy.

Prayerbooks which we have not seen, but the existence of which has been inferred from other sources, are listed here in parentheses, and the sources, on which the inferences are based, are indicated.

Some of the prayerbooks were published without stating their year of publication. The sign (?) placed after a year of publication indicates that, on the basis of internal and external evidence, the year stated here seems to be the most probable one.

The sign (x) placed after a listing indicates that, though not available to this writer, earlier editions of that work must have appeared.

1816(?)

(Gebete am Sabbath Morgens und an den beiden Neujahrs-Tagen.)
This appeared without the name of the editor, and without the mention of the place and the year of publication. It is clear, however, that this prayerbook appeared in Berlin, and that it was meant for the services conducted under Israel Jacobson's auspices in the days when, temporarily, those services took the place of the Berlin Jewish community's synagogue worship. See Ludwig Geiger, *Geschichte der Juden in Berlin*, Part II. Berlin, 1871, p. 222, and the corrections and amplifications of Geiger's description in Simon Bernfeld, תולדות הריפורמציון הדתית בישראל, Cracow, 1900, pp. 240ff.

1817

Die Deutsche Synagoge, ed. Eduard Kley and Carl Siegfried Günsburg. Vol. I. Berlin, 1817.

1818

Die Deutsche Synagoge, ed. Eduard Kley and Carl Siegfried Günsburg. Vol. II. Berlin, 1818.

1819

סדר העבודה—*Ordnung der öffentlichen Andacht für die Sabbath- und Festtage des ganzen Jahres. Nach dem Gebrauche des Neuen-Tempel-Vereins in Hamburg,* ed. S. J. Fränkel and M. J. Bresselau. Hamburg, 1819.

1840

Leopold Stein, חזוק הבית—*Gebete und Gesänge zum Gebrauche bei der öffentlichen Andacht der Israeliten. Oder: Bausteine zur Auferbauung eines veredelten Synagogengottesdienstes.* Vol. I. (New Year and Atonement.) Erlangen, 1840.

1841

סדר העבודה—*Gebetbuch ... nach dem Gebrauch des Neuen Israelitischen Tempels in Hamburg.* 2nd edition. Hamburg, 1841.[1]

סדר התפלות—*Forms of Prayer Used in the West London Synagogue of British Jews,* ed. D. W. Marks. Vol. I. (Daily and Sabbath.) London, 1841.

1842

סדר התפלות—*Forms of Prayer Used in the West London Synagogue of British Jews,* ed. D. W. Marks. Vol. II. (Festivals.) London, 1842.

סדר התפלות—*Forms of Prayer Used in the West London Synagogue of British Jews,* ed. D. W. Marks. Vol. III (New Year) London, 1842.

סדר התפלות—*Forms of Prayer Used in the West London Synagogue of British Jews,* ed. D. W. Marks. Vol. IV. (Atonement.) London, 1842.

סדר התפלות—*Forms of Prayer Used in the West London Synagogue of British Jews,* ed. D. W. Marks and A. Löwy. Vol. V. (Various occasions.) London, 1842.

1844

Das Deutsche in der Liturgie der Braunschweiger Synagoge, eingeführt noch unter dem seligen Landesrabbiner S. L. Egers von Dr. Herzfeld, jetzigem Landesrabbiner. Brunswick, 1844.

1844(?)

Deutsche Gebete und Gesänge für Neujahr und Versöhnungstag. Zum Gebrauche beim öffentlichen Gottesdienste in der Hauptsynagoge zu Frankfurt am Main. Frankfort o. M., n.d.

This volume, published without date of publication or name of editor, contains, on pp. 17ff., the hymn, "O Tag des Herrn," as a substitute for the traditional *Kol Nidré.* The hymn was written by Leopold Stein, and first published by him in *Ḥizzuq Habayith*, 1840. Stein became rabbi of the Frankfort community, in 1844; and it probably did not take him very long to introduce there the reforms he had previously introduced in his earlier congregation.

1845

סדר העבודה—*Gebetbuch ... nach dem Gebrauch des Neuen Israelitischen Tempels in Hamburg.* (Reprint of the 2nd edition, of 1841.) Hamburg, 1845.

Gebete und Gesänge zu dem von der Genossenschaft für Reform im Judenthum eingerichteten Gottesdienst in Berlin, für das Neujahrsfest des Weltjahres 5606. (Printed as manuscript.) Berlin, 1845.

Gebete und Gesänge zu dem von der Genossenschaft für Reform im Judenthum eingerichteten Gottesdienst in Berlin, für das Versöhnungsfest des Weltjahres 5606. (Printed as manuscript.) Berlin, 1845.

1846

Gebete und Gesänge zu dem von der Genossenschaft für Reform im Judenthum eingerichteten Gottesdienst in Berlin, für das Pessachfest des Weltjahres 5606. (Printed as manuscript.) Berlin, 1846.

Gebete und Gesänge zu dem von der Genossenschaft für Reform im Judenthum eingerichteten Gottesdienst in Berlin, für die Zeit zwischen dem Pessach- und Wochenfest des Weltjahres 5606. (Printed as manuscript.) Berlin, 1846.

Gebete und Gesänge zu dem von der Genossenschaft für Reform im Judenthum eingerichteten Gottesdienst in Berlin, für das Schewuoth-Fest des Weltjahres 5606. (Printed as manuscript.) Berlin, 1846.

Gebete und Gesänge zu dem von der Genossenschaft für Reform im Judenthum eingerichteten Gottesdienst in Berlin, für die Zeit zwischen dem Schewuoth- und Roschhaschanah-Fest des Weltjahres 5606/7 (Printed as manuscript.) Berlin, 1846.

Gebete und Gesänge zu dem von der Genossenschaft für Reform im Judenthum eingerichteten Gottesdienst in Berlin, für

Roschhaschanah, Jomkippur und Szuckoth des Weltjahres 5607. (Printed as manuscript.) Berlin, 1846.

1848

Gebetbuch der Genossenschaft für Reform im Judenthum. Part I. (Weekly Prayer and Domestic Devotion.) Berlin, 1848.[2]

Gebetbuch der Genossenschaft für Reform im Judenthum. Part II. (Festivals and Holy Days.) Berlin, 1848.

Israelitisches Gebet- und Andachtsbuch, zum Gebrauche bei der häuslichen und öffentlichen Gottesverehrung von Kirchenrath Dr. Maier, Rabbiner. Stuttgart, 1848.

1849

זמרת יה.—*Gottesdienstliches Gesangbuch eingeführt im israelitischen Tempel zu Prag, nebst Beschreibung des Tempel-Ritus an Feier- und Festtagen.* Von Dr. S. I. Kämpf. Vol. I. Prague, 1849.

1851

Gebetbuch für jüdische Reformgemeinden. Part II. 2nd edition. Berlin, 1851.

1852

Gebetbuch für jüdische Reformgemeinden. Part I. 2nd edition. Berlin, 1852.

1853

סדר עבודת ה׳.—*Gebetbuch nach dem Ritus der israelitischen Gemeinde in Aachen.* Vol. I. (Weekdays, Sabbaths, and Festivals.) Aachen, 1853.

תפלה לעדת ישורון.—*Gebete für die öffentliche Gottesverehrung in der Synagoge zu Mainz.*

Erstes Heft: für den Abendgottesdienst an Sabbath und den drei Hauptfesten. Erstes Heft (sic): für den Hauptgottesdienst an Sabbath und den drei Hauptfesten. Frankfort o. M., 1853.

1854

סדר תפלה דבר יום ביומו.—*Israelitisches Gebetbuch für den öffentlichen Gottesdienst im ganzen Jahre, . . . ,* ed. Abraham Geiger. Breslau, 1854.

1855

Tefillat Jisrael. Das Israelitische Gebetbuch nach dem Braunschweiger Ritus, ed. Levi Herzfeld. Brunswick, 1855.

סדר העבודה—*Israelitisches Gebetbuch . . . zunächst für die israelitische Gemeinde in Mannheim*, ed. M. Präger. Mannheim, 1855.

The Preface of Präger's 1855 edition is reprinted in the 2nd edition of the Mannheim prayerbook, in 1868.

1856

סדר התפלות—*Forms of Prayer Used at the West London Synagogue of British Jews*, ed. D. W. Marks and A. Löwy. Vol. I. (Daily and Sabbath.) 2nd edition. London, 1856.

1858

Gebetbuch für jüdische Reformgemeinden. Die Festgebete. (Festivals and Holy Days.) 3rd edition. Berlin, 1858.

סדר העבודה—*Bönbok för den offentliga gudstjensten inom Mosaiska fürsamlingen i Göteborg.* 3 volumes (covering the entire year). Göteborg, Sweden, 1858/62.

1859

Gebete und Gesänge für das Neujahrs- und Versöhnungs-Fest, zum Gebrauche . . . jüdischer Reformgemeinden, ed. Samuel Holdheim. Berlin, 1859.

Gebetbuch für jüdische Reformgemeinden. Part I. (Weekly Prayers and Domestic Devotion.) 3rd edition. Berlin, 1859.

Das Gebetbuch der Synagoge, für öffentliche und häusliche Andacht, mit besonderer Rücksicht auf Frauen übertragen und bearbeitet von Dr. Joseph L. Saalschütz. Königsberg, 1859.

In 1845, Saalschütz had argued against making changes in the traditional text of the prayers. He suggested, instead, that the traditional prayers be said silently, either in Hebrew or in the vernacular, by the individual worshipper. After each section of silent recitation, the rabbi is to read aloud a German translation or paraphrase, in which, however, he is free to give expression only to the "universalistic" elements. (*Hauptprincipien, bei Entwerfung einer zeitgemässen Liturgie für den Israelitischen Gottesdienst.* Königsberg, 1845). His 1859 prayerbook, in German only, though presupposing the traditional service, paraphrases with that tendency in mind.

1860

סדר העבודה—*Gebetbuch für Israelitische Gemeinden. Nach dem Ritus der Hauptsynagoge zu Frankfurt a. M.*, ed. Leopold Stein. Vol. I. (Sabbath and Festivals.) Frankfort o. M., 1860.

1861

סדר תפלה—*Israelitische Gebetordnung für Synagoge und Schule, wie zur häuslichen Gottesverehrung*: Bearbeitet und aus Auftrag der Königl. Württemb. Oberkirchenbehörde, ed. Joseph Maier, Kirchenrath und Rabbiner zu Stuttgart. Vol. I. (Weekdays, Sabbaths, and Festivals.) Vol. II. (High Holy Days.) Stuttgart, 1861.

1862

Gebetbuch für jüdische Reformgemeinden. Part II. (Festivals and High Holy Days.) 4th edition. Berlin, 1862.

1864

Gebetbuch für jüdische Reformgemeinden. Part I. (Weekly Prayers.) 4th edition. Berlin, 1864.

Neues Israelitisches Gebetbuch für die Wochentage, Sabbathe und alle Feste, zum Gebrauche während des Gottesdienstes und bei der häuslichen Andacht, ed. Dr. Ludwig Philippson, emerit. Rabbiner. Berlin, 1864.

This prayerbook presupposes that the worshipper is attending a traditional service, and means him to read the "liberalized" prayers while the traditional service is in progress.

1865

Deutsche Gebete und Gesänge beim Gottesdienste im israelitischen Gemeindetempel zu Leipzig. Leipzig, 1865.

Page 12 contains, in Hebrew and German, the prayer כל סתרי, which is to take the place of the traditional *Kol Nidré*.

Gebete und Gesänge für das Neujahrs- und Versöhnungsfest. Zum Gebrauche für den geregelten jüd. Gottesdienst in Königsberg i. Pr., ed. H. Jolowicz. Königsberg, 1865.

1866

סדר תפלות כל השנה—*Gebetbuch für den öffentlichen Gottesdienst im ganzen Jahre nach dem Ritus der neuerbauten grossen Synagoge in Berlin,* ed. Joseph Aub. 3 volumes (covering the entire year). Berlin, 1866.

1868

סדר העבודה—*Israelitisches Gebetbuch für Sabbath- und Festtage, nach dem Gebrauche des Israelitischen Tempel-Verbandes in Hamburg.* 3rd edition. Hamburg, 1868.

Ditto, with following remark on title-page: "Eingeführt in dem Tempel der Gemeinde *Schaar haschomajim* zu New York." Hamburg, 1868.

סדר העבודה—*Israelitisches Gebetbuch . . . zunächst für die israelitische Gemeinde in Mannheim.* 2nd edition, ed. Bernhard Friedmann. Mannheim, 1868.

1870

סדר תפלה דבר יום ביומו—*Israelitisches Gebetbuch für den öffentlichen Gottesdienst im ganzen Jahre,* ed. Abraham Geiger. Vol. I. (Weekdays, Sabbath, and Festivals.) Vol. II. (New Year and Atonement.) German Rite (i.e., *Minhag Ashkenaz*). Berlin, 1870.

Ditto. Polish Rite (i.e., *Minhag Polin*). Berlin, 1870.

1872

סדר תפלה—*Israelitisches Gebetbuch für die öffentliche Andacht des ganzen Jahres.* Auf Anordnung der Breslauer Gemeinde-Collegien mit Benutzung des bislang eingeführt gewesenen Rabbiner Dr. Geiger'schen Buches neu bearbeitet von Dr. M. Joël. Vol. I. (Weekdays, Sabbath, Festivals.) Vol. II. (New Year and Atonement.) Berlin, 1872.

1874

סדר העבודה—*Israelitisches Gebetbuch für die öffentliche Andacht des ganzen Jahres, zunächst für die israelitische Gemeinde zu Leipzig.* (Ed. A. M. Goldschmidt.) Vol. II. (New Year and Atonement.) Leipzig, 1874.

While the editor's name does not appear on the title page of this volume, it does appear on the title page of Volume I, published in 1876; and it is evident from the Preface to the latter volume that Goldschmidt was responsible for both volumes.

Tefillas Jisrael. Das Gebetbuch der jüdischen Gemeinde zu Braunschweig, ed. Levi Herzfeld. 2nd edition. Brunswick, 1874.

עבודה שבלב—*Der Gottesdienst des Herzens,* ed. M. Levin. Vol. I. (Weekday, Sabbath, and Festivals.) Vol. II. (New Year and Atonement.) Nuremberg, 1874.[3]

1876

סדר העבודה—*Israelitisches Gebetbuch für Sabbath- und Festtage, nach dem Gebrauche des Israelitischen Tempel-Verbandes in Hamburg.* Reprint of the 3rd (1868) edition. Hamburg, 1876.

סדר העבודה—*Israelitiches Gebetbuch für die öffentliche Andacht, zunächst für die israelitische Gemeinde zu Leipzig,* ed. A. M. Goldschmidt. Vol. I. (Daily, Sabbath, and Festivals.) Leipzig, 1876.

סדר התפלה—*Israelitische Gebetordnung.* Unter Zugrundlegung des Kirchenrat Dr. Maier'schen Gebetbuches zum Gebrauche der israelitischen Gemeinde in München, ed. Joseph Perles. Vol. I. (Daily, Sabbath, and Festivals.) Vol. II. (New Year and Atonement.) Munich, 1876.

1878

Gebetbuch der jüdischen Reformgemeinde zu Berlin. Part II. (Festivals and High Holy Days.) "Neu bearbeitete Ausgabe." (Newly revised edition.) Berlin, 1878.

סדר העבודה—*Gebetbuch für israelitische Gemeinden,* ed. Leopold Stein. Vol. II. (New Year and Atonement.) 1878.
Appearance of this volume in 1878 reported in A. Z. Idelsohn, *Jewish Liturgy and its Development,* p. 275.

1880

Gebetbuch der jüdischen Reformgemeinde zu Berlin. Part I. "Neu bearbeitete Ausgabe." (Newly revised edition.) Berlin, 1880.

1881

סדר העבודה—*Bönbok för den offentliga gudstjensten inom Mosaiska församlingen i Stockholm.* Vol. III (New Year.) Göteborg, 1881.

סדר העבודה—*Israelitisches Gebetbuch . . . Mannheim.* 3rd edition, ed. M. Steckelmacher. Mannheim, 1881.

While the Preface of this edition is dated 1882, the title page gives the year of publication as 1881.

סדר תפלות כל השנה—*Gebetbuch für die neue Synagoge in Berlin*. Vol. I. (Daily, Sabbath and Festivals.) Vol. II. (New Year and Atonement.) Berlin, 1881.[4]

1882

סדר העבודה—*Gebetbuch für israelitische Gemeinden*, ed. Leopold Stein. Vol. I. (Sabbath, Festivals, and Weekdays.) Mannheim, 1882.

1885

Gebetbuch der jüdischen Reformgemeinde zu Berlin. Neue Ausgabe. (New edition.) Berlin, 1885.

סדר התפלות—*Forms of Prayer Used in the West London Synagogue of British Jews*, ed. D. W. Marks and A. Löwy. Vol. III. (New Year.) 3rd edition. (x) London, 1885.

1887

סדר תפלות כל השנה—*Gebetbuch für die neue Synagoge in Berlin*. Part II. (New Year and Atonement.) 2nd edition. Berlin, 1887.

(סדר תפלה—*Israelitisches Gebetbuch für die neue Synagoge in Danzig*, ed. C. Werner. Vol. I. Danzig, 1887.)
Preface to that edition reprinted in the 1905 edition.

1889

Gebetbuch der jüdischen Reformgemeinde zu Berlin. Reprint of the new (1885) edition. Berlin, 1889.

סדר תפלות כל השנה—*Gebetbuch für die neue Synagoge in Berlin*. Part I. (Daily, Sabbath and Festivals.) 2nd edition. Berlin, 1889.

1890

סדר תפלות כל השנה—*Gebetbuch für die neue Synagoge in Berlin*. Part II. (New Year and Atonement.) 3rd edition. Berlin, 1890.

סדר התפלות—*Forms of Prayer Used in the West London Synagogue of British Jews*, ed. D. W. Marks and A. Löwy. Vol. IV. (Atonement.) 4th edition. London, 1890.

1891

סדר תפלה דבר יום ביומו—*Israelitisches Gebetbuch für den öffentlichen Gottesdienst im ganzen Jahre,* ed. Abraham Geiger. Volumes I and II. "Im Einverständnisse mit der Gemeinde-Verwaltung in Frankfurt a.M." 2nd edition (of Geiger's 1870 prayerbook). Frankfort o. M., 1891.

סדר תפלה—*Israelitische Gebetordnung.* Unter Zugrundlegung des Kirchenrat D. Maier'schen Gebetbuches zum Gebrauche der israelitischen Gemeinde in München, ed. Joseph Perles. Vol. I. (Daily, Sabbath, and Festivals.) Munich, 1891.

1892(?)

Israelitisches Gebetbuch für Werktage, Sabbate und Feste. Glogau, n.d.

This prayerbook does not indicate the name of the editor or the year of publication. Yet, in 1894, Vogelstein mentions the Glogau prayerbook in his Introduction to the Westphalian prayerbook. Assuming that Vogelstein wrote his Introduction a year before the prayerbook was actually published, we would have 1893 as the *terminus ad quem* for the publication of the Glogau prayerbook. But the year 1892 marked the dedication of Glogau's New Synagogue. (See *Jewish Encyclopedia,* Vol. VII, p. 442.) The publication of the new prayerbook may well have coincided with that event.

1894

סדר תפלה—*Israelitisches Gebetbuch. Im Auftrage des Verbandes der Synagogen-Gemeinden Westfalens,* ed. Heinemann Vogelstein. Part I. (Weekdays, Sabbath and Festivals.) Verband der Synagogen-Gemeinden Westfalens, 1894.

Beilage zu . . . dem . . . Vogelstein Gebetbuche. (Contains Scripture readings for Festivals and fast days, in part deviating from the traditional lectionary.) Verband der Synagogen-Gemeinden Westfalens, 1894.

1895

Gebetbuch der jüdischen Reformgemeinde in Berlin. Jubiläumsausgabe zur Deier des fünfzigjährigen Bestehens der Gemeinde. (Jubilee Edition.) Berlin, 1895.

1896

סדר תפלה—*Israelitisches Gebetbuch. Im Auftrage des Verbandes der Synagogen-Gemeinden Westfalens,* ed. Heinemann Vogelstein. Part II. (New Year and Atonement.) Verband der Synagogen-Gemeinden Westfalens, 1896.

סדר תפלה—*Israelitisches Gebetbuch für Schule und Haus.* Im Auftrage des Verbandes der Synagogen-Gemeinden Westfalens, ed. Heinemann Vogelstein. Bielefeld, 1896.

This is a school edition of Volume I of Vogelstein's prayerbook. The greater part of it is in Hebrew only.

סדר תפלה—*Israelitisches Gebetbuch für die öffentliche Andacht des ganzen Jahres,* ed. M. Joël. Part I. (Weekdays, Sabbath, and Festivals.) 4th edition. (x) "Für den Gebrauch der neuen Synagoge zu Königsberg i. Pr." Breslau, 1896.

1897

עבודה שבלב—*Der Gottesdienst des Herzens.* Vol. I. (Weekdays, Sabbath, and Festivals.) 2nd edition, ed. Bernhard Ziemlich. Nuremberg, 1897.

1898

עבודה שבלב—*Der Gottesdienst des Herzens.* Vol. II. (New Year and Atonement.) 2nd edition, ed. Bernhard Ziemlich. Nuremberg, 1898.

1899

סדר תפלה—*Israelitische Gebetordnung.* Unter Zugrundlegung des Kirchenrat Dr. Maier'schen Gebetbuches zum Gebrauche der israelitischen Gemeinde in München, ed. Joseph Perles. Vol. II. (High Holy Days.) Munich, 1899.

1902

Gebetbuch der jüdischen Reformgemeinde in Berlin. Der Jubiläumsausgabe zweite Auflage. (Second printing of the Jubilee Edition of 1895.) Berlin, 1902.

This is practically identical with the "Jubilee Edition" of 1895. But some Hebrew phrases of the *Kaddish* have been added in the Memorial Service.

A Selection of Prayers, Psalms and Other Scripture Passages, and Hymns for Use at the Services of the Jewish Religious Union. Provisional edition. London, 1902.

1903

A Selection of Prayers, Psalms and Other Scriptural Passages and Hymns for Use at the Services of the Jewish Religious Union, London. 2nd edition. London, 1903.

1904

סדר העבודה—*Gebetbuch herausgegeben vom Israelitischen Tempelverband in Hamburg*. Hamburg, 1904. 6th edition.

Neues Gebetbuch für Neujahr und Versöhnungstag, ed. Caesar Seligmann. (Printed as manuscript.) Frankfort o. M., 1904.

סדר תפלה—*Israelitisches Gebetbuch für die öffentliche Andacht des ganzen Jahres. Bearbeitet von Rabbiner Dr. M. Joël*. Part I. (Weekdays, Sabbath, and Festivals.) 4th printing of the edition for the Breslau *Synagogengemeinde*. (x) Ed. J. Guttmann. Breslau, 1904.

1905(?)

סדר תפלה—*Israelitisches Gebetbuch für die öffentliche Andacht des ganzen Jahres. Bearbeitet von Rabbiner Dr. M. Joël*. Part II. (High Holy Days.) 5th edition (x), with minor changes, ed. J. Guttmann. Breslau, n.d.

1905

Gebetbuch. Erster Teil. Für Werktage, Sabbathe, Befreiungsfest, Offenbarungsfest und Laubhüttenfest. Herausgegeben von dem Grossherzoglich Badischen Oberrat der Israeliten. Als Manuskript gedruckt. Karlsruhe, n.d. (Actually edited by David Mayer, and published in 1905.)

Name of the editor and year of publication are given in the Preface to the *Einheitsgebetbuch* of 1929.

סדר תפלה—*Israelitisches Gebetbuch für die Neue Synagoge in Danzig*. Part I (Weekdays, Sabbaths, and Festivals.), 2nd edition, ed. Max Freudenthal. Danzig, 1905.

1906

Gebete und Lieder für die Sabbate und Festtage nebst Synagogen- und Gebet-Ordnung für die Synagogen-Gemeinde Beuthen O.-S. Beuthen, 1906.

Includes revised version of *Kol Nidré*.

סדר תפלות כל השנה—*Gebetbuch der jüdischen Gemeinde zu Braunschweig*. Part I. (Weekdays, Sabbaths, and Festivals.) Brunswick, 1906.

1907

תפלת ישראל—*Bönbok för den offentliga Gudstjänsten inom Mosaiska Församlingen i Stockholm*. (Sabbath and Festivals.) 2nd edition (x). Rödelheim, 1907.

1908

סדר תפלה—*Israelitische Gebetordnung. Unter Zugrundlegung des Kirchenrat Dr. Maier'schen Gebetbuches herausgegeben vom Israelitischen Kirchenvorsteheramt Stuttgart.* Vol. I. (Weekdays, Sabbath, and Festivals.) Stuttgart, 1908.

1910

Israelitisches Gebetbuch, ed. Caesar Seligmann. Part I. (Sabbath, Festivals, and Weekdays.) Part II. (New Year and Atonement.) Frankfort o. M., 1910.

סדר תפלות כל השנה—*Gebetbuch für die neue Synagoge in Berlin.* Part II. (New Year and Atonement.) 11th edition. (x) Berlin, 1910.

סדר התפלות—*Forms of Prayer Used in the West London Synagogue of British Jews.* Edited by the Ministers of the Congregation. Vol. IV. (Atonement.) 5th edition. London, 1910.

1911

בית יעקב—*Gebete für den Gottesdienst im "Tempel" der Jacobsonschule zu Seesen am Harz,* ed. A. Strauss. Seesen am Harz, 1911.

1912

סדר תפלות כל השנה—*Gebetbuch für die neue Synagoge in Berlin.* Part II. (New Year and Atonement.) 12th edition. Berlin, 1912.

סדר תפלות כל השנה—*Gebetbuch für die Synagoge in der Fasanenstrasse.* Part I. (Weekdays, Sabbath, and Festivals.) Berlin, 1912.

There were only minor variations among the services of the Liberal synagogues in Berlin. The "Fasanenstrasse" ritual is almost identical with that contained in the prayerbook of the "Neue Synagoge."[5]

1912(?)

Sabbath Afternoon Services. Liberal Jewish Synagogue. (London), n.d.

1913

סדר העבודה—*Israelitisches Gebetbuch.* Vol. II. (New Year and Atonement.) (Unchanged reprint of the 1874 edition.) Leipzig, 1913.

כנפים לארץ—*Des Ailes à la Terre. Prières.* Paris, Union Libérale Israélite, n.d.

Date of publication supplied by Rabbin André Zaoui of Paris.

1914

עבודה שבלב—*Der Gottesdienst des Herzens.* Vol. I. (Daily, Sabbath, and Festivals.) 3rd edition, ed. Max Freudenthal. Nuremberg, 1914.

1915

עבודה שבלב—*Der Gottesdienst des Herzens.* Vol. II. (New Year and Atonement.) 3rd edition, ed. Max Freudenthal. Nuremberg, 1915.

1916

Sabbath Morning Services. Liberal Jewish Synagogue. London, 1916.

1917

סדר העבודה—*Gebetbuch für israelitische Gemeinden,* ed. Leopold Stein. Vol. I. (Weekdays, Sabbath, and Festivals.) 2nd edition, ed. Richard Grünfeld. Augsburg, 1917.

1918

סדר העבודה—*Gebetbuch für israelitische Gemeinden,* ed. Leopold Stein. Vol. II. (New Year and Atonement.) 2nd edition, ed. Richard Grünfeld. Augsburg, 1918.

1921

סדר התפלות—*Forms of Prayer Used in the West London Synagogue of British Jews.* Edited by the Ministers of the Congregation. Vol. II. (Festivals.) 4th edition. (x) London, 1921.

1922

סדר תפלות כל השנה—*Gebetbuch für die neue Synagoge in Berlin.* Vol. II. (New Year and Atonement.) 17th edition. (x) Berlin, 1922.

1924

סדר תפלה—*Israelitisches Gebetbuch für die Neue Synagoge in Danzig.* Part II. (New Year and Atonement.) 3rd edition, ed. Kälter. Danzig, 1924.

Liberal Jewish Prayer Book, ed. Israel I. Mattuck. Vol. II. (New Year and Atonement.) London, Liberal Jewish Synagogue, 1924.

1925

סדר תפלות כל השנה—*Gebetbuch für die Synagoge in der Fasanenstrasse*. Part I. (Weekdays, Sabbath, and Festivals.) 4th edition (x). Berlin, 1925.

תפלות כל השנה—*Rituel des Prières Journalières*. Paris, Union Libérale Israélite, n.d.
Date supplied by Rabbin André Zaoui.

1925(?)

ראש השנה—*Offices de Rosch Haschanah*. Paris, Union Libérale Israélite, n.d. Approximate date of publication supplied by Rabbin André Zaoui.

תפלות יום כפור—*Kippour*. Paris, Union Libérale Israélite, n.d. Approximate date of publication supplied by Rabbin André Zaoui.

1926

Liberal Jewish Prayer Book, ed. Israel I. Mattuck. Vol. I. (Weekdays and Sabbath.) London, Liberal Jewish Synagogue, 1926.

Liberal Jewish Prayer Book, ed. Israel I. Mattuck. Vol. III. (Festivals.) London, Liberal Jewish Synagogue, 1926.

Israelitisches Gebetbuch, ed. Caesar Seligmann. Vol. II. (New Year and Atonement.) 3rd revised edition. Frankfort o. M., 1926.

1928

Israelitisches Gebetbuch, ed. Caesar Seligmann. Vol. I. (Sabbath, Festivals, and Weekdays.) 2nd revised edition. Frankfort o. M., 1928.

1929

תפלות לכל השנה—*Gebetbuch für das ganze Jahr* bearbeitet im Auftrag des Liberalen Kultus-Ausschusses des Preussischen Landesverbandes jüdischer Gemeinden, (ed. Caesar Seligmann, Ismar Elbogen, and Hermann Vogelstein). Vol. I. (Weekdays, Sabbath and Festivals.) Frankfort o. M., 1929.
This is the *Einheitsgebetbuch* ("Union Prayer Book") of German Liberal Judaism. See the article, *Einheitsgebetbuch,* by Caesar Seligmann, in *Jüdisches Lexikon,* Vol. II, pp. 309ff.

תפלות לכל השנה—*Gebetbuch für das ganze Jahr . . . (Einheitsgebetbuch)* Vol. II. (New Year and Atonement.) Frankfort o. M., 1929.

Prayer Book of the St. George's Settlement Synagogue, ed. Basil L. Q. Henriques. London, 1929.

סדר תפלות כל השנה—*Gebetbuch für die neue Synagoge in Berlin.* Vol. II., Part 1. (New Year.) 20th edition. (x) Berlin, 1929.

1930

סדר תפלות כל השנה—*Gebetbuch für die neue Synagoge in Berlin.* Vol. II. (New Year and Atonement.) 21st edition. Berlin, 1930.

תפלת ישראל—*Bönbok för den offentliga Gudstjänsten.* Stockholms Mosaiska Församling. (Sabbath and Festivals.) Stockholm, 1930.

1931

סדר התפלות—*Forms of Prayer for Jewish Worship.* Edited for the use of their own and allied congregations by the Ministers of the West London Synagogue of British Jews. Vol. I. (Sabbath and Weekday.) London, 1931.

תפלת ישראל—*Bönbok för den offentliga Gudstjänsten.* Stockholms Mosaiska Församling. (New Year.) Frankfort o. M., 1931.

תפלת ישראל—*Bönbok för den offentliga Gudstjänsten.* Stockholms Mosaiska Församling. (Day of Atonement.) Frankfort o. M., 1931.

תפלות לכל השנה—*Gebetbuch für das ganze Jahr . . . (Einheitsgebetbuch)* Vol. I. *Ausgabe für Berlin.* (Edition for Berlin.) Frankfort, o. M., 1931.

1933

תפלות לכל השנה—*Gebetbuch für das ganze Jahr . . . (Einheitsgebetbuch)* Vol. I. *Ausgabe für Berlin.* (Edition for Berlin.) Frankfort o. M., 1933.

תפלות לכל השנה—*Gebetbuch für das ganze Jahr . . . (Einheitsgebetbuch)* Vol. II. *Ausgabe für Berlin.* (Edition for Berlin.) Frankfort o. M., 1933.

[Liberal prayerbook published in Holland, in 1933, as is evidenced by the title page of a 1934 Dutch prayerbook, describing the latter as a "supplement" to the 1933 prayerbook.]

1933(?)

Gebetbuch. Berlin, Verlag der Jüdischen Reform-Gemeinde zu Berlin, n.d.

Page 2 of this volume states: "In the years 1925–1932, the Liturgy Commission of the Berlin Jewish *Reform-Gemeinde,* under the chairmanship of Herr Hans Lachmann-Mosse, created this prayerbook." 1933 is, therefore, the likely date of publication. This little volume is rather unique in the history of European Liberal and Reform liturgy. Its 64 pages contain all the services of the entire year!

1934

Gebeden en Gezangen voor de Godsdienstoefeningen op den Grooten Verzoendag. (Day of Atonement.) (Supplement to the 1933 edition of the prayerbook.) Amsterdam, Verbond van Liberaal-Religieuse Joden in Nederland, 1934.

1937

Liberal Jewish Prayer Book, ed. Israel I. Mattuck. Vol. I. (Sabbath and Weekdays.) 2nd edition. London, Liberal Jewish Synagogue, 1937.

193?

Gebeden en Gezangen voor de Avonddiensten, ed. H. Hirschberg. (Evening Services for Sukkoth, Shemini Atzereth and Simḥath Torah.) Verbond van Liberaal-Religieuse Joden in Nederland, n.d.

Gebeden en Gezangen voor den Grooten Verzoendag, ed. H. Andorn. (Atonement Morning Service.) Kerkgenootschap Liberaal Joodsche Gemeente, 'S—Gravenhage, n.d.

Gebeden en Gezangen voor de Godsdienstoefeningen op de Nieuwjaarsdagen, ed. H. Hirschberg. (New Year Service.) Verbond van Liberaal-Religieuse Joden in Nederland, n.d.

1948

תפלות יום כפור—*Kippour*. Paris, Union Libérale Israélite, 1948. Offset of 1925(?) edition.

1952

סדר התפלות—*Forms of Prayer for Jewish Worship. First Supplement to Volume I. Evening Prayers.* Edited by the Ministers of the Association of Synagogues in Great Britain. London, 1952.

This is a supplement to the prayerbook of the West London Synagogue. That prayerbook had by then become the prayerbook of the Association of Synagogues in Great Britain, an organization which later changed its name to that of Reform Synagogues of Great Britain.

1957

Liberal Jewish Prayer Book, ed. Israel I. Mattuck. Vol. I. London, Union of Liberal and Progressive Synagogues, 1957.

This is a reprint of the 1937 edition of the prayerbook of the Liberal Jewish Synagogue, London.

1958

תפלות כל השנה—*Rituel des Prières Journalières.* Paris, Union Libérale Israélite, 1958.

Date supplied by Rabbin André Zaoui. This is an offset edition of the 1925 edition, greatly reduced in size, but augmented in its Hebrew section.

סדר התפלות—*Forms of Prayer Used in the West London Synagogue of British Jews and its Associated Synagogues.* Vol. III. (New Year.) 6th edition. (x) Photo-offset. Oxford, 1958.

195?

סדר תפלות לשבת—*Gebeden voor Vrijdagavond en Sjabbat.* Amsterdam, Den Haag, Verbond van Liberaal Religieuse Joden, n.d.

1960

תפלות לכל השנה—*Gebetbuch für das ganze Jahr.* Vol. II. (New Year and Atonement.) (Photo-offset of Vol. II of the *Einheitsgebetbuch,* Hebrew and German.) Verbond van Liberaal-Religieuse Joden in Nederland, 1960.

1961

Service for the Eve of Sukkot. South-West Essex Reform Synagogue (England), 1961.

1962

תפלות לכל השנה—*Prayer Book for Jewish Worship Throughout the Year.* Revised Edition with English Translation and

Supplementary Prayers by Rabbi Jakob J. Kokotek. Part II. (New Year and Day of Atonement.) London, New Liberal Jewish Congregation, 1962.

An English translation of Vol. II of the *Einheitsgebetbuch*.

1964

סדר טוב להודות—*Gebeden voor Sjabbat en Feestdagen ten gebruike in de Liberaal-Joodse Gemeenten in Nederland.* (Sabbath and Festivals.) (Amsterdam), Verbond van Liberaal Religieuze Joden in Nederland, 1964.

סדר טוב להודות—*Gebeden voor Rosj Hasjanah en Jom Kipoer ten gebruike in de Liberaal-Joodse Gemeenten in Nederland.* (High Holy Days.) (Amsterdam), Verbond van Liberaal Religieuze Joden in Nederland, 1964.

1965

תפלת ערבית לשבת—*Gebetbuch für den Freitagabend,* ed. Eugen J. Messinger and Lothar Rothschild. Vereinigung für Religiös-Liberales Judentum in der Schweiz, 1965.

מחזור לשלש רגלים—*Prayers for the Pilgrim Festivals. New edition.* Edited by the Assembly of Ministers of the Reform Synagogues of Great Britain. Amsterdam, 1965.

Prayer Book of the St. George's Settlement Synagogue, ed. Basil L. Q. Henriques. 2nd edition. London, 1965.

This is basically a reprint of the first, 1929, edition, with some additional Hebrew prayers and English hymns.

1967

עֲבודת הלב—*The Service of the Heart.* London, Union of Liberal and Progressive Synagogues, 1967. (Sabbath, Festivals and Weekdays.)

The galley proofs of major parts of this prayerbook have been available to us.

To the above list we must add a prayerbook published in Coblenz, to which reference is made in the Introduction to the *Einheitsgebetbuch,* although we have been unable to inspect a copy, or to determine the year of its publication. We have also been informed by Dr. Alfred Karger, of Quito-Ecuador, that the Magdeburg congregation used an edition of the Joël prayerbook, edited by Moritz Rahmer, but, again, we have been unable to locate a copy of that ritual.

In surveying the multiplicity and diversity of European Liberal and Reform liturgical productions, stretching over a century and a half, two reactions are possible. On the one hand, one could rue the lack of unity in the progressive camp, and regret the inability of Liberal and Reform Jews to agree to a common prayerbook. In a way, that was the sentiment reflected by the editors of the *Einheitsgebetbuch,* who, in their Introduction, traced the painful efforts which, at long last, had led to this attempt at a "Union Prayer Book." On the other hand, however, one might also view the liturgical divergences with a certain equanimity, and voice the sentiments expressed by Joseph Aub, in the Preface to his 1866 edition of the prayerbook:

> We must not bemoan nor find fault with the fact that so many new prayerbooks are being published in our time. The newly published prayerbooks are the best testimony to the newly awakened religious spirit. Every one of them contributes to the ennoblement of our worship service, and will serve as a building stone in the rearing of the complete sanctuary of our devotion—once the time has come when our congregations will have come close to one another on the level of their religious education.

TWO

Some Characteristics of Jewish Liturgy

THE HISTORY OF JEWISH LITURGY AS RECORDED BY THE EXPERTS IN THE field need not be repeated here. It must be taken for granted in the present inquiry.[1] But the labors of the pioneers in this field do suggest certain topics which should be borne in mind before we can adequately deal with the liturgical developments of Liberal and Reform Judaism.

There is, first of all, the very fact that we can speak of something as definite as a "Jewish Liturgy." Judaism, in other words, is a liturgical religion. Herein Judaism differs from some other religions which rely on hymns and *ex tempore* prayer exclusively. Judaism has its prayerbook. It, too, knows of the free outpourings of the pious heart, of the prayer uttered by the individual in his joy and in his anguish. But, in addition to those private expressions of devotion, Judaism has, for use in both synagogue and home, the fixed liturgy which is known as the *siddur*. The name itself (meaning "order") indicates that Jewish prayer follows a definite and established order or arrangement. So much indeed has the *siddur* become a part of Judaism that even sects which have broken away from Judaism have taken with them the idea that there should be a fixed liturgy. The Samaritans have a fixed liturgy. So do the Karaites. Even the liturgical tradition of the early Christian Church was, at least in part, indebted to the worship services of the synagogue.

The second fact to be borne in mind is that scholars are able to speak of a *history* of Jewish liturgy. History implies development. It means growth and change. The *siddur* did not come into existence all at one time. Many generations contributed to its evolution, and perpetuated within its pages their love of God, Torah, and Israel, their joys and their sorrows, their contrition and their exaltation, their memories and their hopes.

Biblical psalmists, Pharisaic interpreters, Rabbinic sages, medieval bards, commentators and philosophers, and more recent mystics and poets—all had their share in the formation of the *siddur*. Moreover, the existence of various rites—such as the Sepharadi, the Ashkenazi, the Italiani, the Yemenite, etc.—within the Tradition itself testifies to the important role played by local needs as well as by local talent. Yet all of the rites, with all their divergences and unique *minhagim* (local customs), have enough basic material in common to be recognizable as mere varieties of the same fundamental structure of Jewish prayer which was laid down in Mishnah and Gemara, and formalized in the Geonic period.

The fact of evolution and change, moreover, must not be misunderstood. With a few rare exceptions in the realm of synagogal poetry, the evolution of the *siddur,* until the rise of modern Reform Judaism, has been in one direction only. It has always been a case of adding more, never one of omitting. Every age would leave traces of its own devotional experience, but never at the expense of that of its predecessors. There are pages in the Talmud which take us straight into the liturgical workshop of Rabbinic Judaism, and demonstrate to us how the liturgy came to be fixed. Different rabbis suggest different prayers for the same occasion. In doing so, each one tries to do justice to one, rather than to another, tradition. But the final decision is not couched in terms of "either/or," but of "let us say all of them!"[2]

Then, again, there are prayers which were, at first, nothing but the private prayers of individual teachers. But, on account of the reputation of the teachers, or of the intrinsic merit of the prayers, or on account of both, such prayers found their way into the statutory service and became part of the fixed liturgy. We can illustrate this with the following example. "Prayer" *par excellence* for the ancient Rabbis was the prayer of the so-called Eighteen Benedictions. After the structure of the Eighteen Benedictions had become formalized, provision was made in the daily service for the private prayer of individuals. This rubric was called "Supplications," or "The Falling on one's Face," in view of the posture of prostration assumed by the worshipper for this section of the service—the Eighteen Benedictions having been recited in a standing position. While, at first, this rubric of the service was meant to enable the individual to couch his private prayer in his own words, the Talmud records the prayers which some of the teachers used to offer on that occasion.[3] After a while, the private prayer of Mar the son of Rabhina—"O my God, guard my tongue from evil, and my lips from speaking guile . . ."—was incorporated into the liturgy at this point. As a consequence, the period for private "Supplications" was shifted to a position *after* the recitation of Mar's prayer. For a time, the period set aside for "Supplications" was still regarded as the domain of private prayer. In due course, however, official liturgical texts were provided for the "Supplications" as well.

This illustration may serve to highlight two problems in connection with the traditional liturgy. On the one hand, it shows how the service grew by constant additions. On the other hand, it raises the question of the place of individual prayer within the framework of a liturgical service. Both of these problems are related to the apparently contradictory claims, known already to the Talmud, of *qebha'* (fixed times and fixed liturgy) and of *kawwanah* (inwardness and spontaneity). Yet traditional Judaism affirms both principles, and Abraham J. Heschel has shown how they are reconciled.[4] The fixed times of prayer, he says, are part of "the order of the divine will." They are an immeasurable aid to us when we are in no mood to pray, and by thus forcing oneself to pray he may be saved from the danger of losing the ability to pray altogether. Again, the fixed liturgy may admittedly be nothing more than a makeshift arrangement. Ideally, perhaps, man should pray in his own words, and the liturgical formulae were fixed only when, because of the Exile, men had lost the art of spontaneous prayer. But that is only part of the story. If reciting the words of the liturgy is a "prayer of empathy" (man deriving inspiration from the words on the page in front of him), and is thus contrasted with the prayer of "self-expression," we ought to remember that even in the latter man is making use of *words,* and words are by nature external. Why not, then, use the words which have been proved to be efficacious by millennial use?

But the synthesis of *qebha'* and *kawwanah*, of the fixed and the spontaneous, of the printed word and the inward intent, is a synthesis which gives birth to its own dialectic. One generation's expression of *kawwanah* becomes the next generation's heritage of *qebha'*. The example we have given above of the daily rubric called "Supplications" demonstrates this. So does the history of the *piyut,* that artistic creation of the medieval synagogal poets, which, at first, aimed at an alleviation of the routine character of the service, and which, in due time, was itself to become so much a matter of liturgical routine that its removal was demanded in the very name of *kawwanah*. And, when we come to the nineteenth century, to the rise of Reform Judaism, the old balance between *qebha'* and *kawwanah* had to be struck all over again, and a new synthesis came into being.

The basic structure of the Jewish public worship service is simple enough. In its original form it consisted of "The *Shema* and its Blessings," and of—what the Rabbis called—"The Prayer," i.e., a composite of eighteen (later, nineteen) benedictions on weekdays, and of seven benedictions on Sabbaths and festivals. The *Shema* comprised Deuteronomy 6: 4–9 (which the Rabbis called, "The Acceptance of the Yoke of God's Rulership"); Deuteronomy 11: 13–21 (which the Rabbis called, "The Acceptance of the Yoke of the Commandments"); and Numbers 15:37–41 (which, on account of its last verse, the Rabbis referred to as "The Exodus from Egypt"). The three Biblical passages were surrounded by a framework of "blessings," i.e., really eulogies in which God was praised for various aspects of His dealings with the world in general, and with Israel in particular.

The first "blessing" before the *Shema*, in the morning service, praised God as the Creator of light, who daily renews the work of creation. In the evening service, this "blessing" took the form of praising God, who, "by His word, brings on the evening twilight." The second "blessing" before the *Shema*, identical in content for both morning and evening services, though differing in the wording employed, praised God for the love He has shown Israel—a love manifest in Israel's possession of the Torah. In the morning service, the *Shema* was followed by one "blessing," in which the contents of the *Shema* were affirmed as true and enduring, and in which the theme of the Exodus from Egypt, mentioned in the third paragraph of the *Shema*, was developed—both in terms of the memory of God's past redemptive acts, and in terms of the future messianic hope. A similar "blessing" followed upon the *Shema* in the evening service, where, however, yet another "blessing" followed—one which invokes God as the Guardian "who spreads out the tabernacle of peace."

The rubric, "The *Shema* and its Blessings," thus constituted the creedal affirmation within the Jewish worship service. It proclaimed the monotheistic faith, and Israel's loyalty to the divine commandments; and it linked that proclamation with an affirmation of the doctrines of Creation, Revelation, and Redemption.

That the *public* worship originally began with the first "blessing" before the *Shema* is still evidenced by the fact that, to this day, the first "blessing" before the *Shema* is preceded by the Call to Worship ("Praise ye the Lord, to whom all praise is due!"), even though, for many a century now, this Call to Worship has been preceded by a great deal of other liturgical material. Prayers which were originally meant to be recited by the individual in his own home, prayers connected with rising from one's bed, washing one's hands, putting on one's belt, etc., were transferred to the beginning of the synagogue service. So were passages from Scripture and Rabbinic literature which the pious Jew was meant to study every day before he began his statutory prayer. And so were psalmodic passages from Scripture which, at first, were likewise a matter of private, rather than of public, worship.

Nor did the actual "blessings" of the *Shema* remain in the short and simple form in which they were originally couched. For example, the first "blessing" before the *Shema*, dealing, as we have noted, with God as the Creator of light, was elaborated by later mystics who saw the heavenly luminaries as angelic beings, and who, therefore, gave free rein to their fancy in describing the praises uttered by the angelic choirs.

"The Prayer" which followed the "*Shema* and its Blessings" was the rubric which provided petitionary prayer, prayers for forgiveness, for instruction, for personal and national welfare, etc. That is to say, it provided that on weekdays. On Sabbaths and Festivals, the petitionary prayers were replaced by a single one of gratitude for the gift of the Sabbath or the festival. Yet the first three and the last three benedictions of "The Prayer" remained the same for Sabbaths, festivals, and weekdays. Those six benedictions dealt with (a) the God of the fathers, who would send a redeemer to their children; (b) the mighty acts of the Lord, manifest particularly in the resurrection of the dead; (c) the holiness of God which is proclaimed by Israel on earth even as it is by the angels on high; (d) the request that the worship service be acceptable to God; (e) gratitude for God's providence; and (f) a prayer for peace.

The benedictions making up "The Prayer" also underwent elaborations, and they were changed to take into account the changed circumstances of Jewish life. For example, the benediction we have mentioned under (d), above, originally read as follows: "Have pleasure, O Lord our God, in the service of Thy people Israel, and accept in favor the fire-offerings of Israel and their prayer." It concluded either with "Praised art Thou, O Lord, who accepts the service of His people Israel," or with "Praised art Thou, O Lord, whom we serve in reverence."[5] This benediction goes back to the days when the sacrificial cult of the Jerusalem Temple was still practised. After the destruction of the Temple, a prayer for the acceptance of sacrifices was no longer in order. Instead, it was changed into a plea for the acceptance of *prayer* and for the *restoration* of the sacrifices. It now reads as follows:- "Have pleasure, O Lord our God, in Thy people Israel, and in their prayer. Restore the sacrificial service to the inner sanctuary of Thy house; and receive in love and favor both the fire-offerings of Israel and their prayer. And may the service of Thy people Israel ever be acceptable to Thee. And let our eyes behold Thy return in mercy to Zion. Praised art Thou, O Lord, who restorest Thy divine presence to Zion."

If "The *Shema* and its Blessings" and "The Prayer" were the original components of the public Jewish worship service, they did not remain its sole contents. We have already seen that the rubric of "The *Shema* and its Blessings" is now preceded by a number of other rubrics. Likewise, "The Prayer" came to be followed by other liturgical materials. Reference has already been made to the history of the rubric called "Supplications." This was followed by other prayers as well. It almost seems that Jews were reluctant to bring their service to a conclusion. The actual end was postponed more and more—by the addition of more psalms, more prayers, and the repeated recitation of the *kaddish*.

Yet, even before those latter additions were reached, there came other components of the worship service. There was a reading from the Torah on the mornings of Sabbaths, festivals, Mondays, Thursdays, New Moons, and all special feast and fast days. There was also a Torah reading on Sabbath afternoons; and a lesson from the Prophets followed the Torah reading on the mornings of Sabbaths and festivals and on some special days during the afternoon service as well. The custom in Palestine had been to read through the entire Pentateuch within a period of three years or three and a half years. The Babylonian custom was to read through the entire Pentateuch in one year; and the Babylonian custom ultimately prevailed everywhere. It was left to some congregations espousing the cause of modern Reform Judaism to revert to the old Palestinian custom. It should furthermore be remembered that, in the early Rabbinic period, the Hebrew readings from the Scriptures were followed by an Aramaic translation or paraphrase. There was also an exposition of the Scriptures—the antecedent of the modern sermon. The Aramaic paraphrase ultimately lapsed, and the homilies, too, fell into oblivion before the beginning of the modern period. There were, indeed, wandering preachers who entertained and edified congregations in Eastern Europe on Sabbath afternoons. But the regular rabbis confined themselves to legal expositions twice a year, on the Sabbath before Passover, and on the Sabbath before the Day of Atonement.

The place of homiletics was taken by inserts into the prayers, the *piyutim*. In the Palestinian rite, there seem to have been *piyutim* for every Sabbath of the year. Elsewhere, *piyutim* were recited on the festivals and on special Sabbaths only. *Piyutim* are poetic compositions which develop the themes of the particular occasion, weaving the law and the lore of the day into the warp and woof of the liturgy. Scholars are still debating the precise occasion in Jewish history which gave rise to the introduction of *piyutim*. Was it the legislation of the Emperor Justinian, in the sixth century, prohibiting the exposition of Scripture in the synagogue? In that case, the Jews circumvented this prohibition by incorporating this exposition into the prayers which they were allowed to recite. Or was it some other manifestation of government interference with Jewish practice, perhaps in Babylonia rather than in the Byzantine Empire? Perhaps we shall never know for sure. But one thing we do know. Quite apart from any external pressure, there was an inherent dynamic in the Jewish liturgy which led to constant elaborations. We have already referred to the mystical embellishments of the first "blessing" before the *Shema* in the morning service. This had nothing to do with government interference. Other liturgical poetry was likewise independent of such considerations. It is the old conflict between *qebha'* and *kawwanah*, between the fixed and the spontaneous elements of the worship service which is, at least in part, responsible also for the introduction of *piyutim*. The Jewish worshipper was not satisfied merely to recite his father's prayers. He wanted to pour out his own heart before God, to "sing unto the Lord a new song."

The classical structure of the liturgy makes no distinction between one festival and another. The service is the same for Passover as it is for Pentecost and Tabernacles. Only the mention, by name, of the particular festival in question—and sometimes, though not always, the Scripture lesson being read—distinguishes one festival service from another. By means of the *piyutim*, the meaning of each and every festival was brought out more clearly in the liturgy; and a service on Passover was truly a Passover service, a service on Tabernacles was distinctly a Tabernacles service, and so forth. The *piyutim*, therefore, served the purpose of revitalizing the synagogue service.

That is not to say that the *piyutim* were, at first, universally welcomed. Any *addition* to what has become traditional is as much of a *reform* as any *omission* from what has become customary. The legal authorities of Judaism fought fiercely against the introduction of the *piyutim*—quite as fiercely as they were to fight, centuries later, against any suggestion that the *piyutim* be omitted. For one thing, there was objection to introducing one kind of subject matter into a prayer which deals with something else. This was a general objection, and, as such, it was not even specifically directed against the *piyutim*, although, of course, it lent itself to that purpose. Take, for example, the case of the first "blessing" before the *Shema* in the morning service. We have described it as a praise of God who is the Creator of light. Not in its original version, but before the time of Saadia Gaon (10th century), this "blessing" was made to include the wish, "O cause a new light to shine upon Zion, and may we all be worthy soon to enjoy its brightness." Saadia Gaon objected to the insertion of that wish—not, be it understood, because he objected to the messianic hope as such, but because he regarded the first "blessing" before the *Shema* as a prayer dealing with the *physical* light, which must not be interrupted by mentioning the quite different—and metaphorical—messianic light.[6] If a mere sentence, voicing the messianic hope, could be regarded as an illegitimate interruption of a prayer, it is easy to imagine how much greater must have been the objection to the insertion of long and involved poetic passages which, to give but one example, discuss in great detail the various aspects of the Sinaitic Revelation *within* the structure of the first three benedictions of the Prayer of the Seven Benedictions in the morning service of Pentecost.

But the legalistic objections had to give way to the strong popular desire for this innovation in the liturgy. A compromise was reached by insisting that, whatever the subject matter of the poem, towards its end it must lead into the theme of the prayer in which it is inserted. With this proviso more or less followed, the *piyutim* became an integral part of the traditional Jewish liturgy. They represented the victory of *kawwanah* over the exclusive domination of *qebha'*. Yet, as we have already had occasion to see, one generation's expression of *kawwanah* becomes the next generation's heritage of *qebha'*. This was in a very special sense the case with the *piyutim*. Most of the poets who wrote *piyutim* must have had very learned congregations in mind. Their compositions presuppose an intimate knowledge on the part of the worshipper of the totality of Biblical and Rabbinic literature, an ability to catch the slightest hint, and a mind which is a veritable concordance and cross-index.

To illustrate this latter point, it suffices to take but one line of a very early composition for the Festival of Tabernacles. The Hebrew text, literally translated, says: "As Thou hast saved the mighty ones in Lud with Thee, when Thou didst go forth to the salvation of Thy people, so do Thou save us."[7] What the poet *intends* to say is the following: "As Thou hast saved Israel together with Thyself in Egypt, when Thou didst go forth etc." The word for "mighty ones" (*elim*) can also be read as "terebinths," and, in Isaiah 61: 3, Israel is called "terebinths of righteousness." Consequently, the word *elim* (terebinths) can be used as a name for Israel. As for Lud, we read in Genesis 10: 13 that "Mizraim begot Ludim, etc." But *Mizraim* is Hebrew for Egypt, and, if Ludim be the offspring of Egypt, then Ludim (or, in the singular, Lud) could likewise be used as a name for Egypt.

That this kind of style fascinates the scholar and challenges his ingenuity goes without saying. He either has the requisite knowledge at his finger tips, or he can study the various commentaries which have been written on the *piyutim*, supplying the necessary cross-references. (Yet no less an expert in the classical sources than the twelfth-century Bible commentator Abraham Ibn Ezra was quite vehement in his objection to the very style of the *piyutim.*)[8] But it is also clear that the worshipper without the requisite background in Hebraic scholarship can only experience the height of boredom during the recitation of the *piyutim*—a boredom which will lead to conversation with his neighbor, and to an inevitable disturbance of the decorum. Or—and this is hardly any better—he may devoutly recite page after page of words which are utterly incomprehensible to him, regarding them as some kind of magical incantation. In either case, the inclusion of *piyutim* in the liturgy of necessity leads to a considerable prolongation of the worship service.

If we have devoted, what might appear to be, an undue amount of space to a discussion of the *piyutim*, then the explanation for that is to be found in the fact that, long before any more thoroughgoing reforms of the worship service were undertaken, nascent Reform Judaism directed its major offensive against the *piyutim*. They were the *bête noire* of the early Reformers. There is something ironic, and even pathetic, in the spectacle of Reform Judaism—the champion of *kawwanah*—declaring war on what was, after all, the major expression of *kawwanah* in an earlier age, and in seeing the arch-traditionalists, the spiritual heirs of those who initially opposed the introduction of *piyutim* with all their might, as the zealous defenders of the *kawannah* which, in the course of the centuries, had itself become *qebha'*. (A rather lone Reform voice was that of Gustav Gottheil who, at the 1869 Israelite Synod in Leipzig, pleaded: "I fully recognize the rights of the present to change the prayer, but I believe that the religious consciousness of other times also has the right to find expression in our prayers. I do not believe that our time, with its cold rational direction, is especially suitable to create warm, heart-stirring prayers. And for these I would rather go back to the warmer religious sentiment of antiquity, and let it supply us with such prayers. Therefore, I must speak out against the generally condemnatory judgment against *piyutim.*")[9]

The very struggle about the *piyutim* underlines one of the major features of the evolution of the traditional Jewish liturgy. There was, indeed, evolution. There was development, and there was growth. But, as we have already noted, it was all in one direction only: that of constant *addition*. Once something had been incorporated into the liturgy, one did not let go of it any more. To this day, the Orthodox Jew prays, on every Sabbath, for the welfare of the Babylonian exilarchs and the heads of the Babylonian academies[10]—institutions which have ceased to exist many centuries ago. But the prayer remains!

It was this kind of extreme conservatism in our liturgical development which, by the time the nineteenth century had come around, set the stage for the liturgical task of modern Reform Judaism.

THREE

Reform from Within

BEFORE WE CAN UNDERSTAND WHAT REFORM JUDAISM IN EUROPE SET out to achieve, and how it went about achieving it, some clarification is necessary with regard to the organizational structure of European Jewry. In the Anglo-Saxon world, we have become accustomed to viewing Jewish congregations as voluntary and independent societies. They may spring up, or fade away, to the extent to which a need for them either is, or is not, being felt. Since any number of Jews can get together and establish a congregation for themselves, it follows that, in the majority of cases, such congregations will be established by like-minded spirits. In this way, we have congregations established expressly as Reform congregations, as Conservative congregations, or as Orthodox congregations. Such congregations decide for themselves what prayerbook they want to use, and to what degree they wish to be bound by traditional

Jewish law. It has also happened that Jewish congregations which began with one "denominational" allegiance changed their theological direction in the course of time—an eventuality which is as likely as not to lead to the formation of a secessionist splinter congregation, composed of those who maintain their loyalty to the original philosophy. Nor has the other possibility remained unknown, where a congregation maintains its original position, and splinter groups, espousing a different outlook, break off from the original congregation.

In all such situations, there may remain the feeling of belonging to an overall local Jewish community, and there will indeed be many activities, particularly in the philanthropic realm, in which Jews of all shades of opinion participate. But in the religious sphere every congregation goes its own way. The Reform Jew need not be too much concerned with what the Orthodox Jew thinks about the liturgical innovations in the Reform synagogue, and the Conservative Jew cannot interfere with the practices of the Orthodox synagogue.

All of this, of course, applies only to the case where we are dealing with separate congregations for the three "wings" of Judaism. The situation is quite different where, on account of the smallness of the number of Jews involved, there are not enough synagogues in a locality to cater to all the variations in religious belief and practice. Here, the Conservative Jew may have to share the same synagogue with either the Orthodox or the Reform Jew. Or there may altogether be only one synagogue to cater to the religious needs of all. In such an eventuality, extremism of either the traditionalist or the modernist variety is ruled out. Instead, there will be a process of "give-and-take" and mutual accommodation in the cause of the greater unity. Such instances, though not the rule, have been known to occur on American soil.

In Europe, on the other hand, such instances were not the exception, but the rule. *Vis à vis* the government, and in terms of Jewish self-identification, the local Jewish community was a united Jewish community—however much the individual members might differ in religious belief and observance. Indeed, as far as Germany is concerned, it was legally impossible, until the year 1876, for any Jew to leave the Jewish community structure without, at the same time, officially indicating his rejection of Judaism as his religion. Not before July 28th, 1876, did the Prussian government pass a law which enabled Jews to resign from their local Jewish community without, at the same time, abandoning Judaism.

Two considerations should be borne in mind in connection with that Prussian law of 1876: (1) Until 1876, i.e., sixty-six years after the first Reform endeavors, the arena of the struggle for liturgical reform is the total Jewish community. (2) The law of 1876 came about as a result of strong ultra-Orthodox agitation. The ultra-Orthodox Jews claimed that they could no longer remain members of the local Jewish communities, since the Reform element had become predominant in them—in itself a testimony to the victory of Reform Judaism *within* the established communities!

All of which is not to say that there had been no "separatist" Orthodox congregations before 1876. There had been. But the members of such "separatist" congregations, until 1876, had been obliged to be members of the general Jewish community at the same time, and, through communal taxation, to support religious institutions. Yet, even after 1876, most Orthodox Jews in Germany refused to avail themselves of the provisions of the new "law of secession."

Just as, originally, the ultra-Orthodox were members of the general Jewish community, so were the Reformers. The men who founded the Hamburg Temple, in 1818, continued to be members of the general Jewish community of Hamburg. They were as eager to demonstrate their compliance with traditional Jewish law to the Orthodox rabbinate as the latter was to warn the whole community that the new prayerbook did not meet the traditional requirements. Even the Berlin *Reformgemeinde,* which came into existence, in 1845, with an avowed radical Reform program, consisted of Jews who retained their membership in, and paid their taxes to, the general Jewish community of Berlin.

The Hamburg Temple and the Berlin *Reformgemeinde* were unique in that they represented instances where Reform Jews, without leaving the general Jewish community, assumed the additional responsibility of maintaining synagogues in which, from the beginning, the liturgy was of a reformed character. In all other instances, in Germany, the striving for Reform manifested itself not only within the structure of the general Jewish community, but within the established synagogues of that community. It was, in other words, a Reform from within the community, rather than a sectarian growth on the periphery. Some of the great leaders of Reform Judaism would have it no other way.

Two events in the life of Abraham Geiger, one of the leading theoreticians of Reform in Judaism, may help to clarify this point. Geiger was called to the pulpit of the Breslau community in 1838. He preached his inaugural sermon there on January 4th, 1840—after he and his supporters had been able to overcome the fierce opposition of the old rabbi of Breslau, Solomon Tiktin. The latter had objected to Geiger's appointment as second rabbi of the community on the ground that no university graduate was fit for a rabbinical position. Geiger was nevertheless engaged as Tiktin's colleague. But Tiktin, the champion of unbending traditionalism, refused to serve together with his newly elected colleague. At that point, the officers of the community, looking for a way out of the impasse, suggested to Geiger that he confine himself to the homiletical and educational aspects of spiritual leadership, leaving the *beth din* and the *halakhic* functions to Tiktin. It is characteristic of

Geiger's approach to Reform Judaism that he refused to accept that compromise. He wanted to be as much the rabbi and *halakhic* authority of the total community as was his more traditionalist colleague. "He claimed that the division of Judaism into two parts, the one quick and the other dead, which this arrangement presupposed, harmed the religion incalculably in the estimation of its own followers. It made the formation of two parties inevitable, the one, following the leadership of the rabbi, must look upon the preacher as an unbeliever, while the other, adhering to the preacher, would consider the rabbi an ignorant obscurantist. Such states of mind must lead without fail to a schism in fact as well as in thought, and Judaism would be in a sorrier condition in the end than it had been at the beginning."[1]

Geiger remained true to this conviction to such an extent that he preferred the struggle for Reform *within* the Breslau Jewish community, with all of the irritations which that entailed for him personally, to the spiritual leadership of a congregation which, from its very beginning, was founded on pronounced Reform principles. The Berlin *Reformgemeinde,* founded in 1845, was, as we have seen, such a congregation; and it was the Berlin *Reformgemeinde* which turned to Geiger in its search for rabbinical leadership. "Twice he declined an urgent call to serve that congregation—primarily because he did not want to be the rabbi of a private congregation, which had separated from the total community. He did not want Reform to separate from the totality of Jews, and to organize separatist congregations. He wanted to avoid a schism in German Judaism. At the very least, he wanted to prevent Reform from initiating such a schism."[2]

We have intentionally singled out the case of Abraham Geiger, one of the central figures of the nineteenth-century struggle for Reform in Judaism, and a man of relatively radical views. While it is true that an even greater radical, Samuel Holdheim, eagerly accepted the pulpit of the *Reformgemeinde,* it is also true that the majority of the German rabbis who were sympathetic to the cause of Reform—most of them somewhat less radical than Geiger—conceived, like Geiger, of Reform as something which had to take place *within* the established Jewish congregations, and not in separatist Reform synagogues. That is why the Rabbinical Conferences of the 1840's, though they came to be dominated by the Reform element, were not called as conferences of Reform rabbis, but as conferences of German rabbis as such. (The Orthodox element, by staying away, had as much to do with giving those conferences their Reform character as did Zacharias Frankel's demonstrative departure from the Frankfort Conference in 1845.) Thus, as late as 1845, curious as this may appear to us from our vantage point, rabbis like David Einhorn and Samuel Hirsch, at the Frankfort Conference, addressed themselves in all seriousness to the question submitted by one of the congregations: whether, for purposes of fulfilling the commandment of the ritual bath (*miqwah*), women could use the municipal bath where "drawn waters," rather than "living waters," were utilized?[3] That is also the reason why, when the abolition of *Kol Nidré* was decided by the Brunswick Conference of 1844, one of the participants expressed the fear "that he would not be able to make any headway with this in his congregation."[4] Note that the rabbi in question did not voice his disagreement with the Conference decision to abolish *Kol Nidré,* but merely his apprehension about his own ability to carry it out in his local congregation. For District Rabbi Goldmann—that was his name—did not attend the conference as the representative of a Reform congregation. He was present as one of the German rabbis who hoped, ultimately, to bring about a reform within their congregations. Meanwhile they themselves had to be won over to the cause. And that was to be a rather gradual process.

The German Jewish congregations were not of today or yesterday. Many of them could look back upon a history of many centuries. The congregation of Worms, for example, went back to Roman days, as did the congregation in Cologne. Not only were the German congregations deeply attached to the traditional Jewish liturgy as such, but even—and, perhaps, particularly so—to their own long-established local customs and rites. Thus, Rabbi Solomon Zalman Geiger, an Orthodox brother of Abraham Geiger's, published, in 1862, his *Dibhré Kehilloth,* a book which, in 478 closely printed pages, lists the liturgical variations and peculiarities of the Frankfort congregation alone! And, long after the *principle* of liturgical reform had gained wide acceptance in the German congregations, the German Jews' attachment to their local rites effectively prevented the introduction of a uniform Reform prayerbook. This, rather than niceties of theological distinctions, accounts for the fact that most of the major congregations found it necessary to publish their own reformed prayerbooks. And where, as in the case of Abraham Geiger's prayerbook of 1870, a prayerbook appeared which was meant to be of use to more than one congregation, it appeared in two separate editions—one for the "German Rite" (used in Southern German congregations), and one for the "Polish Rite" (used in Northern German congregations). As late as 1929, when the Liberal Jews of Germany at long last succeeded in producing their own "Union Prayer Book" (*Einheitsgebetbuch*), the latter appeared in three different editions—one for Berlin, one for Frankfort, and one for Breslau!

With the exceptions, therefore, which have already been noted, and with those yet to be mentioned in a subsequent chapter, the struggle for liturgical reform in Europe was a struggle which took place within, and not outside of, "the Establishment." It was not a question of providing prayerbooks for those Jews who, as a matter of principle, had broken with the beliefs and practices of Rabbinic Judaism—as was the situation which obtained in the United States. Rather was it a question of swaying whole Jewish communities, rooted in the Rabbinic tradition, and attached to their own local liturgical rites, towards the acceptance of liturgical reforms. Usually, of course, the arguments were not confined to the particular community in which the reforms were to be introduced. Both traditionalists and modernists sought and found their allies in all parts of the country.

For example, the Union of Synagogue Congregations in Westphalia, at its convention (*Gemeindetag*), held in Bielefeld, in 1892, entrusted Rabbi Heinemann Vogelstein[5] with the task of editing a prayerbook along progressive lines. In 1893, the Union adopted Vogelstein's draft. In 1894, the first volume of the prayerbook appeared.[6]

Now, Westphalia already had an old "Reform" tradition. It was there that Israel Jacobson had been active in the early part of the century as head of the consistory. It was there, too, that, in 1810, the first modern "Synagogue Order (*Synagogenordnung*) was published.[7] But that did not mean that there were no traditionalists in Westphalia, or that the views of the traditionalists did not have to be reckoned with. And not only the views of the local traditionalists! As soon as the Vogelstein prayerbook had appeared, Dr. Adolf (Abraham) Berliner, professor at the Orthodox Rabbinical Seminary in Berlin, launched an attack against it.[8]

Berliner began his attack as follows:

> An outrage committed against the sanctuary of the whole of Israel—as such, and in no other way, must we regard the 'prayerbook' which Dr. Vogelstein has edited by order of the Union of Synagogue Congregations in Westphalia. We have in front of us the first volume, recently published, which contains the prayers for weekdays, Sabbath, and the three festivals. The prayers appear in a changed form which lets us recognize throughout the tendency to fly in the face of our past and our history, and to obliterate, without further ado, its promises for the future.[9]

Specifically, Berliner is upset by Vogelstein's treatment of the Election of Israel. Vogelstein, in an attempt to eliminate invidious comparisons, had, like several editors of reformed prayerbooks before him, consistently omitted the words, "from all the peoples," when mentioning God's choosing of Israel. Berliner argues the futility of that procedure, seeing that the non-Jews, for whose benefit Vogelstein had undoubtedly undertaken the excision, continue to read about the true nature of the Election of

Israel in their own Bibles! Apart from accusing Vogelstein of a number of inconsistencies—even by Vogelstein's own standards!—Berliner, as is to be expected, finds much fault with Vogelstein's treatment of the Return to Zion and the Rebuilding of Jerusalem.

While Berliner was rendering his judgment from distant Berlin, a layman, A. Lewertoff, who resided in Westphalia itself, saw fit to obtain and to publish "Fifty Responsa about the new 'Westphalian Prayerbook' by Rabbi Dr. Vogelstein."[10] Characteristically enough, and indicative of the dimensions which such polemics always produced, the leaflet states on its title page that it was published with a subvention from the Free Association for the Interests of Orthodox Judaism, in Frankfort o. M.[11]

In his Preface, Lewertoff tells us why he has seen fit to publish this collection of responsa:

> After there was talk in our local congregation, too, of introducing the 'Israelite Prayerbook,' edited by Dr. Vogelstein of Stettin, by order of the Union of Synagogue Congregations in Westphalia, I turned to a considerable number of the most famous rabbis in this country and abroad. I requested them to send me as brief a responsum as possible to answer the question, whether the above-named 'Vogelstein Prayerbook' may be used for a Jewish worship service, and whether one may attend a service conducted on the basis of that 'prayerbook.'

To show that far more than mere academic interest in the matter is involved here, Lewertoff appends the following note to his Preface:

> Please let this collection of responsa circulate among your friends and acquaintances. At your request, it is being made available for free distribution.

Considering the sponsorship, it is not hard to guess the kind of answer given in those responsa. Dr. M. Cahn, Provincial Rabbi of Fulda, speaks about the "arbitrary changes introduced into those prayers of the Israelites which have been transmitted by the religious law," and about the "denial of fundamental religious doctrines." He comes to the conclusion that "a worship service conducted on the basis of the Vogelstein Prayerbook cannot be regarded as a Jewish worship service, so that an Israelite, true to his faith, cannot fulfil his religious obligation by attending such a service."

Provincial Rabbi Dr. M. Koref, of Hanau, writes: "Both according to the rulings of the ritual code and according to the decisions of the authoritative legalists, *any change* in the benedictions and prayers ordained by our ancient sages is *strictly prohibited*. With that, we have already pronounced the verdict on the prayerbook in question." Yet Koref continues to single out some points for special attack. The remaining forty-eight responsa are written in the same vein.

Thus challenged, the Union of Synagogue Congregations in Westphalia retaliated with a responsa collection of its own.[12] The replies of sixteen rabbis were included in that collection. The Preface quotes from the initial request which was addressed to them:

> We request neither a judgment about the value of the work, nor any statement which might refer to the author, Dr. Vogelstein. We are merely interested in obtaining a declaration to the effect that our new prayerbook does not, in any way, contradict the doctrines of Judaism.

Fourteen of the sixteen rabbis whose replies are included in this responsa collection showed themselves willing to make that declaration. The two who abstained had their own reasons for abstaining. Blumenstein of Luxemburg, as a rabbi officiating abroad, excused himself from intervening in an affair beyond his own boundaries, but he nevertheless "condemned the Orthodox agitation."[13] Benjamin Rippner of Glogau is more to the point:

> The presumption of the fifty gentlemen in judging the Union and Dr. Vogelstein is, in my opinion, utterly improper. They must be rebuffed *a limine*. In a certain sense, it would be an approval of this impropriety if one were to deal with the objective contents of those responsa. I, therefore, find it impossible to comply with your request.[14]

All the others furnished the expected reply. Maybaum of Berlin, for example, declares that the prayerbook "does not only not contradict the doctrines of Judaism—as Orthodoxy, in alliance with ignorance, constantly dares to assert—but, on the contrary, the prayerbook faithfully follows the tradition of those prayerbooks which have already been introduced, decades ago, in prominent congregations of Germany."[15] Kayserling in Budapest finds it hard to believe that "such an agitation should still be possible at this time." He regards Vogelstein's prayerbook as essentially identical with the prayerbook previously published by Abraham Geiger—a prayerbook about which the traditionalist scholar, Samuel David Luzzatto, had written to Geiger himself: "I must tell you that I have met Orthodox Jews who approved of your prayerbook, and who intend to purchase it."[16]

Apparently, the Union of Synagogue Congregations in Westphalia found sufficient support in the views of the rabbis who came to the defense of Vogelstein's prayerbook to remain unaffected by the opposition of the fifty Orthodox respondents. Vogelstein's prayerbook remained the official prayerbook of the Union—a state of affairs which, of course, did not prevent the more pronounced Orthodox congregations from continuing to use the traditional liturgy in an unchanged form.

In the Grand Duchy of Baden, on the other hand, a story of similar beginnings was to have quite a different outcome. In 1895, the Supreme Council of the Israelites of Baden (*Grossherzoglich Badische Oberrat der Israeliten*) voted unanimously to ask its "conference rabbis" to work out a new edition of the prayerbook, one which would do justice to the modern spirit.[17] The first proof sheets of the new prayerbook were published in 1903. Even though the prayerbook was meant only for congregations willing to use it, and guarantees were given that the prayerbook would not be imposed upon congregations unwilling to accept it, the publication of the proof sheets gave rise to very violent opposition. In September 1903, an appeal was launched which led to the foundation of the Union for the Protection of the Interests of Law-Abiding Judaism in Baden (*Verein zur Wahrung der Interessen des gesetzestreuen Judentums in Baden*), an appeal which included an attack on the prospective new prayerbook.[18] Elections for the forthcoming fourth "regular synod," the executive body of the Baden Jews, were held in July 1904. The elections resulted in some changes of representation, the traditionalists winning some seats from the liberals.[19] And then, after some ten years of work, the draft of the new prayerbook was finally "printed as manuscript." It appeared without a date of publication. Elbogen, the historian of Jewish liturgy, gives the date as 1905.[20] Lewin, the historian of Baden Jewry, says that the *Oberrat* distributed the draft of the new prayerbook "already in the middle of 1907, so that it could be thoroughly examined by the forthcoming synod."[21] While we have been unable to find evidence to corroborate Elbogen's dating (though *prima facie* we would have a right to assume that Elbogen had all the relevant facts at his disposal), we can be certain that, contrary to Lewin's statement, the prayerbook must have been available *before* the middle of 1907.

With a dateline, Frankfort o. M., December 30th, 1906, the Orthodox newspaper, *Der Israelit,* of January 3rd, 1907, brings the following report:

> The rabbinical commission of the Free Association for the Interests of Orthodox Judaism has given the following requested opinion about the prayerbook of the Baden *Oberrat:*
>
> The prayerbook published by the *Grossherzoglich Badische Oberrat der Israeliten,* on account of the changes it contains, and on account of the omission of individual prayers as a whole or in part, cannot be used for the statutory prayer of the Jew, in accordance with the provisions of religious law.
>
> In addition, the prayerbook shows such a lack of plan and such arbitrariness—and, as a consequence, such a lack of respect

for prayer in the merely external sense—that, quite apart from its intrinsic deficiencies, the use of that prayerbook is irreconcilable with a recognition of the sanctity of the worship service.

Of the many proofs for the above judgment, only the following are here singled out:

I. The changes in and by themselves, quite irrespective of the tendency expressed in the "Preliminary Remarks" and obvious in the prayerbook itself, are a breach of the provisions of religious law which provides that the form of the prayer ordained by the original arrangers of the liturgy must be retained. (*Babli Berakhoth* 40b.)

II. In many of the changes and omissions there is an obvious denial of the basic truths of Judaism, particularly of the Prophetic promises regarding the future of Israel and of all mankind. For example, the following is being denied:

(a) the future ingathering of all members of the people of Israel, . . . ;

(b) the promise of the personal Messiah, . . . ;

(c) the restoration of Jerusalem and the Temple, . . . ;

(d) the resurrection of the dead, ...

III. [The rabbinical "opinion" goes on to instance a number of inconsistencies which appear in the new prayerbook, i.e., basic truths which, according to the "opinion," have been "denied," do figure in some of the prayers which have been retained in an unchanged form. There are also unsurmountable contradictions between the Hebrew text and the German translation.]

From all of this it follows that the prayerbook published by the *Grossherzoglich Badische Oberrat der Israeliten* must not be used in a Jewish worship service, and no Jew, who knows and respects the duty of prayer and its holiness, is allowed to participate in a worship service based on the above-mentioned book.[22]

So much for the "opinion" of the rabbinical commission of the Free Association for the Interests of Orthodox Judaism. We have quoted it here to show that, at the end of 1906, there was already an Orthodox reaction to the specifics of the new prayerbook—a fact which would definitely indicate that the new prayerbook had become available *before* the middle of 1907. It should also be noted that the Orthodox reaction came from Frankfort, i.e., from beyond the borders of Baden. Even more than the Westphalian prayerbook, the new Baden prayerbook became an issue involving German Jewry as a whole.

About one third of all German rabbis—although, with a few exceptions, not including rabbis serving major German congregations—were to express themselves against the Baden prayerbook.[23] A literary warfare of considerable dimensions was the result, and we shall devote a special chapter to the arguments on both sides. At that, the new Baden prayerbook was one of the most "conservative" of all the new rituals. What the Frankfort "opinion" criticized as "inconsistencies" were really attempts to make the book acceptable even to those of a more traditionalist bent of mind. The prayerbook contains a rather full Hebrew text, and even includes a number of *piyutim* for the festivals. Yet it is, in part at least, "guilty" of the "denials" with which it is charged by the Frankfort "opinion"—though certainly not any more so than the prayerbooks which had already been introduced in major congregations elsewhere.

The Zionists joined the Orthodox in the opposition to the new prayerbook. The attempts, made in the new prayerbook, to "universalize" some of the "particularistic" passages of the traditional liturgy were felt to be an affront to Jewish nationalism, quite apart from any theological considerations. Thus it came about that both the Orthodox and the Zionists of the whole of Germany regarded the elections to the next Baden "synod" as their most personal concern. Not only in the press, but also by means of the mass distribution of pamphlets and leaflets, and by making available speakers and funds, they took part in the electioneering.[24]

The elections finally took place on March 15th, 1908. When the election results were in, it turned out that only eleven protagonists of the new prayerbook had been elected—as against fifteen decisive opponents.[25] It was, therefore, inevitable that the following resolution was adopted by the Synod that year:

> The Synod appreciates both the intentions which have led the *Oberrat* and its religious Conference to the working out of the plan for a new prayerbook to satisfy the religious needs of one part of the religious community in Baden, and the extraordinary care which has been devoted for years to the attainment of that goal.
>
> The Synod likewise appreciates the fact that the *Oberrat*—even after the election results—has felt the need, in the spirit of the adherents of the new prayerbook, to submit to the Synod a plan about the presuppositions of the introduction of the prayerbook in the individual congregations. The Synod has complete confidence that, in case of the adoption of this plan, the *Oberrat* would strive for its execution with the avoidance of any kind of coercion of conscience.
>
> Nevertheless, the Synod cannot escape the realization that, with regard to the basic evaluation of the draft, no unanimity could be achieved either within the Synod itself or within the *Oberrat*.
>
> With the intention of maintaning the past harmonious relationship within the Synod and *vis à vis* the *Oberrat*, in the inter-

> est of the synagogues of the whole country, and with the recognition that, above all, there is a need in the land to calm down the spirits which have been aroused by the Prayer Book Struggle, the Synod declares that the *Oberrat* would deserve well of the synagogues of the whole country if it were to forgo the further deliberations about its draft prayerbook as well as the vote about it.[26]

The proposed Baden prayerbook failed to win approval, and was, therefore, not introduced in the Baden congregations. The Westphalian prayerbook did win approval, and was introduced in some major Westphalian congregations. The two examples show the two different possibilities in the matter of introducing a new prayerbook, even as they show what is involved in producing a prayerbook not for a sectarian group, but for a whole Jewish community—or even all of the Jewish communities of a whole country. For one thing, there is, as the case of Baden shows, the risk of non-acceptance. For another, there is the need to keep radicalism within bounds, and not to offend traditionalist susceptibilities unnecessarily. The latter requirement has brought it about that most of the European reformed prayerbooks have a distinct "traditional" appearance. This, in turn, has led American observers to the conclusion that, while Reform Judaism flourished in the United States, it "stagnated" in the Europe where its cradle stood. Such a judgment not only takes too narrow a view of Reform Judaism, but it is also misled by externals and mere appearances.

Take, for example, Vogelstein's Westphalian prayerbook.[27] Dogmatically it is no less "Reform" than, say, the American *Union Prayer Book*. Like the latter, it contains no petitions for the return to Zion or the restoration of the sacrificial cult. It replaces the concept of the personal Messiah with that of a (depersonalized) "redemption." It eliminates angelology completely, and it removes all "invidious comparisons" between Israel and the non-Jews. While it does retain (unlike the *Union Prayer Book*) the Hebrew benediction, in the Eighteen Benedictions, which, if understood literally, could be taken to refer to the physical resurrection of the dead, it paraphrases it in German in a way which expresses spiritual immortality rather than physical resurrection. It is, in other words, a "Reform" prayerbook in every sense of that term, as its Orthodox opponents were quick enough to point out.

Indeed, much more than many other European reformed prayerbooks, Vogelstein's was designed in a way which would enable congregations desiring to do so to conduct major portions of the service in the vernacular. Nevertheless, the book has the appearance of a traditional *siddur*. It opens from right to left. It remains faithful to the rubrics of the traditional service, in spite of the changes and abbreviations which it introduces. And, above all, whatever appears in German on the left-hand page appears in Hebrew on the right-hand page, thereby enabling congregations to include as much Hebrew, or as little Hebrew, in their worship service as circumstances warranted. Moreover, for purposes of religious instruction, a separate edition of Vogelstein's prayerbook was published,[28] which, apart from the German translation of the "Ethics of the Fathers" and of a special Youth Service for Sabbath Afternoon, contains the full Hebrew section of Vogelstein's 1894 prayerbook without any German at all. This volume of 306 pages looks more like an Orthodox *siddur* than perhaps any other Reform prayerbook, and the casual viewer might easily mistake it for such. Yet a closer inspection of this prayerbook "for school and home" will leave no doubt that the Hebrew text has been edited from a pronounced "Reform" point of view. And the same could be said about the (rejected) Baden prayerbook, which, however, took fewer liberties with the traditional text than Vogelstein did.

The case of Baden notwithstanding, most of the major German congregations, by the beginning of the twentieth century, were either using prayerbooks of the Vogelstein or Baden type, or exercised a judicious selection in the use of the traditional prayerbook, supplementing the latter with German prayers recited by the rabbi. If we, furthermore, bear in mind that German Orthodox Jews in several of the larger cities felt compelled to organize their own separatist congregations, because the communities had become "dominated" by the Reform element, the conclusion which forces itself upon us is that, so far from stagnating within its cradle, Reform Judaism in Europe had actually become the dominant form of the faith in that part of the world. If, in its forms and in the language of its prayers, it remained more "traditional" than its American counterpart, then the reason must be sought in the fact that, unlike the American Reform movement, European Reform was by and large a "Reform from *within*."

FOUR

Independent Reform

THE PROCESS OF "REFORM FROM WITHIN," WHICH WE HAVE DESCRIBED in our last chapter, was brought to fruition in most of the larger German Jewish communities. Reformed rituals were the "official" prayerbooks of Breslau and of Glogau, of Leipzig and of Nuremberg, of Frankfort o. M. and of Berlin, of Munich and of Aachen, of Brunswick and of Mannheim, of Danzig and of Königsberg. And, from the second half of the nineteenth century, a reformed ritual became the "official" liturgy of Judaism in Sweden.[1] Those prayerbooks may not have incorporated all of the reforms suggested by the rabbis meeting in conference,[2] but, then, the rabbis themselves never achieved unanimity in their deliberations, and local needs always took precedence over the theoretical resolutions of the Rabbinical Conferences. This applied particularly to what the rabbis had to say about the far-reaching substitution of the vernacular for Hebrew. This had been decided by majority vote at the Frankfort Conference of 1845, a decision which induced Zacharias Frankel to walk out of that Conference, and to become the leader of a "third force," Conservative Judaism.[3] But that decision was never implemented on any large scale. At the 1930 Conference of the World Union for Progressive Judaism, the sub-committee on Liturgy reported that "there is a preponderance of Hebrew in the German congregations, some estimates being 9/10 and 2/3 Hebrew."[4] That was eighty-five years after the Frankfort Conference! Yet this conservatism in the retention of Hebrew, and in following the major outlines of the traditional worship service, went hand in hand with a rather consistent liturgical reform. What all the new prayerbooks had in common was (a) the shortening of the worship service, (b) the elimination of all or most of the *piyutim,* (c) the introduction of some German prayers and hymns, (d) the emendation of traditional texts based on dogmatic considerations, i.e., in the case of prayers dealing with the personal Messiah, the Return to Zion, and the sacrificial cult. It is in view of those changes, therefore, that the movement of "Reform from Within" must be regarded as successful.

However, "Reform from Within" was not the only kind of Reform endeavor which history has to record. For one thing, it was conditioned by the peculiar form which the organization of Jewish communities in Germany had to take *vis à vis* the government. The situation was quite different in England, France, and Holland. For another, as has already been hinted at, within Germany itself, the liturgies of the Hamburg Temple and of the Berlin *Reformgemeinde* were, from the very beginning, designed for homogeneous groups committed to the principles of Reform Judaism. In contradistinction to what we have called, "Reform from Within," we might call this the manifestation of "Independent Reform." Moreover, if by "Independent Reform" we mean those attempts at reforming the liturgy which were not made through "official channels," and which were content with an application to a limited circle, without insisting on universal acceptance, then we must seek the origin of liturgical innovation long before the nineteenth century.

(1) The Precursors

When, in the eighth century, the sect of the Karaites rejected the totality of the Rabbinic Tradition, they, of course, also rejected the Rabbinic liturgy, and they proceeded to create their own. According to their founder, Anan ben David, prayer was to consist of a number of Psalms only. He argued that what was good enough for King David was good enough for the Karaites.[5] But Karaite liturgy did not confine itself to Psalms for too long. It became quite voluminous in its own right, and, in the course of time, it increasingly adopted borrowings from Rabbinic liturgy.[6] What is of significance within our present context, however, is the mere fact that a group of Jews challenged the authority of the Talmud in laying down liturgical rubrics and texts, and strove for a more simple and "Biblical" kind of worship. While there was no direct influence of Karaism on modern Reform Judaism, some quasi-Karaite sentiments were occasionally voiced in the Reform polemics of the nineteenth century, and early Reform Judaism showed, to say the least, some interesting parallel developments.[7]

If Karaism, at any rate in its first stages, represented the taking away of something from the traditional liturgical structure, the incorporation of *piyutim,* throughout the Middle Ages, represented a kind of "Independent Reform" by means of additions to the established structure. Nor was there any lack of Rabbinic opposition to this innovation. A. A. Wolff has collected and published the views of twenty-one Rabbinic authorities who expressed opposition either to the *piyutim* as such, or to the particular *piyutim* which have found their way into the accepted liturgy. Those authorities range from Ibn Ezra to the Vilna Gaon, and from David Kimḥi to Jacob Emden.[8] Wolff, who, as Chief Rabbi of Denmark,[9] was trying to bring some order and decorum into the traditional worship service, was engaging in more than disinterested scholarship when he published his tract on the *piyutim.* As he stated in his Preface:

> Who does not know how much talk there is today in the various congregations about the *piyutim?* That is so because so many rabbis are too weak to do the right thing or to recognize it, and because the congregations know too little about it to demand of their clergymen the kind of action which, after a more searching examination, they should feel compelled to undertake.[10]

Wolff, in other words, though not in any technical or organizational sense one of the Reformers, shared the modern Reformers' aversion to the *piyutim,* and provided justifications for their abolition. All of which should not make us overlook the fact that, while, in the nineteenth century, it was a "reform" to abolish the *piyutim,* in earlier centuries it was a "reform" to introduce them—in the face of all the Rabbinic opposition which was marshalled against them. For the *piyutim* represented not only, negatively, a departure from the sanctioned pattern of the past, but also, positively, an expression, in worship, of the needs and the concerns of changing times and environments.

At the opposite pole from those who added to the liturgy by incorporating *piyutim* stood the seventeenth-century author of the heretical tract, *Kol Sakhal.*[11] That author, in his demands for liturgical reforms, was more extreme than the most radical Reformers of the nineteenth and twentieth centuries. He would even do away with the recitation of the *Shema,* arguing that what the *Shema* is supposed to achieve it does not achieve. The purpose of the *Shema,* according to the *Kol Sakhal,* is Moses' admonition to Israel (a) that they recognize the Unity of God, and love Him; (b) that they walk in His Torah and commandments knowing that there is a reward for him who keeps the commandments, and punishment for him who transgresses them; (c) that they should always make mention of the fact that God brought them forth out of Egypt. All this, says the *Kol Sakhal,* would be best achieved not by the rote repetition of three Biblical paragraphs, but rather by the recitation of some such formula as the following:

> ה׳ אלהינו אחד ואני מקבל עלי תורתו ומצותיו כי יגמול עושה טוב
> וייסר עושה רע כי הוא הוציאנו ממצרים ואזכרנו כל ימי חיי:
>
> *The Lord our God is One; and I accept upon myself His Torah and His commandments, for He will reward him that doeth good, and chastise him that doeth evil. For it was He who brought us forth out of Egypt; and I will remember it all the days of my life.*[12]

If anything, the author of the *Kol Sakhal* has even less use for the three daily recitations of the Eighteen Benedictions. He does accept the obligation to pray three times every day. But all that is called for is a brief prayer, containing the essentials; and the following version is suggested:

> ה׳ אלהי ואלהי אבותי בורא עולם ומנהיגו יוצר אור ובורא חשך
> יכול ורואה אשר הוצאתנו ממצרים ונתת לנו תורת אמת על ידי
> משה עבדך, חוס עלי ותן לי חיים ובריאות פרנסה וכלכלה ושכל
> טוב לעשות רצונך ולהדבק בך, ולחטאי מחול ברחמיך כי נחמתי
> כי עשיתים, הצילני מכל פגע ומקרה רע, רחם על עמך ישראל
> והשב שבותנו למען שמך הגדול המבורך המפואר והמשובח לנצח
> נצחים אמן:
>
> *O Lord, my God and God of my fathers, Creator and Guide of the world, who fashionest light and createst darkness, who art omnipotent and all-seeing, who hast brought us forth out of Egypt, and hast given us the Torah of truth through Thy servant Moses! Have pity upon me, and grant me life and health, sustenance and support, and a good mind, that I may do Thy will and cleave unto Thee. In Thy mercy, forgive my sins, for I regret having committed them. Save me from all plagues and evil occurrences. Have mercy upon Thy people Israel, and restore our captivity, for the sake of Thy great Name, which is blessed, glorified and praised unto all eternity. Amen.*[13]

The two prayers just quoted did not find their way into any Liberal or Reform prayerbook, but the general anti-Rabbinic attitude of the *Kol Sakhal* exercised an irresistible fascination on some of the nineteenth-century Reformers, once the text had been published.[14] In many ways, and not just in the field of liturgy, the author of the *Kol Sakhal* may be regarded as a precursor of modern Reform Judaism. Whether there was a direct connection between the *Kol Sakhal's* world of thought and the rise of Reform Judaism two centuries later, has not yet been established. We have drawn attention, in a different context,[15] to the fact that members of the very circles of ex-Marranos who "regarded the *Kol Sakhal* as their *Shulḥan 'Arukh*" constituted the group in London who voiced their opposition to the Rabbinic Tradition in the early eighteenth century. We have also noted that, a hundred years later, opposition to the Oral Law was the distinguishing feature of the nascent Reform movement in England, and we have ventured the conjecture (no more than that) which would link, through family ties, the nineteenth-century opponents of the Oral Law with their eighteenth-century predecessors.[16] A very similar conjecture was voiced by Professor Lou H. Silberman with regard to the beginnings of the Reform movement in the United States.[17] Be that as it may. Whether there was a direct influence or not, it must be said, from a historical perspective, that those who set out to reform the traditional liturgy in the nineteenth century certainly had a very radical precursor in the author of the *Kol Sakhal,* two centuries before.

It was in Amsterdam, another center of ex-Marranos, that, at the end of the eighteenth century, a congregation was established which, by the standards of that time, was considered "Reform." When Emancipation came to the Jews of the Netherlands, the Jewish community of Amsterdam, as a whole, did not particularly welcome it. But there were some members of both the Ashkenazi and the Sepharadi congregations who, holding liberal views, were in favor of full Emancipation. They combined their political liberalism with liberal views on religion; and, in 1796, they established their own congregation, *Adath Yeshurun*.[18] The liturgical procedures in which that congregation differed from other congregations were collected and published in a tract by Aaron Moses Isaac ben Abraham Graanboom, in 5569 (1808/9).[19] How moderate, almost innocent, the *Adath Yeshurun* Reforms were may be gathered from the following characteristic quotations from that tract:

> Everyday one says one division of the thirty divisions of the Book of Psalms,[20] so that it can be said quietly and with devotion, and not in confusion and·haste. About this they said: "Better a little with devotion than much without devotion."[21]
>
> One says *'Alenu* between the afternoon and the evening services, so that people can concentrate their minds (on the two different services). See *Oraḥ Ḥayyim* 93:105.[22]
>
> On Sabbath Eve, the whole congregation sings Psalm 29, *Lekhah Dodi,* Psalm 92, *Yigdal* and *Adon 'Olam,* word for word, in one tune, aloud and musically. And on Sabbath and festivals

> they recite the Verses of Song, word for word, and the cantor concludes every single Psalm .... [23]
>
> The priests recite the Priestly Benediction only once on every Sabbath and festival.[24]
>
> It is not our custom to have the priests recite the Priestly Benediction during the *Musaph* Service, so as not to bother the congregation.[25]
>
> One does not say *yotzeroth, piyutim, qerobetz,* and *zuloth.* (Proofs from Rabbinic literature are furnished.)[26]
>
> It is not acceptable among us to decorate the synagogue with blossoms and flowers on Pentecost, so as not to distract the concentration on prayer.[27]
>
> The whole Eighteen Benedictions are recited silently.[28]

The above quotations should suffice to convey an idea of the kind of liturgical reform introduced in that Amsterdam congregation. There is also a lengthy paragraph giving detailed reasons why certain Kabbalistic prayers are omitted from the services. However, there is no mention of the fact that the twelfth of the Eighteen Benedictions, the malediction against slanderers, was eliminated by the *Adath Yeshurun* congregation, although Graetz mentions that specifically as one of the reforms introduced in 1796—together with the abolition of the hasty burial of the dead, and the establishment of a new and clean congregational bathhouse.[29]

The reforms introduced in the *Adath Yeshurun* congregation, innocent and moderate as they may look to us from our vantage-point, were "radical" enough in those days to lead to the excommunication of the members; and even physical violence was prevented only by the interference of armed officials.[30] As a challenge to the rigidity of the Establishment, the *Adath Yeshurun* congregation, therefore, deserves a place among the precursors of modern "Independent Reform." But, in its own right, it exercised no influence on the Dutch Liberal Judaism of the nineteen-thirties. Rabbi Dr. J. Soetendorp, the present rabbi of the Liberal Jewish Congregation in Amsterdam, writes: "The leaders of the new progressive movement were much more influenced by the English movement and, a few years later, by the German movement than by an unknown Dutch progressive congregation. I think that I would have preferred to claim a link, but history could not be altered."[31]

(2) The Hamburg Temple Prayerbook

The Hamburg Temple congregation was the first congregation in the nineteenth century which was founded on a declared Reform basis. To that extent it differs from the minor liturgical reforms introduced by Israel Jacobson in Cassel and in the services held in private Berlin homes from 1815 on. The Hamburg Temple Association was formed in 1817, the Temple was dedicated in 1818, and the first edition of the Hamburg Temple Prayerbook appeared in 1819. As the first prayerbook specifically designed for a congregation founded on the principles of Reform, the Hamburg Temple Prayerbook of 1819 is of great historical significance. To some extent, a number of its innovations are still being perpetuated by the latest Liberal and Reform prayerbooks in all parts of the world. As was to be expected, the Hamburg Temple Prayerbook aroused some fierce Orthodox opposition—although possibly even more so in its second edition, in 1841. Interestingly enough, the fact that the book opened from left to right, like a German book and unlike the traditional *siddur,* does not seem to have aroused the severe criticism which was aroused by the Hamburg Reformers' adoption of the Sepharadi pronunciation of the Hebrew, in place of the Ashkenazi one.

Yet the innovations of the Hamburg Temple, however, were more noticeable in the introduction of an organ, of choral singing, and of a regular sermon in the vernacular than in any radical changes of the standard prayers of the traditional liturgy. The fact that some prayers were recited in German was, on the other hand, a remarkable feature, as was the substitution of Sepharadi for Ashkenazi *piyutim* in those few instances where *piyutim* were retained at all.

The nature of the Hamburg Temple Prayerbook will be better understood on the basis of a comparison between two of its services and their traditional prototypes.

Service for the Eve of the Sabbath

TRADITIONAL [32]	HAMBURG TEMPLE 1819 [33]
Psalms 95, 96, 97, 98, 29.	German version of *mah tobhu,* without the first sentence.
Lekhah Dodi.	German hymn.
Psalm 92.	Psalm 92 (Hebrew).
Psalm 93.	—
Mourners' Kaddish.	Half Kaddish. (Hebrew)
Barekhu.	*Barekhu.* (Hebrew)
Ma'aribh 'Arabhim.	German version of *Ma'aribh 'Arabhim.*
Ahabhath 'Olam.	German version of *Ahabhath 'Olam.*
Shema, 3 paragraphs.	*Shema,* 3 paragraphs. (Hebrew)
Emeth We-emunah.	German version of *Emeth We-emunah.*

Hashkibhenu.	German version of *Hashkibhenu.*
Weshameru.	German version of *Weshameru* with newly composed introduction.
Half Kaddish.	Half Kaddish. (Hebrew)
The Seven Benedictions.	German version of The Seven Benedictions, containing no other "dogmatic" change than the substitution of "redemption" for "redeemer" in the first benediction.
Wayekhulu.	*Wayekhulu.* (Hebrew)
Birkath Me'en Shebha'.	*Birkath Me'en Shebha'.* (Hebrew)
Full Kaddish.	Full Kaddish. (Hebrew)
Bameh Madliqin etc.	German hymn.
Kiddush.	*Kiddush.* (Hebrew)
'Alenu.	—
Mourners' Kaddish.	Mourners' Kaddish with newly composed introduction. (Hebrew)
Yigdal or *Adon 'Olam.*	German version of *Adon 'Olam.*

Sabbath Morning Service

TRADITIONAL[34]	HAMBURG TEMPLE 1819[35]
Adon 'Olam, Yigdal.	German hymn.
Morning benedictions.	—
Elohai Neshamah.	German version of *Elohai Neshamah.*
Benedictions.	—
Wihi Ratzon.	German version of *Wihi Ratzon.*
Yehi Ratzon.	—
Le'olam Yehé and *Ribbon Kol Ha'olamim.*	German version of *Ribbon Kol Ha'olamim.*
Abhal Anahnu, Shema, Attah Hu.	German version of *Abhal Anaḥnu, Shema', Attah Hu.*
Attah Hu Adonai Elohenu.	German version of *Attah Hu Adonai Elohenu,* omitting last part.
Biblical and Rabbinic Passages dealing with the sacrifices.	—
Kaddish DeRabbanan.	—
Psalm 30.	—
Mourners' Kaddish.	—
Barukh She-amar.	German version of *Barukh She-amar.*
I. Chr. 16: 8–36, Scripture verses.	—

Psalms 19, 34, 90, 91, 135, 136, 33, 92, 93.	—
Yehi Khebhod.	—
Psalms 145–150.	German version of Psalm 148.
I. Chr. 29: 10–13; Neh. 9: 6–11.	—
Exodus 14: 30–31; 15: 1–18.	—
Nishmath.	German version of *Nishmath*, followed by German hymn.
Yishtabbaḥ.	*Yishtabbaḥ.* (Hebrew)
Half Kaddish.	Half Kaddish. (Hebrew)
Barekhu.	*Barekhu.* (Hebrew)
Yotzer Or and *Hakkol Yodukha.*	*Yotzer Or* and *Hakkol Yodukha.* (Hebrew)
El Adon.	—
Kedushah deYotzer.	*Kedushah deYotzer.* (Hebrew)
Le-el Barukh.	*Le-el Barukh* (Hebrew), omitting *Or Hadash.*
Ahabhah Rabbah.	*Ahabhah Rabbah* (Hebrew), omitting Return to Zion.
Shema, 3 paragraphs.	*Shema,* 3 paragraphs. (Hebrew)
Emeth Weyatzibh, Al Harishonim.	*Emeth Weyatzibh, Al Harishonim.* (Hebrew, with German choral parts.)
'Ezrath Abhothenu.	*'Ezrath Abhothenu.* (Hebrew, with German *mi khamokhah.*)
Tzur Yisrael.	*Go-alenu.* (Hebrew, as in the Sephardi rite.)
The Seven Benedictions.	The Seven Benedictions. (Hebrew) Traditional text unchanged, except that *Musaph Kedushah* is used, and the paragraph *welo nethato* is emended to *uleyisrael 'ammekha nethato.*
Full Kaddish.	Full Kaddish. (Hebrew)
Torah Service.	Torah Service. (Shorter than in traditional rite.)
Reading of Haftarah.	—
Yequm Purqan etc.	—
Prayer for the Government.	
Psalm 145.	Psalm 145. (Hebrew)
	German hymn.
	Sermon.

	Prayer for the Government.
	German hymn.
Half Kaddish.	Half Kaddish. (Hebrew)
The Seven Benedictions.	The Seven Benedictions. (Hebrew)
	No prayer for restoration of sacrifices.
Full Kaddish.	Full Kaddish. (Hebrew)
En Kelohenu.	—
Pittum Haqetoreth etc.	—
Kaddish deRabbanan.	—
'Alenu.	—
Mourners' Kaddish.	Mourners' Kaddish with newly composed introduction. (Hebrew)
Adon 'Olam.	German version of *Adon 'Olam.*

While we shall deal with some of the Orthodox opposition to this prayerbook, and with some of the Reform attempts to justify it on the basis of the traditional codes, in a subsequent chapter, it is only fitting that we mention here the rationale behind this prayerbook, as expounded by one of its two editors, Seckel Isaac Fränkel.[36]

Fränkel first explains why so much of the prayerbook has been left in Hebrew:

(1) The prayerbook contains many verses from the Scriptures which are generally known, and may, therefore, be kept in the original.
(2) In order not to let the Hebrew language be eventually forgotten.
(3) An abandonment of the Hebrew language would lead to the suspicion that we wanted to abandon Judaism as well.

Fränkel next addresses himself to the reasons why certain prayers were omitted, and why German prayers have been introduced:

(1) Some of the passages which have been omitted deal with the sacrificial cult.
(2) Others deal with the extermination of the heathens, which is alien to the true spirit of Judaism.
(3) The desire for a return to Jerusalem was omitted, because it is a wish which issues from the heart of only very few. When Cyrus permitted the Israelites to return from the Babylonian Exile, only some 42,000 availed themselves of that opportunity. The rest stayed behind, demonstrating that one can be a good Jew without praying for a return

to Jerusalem. The prayers for a return to Zion which we have retained can be taken in a spiritual sense; but we do not request that God transport us physically to Zion, because we are satisfied with the place where we live.

(4) The use of the vernacular for worship is shown to be justified on the basis of the Rabbinic codes.

Next, Fränkel elaborates on the theme that prayer must change according to the circumstances of the times:

(1) The prayerbook of the Sepharadim differs from that of the Ashkenazim; even where both traditions have the same prayer, e.g., the Eighteen Benedictions, there are differences in the wording.

(2) If only one formula had been accepted, there could not now be such differing usages as those of the Polish and the German rites.

(3) According to the Rabbis, the *Musaph* prayer before the destruction of the Temple was not identical with the *Musaph* prayer after the destruction of the Temple; people always prayed for their needs as the situation of the times demanded it.

(4) Prayers were never fixed for all time. They underwent gradual development.

(5) All benedictions can be recited in any language, as long as they follow the arrangement laid down by the Sages. The formula can be changed as long as the contents remain the same, and the benediction contains the Name of God and the recognition of His Kingdom.

Fränkel also deals with the question of instrumental music in the sanctuary; but that goes beyond the concerns of this chapter.

The second edition of the Hamburg Temple Prayerbook contained some interesting changes. Appearing in 1841, that edition represented, on the one hand, a return to Tradition, and, on the other, an espousal of a more "radical" Reform point of view. Thus, to take but one example, all the Psalms and other Scripture verses, which constitute the Verses of Song in the traditional Sabbath Morning Service, and of which the 1819 edition had retained the 148th Psalm only, reappear—in Hebrew—in the 1841 edition, just as the introductory benediction of this section of the service, *Barukh She-amar,* of which the 1819 edition contained a German version only, is now given in Hebrew. There is also some half-hearted concession to some of the criticisms levelled against the first edition. The phrase, "O cause a new light to shine upon Zion," which had been omitted from the first benediction before the *Shema* in the 1819 edition, makes its appearance in the 1841 edition. But it is a half-hearted appearance: the words are in small print and enclosed in parentheses, and they are left untranslated. The same treatment is accorded some of the phrases which had appeared in large print, and with translation, in the first edition. For example, in the fifth of the Seven Benedictions, which had been left completely unchanged in the 1819 edition, the words, "and restore the service to the inner sanctuary of Thy house; and receive in love and favor both the fire-offerings of Israel and their prayer," are now printed in small type, enclosed in parentheses, and left untranslated. Moreover, and this time in large print, the concluding eulogy of this benediction has been changed from "who restorest Thy divine Presence unto Zion" to "whom alone we serve in reverence." Again, the benedictions preceding the fulfilment of Rabbinic, rather than Biblical, commandments have been given the small print treatment.[37]

The 1841 edition of the prayerbook was evidently meant to satisfy all those who had criticized the 1819 edition—whether from a position of stronger traditionalism or from one of more radical Reform. It was inevitable that this *tour de force* would please neither. The literature to which this edition of the Hamburg Temple Prayerbook gave rise is voluminous.[38] Those who contributed to it, and they included practically all the notable German rabbis of that time, addressed themselves to two questions which, though related, had to be dealt with separately: (a) the Proclamation issued against the use of that prayerbook by the Orthodox rabbi of Hamburg, Isaac Bernays,[39] and (b) the intrinsic merit, or otherwise, of the prayerbook itself. For there were those among the men whose opinion was elicited who, without particularly liking the prayerbook, still felt that Bernays had no right to interdict its use.

Such, for example, was the position of Zacharias Frankel. In a detailed critique, he dealt with—what he considered to have been—all the sins of omission and all the sins of commission of the new prayerbook; and, at the end, he comes to the following conclusions:

(1) Herr Bernays is extraordinarily mistaken in the manner in which he has expressed himself about the new prayerbook of the Temple Association.

(2) Herr Bernays has wrongly decided that one cannot pray the *tephillath ḥobhah* (obligatory prayer) from this book, since all the prayers required for *ḥobhah* are found in it, and since, as has long been known and acknowledged, what is here given in German does not constitute any injury to the prayer.

(3) On the other hand, this prayerbook of the Temple Association does not at all lend itself to use as a popular prayerbook, because the holiest sentiments of the nation are to a

considerable extent suppressed in it, and because, altogether, there are missing from it the soulful and most intimate aspects connected with the Hebrew prayers.

(4) The new prayerbook of the Temple Association lacks a scientific basis, and the kind of dignified seriousness which judges with deliberation. The revision shows haste and hurry, and an inexact evaluation of this important and holy subject. This prayerbook, therefore, on account of its inconsistencies, can claim neither validity nor recommendation.[40]

If Frankel criticized the prayerbook from his own more traditional point of view, Geiger, who wrote a learned treatise of 84 pages about it,[41] was no less critical. But, whereas Frankel would have liked to see a more traditional ritual, Geiger complained that the prayerbook was not radical enough in applying the Reform principle. The Temple, complained Geiger, had remained in its old half-heartedness. Instead of abbreviating the service still further, it had lengthened it. It had increased the amount of Hebrew. It had restored formulæ which had rightly been omitted from the first edition. And it had been somewhat less than honest in its method of printing certain prayers in small type and leaving them untranslated.[42]

That Geiger wanted too much too soon is evidenced not only by the prayerbook which he himself published in 1854, and which was far more "traditionalist" than the Hamburg ritual, but it was also stated, and in so many words, by the most radical Reformer of all, Samuel Holdheim. The latter makes the point that "the position of Dr. Geiger, while not an isolated one in the scientific world, is one which cannot be practically applied to real life."[43] Holdheim, for his part, confined himself to the demonstration that the innovations of the Hamburg Temple Prayerbook could all be justified within the framework of Rabbinic law.

There were also aesthetic criticisms. One of them was voiced by Max Loewengard.[44] Admitting that, while Hebrew is unhesitatingly to be preferred if the worshipper understands Hebrew, it is better, for those ignorant of Hebrew, to pray in the vernacular, he still voices his dislike of the alternation of Hebrew and German prayers in the Hamburg ritual. The German prayers should all have been grouped around the sermon.

> To recite the entire service in the vernacular (with the exception of the Torah reading, which, being a kind of demonstration, and not a prayer, must always take place in the holy tongue) is still no infringement of the Rabbinic *theory*. However, that alternation between Hebrew and the vernacular appears to me —and I do not want to be insulting—as patchwork.[45]

What the editors of the new prayerbook themselves wanted to achieve, they had stated quite simply in their Preface, of which we shall give a translation in a subsequent chapter.[46] That some of the criticisms levelled against this edition was seriously taken into consideration is evidenced by subsequent editions. And yet, those subsequent editions, in their own way, follow the method initiated by this second edition. They become ever more "Reform" in their doctrinal content, and ever more "traditional" in language and form. Thus, the 1868 edition, the next *revised* version of this prayerbook (the 1845 edition having been a mere reprint of the 1841 edition), opens from right to left, and contains the Hebrew text of practically all of the prayers which have been included. But there are no more prayers and benedictions which appear in small print and in parentheses, and remain untranslated. Passages which, for theological reasons, the 1841 edition presented in that form are altogether omitted in the 1868 edition. This dual process of more consistency in the Reform position, on the one hand, and of greater faithfulness to the traditional form, on the other, was carried still further by the 1904 edition, the last edition of the Hamburg Temple Prayerbook which appeared. In the twentieth century, however, an altogether new philosophy of liturgy seems to have been espoused by the Hamburg Temple. Its results have been described in 1937 by Caesar Seligmann, who, at one time, had himself been a rabbi of the Hamburg Temple. He wrote:

> Since then (i.e., the 1904 edition of the prayerbook), partly already under the earlier Temple preachers (who, by the way, since the turn of the twentieth century again called themselves "rabbis") and particularly under the influence of the present Chief Rabbi Dr. Italiener and the Chief Cantor Kornitzer, decisive changes have been made in the liturgy, in a conservative direction. . . . .
>
> (1) Ashkenazi pronunciation, instead of the Sepharadi pronunciation as hitherto.
> (2) Torah reading in the traditional *niggun*.
> (3) Change of the triennial cycle of Torah readings, so that each time one third of the current portion is being read.
> (4) Reading of the *whole Megillah*, in Hebrew, on Purim.
> (5) Introduction of a regular weekday service.
> (6) Introduction of a solemn service on the Eve of Hanukkah, the Eve of Purim, and on the evening, morning, and afternoon of the Ninth of Ab.
> (7) Introduction of *Seliḥoth* Services.
> (8) Youth services which are conducted in their entirety—including the Torah reading—by young people.
> (9) Substitution of the corresponding Hebrew prayers for all

the prayers (printed above the line) hitherto recited in German.

(10) Restoration of all the passages relating to Jerusalem.

(11) Inclusion of *En Kelohenu*.

(12) Musical revision of the entire worship service to bring it in line with the Ashkenazi musical tradition.

By means of those changes, the Temple has established its connection with the Synagogue, and has removed its isolation, which had hitherto existed, from the other German Liberal congregations.[47]

(3) The Liturgy of the Berlin *Reformgemeinde*

The Hamburg Temple was the first regular congregation in Germany (and in the world, for that matter) which was organized for the purpose of conducting worship on the basis of a Reform liturgy. The second such congregation in Germany (being preceded in the wider world by congregations in America and in England) was the *Reformgemeinde* of Berlin, which came into existence in 1845.[48] That congregation had the distinction of applying the radical Reform principle most consistently, and with ruthless logic, to the field of liturgy. It was also, as far as we have been able to determine, the one Reform congregation in the world which revised its prayerbook more frequently than any other. In compiling our Chronological Bibliography,[49] we have come across ten different editions of Volume I of the *Reformgemeinde* prayerbook, published between 1848 and 1933; and the 1848 edition itself had been preceded, between 1845 and 1846, by some seven experimental prayer leaflets.

Yet two entirely different tendencies marked the development of the Hamburg liturgy and the evolution of the Berlin Reform liturgy. While each successive edition of the Hamburg Temple Prayerbook marked a further rapprochement to the traditional rubrics and forms, even though the traditional prayers might be increasingly emended in accordance with doctrinal Reform principles, the successive editions of the *Reformgemeinde* prayerbook fluctuated between greater and lesser faithfulness to the traditional pattern—until the latter was almost completely abandoned in the last edition which was published. The latter was a leaflet of 64 pages, containing the services for the entire year, viz., a weekly evening service (3 pages), a weekly morning service (6 pages), a service for the Pilgrim Festivals (10 pages), a New Year's Eve service (4 pages), a service for the first day of New Year (7 pages), a service for the second day of New Year (7 pages), a service for Atonement Eve (4 pages), a service for the morning of the Day of Atonement

(8 pages), a service for the conclusion of the Day of Atonement (5 pages), a service for Hanukkah (3 pages), and a Confirmation Service (5 pages).[50]

From its inception, that congregation never intended to have any but completely German services, and there was never any departure from that principle, except that the *Shema,* but only the first verse and its response, the responses of the *Kedushah,* and three or four similar verses, as well as the Torah reading, were retained. Immanuel Heinrich Ritter, one of the preachers of that congregation, explained the principle involved:

> Hebrew has become a foreign language for us, and German the language of our homeland. Only the ancient proclamations of Judaism, the *Shema Yisrael* (Hear, O Israel, etc.), the *Kadosh Kadosh* (Holy, holy is the Lord of hosts) and a few similar verses do we also recite in their original language. But those are not prayers. They are the pledge of allegiance and the watchword of Judaism, of which we are preserving the most ancient form—just as the Prussians and the Austrians are preserving their mottoes, *suum cuique* ("To each his own") and *unitis viribus* ("With combined strengths"), in Latin, even though they are speaking German today. By proclaiming those basic truths in both languages, we also want to point to their origin in the times and places of most ancient Asiatic culture, and to remind ourselves of the fact that the bases of Judaism have remained the same, and that the present-day conviction of its adherents coincides with that of its first representatives.
>
> In addition to reading a translation of the Bible, we also read it in its Hebrew original, for, as Holdheim has demonstrated, only the latter can be a source for the knowledge and perception of Biblical religion—only it, but not any given translation which itself is already the result of a definite individual interpretation. In Judaism, no single translation, however successful, can attain binding validity, and none may anticipate and hamper further investigations. It is due to this fortunate circumstance that, until now, the doctrinal and creedal contents of the Bible have not yet been completely determined, and fixed in permanent creedal affirmations. Instead, ever and again we go back to the original text, meditating about its meaning and application. Thus, also in this connection, religious compulsion is excluded, and the freedom of conscience is advanced.[51]

It should be borne in mind that this defense of Hebrew by Ritter contains many more words than the number of Hebrew words in any single volume of the prayerbook of the Berlin *Reformgemeinde.*

At first, the *Reformgemeinde* used to hold services both on Saturday and on Sunday, but, after a very short time, the Saturday services were discontinued. One of the problems, therefore, which faced the liturgists of that congregation was whether the Sunday services should be given the character of weekday services, or whether real Sabbath services should be held on Sunday.[52] The solution of this problem was evaded for a long time, for, even though prayers from the Sabbath liturgy were included in the "Weekly Service," specific references to the Sabbath were omitted, the prayerbook confining itself to thanking God "for the day on which we are able to lift up heart and spirit unto Thee, in Thy house," and praising God "who sanctifiest our celebration."[53] In the nineteen-thirties, however, any inhibitions on that score were giving way, and the Sabbath character of the service was made explicit.[54]

It goes without saying that the tendency to "universalize" the prayers, which has been evident in all modern reformed rituals, reaches its climax in the prayerbook of the *Reformgemeinde*. Jerusalem, Zion, the Messiah, the sacrifices, etc., are simply no problem here.

The 1848 edition of the prayerbook contains a meditation for silent devotion "in preparation for the worship service," a selection of 54 chorales, an "Introductory Prayer for Saturday Worship," a prayer for the Kaiser, and nine different "cycles" for the weekly service, followed by 15 concluding hymns, prayers for special occasions and domestic devotions. Each "cycle" is somewhat reminiscent of the traditional pattern. It includes the first paragraph of the *Shema* and at least the first three of the Eighteen Benedictions. The second benediction is invariably followed by a silent prayer for the dead. However, in order to have enough material for nine different services, the editors of that prayerbook not only composed new prayers, and adapted others from the traditional liturgy for Sabbath and weekdays. They also included in the weekly services prayers peculiar to the liturgy of the High Holy Days. In 1856, Samuel Holdheim, the first rabbi of the *Reformgemeinde,* petitioned for the removal of the High Holy Day prayers from the weekly liturgy, even as he suggested the substitution of Psalm verses for the introductory chorales, which latter he described as "exotic plants which do not flourish on the soil of the Jewish worship service."[55]

Holdheim's suggestions were not completely implemented in the 1859 edition of the prayerbook. But, beginning with the 1885 edition, a number of editions definitely show that Holdheim's views had been taken to heart. The opening hymns are now Psalms, the High Holy Day elements have been removed from the weekly service, and the latter, in spite of all of its modifications and omissions, follows the traditional liturgical pattern of Judaism.

Ten years later, in 1895, the "Jubilee Edition" of the prayerbook of the *Reformgemeinde* is essentially identical with the 1885 version. It does, in fact, add twelve Hebrew and Aramaic words from the traditional Kaddish prayer.[56] But this attempt to bring the liturgy of the *Reformgemeinde* in line with the traditional pattern was short-lived. The twentieth century was to see a very radical departure from that pattern. Since the prayerbook of the nineteen-thirties is distinguished by its extreme brevity, we are able to present here the complete morning service.[57] In footnotes we shall refer the reader to such traditional liturgical sources as have been utilized by the editors. A comparison with the original will show to what extent the prayers have been abbreviated and changed in implication, and also the degree to which this liturgy departs from the traditional pattern.

Morning Service

SILENT DEVOTION.

CHOIR:

How goodly are thy tents, O Jacob, thy dwelling places, O Israel! Through Thy lovingkindness, O Heavenly Father, we enter Thy house, and bow down before Thee in reverence, in Thy holy temple.[58]

Praised be He through Whose word
The world came into being.
Praised be He Who speaketh and doeth,
Who decreeth and performeth.
Praised be He Who liveth forever,
And faithfully rewardeth pious deeds.[59]

CONGREGATION:

When creation was completed,
Everything did rest in peace,
Then unto Thy world Thou sendest
The day of Sabbath blessedness.
Merciful Creator, Thou,
Giving Sabbath rest us now.

Light and joy and Sabbath peace
Enter now in our hearts.
May all creatures get their portion
Of Thy Sabbath's radiance.
Lov'd and loving Father, Thou,
Bless our Sabbath resting now.[60]

How great are Thy works, O Lord, with wisdom hast Thou ordered them all. The whole earth is full of Thy gifts.[61]

Pure was our heart when we came into existence; pure shall it be when we depart.[62]

Life, which we received as a gift from God, is to find its fulfilment in Thy service, in the service of righteousness and love, of truth and faithfulness, for the salvation of all of our human brothers, for the blessing of all mankind.

May peace and blessing descend upon all the children of the earth, so that they may all unite in one union of mankind, to do Thy will with a perfect heart.[63]

CHOIR: Now let us praise the mighty Ruler,
CONGREGATION: Who is like unto Thee, O God!
CHOIR: The exalted Master of all beings.
CONGREGATION: Who is like unto Thee, O God!
CHOIR: We would serve Him in reverence,
CONGREGATION: We praise Thee, O God!
CHOIR: And joyfully praise His Name.
CONGREGATION: We praise Thee, O God!
CHOIR: Creator from the beginning of all worlds,
CONGREGATION: We thank Thee, O God!
CHOIR: And faithful Father of all creatures,
CONGREGATION: We thank Thee, O God!
CHOIR: Who is holy in the heavenly heights.
CONGREGATION: Who is like unto Thee, O God!

Selection from the Scriptures

Amen!
Let us glorify the holiness of God.

(The congregation rises.)

We proclaim in the word of the Prophet (Isa. 6: 3):

Holy, holy, holy is the Lord Zebaoth!
The whole earth is full of His glory.

CONGREGATION: קדוש קדוש קדוש יי צבאות מלא כל הארץ כבודו:

CHOIR: Praised be the glory of the Eternal, here and in all the world.
CONGREGATION: ברוך כבוד יי ממקומו:
CHOIR: God reigneth forever, even Thy God, O Zion, for all times.
CONGREGATION: ימלוך יי לעולם אלהיך ציון לדור ודור הללויה:

(The congregation is seated.)

Thine is the kingdom unto eternity, and all the children of man will bow down before Thee, on that day when God will be King over the whole earth—He, the One, and His Name One. [65]

Silent Devotion

(For mourners in the period of mourning:)

Out of the depths I call unto Thee, O Lord, Who art near unto all them that are of a saddened heart. In Thine unsearchable wisdom, Thou hast taken from me the beloved .... Humbly I bow to Thy holy will, O God of life. Thou hast given and hast taken away. Thou bringest down, and Thou raisest up again. Let me find comfort in this thought, and let me revere Thy wisdom. Amen!

(For those remembering a departed relative at a "Jahrzeit":)

I remember you, dear ..., whom the will of the omniscient Guide of the World has called away all too soon. Again a year has gone over your grave. The love which you have shown me, and the joys which you have given me, have not been forgotten by me. I will remember you as long as I live. Praised art Thou, O Lord, Who keepest the departed alive in the memory of their survivors. Amen!

We remember our departed:

(The congregation rises.)

and, with grateful hearts, we renew the memory of their life and deeds. In pious resignation we say:

יתגדל ויתקדש שמה רבא:

May God be praised in the world, which He hath created according to His omnipotent will. May His Kingdom come soon, and may His rule be accepted by all the world. May we become citizens of this Kingdom, together with all the children of man, in the paternal household of God.

And may all those who have departed according to the will of the Almighty rest in peace. Faithfully they will be remembered in the hearts of their loved ones!

God be praised from eternity to eternity!

CONGREGATION: [66]אמן : יהא שמה רבא מברך לעלם ולעלמי עלמיא :

(The congregation is seated.)

(On special days of remembrance, the choir sings the anthem, "All the souls do rest in peace.")

SILENT PRAYER.

Taking the Torah from the Ark

CHOIR:

Highly exalted art Thou, O Lord,
Thy works praise Thee.
All creation praiseth Thy might,
And Thy Kingdom is forever.
The Eternal reigneth throughout all ages.
May He bless His people; praised be He! [67]

(The congregation rises.)

CONGREGATION:

Open and be ye lifted up, O gates of the world,
That the King of Glory may enter!
The Lord is a great God,
The Lord is a great King.
Let all praise His holy Name! Amen!

PREACHER:

Praised be He Who, in His holiness, hath given us the doctrine of truth, and hath planted within us eternal life.[68]

A glorious gift hath been given unto us; may we never forsake it. Length of days is in her right hand; in her left hand are riches and honor. She is a firm support to them that lay hold upon her, and he who supports himself on her walketh steadily.[69]

CONGREGATION:

Praise ye the Lord. He hath given His teaching to the house of Israel, in His holiness.[70]

CHOIR: שמע ישראל יי אלהינו יי אחד :

CONGREGATION: שמע ישראל יי אלהינו יי אחד :

PREACHER:

Hear, O Israel: The Eternal is our God, the Unique and Eternal

One! Thou shalt love the Eternal thy God with all thy heart, with all thy soul, and with all thy might. (The German version of the *Shema* continues, and concludes with "when thou liest down, and when thou risest up.")[71]

CHOIR:

Thine, O Lord, is the might, and the greatness, the glory, and the dominion, O Holy One! All that is in the heaven and in the earth is Thine, O Lord, our King. Praise is Thine, O Lord, and honor and thanks are Thine, O Exalted One![72]

(The congregation is seated.)

From the Torah

A precious good is the word of the doctrine unto us; happy is he that preserveth it!

CONGREGATION:

O hearken unto the word which the world hath received from the children of Israel! Its divine spirit liveth forever.

From the Books of the Prophets

True and faithful is the word from the mouth of the Prophet, like a well of living waters which never runneth dry.

Organ Music

(The congregation rises.)

PREACHER:

The word of God is perfect, restoring the soul;
The testimony of God is truth, turning simplicity into wisdom;
The commandments of God are wise, rejoicing the heart;
The teachings of God are pure, and enlighten the eye.[73]

CHOIR:

Restore us, O Lord, unto Thy teaching.
It is a tree of life.
Its way is bliss, and peaceful is its path.
Its way is bliss and peace.[74]

(The congregation is seated.)

Sermon

(The congregation rises for the prayer and the benediction of the Preacher.)

CHOIR: יברכך יי וישמרך יאר יי פניו אליך ויחנך ישא יי פניו אליך וישם לך שלום:

CONGREGATION: Amen!

(The congregation is seated.)

CONGREGATION and CHOIR sing responsively a German version of *Adon 'Olam.*[75]

(4) The Liturgy of British Reform Judaism

If the prayerbook of the Berlin *Reformgemeinde* represents one extreme of the spectrum of Reform liturgy, the opposite extreme is represented by the prayerbook of the West London Synagogue of British Jews, at any rate by its early editions. The founders of that synagogue[76] were not troubled by the theological problems which agitated the German Reformers. All they initially desired was an abbreviated liturgy and a decorous worship service which, by the side of a Hebrew liturgy, would include a sermon in the vernacular. They had wanted all this within the framework of the existing congregations, that of the Ashkenazim, and that of the Sepharadim. But they also wanted something else. They advocated the abolition of the second (non-Biblical) day of the festivals; and that brought them into conflict with the very structure of Rabbinic Judaism. This, in turn, led to strong rebuffs, the formation of their own congregation, and their excommunication by the Jewish ecclesiastical authorities of England. It also led to a very strong anti-Rabbinic stance taken by the Reformers, which was also to be reflected by their liturgy.[77] But, strongly as they opposed the binding character of the Rabbinic tradition, they equally strongly maintained the divine character of the Scriptures. And, since the Scriptures contained the doctrine of a personal Messiah, a doctrine of the Resurrection of the Dead, a doctrine of a messianic Return to Zion, and a sacrificial legislation and a promise of the ultimate restoration of the sacrificial cult, all of this appears in an unchanged form in the first edition (1841/42) of the *Forms of Prayer* of the West London Synagogue of British Jews.

Among the founders of the West London Synagogue, there were more Sepharadim than Ashkenazim. Under the circumstances, it is not surprising that, in instances where the Ashkenazi and the Sepharadi rites diverge, the prayerbook of the West London Synagogue more often than not follows the Sepharadi rite. Yet, the main feature of that new liturgy is its brevity. Repetitions are eliminated, and so are the *piyutim*—except on the Day of Atonement. And where repetitions cannot be avoided, there is an attempt at abbreviating the prayer in question. For example, while the intermediate section of the *Musaph* Seven Benedictions has been retained (according to the Sepharadi version) in a completely unchanged form,[78] the first three and last three of the Seven Benedictions, which are given in full for the *Shaḥarith* Service, appear in an abbreviated form in the *Musaph* Service. The first three benedictions[79] are given the form they have in the traditional *me'en shebha'* benediction of the Sabbath Eve Service,[80] while the last three benedictions appear in the following contracted form:

רצה יי אלהינו בעמך ישראל ולתפלתם שעה. והשב העבודה לדביר ביתך. ותהי לרצון תמיד עבודת ישראל עמך לפניך: הטוב כי לא כלו רחמיך. והמרחם כי לא תמו חסדיך: מודים אנחנו לך על היינו המסורים בידך. ועל נשמותינו הפקודות לך. ועל טובותיך שבכל עת. כי אתה הוא הטוב שמך ולך נאה להודות: שים שלום. טובה. ברכה. חיים. חן. ורחמים. עלינו ועל כל ישראל עמך. וברכנו אבינו כלנו יחד באור פניך: ברוך אתה יי. המברך את עמו ישראל בשלום. אמן:[81]

Other innovations of this liturgy will be noted in the various relevant chapters of this book. But one further peculiarity must be pointed out here. The English Reformers' antipathy to Rabbinic Judaism extended also to the Aramaic language, in which so much of Rabbinic literature is written. As a consequence, the English Reformers translated a number of Aramaic prayers into Hebrew, including the Kaddish, which they rendered as follows:[82]

יתגדל ויתקדש שם הגדול (sic): בעולם אשר ברא כרצונו. וימליך מלכותו. ויצמיח ישועתו. ויקרב משיחו. בחייכם ובימיכם ובחיי כל בית ישראל במהרה ובזמן קרוב ואמרו אמן:

יהי שם הגדול (sic) מבורך. לעולם ולעולמי עולמים:

יתברך. וישתבח. ויתפאר. ויתרומם. ויתנשא. ויתהדר, ויתעלה. ויתהלל. שם הקדוש ברוך הוא: למעלה מן כל ברכות. שירות. ותשבחות. הנאמרים (sic) בעולם ואמרו אמן:

יהי שלום רב מן השמים. חיים. ושבע. וישועה. ונחמה. ורפואה. וגאולה. וסליחה. וכפרה. ורוח. והצלה. לנו ולכל ישראל. ואמרו אמן:

עשה שלום במרומיו. הוא יעשה שלום. עלינו ועל כל ישראל. ואמרו אמן:

Subsequent editions corrected the grammatical mistakes, and also improved the Hebrew style of this Kaddish.[83] Subsequent editions of the prayerbook of the West London Synagogue however, also did something else. Almost imperceptibly, the prayers for the Return to Zion were somewhat toned down. In 1841, the members of the West London Synagogue still prayed: "O hasten and bring us blessing and peace from the four corners of the earth; and speedily lead us securely to our land."[84] In the 1856 edition of the prayerbook, the word "speedily" disappears from both the Hebrew and the English texts.[85] From 1890 on, if not before, the petition for the restoration of the "fire-offerings of Israel" is no longer included in the *'Abhodah* section of the Eighteen Benedictions.[86] But the West London Synagogue continued to pray for the Return to Zion, the Rebuilding of Jerusalem, the Ingathering of the Exiles, and the coming of a personal Messiah. On the other hand, Volume V of the *Forms of Prayer,* containing the services for the Ninth of Ab, the Fast of Gedaliah, the Tenth Day of Tebeth, and the Seventeenth Day of Tammuz, does not appear to have been reprinted after the first edition was exhausted, and services on those occasions must have fallen into desuetude. In the forties on the twentieth century, such services were no longer conducted, although the service for the Ninth of Ab was revived in the fifties. Over the years, too, an increasing number of prayers began to be recited in English. However, the greater part of the service continued to be in Hebrew, and the prayerbook provided both the Hebrew and the English texts of all the prayers included in the liturgy.

Thus, in spite of the changes which the West London Synagogue had introduced, such as the abbreviation of the prayers, the elimination of repetitions and of *piyutim,* the substitution of Biblical phrases for Rabbinic ones, and the expunging of "the few expressions which are known to be the offspring of feelings produced by oppression, and are universally admitted to be foreign to the heart of every true Israelite of our day,"[87] and even the discarding of references to the sacrificial cult, the liturgy of the West London Synagogue must still be considered as the most "traditionalist" of all Reform liturgies—whether we compare it to the prayerbooks which come under the heading of "Reform from Within," or whether we have in mind the liturgical productions of other "independent" Reform congregations. Such, at any rate, was the position until 1931. In that year, a new edition, the sixth, of Volume I of the *Forms of Prayer* was published. In their Preface to that edition, the editors state: "We have sought to preserve the rich and hallowed values of the inherited Jewish ritual, and at the same time have endeavoured to meet the needs of the present age, by modifying and omitting where this has been deemed advisable, by reintroducing some ancient prayers, and by adding others entirely new."[88]

Concretely, this meant that, while the editors had retained the traditional structure of the liturgy, they had also applied the Reform point of view so consistently that, as far as the prayers for the Return to Zion and the Rebuilding of Jerusalem were concerned, the liturgy of the West London Synagogue no longer contained them. Its "Reform" position had been made evident, even though the first of the Eighteen Benedictions (reduced to twelve in this edition) continued to speak of "a redeemer" (and not of "redemption"), and the second ascribed to God the power to "quicken the dead."[89] All this, however, applied to the liturgy for Sabbath and weekdays only. For the festivals and High Holy Days the older editions of the prayerbook remained in use. They are, at this moment, being revised by the Assembly of Ministers of the Reform Synagogues of Great Britain, the new edition of Volume II (*Prayers for the Pilgrim Festivals*) having already appeared in 1965.

In relation to earlier editions of this volume of the prayerbook, the new edition of the festival prayers shows the influence of the doctrinal

Reform principles which had marked the 1931 edition of Volume I. Yet there is less emending of the Hebrew text in this 1965 edition, and more reliance on paraphrasing in the spirit of Reform. Thus, while the Hebrew text refers to "the Messiah, the son of Thy servant David," the English translation speaks of "the Messianic hope of Israel." [90] The reference to resurrection, unchanged in Hebrew, becomes "Thou endowest man with immortal life" in English.[91]

Far more significant, however, is the fact that this new volume of the British Reform liturgy contains the full text of the traditional Ashkenazi *Kedushah* for the *Musaph* Service,[92] here, in the absence of a *Musaph* Service, included in the Seven Benedictions of *Shaharith*.[93] One of the few radical departures which had distinguished British Reform liturgy from the traditional prayerbook since 1841 had been the total elimination of angelology—to an extent beyond anything attempted in the reformed prayerbooks of Germany. This had resulted in a reduction of the *Kedushah* to the following elements: (a) Psalm 22:4; (b) Isaiah 6: 3, without the first five words ;(c) Ezekiel 3:12b; (d) Psalm 146: 10; and (e) the concluding eulogy, "Praised art Thou, O Lord, the holy God." [94]

Already in 1955, the late Bruno Italiener, then one of the rabbis of the West London Synagogue, and formerly Chief Rabbi of the Hamburg Temple, had argued for the restoration of the traditional *Kedushah*.[95] Rejecting, what he considered to have been, the shallow rationalism of the nineteenth century, he claimed that it was "just the tremendous progress of physical science, during the last decades, which has revealed (the) limits of human knowledge. The more we seem to penetrate into the secrets of the universe, the more new mysteries and unfathomable depths become apparent." [96]

> It is against this background that we, much better than our ancestors a hundred years ago, begin to understand the metaphorical and figurative language of the prophets and poets, preserved in our sacred literature, and not least in our prayers, by which they tried to express their intuitions and visions. Today, if ever, we should try to satisfy in our services both feelings in man: his respect for reason on the one hand and his new awareness of the depth of life on the other. For this reason those passages of our religious literature should be chosen for the re-shaping of our prayerbooks which, in symbolic and poetical form, make us aware of the presence of a mysterious world, which, although unseen and unexplored, nevertheless is real, continuously surrounding and influencing us.[97]

The editors of the 1965 edition of the *Prayers for the Pilgrim Festivals* must have shared Italiener's sentiments. At any rate, for the first time in many a year, they produced a Reform prayerbook which did not anxiously shy away from angelology.

In one other respect, too, the 1965 prayerbook is remarkable. The anti-Rabbinic, quasi-Karaite stance of the liturgy of the West London Synagogue has now been completely abandoned. This may be seen from the fact that, side by side with the Hebrew version of the Kaddish, the old Aramaic version is likewise provided.[98] In this, however, the 1965 edition had already been preceded by a 1952 Supplement to Volume I of the *Forms of Prayer*.[99] It is even clearer in the restoration of the traditional wording of the benediction over the *lulabh*. The early British Reformers had retained the observance of taking a *lulabh* on the Feast of Tabernacles. That was a Biblical commandment, and Biblical commandments were accepted as divine. However, the word *lulabh* itself is Rabbinical, not Biblical. It was, therefore, unacceptable to the early British Reformers. And so was the wording of the traditional benediction which said: "Praised art Thou, O Lord our God, Sovereign of the Universe, who hast sanctified us by Thy commandments, and commanded us concerning the taking of the *lulabh*." In its place, the Reformers had devised the following formula, leaning heavily on Leviticus 23: 40: "Praised art Thou, O Lord our God, Sovereign of the Universe, who hast sanctified us by Thy commandments, and commanded us to take the fruit of goodly trees, branches of palm trees, and the boughs of thick trees, and willows of the brook."[100] The 1965 edition no longer takes umbrage at the vocabulary of the Rabbis, and restores the traditional *lulabh* benediction.[101]

In a way, the history of British Reform liturgy could be characterized as follows: Many of the things which bothered the Reformers of the nineteenth century no longer bother their successors in the twentieth; and many of the things which did not bother the nineteenth-century Reformers do bother their twentieth-century successors. All that this means, however, is that the liturgy of the West London Synagogue has been alive and alert to the religious needs of its users, and that, in spite of its "traditional" format, that liturgy has its rightful place among the prayerbooks of "Independent Reform."

(5) The Liturgy of British Liberal Judaism

While, still in the nineteenth century, the West London Synagogue prayerbook had been adopted by congregations in Manchester and in Bradford, and while, in the twentieth, many more congregations joined the West London Synagogue in the formation of the Association of Synagogues in Great Britain (later renamed The Reform Synagogues of Great Britain), Progressive Judaism in England created for itself yet a second channel, the Union of Liberal and Progressive Synagogues.[102] Beginning in 1902, under the leadership of the Hon. Lily H. Montagu and of Claude G. Montefiore, assisted by some ministers of the Reform synagogue and even of some Orthodox synagogues, an organization called The Jewish Religious Union held services on Sabbath afternoons. Those services were intended for Jews who were prevented, for economic reasons, from attending regular Sabbath morning services, as well as for those who had otherwise become estranged from the traditional services. At that time, as is evident from the participation of some Orthodox ministers, there was no thought of creating a new religious "denomination" within Anglo-Jewry. The services were regarded as "supplementary" to those conducted in the established synagogues.[103] This enabled the organizers of the Jewish Religious Union to feel quite free with regard to the selection of prayers, the language of prayer, the introduction of instrumental music, the singing of hymns written by non-Jewish poets, the choice of preachers, the absence of a reading from the Torah, and the arrangement of mixed seating. But, while this may perhaps not have been thus intended from the beginning by all of the organizers of the Jewish Religious Union, the changes introduced already contained, if only implicitly, the practical application of some "radical" Reform principles. So "radical" indeed were the principles that, after a while, the Orthodox ministers were unable to cooperate, and even the West London (Reform) Synagogue found itself unable to extend the hospitality of its premises to the new group, the latter having been unwilling to modify their practice along the lines suggested by the Reform Synagogue.[104] It was, therefore, inevitable that, sooner or later, the implicit radicalism would be made explicit. That happened when, in 1912, the Jewish Religious Union established the Liberal Jewish Synagogue, calling to its pulpit a Hebrew Union College graduate, Israel I. Mattuck. At the same time, the Jewish Religious Union added the words "for the Advancement of Liberal Judaism" to its name. Within the English setting, "Liberal Judaism" described the point of view which, in America, was called "Classical Reform Judaism"—whereas "Reform Judaism" was the name applied to the far more "conservative" outlook of the West London Synagogue. After several more congregations had been established under the auspices of the Jewish Religious Union, including one composed of German refugees whose liturgy was far more "traditional" than even that of the Reform congregations in England, the Jewish Religious Union for the Advancement of Liberal Judaism changed its name to that of the Union of Liberal and Progressive Synagogues.

The Jewish Religious Union began its liturgical creativity in 1902 with the "provisional edition" of *A Selection of Prayers, Psalms, and*

Other Scriptural Passages, and Hymns. This booklet contained a number of traditional prayers as well as some newly composed ones. Though designed for services held on Sabbath afternoon, the prayerbook did not confine its selection to prayers traditionally associated with that occasion. Petitions for the Return to Zion were omitted. The prayerbook is mainly in English; only the following passages are also given in Hebrew: The *Barekhu*, the first paragraph of the *Shema'*, The Ten Commandments, Psalm 24, selections from Psalm 92, Psalm 96, selections from Psalm 118, and *Adon 'Olam*.

A greatly augmented edition of the *Selection* appeared in 1903. Not only have many more prayers been "selected" from the traditional ritual, but they are also arranged in a pattern more nearly resembling that of the traditional Jewish liturgical structure. There are also more Hebrew passages, including, in addition to those contained in the 1902 edition, Psalm 69: 14 for the opening of the service, *Wihi Ratzon*,[105] Isaiah 6: 3, *Elohenu . . . Retzeh*,[106] *Sim Shalom*, [107] the opening sentences of *Ubha Letziyon Go-el*,[108] the Kaddish,[109] Psalm 8, Psalm 23, Psalm 29, Psalm 117, *En Kelohenu* in the Sepharadi version, and concluding with the words: "Thou wilt save us; Thou wilt arise, and have mercy on Zion, when the time to favour her, yea, the appointed time, hath come," *Hakkol Yodukha* (concluding with *misgabh ba'adenu*),[110] and *'Al Hakkol* (including the references to God's return to Zion).[111] In the history of Liberal Judaism in England, this 1903 edition of *A Selection of Prayers, Psalms, and Other Scriptural Passages, and Hymns* may be said to represent the most "traditional" liturgical production in contents and in form. Later Liberal prayerbooks, edited by Israel I. Mattuck, were to include more traditional material, but no longer in the traditional sequence and pattern. And the 1967 prayerbook of the Union of Liberal and Progressive Synagogues, while reverting to the traditional pattern, also saw fit to give the traditional prayers it retained a more generalized and "universalized," rather than a specific "Jewish," tone. But, then, in 1903, the Liberal point of view, while implicit, had not yet been made explicit; and the Jewish Religious Union had not yet added the words "for the Advancement of Liberal Judaism" to its name.

That was to come in 1912. It was probably in that year that the *Sabbath Afternoon Services* of the Liberal Jewish Synagogue were published.[112] The arrangement of that prayerbook set the pattern for all future liturgical publications of British Liberal Judaism. Though there can be, at most, only five Sabbaths a month, this prayerbook offers six different services. No service, therefore, is in danger of becoming uninteresting by too much repetition. Such, at any rate, must have been the reasoning behind this arrangement. Every single service contains the *Barekhu*, the first paragraph the the *Shema* (which is *not* included in the traditional Sabbath Afternoon Service), a Torah Service, and the Kaddish. Apart from those permanent elements, each service has prayers not included in the other services. The prayers are either adapted from the traditional liturgy (although not necessarily from the traditional Sabbath Afternoon Service) or modern. The traditional sequence of the prayers has been abandoned.

Four years later, a very similar prayerbook was produced for Sabbath Morning Services.[113] This, however, contains four different services only. Here, in addition to the permanent elements already mentioned in connection with the Sabbath Afternoon Services, there is a form of the *Kedushah* in every single service. Invariably, the *Kedushah* is introduced by the paragraph, *Ledor Wador,*[114] which, in the traditional Ashkenazi rite, follows, rather than precedes, the *Kedushah*. While it is used as an introductory paragraph in the Italian rite, its place in the liturgy of the Liberal Jewish Synagogue was probably less an attempt to educate the members of that congregation in comparative Jewish liturgy than an intended demonstrative departure from the accustomed pattern. Such, at least, is the impression one gets from the treatment of other traditional prayers in this prayerbook. For example, the *Mi Khamokha,* in this collection of Sabbath Morning Services, invariably comes before the *Shema,* rather than after *Shema*—which latter position it had occupied in all rites since the days of the Tannaim.

Since this wilful and arbitrary departure from the traditional pattern is one of the chief distinguishing features of the liturgical activity of the late Israel I. Mattuck, which he was to expand considerably in later years, it will be instructive to compare the order of the prayers in a given service of the 1916 prayerbook with the order in which those prayers would be recited in a traditional service. We are selecting Service I for purposes of comparison.[115]

LIBERAL JEWISH SABBATH MORNING SERVICE	TRADITIONAL ORDER
(1) How goodly are thy tents . . .	(1)
(2) *Barekhu* and response	(4)
(3) My God, the soul . . .	(2)
(4) *Mi Khamokha*	(7)
(5) With abounding love . . .	(5)
(6) *Shema*	(6)
(7) Sovereign of all worlds . . .	(3)
(8) Thou art mighty . . .	(8)
(9) Thou favourest man with knowledge . . .	Never on a Sabbath.
(10) *Ledor Wador*	(10)

(11) *Kedushah*	(9)
(12) *Elohenu . . . Retzeh*	(11)
(13) new prayer	—
(14) O my God, guard my tongue . . .	(12)
(15) Selections from Psalm 36	—
(16) new prayer	—
(17) The Ten Commandments	Not a part of public worship.
(18) Torah Service	(13)
(19) Kaddish	(15)
(20) Sermon	(14)
(21) *Adon 'Olam*	(16)

The tendencies adumbrated in the 1912 and 1916 prayerbooks come to full fruition in Mattuck's 1926 edition of Volume I of the *Liberal Jewish Prayer Book.* A detailed discussion of that volume (and of its 1937 augmented edition) is not needed here, since a description of that book and excerpts from its Introduction will be given in another chapter.[116] It should be pointed out, however, that, notwithstanding Mattuck's complete rearrangement of the Sabbath and weekday services contained in that volume, his edition of the High Holy Day prayers (Volume II of the *Liberal Jewish Prayer Book,* 1924), and of the festival prayers (Volume III, 1926), are marked by a far greater adherence to the traditional liturgical pattern. It may well be that, since the occasions for which the latter two volumes provide occur but once a year, the urge to provide for variety and variation was felt less strongly than in the case of the weekly service.

One of the by-products of the *Liberal Jewish Prayer Book* was the prayerbook edited, in 1929, by Basil L. Q. Henriques, for the St. George's Settlement Synagogue. That settlement house had been established under the joint auspices of the West London Synagogue and of the Liberal Jewish Synagogue, and, under the leadership of Henriques, it functioned as an outpost of Liberal Judaism in London's East End. The prayerbook reflects both the philosophy of Basil L. Q. Henriques, a very "universalistic" kind of Liberal Judaism, and the traditional background of the prayerbook's potential users. Wrote Henriques in his Preface:

> I have to thank Mr. C. G. Montefiore, my friend and master, for the personal help he has given me in connection with this book. He is in no way responsible, however, for the form of the Services, which I believe to be of such a kind as to meet the requirements of my congregation in East London.[117]

The form was that of the traditional service, though greatly abbreviated and not consistently so. Yet, compared with Mattuck's prayerbook, Henriques' bears a greater resemblance to the traditional pattern. Moreover, Henriques is more inclined than Mattuck to preserve such Hebrew prayers as are included in an unemended form, while expressing the Liberal point of view in an English paraphrase which often bears very little relation to the Hebrew text. For example, Henriques keeps Numbers 10:35 in his Torah Service. (Mattuck, for obvious reasons, does not.) The verse reads, "And when the Ark set forward, Moses said: 'Arise, O Lord, and let Thine enemies be scattered; and let those who hate Thee flee before Thee.'" That is also what the Hebrew in Henriques' prayerbook says, on page 48. But the English "translation" reads as follows:

> And when the Ark set forward, Moses said, Arise, shine forth, O Lord, that those who have forsaken thee may find thee.

Again, it is instructive to compare the respective treatments accorded the hymn, *Yigdal,* in Mattuck's *Liberal Jewish Prayer Book,* on the one hand, and in Henriques' *Prayer Book,* on the other.[118] Mattuck omits stanzas 7, 8, and 12 of that hymn, and re-writes stanza 13 to read, "He hath implanted eternal life within us." Stanza 9 ("God will never alter, nor change His law to everlasting for any other.") is accompanied by a footnote which reads: "'His law' is here taken in a larger sense than it has in the original."

Henriques, on the other hand, keeps the Hebrew text of *Yigdal* without any changes. It is in his English version that he shows himself to be completely at one with Mattuck in matters theological. Stanza 7 ("Never has there arisen in Israel a Prophet like Moses beholding God's image.") becomes: "The law of Life has He given us through Moses and the Prophets of Israel." Stanza 8 ("The Torah of truth God gave to His people through His Prophet who was faithful in His house.") becomes: "The law of Truth has He revealed to the wise and faithful of every age." Stanza 12 ("At the end of time He will send our Messiah to redeem those that wait for His final salvation.") becomes: "At the end of days shall all men accept the yoke of His Kingdom, and the age of Righteousness and peace shall be established in the world."

Our consideration of the *Yigdal* must suffice as an indication of the manner in which traditional prayers have been handled in the *Prayer Book* edited by Henriques. The permanent value of that book lies perhaps less in its paraphrasing of traditional Hebrew texts than in the "Special Prayers," composed by Henriques himself, under such headings as "For Faith and Strength," "For the Sanctification of Life," "For Courage," etc., prayers which are marked by a profound spiritual quality.

A second edition of this *Prayer Book,* published in 1965, includes "Supplementary Prayers for Festivals," taken from traditional sources, as well as some additional anthems, including some of Christian provenance.

An entirely new venture in the liturgy of British Liberal Judaism is the prayerbook entitled, *The Service of the Heart,* which will be published in 1967 by the Union of Liberal and Progressive Synagogues. Since the galley proofs of that prayerbook have generously been made available to us by the editors, we have been able to include references to its innovations in various chapters of our book. Here we shall confine ourselves to a description, written at our request by Rabbi John D. Rayner, one of the editors:

The Service of the Heart, the new prayerbook of the Union of Liberal and Progressive Synagogues, is expected to be published early in 1967. It will replace all the prayerbooks now in use in most of the congregations of the Union of Liberal and Progressive Synagogues, except the *Liberal Jewish Prayer Book,* Volume II (for the High Holy Days—this is scheduled for revision in due course). Thus it includes prayers and services for weekdays, Sabbaths, the Pilgrimage Festivals and minor feasts, and for special occasions in the synagogue and in the home.

It is the result of about five years of labor, chiefly by Rabbi John Rayner and Rabbi Chaim Stern, with the cooperation of several colleagues, and with the invaluable technical assistance of Miss Peggy Lang. It represents a new departure as far as the liturgy of the Liberal Jewish community in England is concerned, seeking to take into account the changes in religious outlook which have occurred in that community, as elsewhere, in recent decades.

The general aim of the editors has been to satisfy as fully as possible the legitimate demands both of tradition and of modernity. The renewed emphasis on tradition is to be seen both in the contents of the volume and in the structure of the services. Practically all the principal prayers of the traditional liturgy are utilized, occasionally with a slight textual modification. And the traditional service-structure is maintained with only minor variations. For example, the *Shema'* is always accompanied by its full complement of benedictions; the Sabbath *Amidah* is complete; and the weekday *Amidah* consists of eighteen benedictions, a few of them re-written.

But the prayerbook also makes abundant use of material not to be found in the traditional *Siddur.* This includes passages from Scripture and post-Biblical Jewish literature as well as modern poems (of Jewish and non-Jewish authorship), and a considerable number of modern prayers, some adapted from various sources, many newly written for this volume.

The compilers have been bold in modifying the Hebrew text of traditional prayers whenever their theology seemed to them out of accord with the outlook of Progressive Judaism. References to the Messiah, the Ingathering of the Exiles, the Resurrection of the Dead, etc., are amended in accordance with the beliefs of Liberal Judaism, and what seemed to the compilers over-emphatically "particularistic" phrases are given a "universalistic" revision.[119]

The modern character of this prayerbook is also reflected in its typography and orthography—for example, modern punctuation marks are used in the Hebrew text, and, above all, in the use of modern English throughout. The pronoun 'thou' is dropped, and even God is addressed as 'You.'

The translations, except where indicated otherwise, are fairly literal, and have all been newly done, often departing from renderings of the standard Bible translations. Occasionally there appears by the side of the Hebrew text, instead of a translation, a newly composed prayer on the same theme.

Among the novel features of this volume is a selection of "Additional Prayers and Readings" on a number of well-defined themes, such as Loneliness, Sincerity, Righteousness, Justice, Brotherhood, etc.

The book is furnished with ample historical notes and references.

(6) Liberal Jewish Liturgy in France

The Union Libérale Israélite was founded in Paris, in 1903.[120] Its aims and objectives included the holding of "a service of one hour's duration, including a sermon, every Saturday and Sunday morning, from ten to eleven o'clock" as well as the provision that "the principal Hebrew prayers (for example, the *Shema'* and the *Kedushah*) shall be retained; the others shall be read in French."[121]

The prayerbook which appeared ten years later, entitled *Des Ailes à la Terre,* was undoubtedly designed for such a type of service. It begins with two sections, respectively named, "Introductory Prayers" and "Hymns and Exhortations," from which selections were obviously meant to be made for the different services. The "Introductory Prayers" consist of a number of Scripture verses, both in Hebrew and in French, as well as of *Elohai Neshamah*[122] (with the unchanged Hebrew text and a French adaptation), an adaptation of *Wihi Ratzon*[123] (in French, with the first line in Hebrew), a French version of *Barukh She-amar*[124] (with the first line in Hebrew), and a French adaptation of *Nishmath*[125] (also giving the first line in Hebrew).

Of the "Hymns and Exhortations," only the *Adon 'Olam* is given in Hebrew as well as in French. The rest consists of a large number of

Psalms in French, and of French translations of other Biblical chapters and of a section of *Mekhilta* Tractate *Shiratha*.

The next section of the prayerbook contains the weekday service (*Plein-Office*). It begins with a French adaptation of *Yehi Khebhod*[126] (retaining some verses in Hebrew), followed by the *Barekhu*. In addition to the standard response to the *Barekhu*, this prayerbook also provides fragments of the prayer recited silently in the traditional service while the cantor chants *Barekhu*.[127] In this, the French prayerbook is rather unique among Reform liturgies. The service then continues with a French adaptation of the *Yotzer Or*,[128] and it is as part of that prayer that the *Kedushah* is introduced, the responses being both in Hebrew and in French. A French version of the *Ahabhah Rabbah* comes next, with the first three words and the concluding eulogy retained in Hebrew. This is followed by the first paragraph of the *Shema,'* the *Mi Khamokhah*, and *Tzur Yisrael*, in Hebrew and in French. The emended version of the Eighteen Benedictions, which comes next, will be described in greater detail in a subsequent chapter.[129] The Torah Service, which follows, retains the traditional pattern.

The prayerbook then offers a selection of "Concluding Prayers," all of them in French, although a few are also provided with Hebrew opening and closing lines. The "Concluding Prayers" include *Hashkibhenu*,[130] *Yisrael Nosha'*,[131] *Ubhekhen Ten Paḥdekha*,[132] and *'Alenu*,[133] all of them paraphrases rather than literal translations, with a tendency to "universalize" the traditional prayer. Also included among the "Concluding Prayers" is a French translation of some of the prayers found in B. *Berakhoth* 16b. This section of the prayerbook concludes with an introduction to the Kaddish, and the traditional Kaddish itself (in Aramaic and French).

The next section of the prayerbook contains the service for Sabbath Eve. It opens with Psalm 29: 11, followed by *Lekha Dodi*,[134] of which the third stanza has been omitted. Psalms 92 and 93 come next, followed by the *Barekhu*, the two benedictions before the Evening *Shema,'* the first paragraph of the *Shema,' Mi Khamokha*, the concluding eulogy of the benediction after the *Shema,'* the *Hashkibhenu*, with the concluding eulogy changed to "Who spreads the tabernacle of peace upon us, upon His people Israel, and upon all the peoples," and by Exodus 31: 16–17. The Seven Benedictions come next, containing the full traditional text of the first four, a segment of the sixth, and the *Elohai Netzor* prayer. The *Kiddush* follows, and the prayerbook indicates that the "Concluding Prayers" are recited after that. The complete Sabbath Eve Service is printed in both Hebrew and French.

The Saturday Morning Service constitutes the next section. It surprises one by retaining much of the angelology of the *Yotzer* section,[135] as well as the petition for the Ingathering of the Exiles in *Ahabhah*

Rabbah, although the accompanying French versions tend to paraphrase in the "Reform" vein. Again, we have the first paragraph of the *Shema'* and a truncated version of the Seven Benedictions. Although the prayerbook does not say so specifically, one would assume that the Torah Service (not reprinted as part of the Sabbath liturgy), as included in the weekday service, followed the Seven Benedictions and preceded the "Concluding Prayers."

The final section of this book gives a number of quotations (*Sentences*) from Bible, Talmud, *Zohar,* and Abraham Ibn Ezra, all of them in French only.

The whole volume contains but 146 pages of text, and is impressive on account of its aesthetically pleasing layout and typography, and the appropriateness of its selections from the traditional liturgical heritage. The attraction of the volume lies in its simplicity.

A far more ambitious undertaking was the 1925 volume of *Rituel des Prières Journalières.* A lengthy introduction traces the whole history of Jewish liturgy down to the prayerbooks of Caesar Seligmann and the Jewish Religious Union in London. It sees those two prayerbooks as reflecting the influence of the American *Union Prayer Book,* even as this *Rituel* itself, in its arrangement, although not so much in its choice of materials, is strongly influenced by that American ritual. The book contains standard services for Sabbath and weekdays, but each standard service is preceded by variable introductory portions. It is noteworthy that, among the latter, the *Rituel* also utilizes kabbalistic formulae.[136] In this edition of the French Liberal prayerbook many more Hebrew passages are utilized, and the first paragraph of the *Shema'* is always followed by the end of the third paragraph. The Eighteen Benedictions, while still not complete, are fuller than in the previous edition, and all the traditional components not included in the worship services are printed (without translation) at the end of the book. Judging by the French translations and paraphrases, one would say that, doctrinally, the 1925 liturgy occupies the same ground as did its 1913 predecessor. But the Hebrew texts are somewhat confusing, since they appear in their unchanged traditional form in some services, while they are emended and abbreviated in others. Again, while the prayers for the restoration of the sacrificial cult have been eliminated from most services, the rubric for the Counting of the 'Omer[137] contains the Hebrew prayer, "May the All-Merciful One restore the Temple service to its place. May it be Thy will, O Lord our God and God of our fathers that the Temple be rebuilt speedily and in our days . . ." The French paraphrase, on the other hand, confines itself to a petition for the restoration of "Israel to its full spiritual grandeur."

It seems, therefore, that, unlike other prayerbooks which come under the heading of "Independent Reform," the liturgy of the Union Libérale Israélite, while striving for brevity and variety, did not necessarily aim at theological consistency. As the Union specifically stated, "We are pursuing a task, not of separation and revolution, but of spiritual renovation. . . . The spirit, and not the letter; truth and life —that is our motto." [138]

If, compared to the 1913 prayerbook, the 1925 edition represents a move in the direction of greater adherence to tradition, the 1958 edition of the *Rituel* can be said to have moved still further in that direction.[139] Not only have the Eighteen Benedictions been completely restored, but also a further section of the traditional *Shema,'* Deuteronomy 11: 13–14a, has been incorporated into the liturgy.[140] And so has the complete traditional Grace after Meals.[141]

(7) The Liturgy of Dutch Liberal Judaism

Based on the text of the German *Einheitsgebetbuch,* a series of prayerbooks, in booklet form, containing Hebrew and Dutch, was published between 1932 and 1938. The booklets were compiled by Rabbi Dr. H. Hirschberg and Messrs. R. J. Spitz and L. Levisson, under the general editorship of Rabbi J. Norden of Elberfeld. A new series of prayer booklets, both mimeographed and photo-offset, began to appear after the Second World War, and, in our chapter dealing with "The Eighteen Benedictions," [142] we shall discuss the use which was made in those booklets of some of the formulae which go back to the ancient Palestinian rite. In 1960, the Union of Liberal Religious Jews in the Netherlands produced a photo-offset edition of the second volume of the *Einheitsgebetbuch,* in both Hebrew and German. It was not until 1964 that Liberal Judaism in the Netherlands acquired its very own printed prayerbook, *Seder Tobh Lehodoth,* which was published under the leadership of Rabbi Dr. J. Soetendorp. The first volume contains the services for Sabbath and festivals, and the second volume the services for the High Holy Days. One of the distinguishing features of this prayerbook is that the Hebrew prayers and their Dutch translations follow one another in sequence, as contrasted with the more general arrangement of having Hebrew on top of the page and the vernacular at the bottom, or of having Hebrew and vernacular on facing pages of the book. This new arrangement is meant to facilitate the reading of both.

The indebtedness of this new Dutch prayerbook to the *Einheitsgebetbuch* is quite evident; and yet, it also has a distinctiveness of its own. On the one hand, the new prayerbook is much shorter than the *Einheitsgebetbuch*. It omits many of the prayers which the *Einheits-*

gebetbuch contains, and abbreviates others. While the *Einheitsgebetbuch* contains all three paragraphs of the traditional *Shema,'* the Dutch prayerbook omits the second paragraph entirely, and has the end only of the third paragraph. It also is more "radical" in the application of "Reform" theological principles to the liturgy. While the second of the Eighteen Benedictions is retained in its traditional Hebrew form, the Dutch paraphrase praises God "who lets the memory of the dead live on." (The *Einheitsgebetbuch* has God "quicken the dead.")[143] A corresponding change has been introduced into the *Elohai Neshamah* prayer.[143a] Angelology, too, has been eliminated even more completely than it had been in the German source. The Seven Benedictions for Sabbath *Shaḥarith* include the *Kedushah* for *Musaph* (there is no *Musaph* Service in the Dutch prayerbook). But the traditional introductory statement of the regular Sabbath *Musaph Kedushah* has been replaced by a phrase from the High Holy Day liturgy, which, in the form it is given here, does not lend itself to any angelological associations.[144] *Seder Tobh Lehodoth* also provides for greater variety. There is a choice of three different introductions to the fourth of the Seven Benedictions.[145] The introductions themselves are traditional, except that two of the three introductions are assigned by the tradition to different services, and have retained their traditional position in the *Einheitsgebetbuch*.

But if, on the one hand, *Seder Tobh Lehodoth* is less "traditionalist" than its German prototype, it represents, on the other hand, a return to some traditional elements which had by and large entirely disappeared from Liberal and Reform liturgy. The Dutch prayerbook restores the petitions for the Return to Zion, the Rebuilding of Jerusalem, and the Ingathering of the Exiles (but not those petitions connected with the personal Messiah and the sacrificial cult), even as its Prayer for the State of Israel has been adopted *verbatim* from the prayerbook of the Jerusalem Reform Synagogue.[146]

Altogether, therefore, the 1964 edition of the Dutch Liberal prayerbook is seen to have its own emphases and its own characteristics, which distinguish it from other liturgical creations of "Independent Reform."

(8) Common Elements of "Independent Reform" Liturgy

If we leave aside the Hamburg Temple Prayerbook and the early editions of the liturgy of the West London Synagogue, both of them special cases, the former because it tried to show in its apologia that no break with Tradition had occurred, and the latter because it had not really espoused the cause of doctrinal Reform in its early stages, we note some interesting characteristics which all the liturgies of "Independent Reform" have in common. They can be tabulated as follows:

(a) The traditional "three paragraphs" of the *Shema'* are given up. The *Shema'* is reduced to its first paragraph, and, in some cases, is made to include the end of the third paragraph. (The 1958 edition of the French Liberal prayerbook also contains the opening sentence of the second paragraph.) There was, as far as we know, only one other prayerbook, not dealt with in this chapter, which took such liberties with the traditional contents of the *Shema.'* That was the prayerbook published, in 1848, by Kirchenrat Maier. But it was a prayerbook which Maier published ostensibly for private devotion, and with no particular congregation in mind.[147] Otherwise, the presence or the absence of the complete traditional *Shema'* may well be taken as a yardstick in determining whether a given prayerbook belongs to the category of "Reform from Within" or to that of "Independent Reform."

(b) There is no *Musaph* Service, except, in some instances, on the High Holy Days. Prayerbooks of the "Reform from Within" category change the wording and the meaning of the *Musaph*. The prayerbooks of "Independent Reform" omit it altogether.

(c) There is no attempt made to preserve the full complement of the Eighteen (or the Seven) Benedictions. Other reformed rituals retain the traditional number of benedictions, even if some of the latter have to be reworded on account of doctrinal considerations. The prayerbooks of "Independent Reform" omit rather than reword. (The 1967 English Liberal prayerbook, *The Service of the Heart,* is an exception to this rule, which is all the more noteworthy in that its immediate predecessor was one of the least faithful to the traditional pattern.)

(d) More variety is made possible in the selections used for the different services, either by having different services altogether on successive weeks, or by providing different introductions to a standard service.

(e) The vernacular is more extensively used in prayer.

(f) The influence of the American *Union Prayer Book* is more strongly felt—at least in many instances.

Unlike the Reform editors of prayerbooks designed for whole Jewish communities, the editors of prayerbooks for "Independent Reform" congregations did not have to compromise, or to placate the susceptibilities of the "traditionalists." They could afford to follow their more "radical" inclinations; and most of them did—for a while. It is indeed a remarkable phenomenon that, with the exception of the Berlin *Reformgemeinde* which, after a temporary acceptance of a relatively more traditional pattern in the eighteen-eighties, was at its most "radical" in the nineteen-thirties, and with the exception of the West London Synagogue, which, in the nineteen-thirties, first "reformed" its liturgy from a consistent doctrinal perspective—that, with the two exceptions just named, the general pattern of the liturgy of "Independent Reform" has been an increasing return to the traditional mode—in form, if not always in content. One gets the impression that radicalism in liturgy is very often but a weapon in the arsenal of progress, essential for a certain type of combat, but also dispensable once the battle has been won. The explicit anti-Rabbinism of the early liturgists of the West London Synagogue is really explicable in terms of the same psychology which made an Israel Mattuck arbitrarily upset the time-hallowed sequence of the traditional prayers. Both, at different times, and using different models of the weapon, tried to make the same point: the right of a modern Jewish congregation to break through the rigidity of the established pattern. But once the point has been made, and both of them made it well, the realization begins to dawn that rigid traditionalism and innovation-for-innovation's-sake are not really the only alternatives. And out of this realization comes a re-appraisal of the Tradition and a more critical look at the innovations. And more often than not the fruit of such reflection is that blending of Tradition and modernity which tends to obliterate the distinctions between those prayerbooks which reflect "Reform from Within" and those which are the creation of "Independent Reform."

FIVE

The Battle of the Proof Texts

SOME TIME, BETWEEN 1815, WHEN UNDER ISRAEL JACOBSON'S DIRECTION, reformed worship services were instituted in Berlin,[1] and 1818, an anonymous pamphlet was circulated, which attacked the Reformers on the following grounds:

(1) They have invented the practice of having most of their prayers in German.[2] Their sin is twofold: (i) They have forsaken the source of life, our Holy Tongue, which we have inherited from our fathers since the time when God created the world. (ii) It is stated in the Talmud and in the Codes that whoever departs from the formulation which the Sages have given to prayer does not fulfil his obligation.

(2) They have interpreted the law too leniently by abolishing

the silent recitation of the Eighteen Benedictions. This is against the law of the Talmud and the Codes.

(3) They skip over the traditional version of the *Kedushah* in the Sabbath Morning Service.[3]

(4) As far as their use of organ music is concerned, this is an absolute prohibition, the like of which must not be done in Israel.

(5) Their innovation of using the Spanish and Portuguese pronunciation of Hebrew, of which their fathers knew not until this day.

(6) Their custom of reading the Torah without cantillation, which is against the law of the Talmud and the Codes—apart from other things, such as not calling people to the Torah by their Hebrew names, which is a new custom.

(7) Their profanation of the Name of God by setting up different customs, thereby making the one Torah appear like two, and transgressing the law against the formation of sects.[4]

(8) They transgress the law, "Forsake not the teaching of thy mother,"[5] by changing what had been the custom of our fathers to this day. This is not the correct and upright way in the sight of the Lord. If it were, why did not our sainted fathers conduct themselves like this, seeing that they were more intelligent than we are?[6]

If we discount the value judgments and the supposed references to the sources, the eight points quoted above give us a fairly accurate description of the liturgical reforms which had been introduced in Jacobson's Berlin services. When, in the eighteen-forties, similar accusations had been made against the Reformers in England, the latter chose to declare, openly and belligerently, their break with the Rabbinic tradition.[7] It is, therefore, highly significant (and an omen for the course of Reform in Germany) that Israel Jacobson and his followers decided to take up the Orthodox challenge, and to demonstrate that the charges levelled against them had no basis in the Talmud and in the Codes—that, in fact, such reforms as had been introduced could be fully justified on the basis of the very sources which the Orthodox opponents had led into the field.

The Reform reply took the form of two publications, issued by Eliezer Libermann[8] in 1818, *Or Nogah* ("The Shining Light") and *Nogah Hatzedek* ("The Splendor of Righteousness"). The former was a treatise, in two parts, in which Libermann himself, in Rabbinic Hebrew and in the traditional Rabbinic style, marshalled the arguments from traditional sources in support of the innovations. The latter was a collection of responsa, again in the traditional style, by Moses Kunitz, rabbi of Ofen, Hungary, Shem-Tob Samun, rabbi of Leghorn, Italy, Jacob Vita Recanati, rabbi of Verona, and Aaron Choriner, chief rabbi of Arad, Hungary. It also contained an "approbation" by some rabbis of Jerusalem, temporarily resident in Leghorn. But that "approbation," together with some other items in *Or Nogah*, was later declared to have been a forgery. Most of the responsa confined themselves to the question of the permissibility of organ music, but Aaron Choriner[9] also dealt at length with the liturgical innovations.

The year of the publication of *Or Nogah* and *Nogah Hatzedek* was, of course, also the year of the opening of the Hamburg Temple—a coincidence which has led some popular historians to the assumption that Libermann's works represented a defense of the Hamburg Temple. It is, of course, true that the publication of the two tracts was "timely," and that, in their counter-attack, the Orthodox coupled their "refutations" of Libermann's tracts with condemnations of the Hamburg Temple. But it should be borne in mind that the Hamburg Temple Prayerbook (which, from the point of view of dogmatic considerations, was far more "radical" than the Berlin innovations) appeared in 1819, while Libermann's tracts were already published in 1818. The latter, therefore, must be understood as a defense of the Berlin reforms, although the same arguments could undoubtedly also be used by the Hamburg Reformers.[10]

From the abundance of source material given in *Or Nogah* and *Nogah Hatzedek*, we bring the following selections:

(a) MAIMONIDES, *Hilkhoth Tephillah* 1:1,2.[11]

It is a positive commandment to pray every day, as it is said: "And ye shall serve the Lord your God." They learned from Tradition that this "service" is prayer, as it is said: ". . . and to serve Him with all your heart." The Sages said: "Which is the heart? It is prayer!" But the number of prayers is not derived from the Torah; and the formula of this prayer is not derived from the Torah; and the fixed time for prayer is not derived from the Torah. . . . A man should entreat (God) and pray every day, and proclaim the praise of the Holy One, praised be He. And afterwards he should, in plea and supplication, voice his needs. After that, he gives praise and thanksgiving to God for the goodness which He has abundantly bestowed upon him. Every individual does this according to his own ability.

(b) SHULḤAN 'ARUKH, *Oraḥ Ḥayyim* 101:4.[12]
A man can pray in whatever language he desires. This applies to prayer offered in a congregation; but an individual should pray only in the Holy Tongue. However, there are those who say that the latter provision solely applies to him who voices his own needs, such as one who prays for the sick or on account of pain in his own household, but that, in the case of the prayer which is fixed for the whole congregation, even the individual may recite it in any language. And there are those who say that even the individual voicing his own needs may do so in any language he desires, except in Aramaic.

(c) MAIMONIDES, *Hilkhoth Berakhoth* 1:6.[13]
All of the benedictions (*berakhoth*) may be said in any language, provided one says them according to their essential character, as ordained by the Sages. And, if one has deviated from the formula, as long as he has mentioned the Name of God and His Kingdom, and the subject matter of the benediction, even in the vernacular, he has fulfilled his obligation.

(d) SEPHER ḤASIDIM, Chapter 588.[14]
If someone who does not know Hebrew comes to you, and he is a God-fearing person, or if a woman comes to you, tell them to learn the prayers in the language which they understand. For prayer only takes place when the heart understands. And, if the heart does not know what a man utters with his mouth, of what use is such a prayer to him? Therefore, it is better for a man to pray in the language which he understands.

(e) SEPHER ḤASIDIM, Chapter 785.[15]
It is better for a man to say his prayer, and to recite the *Shema'* and the benedictions, in a language which he understands than for him to pray in the Holy Tongue, if he does not understand it.

(f) B. *Sotah* 32a (i.e., *Mishnah Sotah* 7:1).[16]
The following may be recited in any language: the section concerning the suspected woman, the confession made at the presentation of the tithe, the *Shema,* the Prayer (i.e., the Eighteen Benedictions), the Grace after Meals, ...

(g) MAIMONIDES' Letter, quoted by Rabbi David ben Zimrah.[17]

> Because people do not listen to the reader's repetition of the Eighteen Benedictions, but talk and otherwise behave themselves unsuitably, it is enough if the reader alone recites the Eighteen Benedictions, and the congregation listens to him—(a) because the talking of the people makes a bad impression on the non-Jews who sometimes visit the synagogue, and (b) because the ignorant man, for whose benefit the reader's repetition was ordained in the first place, will see the diversions in which the others are engaging, and he, too, will refrain from listening to the reader.

This selection of Rabbinic source material should suffice as an indication of the type of source used, and of the implications of the sources. To the specific charge concerning the "skipping over the traditional version of the *Kedushah* in the Sabbath Morning Service," Libermann replies as follows:

> The argument about the *Kedushah* on Sabbath is no argument, and there is no need to reply to it. The text of *az beqol* is not found at all among (the sources left by) the arrangers of the liturgy. Some man, whose name we do not even know, has ordained it; and we do not owe him any obedience, for this text is not a part of the (original) *Kedushah* at all. Thus did the author of *Yesh Noḥalin* write: "The fundamental part of the *Kedushah* is only *na'aritzekha, le'umatham,* and *ubhedibhré.* The rest of the text which we add on the Sabbath is not an integral part of the *Kedushah.*" . . . And look, the version used by the people in the West is not known to the Sepharadi rite[18] and in Palestine.[19]

As for the language of prayer, seeing how much Hebrew was actually used in the Berlin services, the Orthodox claim that "most of the prayers were recited in German" was exaggerated to begin with. From the *barekhu* through the end of the Seven Benedictions everything was recited in Hebrew. Nor do Libermann and Choriner wish to create the impression that Hebrew is to be ruled out altogether—even though the sources which have been quoted in justification of a partial use of the vernacular could be used to justify an even more extended use of the vernacular. For one thing, Libermann makes it quite clear that he is invoking the sources on behalf of *German* Jews only.

> Whatever we have said thus far about prayer in the vernacular . . . applies only to the majority of the inhabitants of Germany, who, from their youth on, are accustomed to speak pure German. Great and small, men and women, children and old men, they all speak and understand that language, while they do not un-

> derstand our Holy Tongue, which is known by but a few. The majority, and particularly women and children, do not know its worth, nor do they understand its essence. It is for their sake that we have adduced the evidence, both religious and rational, to the effect that it is better to pray in German, which they understand, than in Hebrew, where the heart does not understand what the mouth utters. But this does not apply to the Jews who live in other countries, within their own environments, such as the people of Poland etc., who do not know pure German, but who are very proficient in the Holy Tongue. . . . For them, it is better to pray in the pure Hebrew, which they know, than in their broken German. . . .[20]

And to the German Jews themselves, Libermann addressed this appeal:

> Even though the commandment we have to observe requires every man to pray in the language which he understands, it is nevertheless right and appropriate to recite some of the prayers in the Holy Tongue—as you indeed do. . . . Among our prayers there are some holy and lofty ones, and it is fitting to recite them in the language which is ours by inheritance from our sainted ancestors, such as the acceptance of the yoke of the Kingdom of Heaven (i.e., the *Shema'*). Even though the Rabbis have ruled that the *Shema,* too, may be said in any lanugage, . . . it is nonetheless fitting and proper for us to accept the yoke of the Kingdom of Heaven in the Holy Tongue. But if someone should object and say, "How can we have any prayer in the Holy Tongue? What shall I do with my son who does not understand it in the least?," then, brethren, I shall retort in amazement: "Why do you not teach your young children our Holy Tongue, the Hebrew language, which was the first of all the languages? Do you not scatter fortunes and possessions in order to teach them the wisdom and the language of every single people? Why, then, do you deprive your children of the study of this precious language, the language of our exalted ancestral tradition? Let it not be forgotten among us until the end of all the generations!" . . . At the very least, you could teach them the acceptance of the yoke of the Kingdom of Heaven and similar passages in the Holy Tongue, since this is easy for everybody to learn and to understand—particularly in his childhood.[21]

Aaron Choriner, too, was careful to limit the applicability of the sources he had adduced:

> At any rate, I say that we do not have the power to change to another language in the case of the Eighteen Benedictions, the

> *Shema,* and the benedictions of the *Shema,* because those prayers are traditional, and it is easy for anyone who calls himself an Israelite to follow the established practice. He should learn the translation of the words and their contents. For, in changing them (into another language), it is easy to fall into the net of error, altering the formula coined by the Sages. See what Maimonides wrote in *Hilkhoth Tephillah* 1:4. . . . And, since it is easy for every man to learn the translation of the words and the intended meaning of the benedictions—for the Men of the Great Assembly have arranged them in a clear and lucid language which is easily intelligible, Hebrew being the most honored language in which God spoke to our fathers and to His Prophet, and which was the language in which He gave us His Torah, the tree of life to them that lay hold of it—let it (i.e., our use of Hebrew for the prayers mentioned above) be a sure sign of our faith in the Ingathering of the Exiles, when, as we hope, the crown of our kingdom will return, and our Temple will be rebuilt, in which we shall offer our prayers before God in the Hebrew language. . . . Why should we leave and forsake a tradition going back to Ezra . . . without a compelling reason? Just because of a fool or two in a city, who does not want to learn, we shall not leave nor forsake a correct practice which goes back to the Men of the Great Assembly. [Choriner then goes on to say that the Verses of Song and similar components of the liturgy, written in poetic form, had, unlike the passages mentioned above, better be recited in the vernacular.] [22]

The Orthodox reaction came a year later. It took the form of a collection of responsa, edited by the Hamburg Rabbinical Court. Under the title, *Eleh Dibhrę Haberith* ("These are the Words of the Covenant"), published in Altona, in 1819, a number of rabbis of the "old school" in Germany, Poland, France, Italy, Bohemia, Moravia, and Hungary, expressed their considered judgment that

(a) It is forbidden to alter the customary form of Jewish prayer, from the Morning Benedictions until after the *'Alenu;* and it is all the more forbidden to abbreviate it.

(b) It is forbidden to recite this order of prayers in any language but the Holy Tongue; and any prayerbook published in any but the established form, and departing from our accepted custom, is ritually unfit, and it is forbidden to pray from it.

(c) It is forbidden to play any musical instrument in the synagogue on Sabbath and Festivals, even when this is done by a Gentile.[23]

More specifically, *Eleh Dibhré Haberith* undertook a detailed "refutation" of *Or Nogah* and *Nogah Hatzedek,* and a vituperative attack on the Hamburg Temple and its prayerbook. Libermann and his associates were accused of being ignoramuses, of misquoting and misinterpreting sources, etc., etc. The tone in which the responsa spoke hardly accorded with the Preface of the Hamburg Rabbinical Court:

> Let this be known: that these letters are printed to the glory of the Holy One, praised be He, and of His Torah; and not, God forbid, to reproach or to provoke a single man of Israel. And also to the glory of our community, the Congregation of Jacob—to make known that they are but a few, who have stumbled in the error and the mistakes of the new sect. They represent less than one out of a hundred. But the whole congregation consists of holy ones. Most of them are God-fearing and faithful, holding fast to the Law of the Lord, both Written and Oral, and they carefully observe the minutiae of the Scribes, even as they have been doing, the Lord be praised, from the day of the community's establishment. Only the minority of a minority have been made to stumble by some enticers and seducers, strangers who have come to destroy the inheritance of the Lord. May the Good Lord grant them atonement, and may He establish peace in our congregation, so that we may serve Him in one accord.[24]

In their rejection of the sources adduced by *Or Nogah* and *Nogah Hatzedek* (or, at any rate of the interpretation given to those sources), the various contributors to *Eleh Dibhré Haberith* all seem to be influenced by the mystical and numerological considerations with which the later Kabbalah had invested the traditional liturgy. In any event, it is only by a recourse to mystical doctrines that the Reformers' interpretation of the Rabbinic sources could be gainsaid. The following passage, from the responsum of Moses Sopher, the famous rabbi of Pressburg, is characteristic:

> As far as their using a language other than the Holy Tongue for congregational worship is concerned, this is impossible under any circumstances. Even though there is a specific *mishnah,* permitting, among other things, the recitation in the vernacular of the obligatory Eighteen Benedictions, this specifically refers to a chance occurrence, to the case of an individual. But to do so permanently, and, above all, to appoint a prayer leader who would lead congregational worship in the language of the nations—that is certainly an absolute prohibition. For, if it were not, then the Men of the Great Assembly would not have composed the Eighteen Benedictions in a pure and elegant Hebrew. After all, in their days, half of the people were speaking the

> language of Ashdod (Nehemiah 13: 24). It would, therefore, have been better to compose the Eighteen Benedictions in the language of the Chaldeans to which they were then accustomed. . . . It is written (in Nehemiah 8:8): "And they read in the book of the Law of God, distinctly; and they gave the sense." The Sages (in b. *Megillah* 3a) said: "This refers to the *Targum* (i.e., the Aramaic translation). It follows from this that the people at that time did not understand the Holy Tongue, and that it was, therefore, necessary to appoint a translator who would translate the Torah for their benefit. But, if this was so, why, then, did they not compose the Eighteen Benedictions in the language of the *Targum,* which they understood at that time? Why did they specifically compose the Eighteen Benedictions in the Holy Tongue, which the people at that time did not comprehend? We are compelled to conclude that the Men of the Great Assembly, among them also some *Prophets,* who composed the Eighteen Benedictions, must have known from the Lord Himself that the Eighteen Benedictions could not be recited in just any kind of language, and that there cannot be any arbitrary substitutes for the Temple cult. If such substitutes could so easily be found, why have a Temple and a sacrificial cult in the first place? It follows, therefore, that nothing can be a complete substitute for the Temple cult. What the Men of the Great Assembly did compose was the best they were able to compose, to create as much of a substitute as was possible. They did so by means of certain words and acceptable meanings (*kawwanoth*—a mystical concept). They voted on every single word and on every single letter; and it is absolutely impossible to transfer their intent (*kawwanah*) into any other language. But if we, even though we do not know their intent (*kawwanah*), recite the words which the Men of the Great Assembly have composed, our prayer will nevertheless meet with divine acceptance—which is not the case if we pray in any other language.[25]

But Moses Sopher was capable also of more rational arguments. To Libermann's defense of the substitution of the *Kedushah* of *Musaph* for the *Kedushah* of *Shaḥarith,* a defense which had taken the form of going into comparative liturgy, Moses Sopher replies as follows:

> What does it matter if we do not know the author of that passage? . . . What harm is there in saying it? Behold, it is an addition to the praises of God, an addition inserted on a day (when the service can be longer because) there is no stoppage of work involved for the people (i.e., they are not waiting to

> return to work on the Sabbath). For hundreds of years we have already been accustomed to say that passage in the synagogues of our countries. (I.e., what the Sepharadi rite does about it is irrelevant in this context.) Through long usage we have already made it like an obligatory prayer.[26]

We may note in passing that Moses Sopher's rebuttal is quite irrefutable. The fact that a certain prayer is not included in the Sepharadi rite is not, in and by itself, sufficient reason to discard it in a Berlin congregation, which is in "Ashkenazi territory." The *Musaph* version of the *Kedushah,* which the Reformers did use, was not that of the Sepharadi rite, either.[27] But if, as we suspect, the real reason for discarding the *Kedushah* of *Shaharith* was the fervent plea which it contained for the establishment of God's Kingdom in Zion, Libermann did not say so. At that stage of the struggle, the Reformers had not yet come out into the open with their reservations in more doctrinal matters.

Moses Sopher also takes Aaron Choriner to task for the latter's recommendation that the Verses of Song be recited in the vernacular, while *Shema* and Eighteen Benedictions should continue to be recited in Hebrew.

> And, behold, the author of that responsum instructs them to recite the Eighteen Benedictions in the Holy Tongue, and to say the Verses of Song in pure German. I, too, would say that it is not such a terrible thing (lit., "an earthquake") to use the vernacular in the recitation of praises and songs. But what does he really want? If the people do not understand the words of the *Shema* and of the Eighteen Benedictions at all, why does he not order them to study the Holy Tongue? After all, they do study the languages of the Gentiles. Why, then, should they not learn to understand what they say when they accept the yoke of the Kingdom of Heaven, and recite the Eighteen Benedictions? But, if he really does teach them (enough Hebrew for the *Shema* and the Eighteen Benedictions), why does he make a distinction in the case of the Verses of Song? Why, indeed, seeing that it is impossible to find an adequate vernacular translation for the Names of God and for His attributes?![28]

But the *pièce de résistance* in *Eleh Dibhré Haberith* was undoubtedly Aaron Choriner's retraction of his earlier pro-Reform responsum. That retraction was submitted to *Eleh Dibhré Haberith* through the good offices of Moses Sopher, who, be it noted, is represented in that collection by three different letters. Choriner wrote in part:

> Now that I have heard that they have also abbreviated the benedictions and the prayers, that they do not pray for the In-

> gathering of the Exiles—the belief in which is the very foundation of our holy Torah—and that they alter the text of the prayers, I apply to myself the verse (Isaiah 3:6): "And let this ruin be under thy hand." I, therefore, declare in public: All my words in *Qin-ath Ha-emeth* (i.e., Choriner's contribution to *Nogah Hatzedek*) are null and void, and that I am not entitled to deal with this matter and to reach decisions. The Sages of Israel, the great scholars of the age, they alone have the right to do so; and my own views must be considered as naught and nothing as against theirs.[29]

Choriner's change of heart may indeed be due to the differences between the Berlin service, to which he had given his original approbation, and the Hamburg Temple Prayerbook, which had introduced changes based on dogmatic considerations. He might well have approved of the former, but, when he found out that his approbation was also invoked by the Hamburg Reformers for their more far-reaching reforms, he withdrew it. But, in the light of Choriner's own religious development—he was to become ever more radical in his championship of the Reform position, towards the end of his life even denying the Return to Zion[30]—this seems unlikely. Besides, a year later he retracted his retraction. Under the circumstances, it would be more reasonable to assume that Choriner had acted under pressure. There were limits to the freedom of expression enjoyed by the chief rabbi of a Hungarian Jewish community in those early days.

Not included in the collection *Eleh Dibhré Haberith* were the views of Abraham Loewenstamm, the rabbi of Emden. They filled a whole volume which was published in Amsterdam, a year later.[31] Loewenstamm reaches the same conclusions arrived at by the contributors to *Eleh Dibhré Haberith,* but he is both more systematical (and verbose) and more urbane in doing so. He does not go to the lengths to which the others had gone in denying that the sources actually say what the Reformers had presented them as saying. As far as he is concerned, for example, prayer in the vernacular is, under certain limited circumstances, permissible. But a prayer in Hebrew not understood is nevertheless better than a prayer understood in the vernacular. To reach this -to us- astonishing conclusion, Loewenstamm has to indulge in the following kind of reasoning:

> In the matter of prayer and benedictions, there are four degrees, one below the other.
>
> The first degree is the highest and most important one. It is that a man should pray and recite the benedictions in the Holy Tongue, in such a way that his whole power of concentration is firmly attached to the prayer which he prays and to the benediction which he recites. He enunciates every word grammati-

cally, with the inward concentration of his heart, and with the appropriate intervals. He bears in mind, in connection with every single word and with every single utterance, the holy (mystical) concentrations and meditations on the Divine Name, which our sainted ancestors, the Men of the Great Assembly, have intended for them. That kind of prayer is certainly the most precious and acceptable prayer in the sight of the Lord of all. Happy are they, and happy is their portion, who have achieved that degree! It was in this manner that the pious ones and the Prophets used to pray. . . .

However, a man is allowed to pray in this holy manner only after he has examined his heart, and has found himself to be faithful in the service of the Lord. That is to say, after he can be sure of his ability to pray and to concentrate on such holy matters, without letting extraneous thoughts and worries intrude upon his holy thoughts. . . . But he who cannot be sure of himself is not allowed to engage in such mystical meditations—lest profane thoughts make an abomination of these most holy things . . .

The second degree is the more appropriate and the more regular one. It is that a man should not immerse himself in such holy mysteries at the time of his prayer. Rather should he concentrate, in the case of every single utterance, on the meaning of the words and the subject matters (of the prayers), until he knows what he prays and before whom he prays. When he recites a benediction, he should know to whom he addresses it, and about what he is reciting it. . . .

The third degree, which is below the first two, is that of the man who knows Hebrew well, and is able to concentrate well on his prayer. But he does not do so. Instead, when he stands up to pray, his heart is not freed from temporal thoughts, and, while, with his mouth, he glorifies the God of Glory, his heart is not upright with Him, and he does not know what he is saying. Behold, this degree of prayer is certainly far inferior to the other two degrees; and, according to the appropriate law, he should not be praying at all in this manner. . . . Nevertheless, praying in this way, he has fulfilled the obligation of prayer.

However, the fourth degree is the lowest of them all, and of the least value. It is the one about which I have been asked the question: "Should someone who can read Hebrew, but does not understand it, pray from a Hebrew prayerbook?" Behold, common sense would tell us that such a man has not fulfilled his obligation. For how could he do his duty by prayer when only his lips are moving, while his heart knows that it does not understand what he is saying? Would a man undertake to send a petition to a human king, written in a foreign language which he, the petitioner, does not understand? Would not the king, once this became known to him, get very angry? How much the more so in the case of God, Who knoweth the hidden secrets of the human heart! Should a hypocrite come before God, entreating Him with his mouth and lips, while not having the slightest idea of what he is saying?!

Thus, at any rate, would human beings argue, who can argue only on the basis of their own analysis, and who do not understand anything which exceeds the power of their own comprehension. But God is not a human being, and His thoughts are not our thoughts. He is the merciful Father of all His creatures, and particularly of His chosen people . . . whom He has called, Israel. Even to the lowest and the least of Israel, He has opened the gates of heaven. He who is unable to clothe his thoughts in words, let him fill his mouth with the prayers arranged before him, and let him lift up his concerns to his Father Who is in Heaven, Who will grant whatever is requested in the prayer. . . .

We have already demonstrated above . . . that he who has not concentrated on his whole prayer, not even on the meaning of the words, except for the first verse of the *Shema* and the first of the Eighteen Benedictions, has nevertheless fulfilled his obligation. . . . Even someone who has said his prayers in a state of drowsiness has fulfilled the obligation of prayer. And this, in fact, did occasionally happen to the early saints. But, if this is so, then, for what reason and by what logic should he who does not know what he is saying, because he does not know Hebrew, be considered inferior to him who does understand Hebrew, but nevertheless does not know what he is saying, because he does not pay attention to what he is saying? And even though the latter could understand, if he wanted to, at any rate, in the case under discussion, he does not do so, because he is letting his mind wander.

Reason asserts the opposite: The one who does not understand Hebrew, and is praying (in Hebrew), is more likely to fulfil his obligation than the one who knows Hebrew, but lets his mind wander from his prayer. For the one who knows Hebrew, and does not know what he is saying, because he lets his mind wander, not only does not know what he is praying. *He does not even know whether he is praying.* If he but knew *that* he is praying, he would also know *what* he is praying, seeing that he does understand the meaning of the words. But as to the one who does not understand Hebrew, he may not know *what* he is praying, but at least he knows *that* he is praying.[32]

It is not surprising that Loewenstamm, having rated a non-understood Hebrew prayer that highly, should also have ruled:

> He who knows and understands Hebrew and also another language must obviously pray in Hebrew only. And if he prays in the other language, he has not fulfilled his obligation.[33]

Nevertheless, Loewenstamm concedes that the individual, after he has recited the statutory service in Hebrew, may offer his private prayers and supplications in the vernacular. But that is as far as he is prepared to go.[34]

The Reformers remained unconvinced by the Orthodox arguments. In a masterpiece of Hebrew satire, *Ḥerebh Noqemeth Neqam Berith* ("The Sword which Avenges the Covenant"), M. J. Bresselau, one of the founders of the Hamburg Temple, and an editor of its prayerbook, replied to *Eleh Dibhré Haberith,* already in 1819.[35] He confronted the contributors to *Eleh Dibhré Haberith* with those Rabbinic sources which they had, in his opinion, either misinterpreted or ignored. Basically, then, Bresselau's tract consists of a restatement of the source material which had already been led into the field in *Or Nogah* and *Nogah Hatzedek,* only this time in juxtaposition to—what Bresselau considered to have been—the perverted interpretations given in *Eleh Dibhré Haberith.* The reader was to judge between the plain meaning of such passages as state specifically that certain prayers may be recited "in any language" and the attempts to deny that the passages were saying what they appear to be saying.

No less emphatic in his rejection of the arguments put forward in *Eleh Dibhré Haberith* was another Hebrew polemicist, David Caro, who, in *Berith Emeth* ("The Covenant of Truth")—Dessau, 1820—dealt *seriatim* with the various contributors to the Orthodox responsa collection.[36] Thus, for example, he took Moses Sopher to task, in connection with Sopher's recommendation that prayer be recited in Hebrew, even if Hebrew is not understood.

> Woe unto the ears which have to hear this! Before a human king, it would not be fitting to do so, even though he does not know the feelings of our heart. How much the less before Him Who knoweth the secrets and understandeth the thoughts! Our mouth is supposed to be full of prayers, while our heart is to think strange thoughts! Truly, the very opposite is made clear in the words of our Sages: "Prayer requires inward concentration." And thus did Maimonides write in *Hilkhoth Tephillah* 4: 15: "Any prayer which is recited without inward concentration is not a prayer." And thus did the Sages say specifically: "Prayer is a manifestation of love; that is why a man must concentrate on it." . . . Thus, according to his (i.e., Moses Sopher's) own

> words, he himself is going against the decisions of the Talmud and the Codes; and, as he writes himself, he knows what the punishment for that transgression is.[37]

Of such a kind, then, were the arguments presented by both sides. By 1820, the literary "Battle of the Proof Texts" was practically over, although, here and there, for the next one hundred years, some of the arguments and counter-arguments were to come up again. But then it was always a case of going back to the source material which had figured so prominently in the literary warfare between 1818 and 1820. That warfare, in a way, was inconclusive. Neither side convinced the other. Reform was ultimately to be successful on a large scale—but not because the Orthodox opponents of the early decades of the nineteenth century conceded defeat. The battle had to be fought all over again in instance after instance—only the weapons chosen in subsequent decades were different, the polemics and apologetics more sophisticated, and the Reform endeavor more far-reaching. What remains of abiding interest is the fact that the early Reformers should have felt the need to defend themselves in that particular arena, and with those particular weapons. Nothing demonstrates more clearly than this that the farthest thing from their mind was the formation of a new Jewish sect, let alone the founding of a new religion. The Judaism to which they wanted to bring liturgical reform was a Judaism based on Bible, Talmud, and Codes; and it was by an appeal to those accepted bases of Jewish life that they sought to justify their place *within* Judaism. Did they succeed in doing so?

The historian Graetz, by no means a friend of the Berlin and Hamburg Reform endeavors, seems to think that they did—on one level, at any rate.

> The reasons which the (Orthodox) rabbis had adduced against the worship service of the (Hamburg) Temple were mostly not valid, and some of them were downright childish. The letter (of the Law) was against them (i.e., the Orthodox). The multiplicity of Rabbinic authorities, belonging to such different times and countries, always enabled one to bring apparent proofs for and against a specific case. The rabbis should have said that, even though the letter could be adduced in favor of the innovations, the spirit of Talmudic Judaism must nevertheless condemn them. But they did not stand on that level; and, in their desire to utilize the letter also for their position, they revealed many a weak spot.[38]

One does not necessarily have to share Graetz's understanding of—what he calls—"the spirit of Talmudic Judaism" to realize that, in a back-handed kind of way, the great historian was here awarding the palm of victory to the Reformers. But the distinction between the "letter" and the "spirit" of Talmudic Judaism, particularly as applied to the case of Reform Judaism, was not original with Graetz. It was first pointed out by one of the Reformers themselves.

Writing in 1844, Ludwig Philippson had this to say:

> We now have Reformers who, if they but find a Talmudic passage which supports, or seems to support, a projected reform, consider the matter as closed. They call that, "reforming on an Orthodox basis." It has, of late, been said often enough that this is not in the *spirit* of the Talmud; for, in essence, the Talmud is the Reform of its time. For . . . even though its intention was to preserve what it could preserve, in spite of the changing times, this was still a manifestation of the spirit of Reform. The abovementioned Reformers are, therefore, still slaves of the letter—in spite of the fact that they merely want to force the Orthodox to concede the intended reform. But we cannot, on account of the pressure of the times, stand firm by the letter of the Talmud. *We must go beyond it.* On the other hand, there are occasions when we must remain *behind* the letter of the Talmud; that is to say, we must preserve something which, according to the letter of the Talmud, could be changed. We must preserve it once it is a case of meeting a higher need which is now being felt.
>
> This consideration applies particularly to the *language of prayer*. According to the first paragraph of the seventh chapter of *Sotah,* with the exceptions stated in the second paragraph, the language of prayer may be any language. Therefore, he who wants to ban the Hebrew language from the Israelite worship service thinks that he has settled the question. All right, you, who thus go in for shadow fighting, now you have an opportunity of demonstrating your deliberation, and of showing that yours is no mere childish desire to destroy, and to acquire a great name because of your liberalism. . . . [Philippson goes on to argue that, notwithstanding the Talmud's permission to pray in the vernacular, the true modern Reformer should not avail himself of that permission. He should, instead, bear in mind the *emotional* and the *historical* reasons which speak strongly in favor of the retention of Hebrew.] [39]

Yet the appeal to emotional, rather than to legalistic, reasons was a double-edged sword. In 1868, twenty-four years after Philippson's appeal, Abraham Geiger also invoked "emotional" reasons. But he invoked them for the purpose of *banishing* Hebrew. Wrote Geiger:

> All the reasons adduced by the defense (of Hebrew) cannot shat-

> ter the truth that prayer can only flow from the heart in the *mother tongue*. Every utterance in a foreign idiom is something acquired, something mediated by reason—but not developed out of the inner life of the soul.[40]

When, within the Reform camp itself, we have one man's word against another's as to what the needs of the "heart" are, and if we then bear in mind that the prayer life of whole congregations may ultimately depend on the outcome of such a debate, conducted on the basis of intangibles, we cannot help feeling that there was something to be said for the earlier debates, firmly grounded as they were in the exposition of normative texts. Yet the frame of reference of the earlier debates was now gone. Nor should it be thought, notwithstanding the particular illustration we have chosen, that "prayer in the vernacular" continued to be the major bone of contention. Liturgical reform had been followed by doctrinal reform, and doctrinal reform, in its turn, led to new liturgical revisions. By 1841, the second edition of the Hamburg Temple Prayerbook, if somewhat half-heartedly, had given liturgical expression to some radical departures from traditional dogma. (And, even so, most of the apologia, not least Holdheim's share of it, still moved in the grooves of Rabbinic legalism!)[41] The early naiveté was now definitely a matter of the past. In 1818/19, a Moses Sopher and an Aaron Choriner might have differed, and differed violently, in their respective interpretations of the sources. But both of them were agreed on the authoritative character of the sources themselves. Forty years later, the situation was different. In 1857, Geiger had published his *Urschrift* ("The Original Text and Translations of the Bible in their Relation to the Inner Development of Judaism"), a work in which he had espoused the methodology of Biblical criticism.

When the same Geiger, in 1861, wrote about "The Necessity and the Dimensions of a Reform of the Jewish Worship Service,"[42] his Orthodox opponents knew that, with Geiger, it would be futile to re-open the "Battle of the Proof Texts." The common basis was gone. Israel Hildesheimer says so, and in so many words. Attacking Geiger's proposals, and, in particular, Geiger's projected emendation of the prayers expressing the concept of the Chosen People, Hildesheimer wrote:

> We would have been naive enough to ask the author, what, as a consequence (of his liturgical proposals), we would now have to make of such expressions of the Torah as "For thou art a holy people unto the Lord thy God," "The Lord hath chosen thee to be His own treasure from among all the peoples that are upon the face of the earth," etc., if we did not know that the author (of the proposals for liturgical reform) was also the

author of the *Urschrift;* and, as such, is bound to have a very convenient answer to such questions.[43]

Yet, some kind of common basis was ultimately found, after all. If, at the begnining of the nineteenth century, the arena was circumscribed by the dimensions of the legal literature of Rabbinic Judaism, towards the end of that century, and at the beginning of the next, the boundaries were set by the *Wissenschaft des Judentums* (The Scientific Study of Judaism)—an over-all concept which included not only a mastery of the entire range of Jewish literature, but also an awareness of its historical development, and a knowledge of the circumstances which had led to that development. The Reformers had been prominent among the pioneers of that new discipline, but Orthodoxy was not without its representatives among their ranks. In 1818/19, both Orthodoxy and Reform, for example, had unquestioningly accepted the Talmud's report that the Men of the Great Assembly had composed the text of the Eighteen Benedictions. Arguments by both sides were predicated on that assumption. By the end of the century, however, such Orthodox protagonists as still wanted to maintain that assumption had to "prove" it before the bar of *Wissenschaft*. The Reformers had given it up long before.

Already in 1841, D. W. Marks, the editor of the Reform prayerbook of London, had stated in his Introduction: "Nothing can be more incorrect than the current notion, that the whole of the Prayer Book, as we now possess it, was composed by the men of the Great Synagogue, from Ezra to Simeon the Just (among whom are numbered several prophets, as Haggai, Zechariah, Malachi, etc., etc.); and that, being stamped by the authority of these great names, the Prayer Book has as fixed and immutable a character as the Sacred Code itself." "The learned Dr. Zunz" is then quoted to the effect that the Eighteen Benedictions consist of "the labours of five successive epochs, in part at least posterior to the time of its supposed composition, and embracing a period of 300 years."[44]

But the battle in the arena of *Wissenschaft des Judentums* could, on occasion, be just as inconclusive as the "Battle of the Proof Texts" had been in an earlier generation. For one thing, charges of ignorance and misrepresentation could be flung at an opponent quite as much when the argument was supposedly "scientific" as they were in the days of purely legalistic conflicts. For another, the "scientific" arguments of one side did not always suggest the desired conclusions to the other.

Instructive in this connection is the controversy surrounding the Baden Prayerbook of 1905.[45] To defend its new prayerbook, the Supreme Council of the Israelites of Baden had published a lengthy

"Memoir," which was probably written by M. Steckelmacher.[46] In some 140 pages, this work contains a history of the evolution of Jewish liturgy, a theoretical justification—with ample Rabbinic quotations—of abbreviations in the worship service, and theological arguments—again supported by quotations from the entire range of Jewish literature—to defend the omission of prayers for the restoration of the sacrificial cult and of the Davidic dynasty, and the avoidance of "unfounded particularisms." The whole work is, as it were, an encyclopedia of Reform apologetics in the liturgical sphere, from the source material first adduced in the earlier "Battle of the Proof Texts" through the latest established conclusions of the *Wissenschaft des Judentums*.

Yet all that ammunition failed to have the desired effect. One of the Orthodox opponents, Dr. J. Wohlgemuth, of the Berlin Rabbinical Seminary, reacted in this way:

> In eighteen pages, the *Memoir*—supported by an abundance of quotations from the Talmud, the Codes, and the works of Jewish *Wissenschaft*—proves the extraordinary new thesis that our prayers developed gradually, and that, until late in the Middle Ages, changes were still introduced into the traditional prayers. Such is the low level of information which the reader is expected to have! Whoever has but the most rudimentary Jewish education already knows the greater part of the relevant Talmudic statements. In Baer's edition of the *Siddur*, which may be found in all Orthodox synagogues, information is given about the dates of origin of the prayers in question, and about the different forms which they had in earlier times.
>
> What on earth, therefore, is the use of all of those scientific disquisitions? Though unintended, the result, at any rate, is that—on account of the multitude of quotations, and the great display of apparent scholarship—the reader's attention is diverted from the real matter in dispute: *Does the Baden Supreme Council have the right to make changes in the prayerbook?* That is to say, is it the business of an authority *per se to* make changes in the prayerbook, and, secondly, is the Baden Supreme Council in particular the appropriate authority for such an undertaking?[47]

After this opening, the reader already knows how Wohlgemuth is going to answer the questions which he has posed. But note that in a few simple lines Wohlgemuth just brushed aside the whole scholarly apparatus of the Baden Reformers. He did not reject it; and he did not refute it. He merely considered it irrelevant to the central question, which amounted to this: Does the Baden Supreme Council have the same right to make liturgical changes in the twentieth century which earlier authorities had in previous centuries? The Baden Supreme

Council claimed that right. Wohlgemuth rejected that claim—not least because, in his view, the editors of the Baden Prayerbook fell far behind earlier liturgists in their degree of ritual observance.[48]

On a more scholarly level, David Hoffmann, too, attacked the Baden Prayerbook and the "Memoir." He, too, shrugged off the scholarly apparatus of the "Memoir" as an attempt to "force open an open door."[49] Otherwise, Hoffmann's pamphlet is full of invectives against the Baden Supreme Council, whom he accused of ignorance and misrepresentation.

M. Steckelmacher, writing on behalf of the Baden Supreme Council, returned the compliment.[50] Interestingly enough, Hoffmann and Steckelmacher were not only arguing about quotations from the Talmud and the Codes. They were also arguing about Graetz! Hoffmann had quoted Graetz in support of his position. Steckelmacher proceeded to demonstrate that Hoffmann had quoted Graetz out of context. And so, an argument developed about what Graetz had, or had not, said—an argument not unlike those of some ninety years before, when Moses Sopher and Aaron Choriner were arguing about what the *Shulḥan 'Arukh* had, or had not, said. "The Battle of the Proof Texts" had shifted to the field of the *Wissenschaft des Judentums*. The year was 1908.

The Orthodox won that round in Baden. Their victory, however, probably owed less to the cogency of Wohlgemuth's and Hoffmann's arguments than to the "political" coalition of Zionists and Orthodox, as we have shown in an earlier chapter.[51]

What, then, is the lasting significance of such "Battles of the Proof Texts," when seen from the perspective of the subsequent development of Liberal and Reform Liturgy? To one aspect we have already referred. The mere fact that the early Reformers took up the Orthodox challenge was an eloquent testimony to their desire not to separate themselves from the Jewish community. And that testimony was reiterated each time the Reformers entered another battle of that kind. But the same may be said for the Orthodox side. Instead of ignoring the Reformers, and regarding them as apostates beyond the fold, the Orthodox tried again and again to convince the Reformers of the error of their ways.

The arena, as we have seen, shifted from time to time; and each shift in location was itself evidence that both sides had kept up with the developments of the times. The old legalistic way of reasoning gave way to the "scientific" approach. The latter may one day yield to theological "dialogue." The language was often abusive, and the practical results nil. But, in the long run, the inconclusiveness of the "battles" is far less significant than the fact that the "battles" took place at all. They forced one side to justify itself in the light of Jewish continuity. They forced the other side to take at least some cognizance of the realities of modern life. They forced both sides to see—however grudgingly—

their opponents as fellow-Jews. That is why the exact location of the arena is likewise not of ultimate significance. The main thing is, rather, that, in every generation, there be something which Jews have in common, something so important to them, and of such concern, that it is worth fighting over. Perhaps it is at this point that we may regard the "Battle of the Proof Texts" in the light of the teaching of our Sages: "Every controversy that is in the Name of Heaven shall in the end lead to a permanent result." [52]

SIX

Order and Decorum

SIDE BY SIDE WITH THE PUBLICATION OF REFORMED PRAYERBOOKS, AND in many instances preceding such publication, there arose, at the very beginning of the nineteenth century, the literature of *Synagogenordnungen*. The German word, *Synagogenordnung*, means "Synagogue Order," and it carries the implications both of authoritative pronouncements and of the order and decorum which the Reformers wanted to see in the synagogue. The former was achieved by having the *Synagogenordnungen* promulgated by government authorities, though it is quite possible that, in a number of cases, it was the government itself which took the initiative. In one classical case, which we shall consider below, the *Judenordnung* of the Grand Duchy of Saxe-Weimar, much depends on the question where the initiative lay. On the whole, it would be safe to assume that where an enlightened government concerned itself with synagogue affairs—and not all governments taking an interest in Jewish worship services were enlightened—the government's aims and objectives by and large coincided with those of the Reformers. By the same token, however, where the government was not enlightened its interference in internal Jewish affairs could work against the aspirations of the Reformers—as was the case in Berlin, in the 1820's.

More often than not the promulgation of a *Synagogenordnung* preceded the publication of a reformed prayerbook in a given locality. The *Synagogenordnung* must, therefore, be seen in terms of the traditional liturgy—and here the omissions sanctioned or demanded by the *Synagogenordnung* become important—even as some of the later reformed rituals are themselves the outgrowth of worship services patterned in accordance with *Synagogenordnungen*. It will be seen that the various *Synagogenordnungen*, of which we here give a selection in English translation, follow one another's example both in style and in content. The prototype of them all, in as far as we have been able to discover, was the "Proclamation concerning the Improvements of the Worship Service in the Synagogues of the Kingdom of Westphalia" (*Bekanntmachung wegen besserer Einrichtung des Gottesdienstes in den Synagogen des Königreichs Westphalen*), published in Cassel, in 1810, i.e., at the time when Israel Jacobson was the guiding spirit of the Westphalian consistory. It consists of twenty-four pages, of which we here give the preamble as well as some characteristic paragraphs.

KINGDOM OF WESTPHALIA
CONSISTORY OF THE ISRAELITES

Cassel, September 24th, 1810.

If it be the function of the public worship service, in a place specifically devoted to that purpose, and in peaceful union with coreligionists, to demonstrate by means of devotional expressions the feelings of reverence and love for the infinite and merciful Father of all, the feelings of gratitude for the abundant acts of mercy of which we have been the recipients, and to proclaim the vows of faithful loyalty to His blissful commandments,—then the manner of such a solemn action must necessarily correspond completely to its beautiful and lofty purpose. There must be no cause for the disturbance of devotion within the consecrated walls, where the heart, in sweet inspiration, is to lift itself to its Creator, and where the mouth is to proclaim only praise and gratitude, love and reverence, noble desires and promises. Every impure ulterior object, every external advantage, every petty striving must be banned, and must remain banned from the House of the Lord. For one is to appear in this sanctuary only with the intention of humbling himself before the throne of the Almighty and All-Present, to obtain atonement from Him through repentance and holy resolves, and, finally, strengthened with gentle comfort, to rise again with renewed vigor to deal with those aspects of life about which we have been commanded by His holy will.

Vividly, therefore, do we feel the desire to see restored to the synagogues of this kingdom that order and that devotion which are appropriate to the true purpose of the public houses of prayer, and which, at the same time, will insure that the number of those who worship God in public is not going to be further diminished.

We have been entrusted by Royal Order of March 31st, 1808, Article 5, with the supervision of the practice of religion, which includes the rituals or the liturgical arrangements which are to be determined, the worship service itself, the synagogal arrangements, discipline and religious instruction. We, therefore, feel obliged to remove from the synagogues some inessentials which have crept into them. Much of it is no longer understood, and much of it gives cause for strife and disturbances. Indeed, earlier recognized scholars have already declared some of it to be inadmissible, while a number of things are inappropriate to the spirit of our times.

We therefore order the following herewith:

Paragraph 1.

Beginning with the 11th of November of this year, no public worship service may be held in any place in more than *one* synagogue, except with the permission of the consistory. In general, nowhere but in the synagogue, under whatever pretext, may a public worship service (*minyan*) take place without the special permission of the board.

Paragraph 2.

The manner of dedicating new synagogues or a newly written Torah is to be determined by the consistory whenever such cases occur.

Paragraph 3.

The primary task of the warden (*Vorsteher*) is to watch over decorum and peace. His regulations in this respect are to be followed *immediately* by all present, without contradiction. Should someone believe that the warden has done him an injustice, he may *afterwards* make a modest appeal to the board or to the consistory. But the immediate compliance with the regulation must never be withheld.

Paragraph 4.

In future, no cantor or sexton may be employed unless he has previously been approved by us. Those who have already been employed without approval must immediately have the directors submit their names to the board, in order that they may be approved if found suitable.

Paragraph 5.

The knocking on the doors and the calling out in the streets, which is customary in several congregations as a sign of the impending worship service, must altogether cease. Instead, the congregations must follow the times of services which will be determined by their rabbi with our approval. . . .

Paragraph 6.

Everybody should be dressed as cleanly and as decently as possible when appearing in the synagogue. The prayer leader, in particular, must be decently attired.

Paragraph 7.

Children who have not yet passed their fourth year must not be admitted. In general, the parents of the children who come to synagogue are responsible for their quiet and good behavior.

Paragraph 8.

Neither with the beginning of the prayers, nor with the reading of the *Shema,* nor with the Eighteen Benedictions must there be any waiting either for the rabbi or for anybody else.

Paragraph 9.

Nobody except the cantor employed by the congregation may at any time lead the congregation in prayer. If the cantor should be indisposed, his place may be taken by his son, if the latter is suitable. If there be no such son, then one of the other suitable sextons may do so. If none be available, then anybody else who has the ability, and who has been invited to do so by the warden, may take the place of the cantor.

Paragraph 10.

However, the penitential prayers before and after the New Year may also be recited by one who has been designated to lead the prayers on New Year and the Day of Atonement.

Paragraph 11.

On Passover and Tabernacles, only the cantor is to recite the *Tal* and *Geshem* prayers.

Paragraph 12.

No travelling cantor is permitted to lead the congregation in prayer. However, if the congregation intends to employ him, after due approval, he is permitted to lead the congregation in prayer. But this may happen only on *one* Sabbath or festival.

Paragraph 13.

Just as it is not permitted in the case of a resident, so it is not allowed for an itinerant to give public sermons or addresses without the special permission of the consistory.

Paragraph 14.

Every cantor shall endeavor to enunciate every word of the prayers clearly. The unsuitable traditional singing which interrupts the prayer is to be avoided. Every accompaniment by singers and bass-singers, employed by some congregations for that purpose, is to cease altogether. . . .

Paragraph 15.

The members of the congregations are reminded and ordered to follow the cantor's prayers quietly and silently. They must refrain from the illegal and cacophonous *shouting* which so frequently disturbs peaceful and true devotion.

Paragraph 16.

Since rabbinical discussions do not belong in the synagogues, no rabbi is to deliver Talmudic or Kabbalistic or mystical discourses. He should speak about the teachings of religion and ethics only.

. . . .

Paragraph 26.

All who are called up to the Torah, including *shevi'i, aḥaron* and *maphtir,* are called by the cantor by their family name (omitting the name of the father). The same applies to the so-called *mi sheberakh*. For example, if the person to be called up is named *Menhe Heilberg,* the cantor is to call him up as *Menahem Heilberg*. Those Westphalians, however, who have not yet adopted a family name, will not be called up to the Torah.

. . . .

Paragraph 40.

The procession with the Torah on the eve of the festival of Rejoicing in the Law, which has been customary in some congregations, must no longer take place. Nor must there be a reading from the Torah on that night.

. . . .

Paragraph 42.

The so-called "beating of Haman" on the feast of Purim is no longer to be permitted. Nor must the Book of Esther be interrupted by the singing of unsuitable songs; but it should be read decently and quietly.

Paragraph 43.

The undersigned board, with complete trust in the judgment of the Israelite congregants, feels sure that they will contribute with all their strength to the realization of its well-meaning intentions, and that they will punctiliously obey the present regulations. It does not want to be compelled to resort to disagreeable measures of compulsion, including ecclesiastical punishment, temporary closing of the synagogue, proposals for the removal of the cantor from his office, and strict investigations of those who are obstinate.

Paragraph 44.

The syndics are to make known and affix this order in all the synagogues of their districts immediately. Every cantor is to be handed a copy of it by the wardens as a guide-line.

THE ROYAL WESTPHALIAN CONSISTORY OF THE ISRAELITES.

Berlin. Kalkar. Steinhardt. Fränkel. Heinemann.

Merkel, *Secretary.*[1]

Decorum and order in the worship service are the primary objective of this 1810 document, strictly enforced decorum and order. To achieve this aim, some of the ancient built-in informality of the old-time synagogue had to give way—including the lay character of traditional Jewish worship. Only the officially appointed "cantor" now has the right to lead the congregation in prayer. (Paragraphs 9 and 12.) In this way the consistory was able to exercise its control over the conduct of the worship service and also to advance its "Westernization." The latter is evident not only from the prohibition of "cacophonous shouting" (Paragraph 15), but also from the interdict (Paragraph 14) of having the cantor accompanied by "singers and bass-singers." The reference here is to the bass and discant singers who were the standard retinue of the traditional *ḥazzan*.[2] 1810 was, of course, the year in which Israel Jacobson introduced the organ in the chapel of his Seesen school. It should, therefore, be noted that no attempt is made in this "Proclamation" to force the organ on other congregations under Jacobson's jurisdiction. Yet, short of bringing in the organ, everything else is being tried here to bring synagogal singing into harmony with modern Western taste. Interesting and, in a way, pathetic is the attempt made (Paragraph 26) to force Westphalian Jews to adopt the ways of their environment. Those who have not yet adopted a family name cannot be called up to the Torah—a radical reform, if we bear in mind that, in the traditional synagogue, family names do not figure at all, the person being called up to the Torah identifying himself as "N son of N." Paragraph 16 is a landmark in the transition from the traditional *derashah* (Talmudic discourse) to the modern sermon, a transition here enacted in the form of a law! While the pre-Emancipation synagogue was not generally marked by too much decorum, there were two occasions in the year when there was even less decorum than usual: Purim and Rejoicing in the Law. In Paragraphs 40 and 42, the Westphalian "Proclamation" tries to remove the apparent causes of such disturbances.

Above all, it is the first Paragraph which calls for some further comment. That Paragraph, occupying the first place in the order of Paragraphs, has become paradigmatic for many other *Synagogenordnungen*. Its intent is clear enough. By making it impossible for Jews to gather for worship purposes outside of the one official synagogue, the consistory made quite sure that its mandatory reforms would not be evaded by some of the traditionalists. It should be remembered in this context that, according to the provisions of Jewish law, any ten adult male Jews can constitute themselves as a "congregation" for purposes of public worship. By enacting its first Paragraph, the Westphalian consistory thus abolished a right which Jews enjoyed under traditional Jewish law.

At the same time, it must be borne in mind that the Westphalian consistory did not invent that particular restriction. The Spanish and Portuguese Jewish Congregation of London had formulated as early as 1663, and adopted as early as 1664, forty-two laws or *ascamoth*. The very first of those *ascamoth* forbade, under penalty of excommunication, the formation of any other Sepharadi congregation in the City of London or its surroundings, or even the assembly of ten persons for the purpose of worship, except on the occasion of a wedding or in the house of mourners. And the London *ascamoth* themselves were patterned after those of Amsterdam and Venice.[3] Such is the irony of history that, thirty years after Paragraph 1. of the Westphalian "Proclamation" prohibited the free assembly of Jews for worship, the Spanish and Portuguese Jewish Congregation of London invoked their *ascamah* No. 1 against those of its members who, in the 1840's, were involved in the formation of England's first Reform synagogue![4]

The "Regulation of the Worship Service for the Synagogues of the Kingdom of Wuerttemberg, ordained with highest approval by the Royal Israelitish Supreme Ecclesiastical Authority" (*Gottesdienst-Ordnung für die Synagogen des Königreichs Württemberg. Unter höchster Genehmigung festgesetzt von der Königl. israelitischen Ober-Kirchen-Behörde.*), was published in Stuttgart, in 1838.[5]

The preamble and some of the characteristic paragraphs read as follows:

> It is the purpose of the worship service and of the liturgical usages to maintain and to strengthen the faith, to arouse and to animate the religious spirit, and to promote the ethical way of life. At the same time, it is to be a bond which binds and unites Israel as a community of faith. The prayers composed by the Men of the Great Synagogue and the order of service introduced by them were as appropriate to that purpose as, originally, they were most simple and dignified. However, as a consequence of centuries during which the synagogue was without any supervision, there was not only a departure from the old and venerable usages, but many abuses crept into the synagogue as well. Particularly in times of severe oppression and persecution, the order of prayers (*seder tephillah*) was augmented by many components which, happily, are no longer appropriate to our times. At the same time, on account of the differences between the congregations and their religious attitudes and spirit, there arose a remarkable difference between them in their customs (*minhagim*), a difference which also has a most disturbing effect upon the totality. In order to bring relief from these ills, and in order to restore dignity and decorum to the public worship service and to the liturgical usages, and aiming at the achievement of some uniformity, the Supreme Ecclesiastical Authority has ordained the following Regulation of the Worship Service. We specifically expect of the rabbis that they will instruct the members of their congregations in the regulations stated herein, and that they will seek to remove any possible misunderstandings. But of all the rest of our coreligionists we expect that they will accept this *Synagogenordnung* with confidence and in the conviction that, in this as in all other regulations, it is our sole intention to maintain and to strengthen the venerable structure of our religion.

CHAPTER ONE.
About the External Order and Decorum during the Worship Service.

Paragraph 1.

From February 1st, 1838, on, no public worship services may be held outside of the synagogues approved by the royal state authorities. From that time on, every private assembly for liturgical purposes (*minyan*) is prohibited on pain of severe punishment. An exception is made in cases of bereavement in that the customary prayers may be said with the dying, and that, with the exception of the Sabbath, the daily prayers may be recited during the first seven days of mourning in the mourner's house.

Paragraph 2.

The knocking on the doors and the shouting in the streets, which are still customary in most congregations as a sign for the impending worship service, must henceforth cease altogether.

Paragraph 3.

The beginning of the worship service is herewith fixed once and for all for all the synagogues of the country. . . .

Paragraph 4.

Both on weekdays and on Sabbaths and festivals, everybody should appear in the synagogue in a suitable and decent attire. An individual is not permitted to wear a special cloak or biretta either during the service as such or during special liturgical acts.

Paragraph 5.

The rabbi, when he conducts the service, and the cantor, whenever he leads in prayer or is engaged in other religious duties, must wear their canonicals.

Paragraph 6.

The synagogue should be entered with decorum and without noise. He who enters must immediately go to his seat, and remain in it as quietly as ever possible. The sexton should direct foreign Israelites to seats. Any walking around or standing together within the synagogue is prohibited on pain of punishment.

Paragraph 7.

Boys below the age of 6, and girls below the age of 9, are not to be admitted to the synagogue. The parents of children attending the synagogue are responsible for their quiet and good behavior.

Paragraph 8.

Every conversation with one's neighbor, every noise, all jokes and pranks, irrespective of time and occasion, as well as everything else which offends decency or disturbs the peace, are strictly prohibited.

Paragraph 9.

As being offensive to the decorum and to the dignity of the worship service, the practice of the following customs is no longer permitted in the synagogue:

(a) the kissing of the curtain on entering the synagogue or during the service;
(b) leaving one's seat in order to kiss the Scroll of the Law;
(c) the knocking during the reading of the Book of Esther on the feast of Purim;
(d) the *malkoth*-beating on the Eve of the Day of Atonement;[6]
(e) the noisy beating of the *hoshanoth*[7] on the seventh day of Tabernacles;
(f) sitting on the floor on the fast of the Ninth of Ab;
(g) removing shoes and boots in the synagogue on that day;
(h) the procession with the Torah, which is still the practice in some localities, on the eve of Rejoicing in the Law;
(i) the procession of the children with flags and candles on that festival;
(j) the distribution of food and drink in the synagogue on that festival in localities where it is still taking place.

The indebtedness of this *Synagogenordung* to the Westphalian "Proclamation" of 1810 is obvious. If anything, the Württemberg "Regulation" goes further than its Westphalian prototype in detailing the prohibited "abuses" and in proscribing some of the manifestations of traditional Jewish piety. The leading spirit in drafting the Württemberg "Regulation" was Dr. Joseph von Maier, the theological member of the Supreme Ecclesiastical Authority and rabbi of Stuttgart. Evaluating Maier's work some sixty-five years later, one of his successors in the Stuttgart rabbinate, Theodor Kroner, wrote that Maier's "aim was to eliminate completely all non-German elements, and to approach as closely as possible to the culture of the time, maintaining the idea of Jewish unity and morality, while abandoning the specifically Jewish laws of exclusion. . . . Most of the communities in the northern part of the country clung, however, to the Hebrew language and to the Biblical and Talmudic rules of life; and at present (i.e., 1906) the majority of the Jewish children are instructed in Hebrew, while the form of worship has remained almost unchanged." [8]

Five years after the Wuerttemberg "Regulation," in 1843, the "Worship Service Regulations for the Israelites of the Principality of Birkenfeld" (*Gottesdienstliche Anordnungen für die Israeliten des Fürstenthums Birkenfeld*) were published in Birkenfeld. What makes the Birkenfeld "Regulations" of particular interest is the fact that they were enacted at the time when David Einhorn (who later achieved prominence as a radical Reformer in the United States [9]) was chief rabbi of the principality. Noteworthy in these "Regulations" are the paragraphs dealing with the reform of the prayers themselves. Some characteristic paragraphs are presented here:

Paragraph 1.

Assemblies for public worship may, as a matter of law, take place only in recognized synagogues. All so-called *minyanim* (private services) are forbidden. Exceptionally, however, they may be permitted in cases of bereavement during the first seven days of mourning, with the exception of the Sabbath, if the mourner's house is suitable for the purpose. The decision about that is the prerogative of the chief rabbi, and, in his absence, of the presiding board member, whose views must be elicited by those concerned.

Paragraph 4.

Everybody must enter and leave the House of God quietly, without noise and without conversation with others. During the service nobody must enter or leave except in emergencies.

Paragraph 5.

On weekdays, and especially on Sabbaths and festivals, everybody must appear in the House of God properly and decently attired. It is particularly offensive to good manners if mourners appear in the House of God on the Sabbath with torn garments (*keri'ah*-tear). This is not to be tolerated.

Paragraph 6.

Furthermore, everything else which runs counter to the rules of decorum is to be avoided during the service. This includes:

All laughing, talking, joking, irrespective of time and occasion, noisy standing around, or even leaving of the seat, all invitations to weddings, etc.

Furthermore, the following customs and abuses are strictly prohibited as being indecent:

1) Being in the House of God with a bare arm.[10] Everybody is required to put on the phylacteries (*tephillin*) as decorously as possible, and to dress himself decently again immediately afterwards.
2) The loud kissing of the *tzitzith*, the swaying to and fro during prayer.
3) The *malkuth*-beating on Atonement Eve.[11]
4) The noisy beating of the willows during *chibbut 'aravah*[12] on the seventh day of Tabernacles.
5) The taking off of shoes and boots on the Day of Atonement and the Ninth of Ab. The *kohanim*, too, have to avoid this in connection with their benediction.
6) The carrying of the festival bouquet, on Tabernacles, from the men's synagogue to the women's synagogue.[13]
7) The putting on and the taking off in the synagogue of the shroud on New Year and the Day of Atonement after the beginning, and before the end, of the service. Also on those days everybody must come to the service in festive attire and with a decent head covering.

Paragraph 19.

The order of prayers remains the customary one, with the following exceptions:

1) On weekdays, as well as on festivals and holy days, no further Psalm is to be added to the one appointed for each day at the conclusion of the service.
2) The prayer, *shir hayiḥud,*[14] is to be recited only on the High Holy Days and festivals, and on Atonement Eve.
3) The two Chaldaic prayers, *yequm purqan,*[15] are no longer recited. On the other hand, the subsequent prayer for His Royal Highness, the Grand Duke, and for the congregation,[16] is solemnly said by the chief rabbi (and, in his absence, by the cantor) with the Torah in his arm. The whole congregation has to stand during that prayer, and to respond with Amen.
4) On the Sabbath before Pentecost and before the Ninth of Ab, the prayer, *av haraḥamim,*[17] is to be omitted. Instead, a German prayer for those who died in pious

faith and for the martyrs is to be inserted by the chief rabbi or, in his absence, by the cantor.

5) The mystical prayers, *yehi ratzon,*[18] before the taking of the *lulabh* and before the blowing of the *shofar,* are henceforth to be omitted.

6) All the *piyutim* and *zulatoth*[19] inserted before the *shemoneh esreh* on various Sabbaths and festivals[20] are to be omitted, excluding those of the two days of New Year and the Day of Atonement. Also the prayers known as *krobotz* (sic)[21] on Purim and the Ninth of Ab. Furthermore, the passages included in the *musaph* of the Sabbaths before Passover, and, finally, the Chaldaic prayer, *Aqdamuth,*[22] on Pentecost, and the enumeration of the 613 commandments during the *musaph* of the first day,[23] except for *az shesh me-oth.*[24]

Paragraph 24.

In the prayer, *abhinu malkenu,* the sentence, *neqom le'enenu,* is to be omitted.[25]

The year 1843, which saw the promulgation of the Birkenfeld "Regulations," also saw the publication of the *"Synagogen-Ordnung"* for the Synagogues of the Grand Duchy of Mecklenburg-Schwerin. While David Einhorn, at that time, was the chief rabbi of Birkenfeld, it was Samuel Holdheim who, in 1843, served as chief rabbi of Mecklenburg-Schwerin. Holdheim, in 1843, was no longer the Orthodox rabbi he had been in Frankfort-on-the-Oder, nor had he as yet reached the degree of radicalism for which he was later to be known in Berlin. But he had already espoused the progressive cause, and had published his views in favor of the prayerbook of the Hamburg Reform Temple. Here, then, are some selections from the *Synagogen-Ordnung für die Synagogen des Grossherzogthums Mecklenburg-Schwerin,* published in Schwerin, in 1843:

CHAPTER ONE

Paragraph 1.

From now on no public worship service may be conducted except in the synagogues. Every private assembly for the conducting of a worship service, *minyan,* is henceforth forbidden.

An exception is made in the case of bereavement. During the first seven days of mourning, with the exception of the Sabbath, the daily prayers may be recited in the mourner's house.

The traditional so-called "night watches" on the eve of *Shavu' oth* and the eve of *Hoshannah Rabbah*[26] may continue to take place in a private house. However, the morning service, *shaḥarith,* connected with the former, is forbidden.

Paragraph 2.

In the synagogue, too, there must not be any special early morning service, *hashkamah,* in addition to the general *shaḥarith* and *musaph* services—not excluding the first two days of Sukkoth.

Paragraph 9.

Boys under the age of 6, and girls under the age of 9, are not to be admitted into the synagogue. The parents are responsible for the good behavior of their children who are present in Synagogue, unless the children are placed under the special supervision of the teacher.

Paragraph 11.

As offensive to the decorum and the dignity of the worship service, the practice of the following customs is no longer permitted in the synagogue:

(a) The kissing of the curtain upon entering the synagogue or during the service;
(b) The leaving of one's seat in order to kiss the Scroll of the Law, *sepher torah;*
(c) The *malquth*-beating on Atonement Eve;[27]
(d) The noisy beating of the *hoshanoth* on the seventh day of Tabernacles;[28]
(e) Sitting on the floor on the fast of the Ninth of Ab. Whoever wants to use a low stool must have it brought to his place before the beginning of the service;
(f) The taking off and the putting on of shoes and boots in the synagogue. Whoever wants to use felt shoes on the Ninth of Ab and on the Day of Atonement will have to wear them prior to entering the synagogue. The change of foot-gear of the *kohanim* in connection with *duchanen*[29] must likewise take place in the vestibule, and must never be done within the synagogue itself;
(g) The procession of children with flags and candles on the feast of Rejoicing in the Law, where that is still customary;
(h) Leaving one's seat during the *duchanen* in order to stand directly in front of the *kohanim;*

(i) Expressions of thanks, *yiyasher ko-aḥ,* to the *kohanim* after the conclusion of the Priestly Benediction, or to anyone else after the performance of a liturgical act;

(k) Leaving the synagogues during *hazkarath neshamoth* [30] on the part of those whose parents are still alive.

Paragraph 16.

No announcements must be made in the synagogue about any matter not related to the cult, unless there be a special order to that effect by the state authorities.

CHAPTER TWO

Paragraph 6.

On weekdays, the prayers shall be recited according to the accustomed order of the prayerbook, *seder tephillah,* but with the omission of *ezehu meqoman* [31] and *pereq rabbi yishma-el.* [32]

Paragraph 7.

The 12th benediction of the *Shemoneh Esreh* is to be recited in the following form:

ולמלשינות אל-תהי תקוה וכל הרשעה כרגע תאבד וכלה מהרה תכרת והזדון מהרה תעקר ותשבר ותמגר ותכניע במהרה בימינו. ברוך אתה ה׳ שובר איבה ומכניע זדון: [33]

Paragraph 8.

In the prayer, *vehu raḥum,* on Monday and Thursday, in the paragraph, *hapote-aḥ* the following phrase is to be omitted: [34]

אל הביטה דל כבודנו בגוים ושקצונו כטומאת הנדה. עד מתי עזך בשבי ותפארתך ביד צר. עוררה גבורתך וקנאתך על אויביך. הם יבושו ויחתו מגבורתם.

Paragraph 21.

The *av haraḥamim* prayer is to be said only to *she-ar tzaddiqé 'olam.* The whole passage beginning with *veyinqom* to the end is omitted.[35]

About ten years after the publication of the Mecklenburg-Schwerin *Synagogen-Ordnung,* another *Synagogenordnung* was promulgated in the city of Mayence.[36] Joseph Aub was the rabbi of Mayence at that time.[37] He never shared Holdheim's radicalism, yet the liturgical provisions of the Mayence *Synagogenordnung* go far beyond, in their Reform tendency, the minor reforms envisaged by the Mecklenburg-Schwerin document. We bring the Mayence *Synagogenordnung* in full.

SYNAGOGEN-ORDNUNG

I. *External Decorum*

1.

Upon entering the synagogue, and throughout the worship service, everyone has to observe quiet and decency, and must carefully avoid any disturbances through conversation, leaving of his seat, etc.

2.

In order not to disturb the devotion of the congregation, everyone present must pray in silence—with the exception of the cases mentioned in paragraph 4, below.

3.

The congregation must listen silently to the prayers recited by the cantor. By no means must they audibly pray together with him, let alone sing along with him.

4.

In the case of prayers which are recited responsively by rabbi and congregation, or cantor and congregation, prayers which the congregation may and should join in singing, nobody is allowed to begin before, or finish after, the choir. Since, however, it will be impossible at first for the congregation to know how they are to respond and to sing, the choir *alone* is to exercise this function for the time being—until the congregation will have gained knowledge and certainty in these matters.

5.

Nobody is allowed to leave his seat when the Torah is being taken out of the Ark or returned thither.

6.

Children below the age of five are not allowed to be brought into the synagogue.

7.

Apart from the rabbi and the cantor, nobody is allowed to take over the function of leading the congregation in prayer.

II. *Liturgical Order for the Service on Sabbath and Weekdays*

1.

Excluded from the daily prayers are the Talmudical sections

which are lacking the character of prayer: *ezehu meqoman*[38] etc., as well as, on the Sabbath, *bameh madliqin,*[39] *pittum haqetoreth*[40] etc.

2.

Instead of the three benedictions, שלא עשני נכרי, עבד, אשה,[41] the one benediction שעשני ישראל is to be recited.[42]

3.

The prayer *velamalshinim* is to be recited in the following version:[43]

ולמלשינות אל-תהי תקוה וכל-הרשעה כלה כעשן תכלה והזדון מהרה תכניע. ברוך אתה ה׳ שובר איבה ומכניע זדון:

4.

On Monday and Thursday, in the prayer *vehu raḥum,* the last paragraph, *hapote-aḥ,* is omitted, with the exception of the concluding words וחון אום.[44] Also omitted are the verses between the *teḥinnah* and *shomer yisra-el.*[45]

5.

No *teḥinnah* is to be recited on national holidays.[46]

6.

Every service concludes with the prayer *'alenu leshabbe-aḥ.*

7.

All *abhelim* (mourners) and those observing the anniversary of the death of their parents (*Jahrzeit*) recite the *Kaddish* together with the cantor, behind whom they take up their position before this prayer.

8.

Of the six psalms before the Sabbath prayer,[47] two are recited responsively every Friday in rotation.

9.

Of the song *lekhah dodi,*[48] apart from the refrain, only the following stanzas are henceforth to be recited:

שמור וזכור, לקראת, בואי בשלום.

10.

The *tephillah* of the Seven and of the Eighteen Benedictions is to be recited no more than once. The first three and the last three benedictions are recited aloud by the cantor, silently by the congregation. The intermediary benedictions, and, in the case of an evening service, the entire *tephillah,* are recited in silence only.

11.

For the prayers *yequm purqan* and *mi sheberakh*[49] a German prayer is to be substituted, which is to follow the prayer for the government.

12.

All *piyutim* are omitted from the services.

13.

The blessings for women after childbirth, and the prayers for the sick, are to be recited by the rabbi. He must, therefore, be informed betimes by those concerned.

14.

On Sabbath and the three festivals, the *musaph* service is to be separated from the *shaḥarith.* The latter is to begin at 6.30 or 7.00 a.m. in the summer, and at 7.30 a.m. in the winter. The former is to begin at 9.00 a.m. in the summer; at 9.30 a.m. in the winter.

15.

The *musaph* prayer, or the service including that prayer, begins with a song before the taking out of the Torah. This is followed by the reading of the Torah, and this, in turn, is followed by the reading of the Haftarah in German. After that come the sermon and the customary prayer.

16.

A German song is to be sung before and after the sermon. A selection of such songs, together with some German prayers, will be separately printed for this purpose.

The publication of *Synagogenordnungen* went on right into the twentieth century, aiming at both external decorum and liturgical reform. An example of a twentieth-century *Synagogenordnung* is that of the Jewish community of Beuthen, in Upper Silesia, published in 1906.[50] If the Birkenfeld "Regulations" of 1843 insisted upon having the phylacteries put on "as decently as possible" and upon the worshipper's "dressing himself again decently immediately afterwards," the Beuthen *Synagogenordnung* of 1906 is more blunt: "The putting on of the *tephillin,*" it says (Paragraph 3), "may take place in the entrance hall only." It also (Paragraph 13) summarily prohibits the beating of the willows. Above all, it brooks no compromise in connection with the starting time of services. Paragraph 4 states: "The time for all public worship services is determined by the rabbi in consultation with the board. Decisive for the beginning of the fixed time of prayer is the clock of the synagogue."

It must not be thought, however, that the striving for external decorum was confined to those who also aspired to liturgical reform. Bringing order and decorum to the synagogue, and removing abuses, marked the efforts of no less a traditionalist than Samson Raphael Hirsch, the leader of the "counter-reformation" and founder of Separatist Orthodoxy. During the rabbinate of Hirsch, the synagogue of the Israelitische Religionsgesellschaft in Frankfort-on-the-Main published, in 1874, a *Synagogenordnung* which, in many of its provisions, is highly reminiscent of *Synagogenordnungen* which owe their origin to circles of quite different tendencies. The following excerpts will illustrate this:

Synagogen-Ordnung für die Synagoge der Israelitischen Religionsgesellschaft in Frankfurt a. M.

Paragraph 1.

It is expected of those who attend the synagogue that, conscious of the holiness of the place, they preserve good manners and dignity, that, on entering, they go to their seats without noise, and that they leave the synagogue only after the termination of the service, likewise without noise.

Paragraph 2.

Any conversation in the synagogue and any formation of groups, both in the synagogue itself and in the adjoining rooms, is inadmissible—even before the beginning and after the end of the service.

Paragraph 10.

Prayers and all liturgical acts are to be conducted with dignity and decorum. In general, everything is to be avoided which could disturb others in their devotion.

During the recitation of the prayers by the cantor, as well as during the reading of the Torah portion, everybody must refrain from accompanying the recitation or the reading with his own singing or reading.

Paragraph 12.

Only the rabbi is allowed (and, in his absence, the officiating chairman of the synagogue) to draw the attention of the cantor and of the reader to such mistakes as they might possibly be making during the recitation of the prayers or during the reading of the Torah.

Paragraph 25.

The *yiyasher ko-aḥ* (to the *kohanim* after the Priestly Benediction) shall not be said by anyone except, in the name of the congregation, by the synagogue wardens appointed for that purpose.

The *Synagogenordnung* of Hirsch's congregation thus shows that the striving for decorum could be engaged in even without aspiring to a reform of the traditional liturgy. Yet most of the *Synagogenordnungen* manage to combine the two. There was, however, one such "regulation" which seemed to have as its major objective the total transformation of the traditional synagogue service. It was drafted in 1823, and put into operation in 1837. We have not included it in our chronological treatment of *Synagogenordnungen,* because it is rather unique and deserves a more detailed treatment in its own right. We are referring to the *Judenordnung* of the Grand Duchy of Saxe-Weimar.

A newspaper report, dated May 16th, 1837, reads as follows:

The introduction of a *German* worship service, ordered in the *Judenordnung* of the Grand Duchy of Saxe-Weimar of June 20th, 1823, has been put into effect since the beginning of this year—in spite of all the appeals of the Jewish congregations against it. The singing of German chorales has been introduced; all of the prayers are recited in *German;* and the Torah portions, after being read in Hebrew, are being translated into *German.* Dr. M. Hess, chief rabbi in Stadt-Lengsfeld, who has been accused of causing this change in the worship service, is defending himself against this accusation in the *Universale Kirchen-Zeitung* by giving his *approval* to the matter *as such,* yet demonstrating at the same time that this change had been ordered *before* he had assumed his office there. Moreover, as a servant of the state, it was his duty to carry out the order.[51]

From a later issue of the same periodical[52] we gather some further particulars about the details of that particular *Judenordnung*:

CARL FRIEDRICH

By the Grace of God Grand Duke of Saxe-Weimer-Eisenach etc.

Paragraph 1.

The regulation of Paragraph 6 of the *Judenordnung* to the effect that the Jewish worship service must be conducted in the *German* language is to be put into effect immediately. However, until further notice, the following exceptions will be maintained:

(a) Those older Jews whose inability to read German is known to the chief rabbi, or vouched for to him, may, at their request, obtain from the latter a special permission to use, for the reading of the prayers etc., a prayerbook with Hebrew text and accompanying German translation in the synagogue.

(b) During the worship service in the synagogue, the Torah portions and Haftarah may be read in Hebrew, but they must immediately be followed by the German translation according to Moses Mendelssohn or Ottensoser.[53] Excluded from this latter requirement are the following passages only: Gen. 19: 31–37; 35: 22; 38; Exodus 32: 21–35; Leviticus 18: 6; 19; 20: 11–20; Numbers 5: 11–31; 6: 1; 6: 22–27; 25: 6–8; Deuteronomy, all of chapters 27 and 28.

(c) The use of the Hebrew language is furthermore still permitted for the benedictions in connection with the reading of the Torah, at the removing of the Torah from the Ark and its return thither, as well as in connection with the blowing of the *shofar* and the Priestly Benediction.

Paragraph 2.

The selection and sequence of the prayers and Scripture passages to be read, as well as all the other acts of solemnity during the service, must be in accordance with the approved liturgy proposed by the chief rabbi.

Paragraph 3.

The prayers (including the few *piyutim* and *seliḥoth* which have still been retained after a careful sifting) must, in accordance with the general rule of Paragraph 1, *be recited in their entirety in German only*—for the sake of true devotion and with suitable decorum. The sing-song tone which had heretofore been generally used for the recitation of the Hebrew prayers is strictly prohibited. So is the loud repetition of the prayers, the over-hasty responding in responsive readings, as well as the swaying to and fro, and the murmuring.

Paragraph 4.

Singing is to be confined to the real hymns in the German language. The chief rabbi is in charge of the decorous and

> edifying utilization of song during the worship service, and he, therefore, has to enact the appropriate regulations.

Hess, the chief rabbi of the Grand Duchy of Saxe-Weimar,[54] has been accused both by contemporary and by modern writers of having forced this radical reform upon the unwilling congregations under his jurisdiction. Thus Elbogen writes: "The Landrabbiner Hess was filled with such a fanatical hatred of traditional Judaism that he encouraged the government in its undertaking, even though, at the same time, the legal position of the Jews deteriorated. But the congregations were so decisively opposed to the reforms that the latter could be introduced only after fifteen years."[55] David Philipson, who calls Hess "one of the most ardent, yes, one of the most fanatic of the early reformers,"[56] holds Hess completely responsible for the government-enforced reforms in the worship service, and considers him to have been "guilty of the same unpardonable offence as the orthodox party in Berlin, viz., the invoking of the police power of the government in private religious concerns."[57] This seems to have been also the view of Ludwig Philippsohn, Editor of the *Allgemeine Zeitung des Judenthums,* who, in 1837 and later,[58] continued to revert to the responsibility of Hess in this matter.

As against all this, there is Hess' insistence that the *Judenordnung* was drafted *before* he had assumed the office of the chief rabbi of the Grand Duchy.[59] Moreover, Hess claimed that he tried to mitigate the rigors of the governmental provisions, and, in his own periodical, *Der Israelit des neunzehnten Jahrhunderts,* he even printed a letter written by congregants testifying to the fact that "our reverend clergyman is far removed from imposing reforms upon his congregations."[60]

The truth of the matter is that the original *Judenordnung* was drafted in 1823, and that Hess did not become chief rabbi of the Grand Duchy until 1828.[61] Of course, if Hess had really been opposed to those provisions, he could have refused the chief rabbinate under such conditions. Moreover, in the preamble to his 1837 edict, enforcing the *Judenordnung,* Grand Duke Carl Friedrich states that the provisions were enacted "on the basis of responsa given by the chief rabbi of the Grand Duchy and by other Israelitish legal experts."[62] That is to say that, even if Hess had nothing to do with the 1823 draft, he was definitely involved in its 1837 enforcement, and was consulted beforehand. There is also no doubt that Hess "belonged to the most radical wing of Reform," favoring not only radical liturgical reforms, but also the right of rabbis to officiate at mixed marriages.[63] It is, therefore, not at all unlikely that, in the enthusiasm of youth, Hess favored government interference on behalf of Reform, though he may have later come to regret the sins of his youth—without, in any way, wavering in his attachment to the cause of radical Reform. After all, Hess was only twenty-one years old when he became chief rabbi of the Grand Duchy of Saxe-Weimar!

When all is said and done, then, David Philipson's judgment on Hess stands. Hess provided the Reform counterpart to the Orthodox offence in Berlin of invoking the police power of the government in private religious concerns. Whatever the extenuating circumstances in both cases, neither can be justified before the bar of history. *Synagogenordnungen* have played an important role in the advance of Reform Judaism and in bringing dignity and decorum even to the Orthodox synagogue in Western Europe. But when partisan interests combine with government interference, then the limits of the *Synagogenordnung*'s usefulness have been trespassed and the partisan interests compromised.

SEVEN

What They Said About Their Work

WHATEVER THE JUDGMENT OF THE MODERN HISTORIAN OF THE LITURGY might be about the achievements in the field of liturgical reform, about its relation to the past history of Jewish prayer, and about its prospects for the future, it is, to say the least, of no less interest to discover how the reformers of the liturgy looked upon their own work. All the tensions between loyalty to tradition, on the one hand, and the needs of a new age, on the other, between *qebha'*, the fixed forms of the past, and *kawwanah,* the spontaneous outpourings of the human heart, have frequently been verbalized by the editors of reformed prayerbooks. The preface or introduction to a new prayerbook was often the occasion for such a verbalization of the tensions; and few were the prayerbooks which did not offer such a preface or introduction. But the latter tell us more than the inner tensions of a liturgical reformer. In many instances they also tell us about the background against which the striving for reform has to be seen, and not only the general background of the *Zeitgeist,* but also the particular and specific *local* background for which a given liturgy was devised. And that, in turn, becomes expressive of an additional set of tensions. A liturgy had to be created to meet local needs. Yet there is, at the same time, a strong desire to think of all Jews united in prayer and using the same liturgy. All of this finds expression in the introductions to the new prayerbooks.

We are, therefore, devoting this, our longest chapter to a number of the prayerbook introductions, thus letting the Reformers speak for themselves. It is, of course, not possible to include the introduction to every single prayerbook published between 1817 and 1967, but we hope that the selection we offer is truly representative of the various trends and schools of thought which have been in evidence. The German style of writing in the early part of the nineteenth century was highly elaborate, not to say, verbose; and, in the hands of the rabbinical writers of the time, it had a tendency to become even more flourishing, or, as the Germans would put it, *salbungsvoll* (unctious). We have, therefore, frequently found it necessary either to summarize or to quote a prayerbook introduction in excerpts only. On the other hand, to preserve the flavor of the period, we have, in many instances, offered as literal a translation as possible.

Before we come to the prayerbooks themselves, we have to address ourselves to the program mapped out, in 1812, by David Friedländer, for, while that program was far more "radical" than many of the Liberal and Reform prayerbooks would ultimately turn out to be, it did outline the major areas in which liturgical reform was attempted once the new prayerbooks began to appear.

In 1786, Friedländer had published a German translation of the traditional Ashkenazi prayerbook.[1] The fact that a translation in the vernacular was published represented, for that time, a "reform." But, in terms of the contents of the traditional prayers, Friedländer did not permit himself any liberties whatsoever. It was the complete Orthodox prayerbook which Friedländer rendered into German, and which he had printed in Hebrew characters—seeing that German Jews were only then beginning, under Mendelssohn's and Friedländer's influence, to acquire a mastery of the German language. Even in the preface which Friedländer wrote for his German translation of the prayerbook there is nothing inherently heterodox or calculated to arouse the opposition of the traditionalists. Nevertheless, if prayer is what Friedländer says it is, it would follow that, once the traditional service is seen to be deficient in providing that kind of prayer, a reform of the traditional service is obviously indicated. Friedländer did not say so in 1786; but he was to say so some twenty-five years later.

1) DAVID FRIEDLÄNDER, 1786 (Summary of Preface to *Gebete der Juden auf das ganze Jahr.*)

> Every morally conscious man feels a need at certain times to lift his soul toward God. He is dependent upon God. He has need for self-examination. Self-examination leads him to a renewed resolve to keep God's commandments, which religion and reason prescribe for his bliss. As in times of joy and sorrow we share our feelings with our friends, so it is even more pleasant, beneficial and comforting to lay them before the All-forgiving Being. God's abundant love and wisdom are so manifest that only a man devoid of feeling could remain unmoved. At the sight of the marvels of creation, man is reminded of his duty and of his destiny, and he rises to worshipful thoughts which bring him close to God. He is purified. He prays. For true prayer, reason and will must work together. Reason will give us a vivid presentation of God. The will steers us away from extraneous matter, and keeps our thoughts on our conversation with God. Such devout and beneficial prayer will be acceptable to the Lord, and will lead us to the divine qualities of the Almighty, will enlarge our comprehension of them, and will enlighten and correct us. We learn wisdom, kindness, consideration, to deal fairly, to forgive our neighbor's shortcomings, and to make the best use of our own capabilities. Prayer will teach the rich man to put his advantage to noble use, and will soothe the turmoil in the mind of the unhappy man, and teach him that even his sufferings are means towards the best end. Prayer will make man happy, confident in times of sorrow, gentle and modest in times of happiness.

By 1812, Friedländer had despaired of the ability of the Jewish worship service, in its traditional form, to enable the modern Jew to have the kind of prayer experience which he, Friedländer, deemed to be essential. Besides, 1812 was the year in which the Jews of Prussia obtained their Emancipation. In the light of the changed circumstances, Friedländer published a leaflet of forty-seven pages, which appeared anonymously under the following imposing title:
Concerning the Reformation, necessitated by the new Organization of the Jewries in Prussian States, of (1) their Worship Services in the Synagogues, (2) their Educational Institutions and their Subjects of

Instruction, and (3) their Education in general.—A Word in its Season.—Berlin, 1812.[2]
The following are excerpts taken from that leaflet.

2) DAVID FRIEDLÄNDER, 1812.

According to tradition, Ezra, the head of the Great Synagogue, and his learned colleagues wrote prayer formulae, known as The Eighteen Benedictions, and also arranged places for private devotion. . . . The above-mentioned Eighteen Benedictions were, from time to time, enlarged by extensive additions and inserts. The authors, and the time of composition, of those additions are largely unknown, or the reports about them are not sure. But the later additions can be recognized in several places even by one who does not thoroughly know the original language. Style and language are grossly neglected and made ugly by the tinkling of word and rhyme which the Holy Tongue neither knows nor willingly suffers. As one comes down to the later centuries, those prayers become constantly poorer in contents, ever more departing from the pure concepts of antiquity. Finally, they become disfigured by kabbalistic doctrines and mystical expressions. The learned Israelites put them aside, and do not regard them as works of edification. They leave them in the hands of the multitude, so as not to make a fuss. . . .

Praying, in the most common meaning of the word, means to be concerned with the Original Being (*Urwesen*), to elevate one's soul to God, to contemplate the relations of the Creator to the creature. . . .

The sound of jubilation and thanksgiving could only be evoked on festive days, when the people were reminded of their earlier glory. Immediately thereafter, irrespective of the celebration of the day, there sounded forth the voices of lamentation and misery of the present. Sighs and lamentations for the destroyed independence, prayer for the restoration of the kingdom and of the Temple, of the sacrifices and of the priests, etc., had to be the sole contents of those prayers, for this was closest to the heart. Added to this, there was the expectation of a savior, the appearance of an unexpected (*sic*) restorer, a Messiah—an idea which was already predominant in the oldest speeches of the Prophets. Now, more than ever, it had to be preserved as predominant in the soul, if the people was not to despair altogether. Should one, indeed, rob the unfortunate of his hope? In the later centuries, the ignorance of the original language increased. What could no longer be effected by the content itself—devotion and the elevation of the soul to God—was now to be made up by quantity. Prayer was heaped upon prayer, formulae upon formulae; and, in the end, with increasing neglect, the question was no longer, *how* and *what*, but *how much* one prayed.

As long as the Jews were, if not actually persecuted, at least regarded as strangers, and treated as such,—as long as they nowhere formed an integral part of a state,—as long as they were not only made to feel, but actually told, that they were only tolerated and really belonged to Palestine, so long there was neither cause nor reason to change the contents and the language of the prayers. Among both rulers and ruled, one and the same idea had struck roots. Among the former, that the Jews were still hoping for a Messiah, that, because of this, they had no fatherland in Europe, and that, consequently, they could have no love and loyalty. Among the latter, tradition, commandments, and oppression maintained the identical thoughts and expectations. . . . How could anyone think of changing the prayer formulae? Whence the cause? And thus they remained unchanged. . . .

In the meantime, civil society was influenced, in the course of the centuries, by the irresistible force of the light of truth, of progress in the sciences, and of the changed conditions of the states. With Frederick the Great, the realm of ideas was shaken, and a general revolution took place. The light which illumined the churches brought illumination also to the synagogues. . . . Reason, humanity, and freedom of thought came into their own. The progress of the times, closer contacts, and the wisdom of the government aroused both spirit and love. The Jew, too, was aroused out of his slumber, and was no longer *regarded* as a stranger. He ceased *being* a stranger. . . .

The prayers and their melodies became increasingly strange to both father and child, increasingly dispensable, increasingly out of harmony with the newly acquired concepts. The lamentations about persecution, oppression, and maltreatment, could no longer be recited without injustice. The prayer formulae, bearing the sombre color of the time of their composition, became untrue and unjust in the mouth of the worshippers. They had no appeal for him who was ignorant of the language. . . . And for him who did know the language, they stood in sharpest contrast to his convictions, his aspirations, and his hopes.

Only the sacred songs and hymns, and a few passages from the days of the Great Synagogue, appealed to the soul of one conversant with the language. But they became objects of thought and meditation, rather than a conversation with God. They lacked the beauty of recitation, the musical accompaniment, which lends wings to the words, elevates the soul, and kindles devotion. The knowledgeable man of religion fled with them to his lonely chamber, when he was looking for edification.

Man needs hours of consecration, in which he gives an account of himself, . . . in which he directs his attention to his relation with his Creator. If those hours are to be of use to him, true hours of edification, whether in his own chamber or in the temple of the Lord, then his devotional exercises must be performed in a language known to him. . . .

Indeed, it requires no special mental effort, only rectitude of soul, for the religious Israelite to say to himself: "Here I stand before God. I pray for blessing and success for my king, for my fellow-citizens, for myself and for my family—not for a return to Jerusalem, not for a restoration of the Temple and the sacrifices. Such wishes I do not have in my heart. Their fulfilment would not make me happy. My mouth shall not utter them." . . .

But there are limits to the reform of the prayers which, according to tradition, have been handed down to us by the Great Synagogue, limits which must not be transgressed either lightheartedly or out of the mere love of innovation.

It is irrefutable that the lofty and noble songs and hymns of Holy Writ are closely related to the truths of the Israelite religion. Also, several of the prayers and devotional exercises, said to have been composed by the Great Synagogue, have excellent contents, rich in blessings, and have been written for all time, and for all conditions of life. It cannot be denied that the spirit of antiquity, resting upon them, appeals to both head and heart, and that the glowing colors of the Oriental style cast an inimitable splendor upon the whole. It is, therefore, prudent duty not to let go of those advantages, and to utilize, with spirit and selectivity, those glorious memorials of antiquity for the arousing of devotion. This statement is only a modest hint, not a presumptuous demand, addressed to the future compilers of prayers and devotions.

Three years later, in 1815, reformed services were indeed held in Friedländer's Berlin; but they were perhaps less indebted to Friedländer's programmatic tract of 1812 than they were to the fact that Israel Jacobson had moved to Berlin, whither he transplanted the kind of services he had previously conducted in the chapel of his Seesen school.[3] Nor were the references to Zion and Jerusalem, and the prayers for the coming of the Messiah and the restoration of the Temple omitted from those services, though the liturgy was abbreviated, some prayers were recited in the vernacular, sermons were preached, and organ accompaniment introduced.[4] When, in 1817, this new kind of service, held in private homes, temporarily gained recognition as the official worship service of the Berlin Jewish community, the actual synagogue undergoing repairs at that time, a liturgy to go with it was published by Eduard Kley and C. S. Günsburg. Entitled *Die Deutsche Synagoge* ("The German Synagogue"), the new prayerbook appeared in two volumes, Volume I in 1817, and Volume II in 1818. We bring excerpts from the Preface to Volume I.

3) DIE DEUTSCHE SYNAGOGE, BERLIN, 1817 (Excerpts from the Preface).

Give heed, O House of Israel, for I will speak; listen, O Congregation of Jeshurun, to the words of my mouth. My doctrine shall drop as the rain, my speech shall distil as the dew. For I will proclaim in the Name of the Lord; give ye glory and greatness to our God!—Who among us knoweth not that in the days but recently past many adversaries and opponents arose, who sharpened their tongue like a double-edged sword, and cast their words like lightning, to fan the flames of hatred against our house, to pour out the glowing embers of destruction upon the dwelling-places of peace. Hard indeed it was to hear how the spirit of lies and of falsehood let his poisonous speech well up. . . . But, my friends and brethren in faith, it was doubly hard and humiliating to feel that there was some truth in that with which they accused us, that, indeed, it was to those few threads of truth that they tied their tissues of lies. And although they did not intend to work for our good, but for our harm, we should accept that evil as a kindness from the hand of the Lord. We should discern in the chastisement the hand which seeks to work for our improvement and salvation.

Five years have gone by since the Eternal our God has given us the great token of His love and mercy, since He directed towards our good the heart of His anointed, our wise, pious and just king, filling him with His holy spirit, to take from upon us the heavy burden which has weighed upon us for more than eighteen hundred years, . . . and to restore unto us the dignity of man and of the free citizen. How our hearts are glowing with gratitude towards our God and our king! . . . But, my friends, true gratitude, which is worthy of the gift and of the giver, is expressed in the deed, in the use which the recipient is making of the gift in his *life*. . . . To seek truth and to know it, the God-fearing conduct before the Lord, the doing of holy works of piety and love: that is the inner, holy *life,* which comes to man from the Highest, and which is to lead him to the Highest. . . . Five years have already gone by, and nothing has as yet been done. . . . With this divine gift of civil freedom from the hands of our exalted monarch we have also taken over new duties, the holy debt of gratitude, the duty of civil life. For even though we do not as yet enjoy that benefit to its fullest extent,[5] let us nevertheless be deeply convinced that it happened for our good. The Lord desireth to test us whether we be worthy of that which has been received. . . .

But, if the fear of God is to find the way to our heart, . . . it must speak a language which can be understood and comprehended by the child as well as by the man, by the youth as well as by the elder, by the maiden as well as by the woman, by the high as well as by the lowly, by the rich as well as by the poor. It must let holy sounds ring forth which are equally holy, valuable and dear to all, . . . because we are all of equal worth in the eyes of God, and because we are all equally obligated to serve Him, and to obey the law. *Holy* is the language in which God once gave the Law to our fathers, and the divine teaching by the mouth of His faithful servant, Mosheh. That language is *holy* unto us as a memorial from the grey days of antiquity, as a sweet echo from the past days of childhood, from the prime of the human race, as a dear remnant of that which has faded away in the course of the years. Holy, too, and venerable it will remain for everyone who still reveres the past as an experienced mother, as a wise teacher, from whom he can always obtain advice. But seven times more holy unto us is the language which belongs to the present and to the soil whence we have sprung forth, . . . the language in which a mother first greets her new-born child, . . . the language which unites us with our fellow-men in happy fellowship or in serious business, the language, finally, in which our philanthropic and just king speaks to us, in which he proclaims his law to us. . . .

Many an item of the traditional order you will miss here. But let us remember: what can sanctify us is not the number of words and of the prayers, but solely the devotion and the profound meaning. Of the prayers we could have omitted even more; and He who knoweth our hearts will hearken unto us if only we be sincere in our actions. . . .

Let us cast a joyous glance upon our brethren in faith in the Danish states, who, favored by their exalted sovereign, have but recently begun the holy work of the Lord by introducing the holy language of their country, Danish, into both the school and the House of God, for the discourses of religion, thereby sowing the glorious seed of a new generation of pious subjects, reared in the fear of God and in civic virtue. Let us joyously look upon that, and let us follow that glorious example. Let us strive only for the ability to offer, through deeds, the sacrifice of thanksgiving, to make ourselves worthy of the favor of our king, and of the love of our God. (Footnote:- According to a report, dated July 12th—*Hamb. Unparth. Correspond.* No. 113 —the first worship service of the Israelites in the Danish language was held there.—Also religious instruction and Confirmation were publicly held in that language, and several members of the royal house honored this festivity by their most exalted presence. . . .)[6]

And Thou, O Lord, grant honor to Thy people, deserved praise to those who fear Thee, hope to those who seek Thee, and courage to speak to those who hope in Thee; joy to this land, delight to this city, and a bright light to Thy holy anointed one. Let the fear of God be present to all Thy children, so that all men may revere Thee, and all may worship Thee. May they all unite in one single band to do Thy holy will, in unity, with an upright heart, so that the bounty of Thy blessing may be poured over all. Amen!

Berlin, July 1817

K. (i.e., Eduard Kley)

After this kind of introduction, one would expect a worship service which was all but completely in German. As a matter of fact, *Die Deutsche Synagoge* is printed in German only, the one exception being the newly written Hebrew substitute for *Kol Nidré*.[7] But, in reality, most of *Die Deutsche Synagoge* consists of German translations of prayers which are meant to be said in Hebrew! Thus, in the Sabbath Morning Service, after providing selections from the traditional rubrics for recitation in German, *Die Deutsche Synagoge* states (on page 6):

> The subsequent prayers are recited in Hebrew, of which the following is the translation.

And the prayers to be recited in Hebrew include *Barukh She-amar,* Psalm 145, *Yishtabbaḥ,* Half *Kaddish,* The *Shema* and its Benedictions, The Seven Benedictions (*'Amidah*), *Kaddish,* and various responses in connection with the Torah Service. In other words, the basic rubrics of the service, which go back to the early Rabbinic period, have been retained in Hebrew. There is no *Musaph* in the Sabbath Service of *Die Deutsche Synagoge,* but the prayers for the restoration of the sacrifices and of God's presence to Zion have been kept in the *'Amidah* of the Sabbath Morning Service.

In 1817, the very year of the appearance of *Die Deutsche Synagoge,* one of its editors, Kley, moved to Hamburg, where, a year later, in 1818, he was appointed preacher of the Temple established in that year. In 1819, the Hamburg Temple published its famous prayerbook. That prayerbook has no preface or introduction. But it does carry a "Dedication" which affords us a good insight into the inspiration behind this new undertaking. We quote that "Dedication" in full.

4) DEDICATION OF THE HAMBURG TEMPLE PRAYERBOOK, 1819.

Dedicated to the Right Honorable Privy Councillor of Finance I. Jacobson, as a sign of true respect and sincere regard, by the Editors.

Right Honorable Sir!

If we permit ourselves to set *your name* at the head of this prayerbook, it is because we see in it a homage which is due *you* for *your* untiring striving both to promote the good and the noble in general, and, in particular, from the religious point of view, to arouse the wish for it among our coreligionists.

Should we have succeeded in shaping this prayerbook, and the worship service connected with it, in *your* spirit, then *you* may regard it as *your* own work, like a plant of which *you* have sown the seed in the distance, a seed carried hither by a benevolent wind, finding here a fertile soil, and flourishing in it. And if *you* find in it the joy which is brought by a successful undertaking, then may the Good Lord grant *you* the even greater joy of seeing this godly work spread ever more widely in Israel.

Filled with the sincere wish for *your* constant well-being, Right Honorable Sir,

we remain

Your most humble

Fränkel and Bresselau

Hamburg, August 1819

5) PREFACE TO THE SECOND EDITION OF THE HAMBURG TEMPLE PRAYERBOOK, 1841.

The commission charged with the preparation of a revised new edition of the Temple Prayerbook finds it in order to state, in a preface, the point of view which has guided it in its work.

Our Prayerbook, as an expression of a truly Israelite worship service which had been restored to *simplicity* and to *dignity,* has, since its first appearance in 1819, brought much blessing.

The religious sense has been revived through worship, and the ancestral religion has regained an elevating influence upon the soul of many for whom it had almost completely lost its sanctity. Even in congregations elsewhere, our worship service has had a wholesome effect. Notwithstanding those happy consequences, the need was felt, in revising this book, to formulate a number of things in it differently, so that it might fulfil its function better. In addition to the urgent need for a worship service, purified in accordance with the times, a need which, guided by expertise and circumspection, originally brought forth this book, a further important factor was involved in the present revision: the *experience* of many years. The latter has taught us to separate the appropriate from the inappropriate, the effective from the ineffective, the essential from the inessential. The guiding thoughts which called our Prayerbook into existence twenty-five years ago have remained the same. But, at the same time, there have been important changes as far as *form* and *contents* are concerned.

From the point of view of form, the book is now more *complete* than it was previously, because it is no longer confined to Sabbath and festivals. It now contains all the days and seasons when services are being held. It will thus undoubtedly satisfy all those Israelite congregations which are imbued with the spirit of perception and the striving for progress, in addition to that of the true fear of God. Great care has been taken in the practically new translation, to make the latter suitable for private devotion.

With regard to the contents, the editorial board has sought to proceed with consideration and with caution. It has retained the distinction upon which our liturgy is based, between *typical* and *accessory* prayers. (See Notes to page 3 and 70, at the end of the book.) The former have been conscientiously kept throughout, because the Temple Congregation differs from other Israelite congregations only in a few liturgical forms, but not in the doctrines of religion. The conscientious person, who is able to think clearly about the ancestral religion, will find his full satisfaction in this. As far as the accessory prayers are concerned, which have ever been subject to modification in the light of their specific use, the passages which have hitherto remained unused have been omitted, and some unsuitable ones have given way to others. This was all the more in order seeing that, in the liturgy of the Temple, the German Hymnal serves as a substitute for the *piyutim*. All the original German prayers have been newly revised, with particular regard to the truths of religion. There has been an endeavor everywhere to bear in mind the principles of a contemporary Israelite worship, and to introduce into the liturgy a greater consistency and harmony. Whoever does not demand extremes in either direction will certainly use this fountain of blessings with joy.

Our Temple Union gives its full recognition to this Prayerbook, which is the result of its own life and work to date, and the new edition of which was entrusted by its administration to its preachers, a member of the directorate who is trained in theology, and two expert members of the Union. The editorial board is not afraid of any honest evaluation, believing that it can defend the present work before the learned public—both in terms of what has been included, and in terms of what has been changed or omitted. It hopes to have met the religious needs and desires of many of its coreligionists, and it is happy that the acquisition and the adoption of the book have been facilitated by a reduction in price. It will be pleased to furnish information about the manner of conducting the service, about the melodies, and about other relevant details, to such congregations as are inclined to adopt the Prayerbook.

Thus may our Prayerbook, also in its new appearance, work for blessing and the salutory worship of the Lord in Israel!
Hamburg, August 1841

The Notes to which reference is made in this Preface state that only The *Shema* and its Blessings, and the *Tephillah* (i.e., The Eighteen Benedictions), can be considered as the permanent and *typical* components of the worship service, with the reading of the Torah on Sabbath and festivals as a third essential component of public worship. All other prayers aim at some specific edification, and are, therefore, *accessory*. It is also shown, on the basis of the sources, that the "traditional" version of *retzeh* (in The Eighteen Benedictions) is not the original one. The Notes conclude with a quotation from Maimonides (*Hilkhoth Tephillah* 1: 1) to the effect that, while the Torah commands us to pray every day, the wording itself of such prayer is not fixed by the Torah.

The year in which the second edition of the Hamburg Temple Prayerbook was published also marked the appearance of the first edition of the *Forms of Prayer Used in the West London Synagogue of British Jews*. Like the reformed rituals of Germany, the English prayerbook was aiming at greater decorum in the worship service, and, therefore, effected an abbreviation and simplification of the traditional liturgical material. But, unlike the Hamburg Prayerbook, it was not very much concerned with introducing changes derived from doctrinal considerations. The lengthy and very interesting Introduction to that prayerbook has recently been reprinted (with some omissions) in *The Rise of Reform Judaism* by W. Gunther Plaut.[8] We, therefore, refrain from repeating it here in full, and content ourselves with but a few excerpts from it which show the principles upon which that London prayerbook was based.

6) INTRODUCTION TO FORMS OF PRAYER, WEST LONDON SYNAGOGUE, 1841. (Excerpts.)

> The history of the ritual till lately lay buried beneath a mass of critical difficulties; to remove which has only within the last generation become the task of several of our eminent continental co-religionists, such as Zunz, Rapoport, and others; to whose valuable and conscientious labours we are indebted for information that has greatly facilitated the accomplishment of our undertaking. From their researches it becomes manifest that the Hebrew ritual, before reaching its present form, had undergone great and repeated changes; that some portions, fortunately few in number, considered by many as the genuine remnants of our ancient temple worship, owe their origin to an age of persecution, and to a state of suffering and degradation now fast disappearing, and every trace of which will, by divine aid, speedily be effaced, to the honour of religion and for the common welfare of mankind. . . .
>
> History bears us out in the assumption, that it becomes a congregation of Israelites to adapt the ritual to the wants of its members; and it must be universally admitted that the present mode of worship fails to call forth the devotion, so essential to the religious improvement of the people. . . .
>
> We have removed those parts of the service which are deficient in devotional tendency; and have expunged the few expressions which are known to be the offspring of feelings produced by oppression, and are universally admitted to be foreign to the heart of every true Israelite of our day. . . .
>
> In order to render the prayers at once more dignified and more generally intelligible, we have translated the Chaldaic expressions into the sacred Hebrew (the language of the Law), a knowledge of which we trust it will be the pride, as it is the bounden duty, of every Israelite to attain. . . .
>
> The differences which formerly existed between the Portuguese and German Jewish congregations, and which caused them to consider each other as half aliens in religious matters, have happily, by the progress of liberal sentiments, been removed,

in as far as they obstructed that brotherly feeling which the unity of our religious system requires; and the efforts of our newly established Congregation have been directed, we hope successfully, to the obliteration of every vestige of that useless and hurtful separation. We have discarded the names indicating a connection between us, natives of Great Britain professing the Jewish religion, and the countries from which our ancestors immigrated, and we have adopted for our place of worship the sufficiently explicit designation of "West London Synagogue of British Jews." In making this statement, it is expedient to notice that the term "British Jews" has been chosen only with a view to efface the distinction now existing between the German and Portuguese Jews, and not in any way to constitute a new distinction, in a religious point of view, between the Jews of Great Britain and those of any other country. . . .
London, Ab, 5601—August, 1841

Joseph von Maier (1797–1873) was the first German rabbi who, being ennobled by the king of Wuerttemberg, became a member of the nobility.[9] Maier was a member of the Jewish Consistory of Wuerttemberg, and he also served as president of the first Rabbinical Conference in Brunswick, in 1844. He published, in 1848, an *Israelite Book of Prayer and Devotion,*[10] which, in terms of contents and form, of tendency and the relative amounts of Hebrew and vernacular, curiously anticipates by almost fifty years the American *Union Prayer Book,* although it is somewhat less "radical" in theology than the latter. Ostensibly, this prayerbook was written for individuals to use at home, or to bring along to a service conducted on more traditional lines, and Maier published it in his individual capacity—and not as an official member of the consistory. However, in its structure, the prayerbook makes detailed provisions for rubrics to be recited by the reader, passages to be read "in silent devotion," congregational responses and hymns, and parts to be sung by the choir. The book thus represents the kind of service which Maier would have liked to see in actual synagogal use. His Preface is given here in full.

7) PREFACE TO MAIER'S ISRAELITE BOOK OF PRAYER AND DEVOTION, 1848.

We are living in a time of misunderstandings. To prevent such misunderstandings about the present book as much as possible, I feel compelled to speak about my intentions of what the book is to achieve, and about the principles which guided me in editing it.

Above all, I must explain that I have not written this book

either by order of the Israelite Supreme Ecclesiastical Authority, or in the capacity of a member of that body. I have simply written it as a clergyman, desiring to remedy a defect which has been all too visible during his official functions. Contrary to the reports of busybody rumour, therefore, it is not the intention of this collection of prayers forcefully to oust our customary prayerbook (*seder tephillah*), that venerable bequest of the ancients. To do such a thing, the author lacks all authority. Even if he had the authority, he would not make use of it, since the freedom of conscience is, in his view, far too sacred a possession to permit him the use of such disciplinary action, or even merely to advise it. *It is not a question of taking a prayerbook away from those who have one, and who find edification in it, but of giving a prayerbook to those who have none.*

It is a fact which can no longer be denied that a large number of our coreligionists—especially among the young generation—are so little acquainted with Hebrew that they can hardly read it any longer. At the same time, it is this part of the congregation which, having attained a degree of education, would find the customary prayerbook lacking in satisfaction even if the contents thereof were understood. That is because a conflict has arisen between mental attitudes and many of the components of the prayerbook, and because no expression is found therein for the various feelings of sorrow and of joy, for the manifold needs of the heart in the vicissitudes of life. To provide the means whereby this part of the congregation can find edification in their native tongue, and that in a truly Israelite manner, and to revive and promote the domestic devotion, which has so largely been allowed to lapse,—that is the primary and foremost aim of this collection of prayers.

At the same time, this book is not meant for domestic worship alone. It is, rather, my desire that, in addition to the customary prayerbook, it will be used also for public worship services both by the individual and by the congregation as a whole. Very many people are, at present, visiting the synagogue, without actually participating in the worship service. Without a knowledge of Hebrew, and without an interest in the liturgy, it is the sermon alone—if and when it takes place—by which they feel themselves addressed. Thus, at best, the synagogue becomes a *school* for them, whereas, according to its original intent, it was meant to be a *house of prayer* (Isaiah 56: 7). If, then, such people do not disdain to take this book to the House of God with them, it could become for them there a means of edification. It could protect them from the boredom and the distraction to which, at present, they are frequently subject.

As far as its use for the whole congregation is concerned, this book, for the time being, would have the following function: After the prescribed prayer (*tephillath ḥobhah*) has been completed, a service out of this book might be conducted for the edification of those who have been left unsatisfied by the prescribed prayer. The sermon could then be combined with it.

The time does not yet seem to me to have arrived for the exclusive use of this collection, or similar ones, for the public worship service in most congregations. In most of the Israelite congregations there still exists a not insignificant number of members who, out of conviction, feel bound to the tradition. In those instances, a new liturgy could not, at this moment, be introduced without disturbing the peace of the congregations. But harmony is the most beautiful and the most dignified service of God, and all of religion has no other purpose than that of preserving and advancing love and peace among men. *Kol hatorah kullah lo nitnah ella bishebhil hashalom.*[11] I would, therefore, seriously warn against such over-hasty experiments; and if, on account of my book, the peace of only one congregation were to be disturbed, I would have to wish not to have written it. From this point of view, I regard the present collection as but a tentative plan, which, together with the congregations themselves, is destined to advance to maturity and completion.

That much about the purpose of this book. As for its contents, although they will have to justify themselves, I believe that I am obligated to give an account of the selection of the material and of the manner in which it has been treated. As the expert can easily convince himself, this book, apart from the prayers for private devotion and the hymns properly so called, contains little that is new. What it does contain consists of re-creations of older liturgical pieces from the various collections of which we possess a great number. This is due to a twofold reason. In the first place, because it is not easy, as far as religious enthusiasm and the fullness of devotion are concerned, to place a more recent product alongside the older ones. Secondly, because the heritage of the past, as such, is not to be negated, but only to be continued and adapted to the religious needs of the times. In the selection I was guided by the principle: *tephillah tzerikhah kawwanah,* "Prayer must be a matter of devotion." Only that could be included which serves that purpose. On the other hand, everything which has no echo in religious sensitivity, and which has no further connection with religious consciousness, had to be excluded.

In the task of editing, I followed the method which has nowadays again been recognized as the better one, namely, that of rendering the contents rather than the word. This is absolutely essential in liturgical creations if their purpose is to be achieved. Since the older Hebrew prayers, with all of the advantages which they otherwise have, suffer from manifold repetitions, and are seldom free from the kind of anthropopathies and anthropomorphisms which contradict the modern concept of religion, a literal translation would not at all be suited to a promotion of edification. My striving, therefore, was primarily directed to a rendition of the actual religious contents from the point of view of modern consciousness, in a treatment which meets the current need, and to clothe the expression in that form which best satisfies the spirit seeking edification.

That, in the case of some of the prayers, I have included the Hebrew original in addition to the German version should, I trust, bring me no censure. On account of its venerable age, and on account of its general use in the worship service of the Israelites of all countries, the Hebrew language represents a holy bond which unifies the scattered members of the community, a bond which one should never tear completely. Even those, therefore, who consider their native tongue to be the only legitimate language for prayer, cannot but be pleased to see the Hebrew original of those prayers which must be regarded as the most ancient and most important components of our worship service, and which, as such, contain the fundamentals of Israel's divine teaching. Indeed, who would not want to teach his children the *shema yisrael* in Hebrew—that confession of faith for the sake of which we have suffered so much, and of which we hope that it will be universally recognized? Who would not want to teach his children the *shema yisrael* in Hebrew, thereby giving them this legitimation of their faith for their path through life? The fact that I did not give more passages, or all of them, in both versions is due to the whole arrangement and purpose of this book. It is meant neither to contain the *tephillath ḥobhah* (obligatory prayer) nor its translation. Rather is it meant to be an independent project for the revival and the advancement of the adoration of God. Tautologies as well as all expressions which do not coincide with the purified concept of the Supreme Being have been omitted also from this part, since they could only have a disturbing and chilling effect upon the worshipful soul.

I believe that I have the duty of expressing myself particularly about another modification, the one connected with the dogma of Redemption. As is well known, there is no unanimity among the teachers of the Synagogue concerning the doctrine of *geullah aḥaronah* (the Final Redemption). The views of Saadia (*Emunoth Wede'oth* VIIIff.) and Albo (*'Iqqarim* IV, 42) differ considerably from those of Maimonides. The views of the latter, however, have become the orthodox doctrine of the Synagogue, and have remained so until most recent times. Of late, the reawakened study of the Bible and, even more, the felicitous change in the civil status of the Israelites, have again caused a difference of opinions concerning this doctrine—with the result that there are today many pious and believing Israelites who understand the Redemption in a spiritual sense, i.e., as the victory and spread of the true religion (*aḥduth*), of a Kingdom of God (*malkhuth shaddai*), and the reign of justice and truth. The author, who believes his own conviction to coincide with Holy Scripture, does not have the temerity to claim exclusive validity for his own view. Nor does he want in the least to offend anybody's conviction. But he does feel that, after including the dogma in an unabbreviated form in the first benedictions of the *tephillath shemoneh esreh,* in the *ya'aleh weyabho,* and in other prayers, he must, with respect to the actual prayers for the restoration of the nationality etc., do justice to a point of view which, after all, is represented in the congregation, and particularly by that part of it which will be the first to make use of this book.

I do not want to cause a renewal of the fight which flared up so fiercely in the wake of the prayerbook of the Hamburg Temple, if only because this would only lead to an embitterment of spirits, but not to a settlement of the matter. In general, one should beware of dragging dogmatic animosities into life. Let us thank God for the freedom of belief which reigns in the Synagogue, where nobody is compelled to swear to the words of another, but where everybody is free to form his own conviction on the basis of Holy Scriptures. We owe to this freedom the unity and concord which have been preserved among us, in spite of all the differences of opinion which exist among ourselves just as they do elsewhere. The claim to exclusive validity of any one view, and the damning of another view as heresy, would lead to sectarianism and schism, and, therefore, to the death of the congregation. That is why, in this connection, I would call to mind the words of the Prophet: *emeth weshalom ehabhu,* "Love ye truth and peace!"

I have to add a word about the sources from which I have drawn. As already indicated above, most of the prayers in this collection are only paraphrases of older liturgical pieces which belong to the *Tephillah,* the *Maḥzor,* the *Seliḥoth,* etc. The translation of them as well as of the Psalms, and the prayers for private devotion, are my work, and praise and blame are mine. (The translation of the *Kedushah* for the *Musaph* Service of Sabbath and festivals was done by someone else. The four last prayers to be recited at the graveside of departed relatives are those adapted in abbreviated form from Dr. Rehfuss' *Sepher Ḥayyim.*) The hymns properly so called have been taken from the *Israelite Hymnal* of Hamburg, with the exception of a few which are part of the Berlin Prayerbook which was printed as manuscript. This is also the source of a few prayers and of the Memorial Service for the Day of Atonement. A German prayer for the *Ne'ilah* Service of that holy day, and the metrical translation of a *seliḥah,* come from the prayerbook of the Hamburg Temple.

With this, I give the present work to my coreligionists, with the hope that I have rendered a service to the good cause of the worship of God. A book, making its appearance with such modest demands as does the present one, need not fear criticism. I desire instruction, but I desire it in the spirit of love and of peace in which I have written the book. I would be hurt by misunderstanding, by intentional misrepresentation, and by the imputation of impure motives. But even in that case I would be comforted by the knowledge that, through this work as through all my other activities as a teacher of religion, I have striven for nothing else but the preservation of our religion, and that in a formulation suited to the spirit of the times, lest that spirit deny our faith.

Maier

Stuttgart, October 1848

Maier's constant reference to "edification" (*Erbauung*) as the purpose of the worship service is characteristic of the whole period. The concept of "edification," of New Testament origin and applied to the worship experience by the Pietists in German Protestantism, became very influential in the nineteenth-century attempts at reforming the Jewish worship service—both liturgically and homiletically, as Alexander Altmann has shown in detail.[12]

The repeated emphasis on not wanting to *force* his prayerbook on anybody, and the warning against over-hasty experiments in introducing the book for public worship, must have been due to Maier's memory of the uproar caused, some years previously, when a German liturgy was actually forced on the Jewish congregations of the Grand Duchy of Saxe-Weimar, aided and abetted by its chief rabbi, M. Hess.[13] So far, indeed, was Maier from using his official position to force his rather "advanced" liturgical views on unwilling congregations that, as we shall have occasion to see, he appears thirteen years later as the editor of a prayerbook which is basically the traditional *siddur* with but minor modifications. That was the prayerbook he edited in his official capacity.

1848, the year in which Maier published his *Gebet- und Andachtsbuch,* also saw the publication of the prayerbook of the Berlin Association for Reform in Judaism (*Genossenschaft für Reform im Judenthum,* later called *Jüdische Reform-Gemeinde*). That was the most "radical" Jewish prayerbook in Europe, and contained the least amount of Hebrew. The substance of the very interesting and instructive Introduction to that prayerbook has recently been translated by W. Gunther Plaut, and included in his volume, *The Rise of Reform Judaism.*[14]

Joseph Aub published his "Prayers for the Public Worship of God in the Synagogue of Mayence"[15] in 1853. Although Aub's name is not mentioned either on the title page or in the preface, he was the rabbi of Mayence at that time.[16] Moreover, the prayerbook which Aub published in Berlin, in 1866, contains many of the German translations found in the Mayence ritual. It, therefore, stands to reason that Aub was the editor of the latter as well. The 1853 Mayence liturgy appeared in two installments. One contains the services for the eve of Sabbath and festivals; the other contains, what Aub called, the "main service" for Sabbath and festivals, by which he means the Torah Service and the *Musaph.* The Hebrew text of the Mayence liturgy is completely traditional, except that there are no *piyutim* for the festivals other than *az shesh me-oth* for recitation *after* the *Musaph* on Pentecost, and German prayers to be recited by the rabbi on the first day of Passover and the eighth day of Tabernacles, to take the place of the traditional Dew and Rain compositions. The Mishnah passages dealing with wicks and oils (for Friday night) and with the composition of the incense (for the *Musaph* service) have been omitted, and the Mourner's Kaddish contains the additional paragraph which was first introduced in the prayerbook of the Hamburg Temple, in 1819. The twelfth of the Eighteen Benedictions (printed here as part of the Friday afternoon service) changes "slanderers" into "slander," and is given the form in which Aub was to reprint it in his Berlin prayerbook of 1866.[17] Apart from this, the "Reform" tendency of the Mayence prayerbook is manifest in the German paraphrases only—for reasons fully explained in the Preface, which we now quote in full.

(8) PREFACE TO MAYENCE PRAYERBOOK, 1853.

To prevent misunderstandings, and to meet misrepresentations, we preface a few enlightening notes to this booklet.

The title, "Prayers for the Public Worship of God in the Synagogue of Mayence," refers to the *Hebrew* text, seeing that the prayers herewith presented are being recited in Hebrew in our place. Of course, the individual is free to express his prayer, in silent devotion, in the German language which he understands.

We chose the designation, "Main Service" (*Hauptgottesdienst*) for the *Musaph* Service, because the reading from the Torah and the Prophets as well as the sermon are combined with this service, thereby uniting all the essential elements of the cult. Although we admit that, on account of the *Shema* and the *Tephillah* of the Seven Benedictions, the *Shaḥarith* prayer represents the *main prayer,* it can by no means be called the main *service,* because in the morning it is only a case of prayer.

For the passages concerning messianism we have offered *no translation,* but a *free paraphrase* in German. About the nature of the messianic kingdom there are great differences of opinion already in the Talmud. Also, among contemporary Jewish scholars, this dogma is a matter in dispute, concerning which no unanimity has as yet been achieved. Yet all agree that the doctrine of the Messiah is an essential truth of faith in Israeldom (*Israelitenthum*). Furthermore, there can be no Biblical justification for accepting only the *idea,* and not also the *personality* of a Messiah (*bi-ath hamashi-aḥ*). But, whereas the *person* of the Messiah represents the center of the faith in Christianity, in Judaism it is the *kingdom* of the Messiah which constitutes the essence of the promise. Opinions differ as to the nature of that kingdom. In the traditional prayers we encounter everywhere only the twofold desire for the *return of Israel* to the land of the fathers, and for the *restoration of the sacrifices*. The defenders of those desires overlook the fact that those prayers were composed in the Babylonian Exile, and that, therefore, those desires primarily referred to the return to Palestine at that time, and to the building of the Second Temple. Indeed, many Biblical promises, which likewise concerned only the return from Babylon and of the sacrifices, have wrongly been understood as messianic promises. Seen against the historical origin of the above-mentioned prayers, it can be explained why the two *most important* elements of the messianic kingdom receive no appreciation in them: *the diffusion of the true faith in One God,* and the rule of *peace* on earth. If then, in the German paraphrase, we have given the latter elements their due, we were simply guided by the motivation of religious and historical truth. To the possible objection, why we did not also change the Hebrew text accordingly, we would reply that worship is not the occasion to do violence to the conscience of those worshippers who regard those former elements, highlighted in the old prayer, as essential. It is, moreover, that group among our brethren in faith which prefers to pray in Hebrew, while it is the other, larger, group, accepting a more spiritual-religious concept of the messianic doctrine, which prefers to pray silently in German. This is not the place to go into details about this matter. Only two points, with which we have already dealt in other writings, deserve to be singled out briefly: (1) The right to change prayers, as long as the changes do not affect the benedictions, is a right granted by all Rabbinical authorities. (2) Even those Israelites, who, in the messianic doctrine, stress the return to Palestine and the sacrifices, do not fall behind any other citizen in regard to their patriotism and their loyalty to the Regent and the laws of the State, because that doctrinal concept is by no means in conflict with patriotism.

Thus may these prayers promote and maintain devotion and peace in our congregation!

The Editor

Mayence, April 1853

Abraham Geiger's 1854 edition of the prayerbook follows the structure and the rubrics of the traditional *siddur* very closely. Some changes have been introduced into the Hebrew text, particularly in passages dealing with the restoration of the sacrificial cult and the ingathering of the exiles. Zion and Jerusalem, however, continue to be mentioned. The services have been somewhat abbreviated, and a Scripture lectionary is included, according to which the Torah is to be read in a three-year cycle. Withal, in its Hebrew section (and the service for which this ritual was edited continued to be conducted in Hebrew) Geiger's prayerbook by and large provides a traditional service. Geiger's strong Reform tendencies are much more evident in the German text which accompanies the Hebrew prayers. It is not a translation, but a very free paraphrase. The following is the Preface which introduces the prayerbook:

9) PREFACE TO GEIGER'S PRAYERBOOK, 1854 (*Israelitisches Gebetbuch.* Breslau.)

Since about eight years ago, the worship service in the local Great Synagogue has received a form which departs—if only in nonessential points—from the earlier one. Nevertheless, the old prayerbooks were used for it. The inconvenience of having to look for a prayer which had been retained, after skipping another one, was particularly disturbing and confusing on New Year and the Day of Atonement. If, nevertheless, I was unable to decide—in spite of many requests—to issue a new edition of the prayerbook, one which would correspond to our type of service, it was due to the following consideration. The individual changes, introduced thus far, had always been due to a need which was decisively felt at a particular time. One felt compelled to meet it, without consistently establishing the principle which called for the particular change, and without pursuing it to all of its consequences. If they did not cause a special offense, one retained passages which, in principle, would have called for the same decision which led to the removal or rewording of other passages. Consequently, our worship service was liable to suffer some inconsistencies here and there. One reconciled himself to this state of affairs by the knowledge that it suffices for the pious feeling of the worshipper if history always progresses in gradual changes, only slowly bringing the process to completion. The institutions of our worship service satisfied those participating in it—indeed, not only more so than a service of the old and rigid kind, but actually as one reformed in accordance with the new views. But the situation is different when those innovations are now to appear together as a unit. Inconsistencies which, in the *celebration* of a service, can be relegated to the background meet the eye *in book form*, and can no longer be so easily concealed. To remove those inconsistencies completely did not appear to be advisable from the point of view of the congregation—either towards one side or towards the other. This was the reason for my opposition to a new edition of the prayerbook.

However, the demand became more urgent and vocal from year to year, and it finally had to be met. Deliberations took place with the board of the congregation, in order to find a more uniform expression of the religious approach on which our worship service is based—and that without any further far-reaching changes. The result of those deliberations is now expressed in this edition. The principles which have their historical sanction in our worship service for many years already have here been applied with somewhat greater precision. They can be summarized as follows: The lamentation about the lost national independence of Israel, the plea for the gathering of the dispersed in Palestine and the restoration of the cult of priests and sacrifices, that is relegated to the background. Jerusalem and Zion are places whence instruction went forth, and to which holy memories are attached. But, on the whole, they are to be celebrated more as a spiritual idea, as the nursery of the Kingdom of God, than as a certain geographical locale connected with a special divine providence for all times. Likewise, the hopeful look into the future is directed to the messianic kingdom as a time of the universal reign of the idea of God (*Gottesidee*), of a strengthening of piety and righteousness among all men, but not as a time for the elevation of the *People* of Israel. Such prayers, which did not acquire a special value in the pious feeling of the worshipper, demand and allow abbreviation. Those, on the other hand, which enjoy a greater respect, remain, as much as possible, unchanged and unabbreviated. But the prestige of the prayers is not only connected with their contents, but also with the traditional form, with the word in which they have been bequeathed unto us—that is to say, with the Hebrew language. Let it remain, therefore, with a few exceptions, the language of prayer. Only in those instances where the rabbi functions independently as a liturgist is the German language to be preferred. To be sure, nowadays a prayerbook must make provision for the great number of those who either do not know Hebrew at all, or do not know it sufficiently to find edification in a Hebrew prayer. Yet particularly for that segment of the congregation, a mere translation of the existing prayers does not suffice. He who is used to the Hebrew prayer may find himself prevented by his loyalty to a beloved prayer from making criticisms about its religious point of view and its form. But the case is different with him who has become estranged from the Hebrew prayer. He demands from the prayer the kind of contents and expression with which his heart can completely identify. The German part, printed underneath the Hebrew, is, therefore, not a translation, but a completely new reworking of the Hebrew prayers in the German language. As much as possible it is related to the contents of the Hebrew prayers, but it restates the contents independently. Here, then, I was able to give full expression to my demands about the religious idea which must pervade the prayer, and about the aesthetic form. The passages in prose as well as in poetry—closely related to the trend of thought of the Hebrew section—have, therefore, in their entirety, been newly arranged by me. . . .

These few words should suffice to introduce this new edition of the prayerbook to the public. This is not the place to deal at length with the basis of the principles and the justification for applying them. The principles stand firm for the religious consciousness of our synagogue, and, I may say with confidence, of the overwhelming majority of German Jewry. Their application in detail will always be differently evaluated, depending upon individual points of view and tastes. But it is not my intention, least of all in this place, to convince and to refute him who is fundamentally opposed to the basic thought. The prayerbook, like the synagogue, is meant to be the site of peaceful union for common edification, not the arena for mutual attacks.

Thus may this prayerbook, too, not lack the divine blessing; and may it also contribute to the elevation of that devotion which—thanks and praise be to the Lord—our synagogue has found again. . . .

Geiger

Breslau, June 26th, 1854

Far more "traditional" than Geiger's prayerbook was the liturgy published a year later (1855) by M. Präger for the Mannheim Jewish community.[18] It is, in its Hebrew section, to all intents and purposes, an Orthodox *siddur,* except for some very minor omissions and changes which nowhere approach the extent of the changes introduced by Geiger in 1854. But, in the age of rising Reform, even the most minor change in the accustomed ritual contributed to the current polemics. And that all the more so since Präger's German translation clearly showed "Reform" tendencies. Moreover, in his Preface, he acknowledged his indebtedness to Stein, Geiger, Maier, the hymnal of the Hamburg Temple, and others. Präger's Preface, from which we are quoting excerpts, affords us an insight into the communal background against which the Reform endeavors of those days have to be seen.

10) PREFACE TO THE MANNHEIM PRAYERBOOK, 1855. (*Israelitisches Gebetbuch,* ed. M. Präger.) (Excerpts)

Many an Israelite of the Orthodox wing, on seeing this book, might ask in amazement: What? A *Tephillah* for the Mannheim congregation? Does this congregation no longer belong to the congregations of Israel which share the same order of prayers (*Siddur Tephillah*) sanctioned by centuries? On the other hand, the men of determined progress might cry out: How? After all, a *Tephillah?* Is this kind of worship never to cease? Should Hebrew, that language of antiquity, have validity for all future?

Even those who desire to combine the venerable past with the living present, who neither want to remove all of the Hebrew nor retain it in its entirety, and who demand a re-arrangement of the Jewish cult, even they might indignantly proclaim with the Prophet: *ki mispar 'arekha hayu elohekha* (Jeremiah

11: 13),[19] as many prayerbooks as there are cities! There should be unity among the new Israel just as there was in the old. And there should not be different worship services in Frankfort, in Mayence, in Coblenz, in Aachen, in Breslau, and in Hamburg! There should be some kind of understanding, so that every congregation desiring to join the new order would, at the same time, enter into cordial relations with like-minded congregations!

Such views are certainly correct and worthy of attention. And union and common practice are indeed the aim for which we are all striving. Still, at the moment, the reform of the synagogue is only just coming about and developing. As little as the old cult became suddenly what it now is, so little can the new cult appear immediately as something universally accepted and completed. It lacks authority. It must first of all win adherents. It must take into account special conditions. It must become aware, through experience, of individual deficiencies. Only when different experiments will have been made in different places, can mutual consent be successful and salutary.

In our local congregation we had to consider the particular circumstance that, here, the desire was general to combine the dedication of the new and splendid House of God with the introduction of an appropriate and worthy form of worship. The Orthodox rightly hoped to bring new validity and new participants to the Jewish worship service, while the so-called modernists were happy at the prospect of finding the synagogue open to them, and particularly to their wives and children.

Through this mediating and mutually respectful consideration of the various religious points of view, our congregation remained completely united. In the composition of this prayerbook, attention was paid to this beautiful unity (which cannot be praised highly enough) *of a very numerous congregation*[20]—so far a rather rare example. Indeed, the worship service, introduced since the dedication of the synagogue, a worship service beautified with . . . choral singing and the . . . sounds of the organ, has met with the most general participation and satisfaction. . . .

M. Präger
City Rabbi

Mannheim, August 8th, 1855

The liturgical reforms, attempted in various parts of Germany since the founding of the Hamburg Temple in 1818, were taken for granted when, in the late fifties of the nineteenth century, the official Judaism of Sweden revised its liturgy and published its prayerbooks 1858/62. This liturgy, showing the influence of the Hamburg Temple, of Stein, and of Geiger, undergoing various revisions in the course of time (in the thirties of the present century the revisions being in the direction of greater adherence to tradition), has remained the liturgy of official Swedish Judaism to this day. The Swedish Chief Rabbi conducts services according to that liturgy. While Orthodox services are also being held in Sweden, they are functions of private organizations. Sweden, then, represents an instance of a whole country's "going Reform"—so much so, in fact, that no need is felt to stress that adjective.

The cradle of Swedish Reform is Göteborg, where the new prayerbooks began to be published in 1858. The Göteborg prayerbooks were reprinted a number of times, also for the use of the Stockholm synagogue. The Preface of the Göteborg prayerbook is simply signed, "The Commission on Worship (*Cultuscommissionen*), but we are given to understand that the guiding spirit behind that Commission was Maurice Wolff, who had been called to the Göteborg rabbinate, from Germany, in 1857.[21]

11) PREFACE TO THE GOTEBORG PRAYERBOOK, 1858. (*Bönbok,* Göteborg.)

> Prayer, the service of the heart, as our Sages called it, this elevating of the human soul to its eternal source for the purpose of finding peace, comfort and hope, must be a true expression of the feelings and thoughts which exist within the one who is praying. It can fulfil its purpose, and bring blessing, only when it is said with true devotion. For this reason, there must be full agreement between the contents of the prayers and the religious consciousness; and anything which in some way could detract from sincere devotion must be removed from the public worship service.
>
> It is this conviction which has given the impetus to the changes in public worship, which, in agreement with the wishes of the congregation, have been effected during the last three years; and it is this conviction which will justify the changes. But, fortunately, there is no need for justification, since the changes have contributed to the awakening and heightening of the religious spirit within our faith. They have met a long and deeply felt need, and, with deep joy, we can point to a brief, though nonetheless satisfying, experience. In essence, this prayerbook adheres to the order of prayer which was decided on three years ago; and the exceptions consist of the removal from the prayers of everything which is no longer in agreement with our hopes, our desires, and our religious beliefs. But we have not done this arbitrarily, and we have not depended on our own judg-

ment. What the earlier assemblies of rabbis and the later Rabbinical Conferences have almost unanimously decided, what the congregation of the Hamburg Temple and the congregations of Frankfort on the Main, Breslau, and several other places have already achieved and put into practice,—all this has been accepted as a guide for every change.

When translating the Hebrew prayers, we have been less concerned with making a literal translation than with reproducing faithfully the spirit and the meaning of the original; and the Commission hopes that they have, to some extent, succeeded in this undertaking.

Regarding the *Haftarah,* the views voiced in *Der Volkslehrer,* Vol. II, page 208, have been adhered to, and, with very few exceptions, the selection adopted in Frankfort o. M. has here been followed. The Announcement of the New Moon takes place in connection with the prayer following the sermon. . . .

With faith and hope, the Commission is now submitting to the congregation this part of the important work, the publishing of which the congregation has entrusted to the Commission. The Commission knows all too well the difficulties it has had to cope with and the frailty of its powers; and it, therefore, does not imagine that the work is without shortcomings and mistakes. But it hopes that God will give the work His blessing, and that the work will aid in preserving and increasing the love of the faith, and effect a *true* worship of God. Rarely has a work of this kind been established with more agreement and peace among the members of a congregation. May it long continue to serve the edification of both young and old, when they gather in the holy temple to bring unto the Lord the offering most pleasing to Him: a pure heart, full of love and gratitude.

The Commission on Worship

Göteborg, September 1858

Leopold Stein (1810–1882) was called to the rabbinate of the Jewish community of Frankfort o. M. in 1844.[22] A contemporary newspaper report, dated 1846,[23] describes the changes which Stein had introduced by that time in Frankfort's Main Synagogue. They included the adoption of the triennial cycle of Torah readings, a German exposition of the Torah portion on Sabbaths when no sermon was preached, the reading of the *Haftarah* and its benedictions in German (omitting the benedictions referring to the Messiah and the rebuilding of Zion), the omission of the *piyutim* throughout the year, and their reduction to one third of the traditional bulk on the High Holy Days. The report concludes by saying:

> The whole service (on a Sabbath morning) takes 1¾ hours when there is a sermon, and 1½ hours when there is a German exposition of the Torah portion (*Methurgemanvortrag*), and can be conducted, from beginning to end, with suitable devotion and order. All we are still lacking is the organ, which, however, is definitely expected to be placed in the old synagogue within the near future. ... Rabbi Dr. Stein has declared the second day of the festivals to be abolished.

The services described in the 1846 report were apparently conducted out of the traditional prayerbook. But, in 1854, Stein began working on a new prayerbook which was published in 1860. The new prayerbook makes provision for the inclusion of a number of German prayers and hymns. Its over-all approach is made explicit enough in the Preface which we bring below. It should be borne in mind that Frankfort o. M. was an old established Jewish community, going back to the twelfth century,[24] and that Stein's prayerbook was designed for the Main Synagogue (*Hauptsynagoge*) there.

12) PREFACE TO STEIN'S FRANKFORT PRAYERBOOK, 1860.
(*Gebetbuch für Israelitische Gemeinden*. Frankfort o. M.)

> God be praised!
>
> We herewith present to the synagogue the *first part* of our new prayerbook. The following has to be prefaced about the history of this work:
>
> Already at the beginning of the year 1854, before the demolition of the *old* synagogue, I was commissioned by the board of our congregation to work out the plan of the liturgy for our *new* House of God. This I did by drawing up the basic principles which were inherent in the reforms which had already been introduced, and after bringing up the subject at the first Conference of Rabbis at Wiesbaden (November 8th, 9th, 1854). There, the thought of the widest possible agreement in the area of the improved worship service was the basis of all the discussions. On December 1st, 1854, then, I submitted the report about the new prayerbook. The relevant principles (eighteen in number) were approved by the commission elected for this purpose, and, later, by the directorate of the congregation itself. With the approval of the latter, the principles were submitted for the approval of the second Conference of Rabbis at Giessen (June 11th–13th, 1855). That Conference examined the principles during three days of discussion. With suitable modifications, it approved of them, and then charged an executive, consisting of seven

members, with the detailed working out of the plan. The following rabbis were members of that executive: Doctors Adler of Alzey (now of New York), Aub of Mayence, Formstecher of Offenbach, Levi of Giessen, Präger of Mannheim, Süsskind of Wiesbaden, and the undersigned as chairman. In many discussions, and with a great deal of zeal and concern, that executive dealt with the plan worked out by me, a plan which aimed at the refining of the worship service while sparing the existing practice as much as possible. That scheme was then printed as manuscript, at the expense of the board of the local congregation, and sent to all the members of the Conference.[25] After that, the third Conference of Rabbis (meeting here on October 19th–22nd, 1857) gave its approval to the above-mentioned plan, after further modifications had been incorporated. The plan then went to the board of the local congregation, which appointed a new *liturgical commission,* composed of men holding various views, but all of them familiar with the spirit of Judaism and its manner of religious observance—thereby, in considerate wisdom, vindicating the *right of the congregation* to have a say in all improvements to be introduced. The commission consisted of the following honorable gentlemen: Dr. Jakob Weil, chairman, J. S. Adler, Dr. Jakob Auerbach, Jakob Bechhold, Leopold Beer, Dr. Michael Hess, and Professor Moritz Oppenheim. That commission, too, in the year 1858, examined the matter with full devotion and conscientiousness. It then informed the undersigned of its proposals and reservations. With mutual concessions, it was possible to achieve unanimity on the majority of issues. Where differences of opinion remained, the directorate of the congregation itself reached the decisions—in favor of the greatest possible conservation of the old forms. The decisions of the Conference of Rabbis have, therefore, been occasionally modified. But the *basic principles* enunciated in Giessen, which corresponded to those accepted here by the Second Rabbinical Conference, in the year 1845, have remained untouched.

The present work thus came into being, as far as the reforms in the Hebrew section are concerned, with very careful consideration, and with a common appreciation of the circumstances—as is mandatory and essential particularly in religious matters.

As to the reforms themselves, they are, first of all, concerned with *the request for a return to Palestine* and for a restoration there of a Jewish national state. Such a request, today, comes from the heart of very few people indeed; yet prayer demands *truth* above all. To an even greater extent, the same applies to *the request for the restoration of the cult of bloody sacrifices.*

That cult, according to many statements of the Scriptures, of the Talmud, and of later teachers of the Synagogue, was only a secondary factor; it was commanded—or, rather, it was conceded—to the ancient Israelites merely as a means of preventing them from sacrificing to the idols. In the Talmud itself the assertion is made that prayer stands on a higher level than sacrifice; indeed, the opinion is expressed that, in the new order of things in the messianic kingdom, the sacrifices will be abolished. Besides, in order to spare the conscience, we have, throughout, also given the older form, and we have relegated the prayers where such differences obtain, to the silent devotion. For this reason, too, in the case of *retzeh* (pp. 182 and 234), where this could not be done, we have retained the older form with as little change as was possible.

On the other hand, we have maintained the basic principles which I drew up for the Second Rabbinical Conference, held here,[26] according to which those prayers were to be retained which petitioned for a renewed glory of Zion and Jerusalem as the place whence all of the light went forth unto mankind. Similarly, we have retained the prayer for the establishment of the messianic kingdom of God through the promised Messiah. We have thus, faithful to our convictions, done justice to religious feelings and modes of expression.

If, in this way, we have done justice to the greatest possible extent to Tradition as far as the *Hebrew* prayers are concerned (even though we have most decidedly excluded such prayers as have their origin in the religious persecutions of earlier times, and in the oppression from which the Jews suffered in those days), we have done no less justice to the definite right of the modern period and *its* demands, by including numerous *prayers and hymns in German*. To give a specific reason for this would be to despair of common sense. According to the Talmud, the whole worship service—with the exception of some very few liturgical formulae—may be conducted in any language, and particularly so the *public* worship service. [Stein here refers to his Notes on pages 298 and 378, in which he draws attention to the Aramaic language in which parts of the traditional liturgy were composed.] We are nevertheless profoundly convinced that a removal of the Hebrew language from the synagogue would constitute a breach in the very foundations of the structure of our religion; and such attempts have nowhere been successful. However, to allocate a significant area in the worship service to the vernacular *by the side of the Hebrew*—that, under present conditions, is not only permitted, but a duty. We have presented the German prayers and hymns, together with the sermon, as the conclusion of the worship service, in order to do justice, also by this means, to the religious needs and circumstances, without any compulsion.

In the case of the German prayers, we have given prominence to the *Psalms,* partly in a free paraphrase and partly in translation, in which latter we have made use of the ever glorious version by *Mendelssohn.* In the case of the chorales, of the prayers for silent devotion, and of the meditations, much use has been made of the prayerbooks and hymnals of Mannheim, Hamburg, and Berlin, and of the collection published locally, some time ago, by Doctors Auerbach and Jost. But the greater part comes from the undersigned himself, both from material previously published and from unpublished material. May we, then, hope that, by making this material available, we have furnished some building material for the renewal of the liturgical life of Israel.

The translation of the Hebrew prayers is entirely new. In it, we were striving, with all loyalty to the spirit of the original, for a higher German way of expression. ... In the plan of our book, we have been greatly aided by the excellent Mannheim prayerbook. We would be very happy indeed if, sooner or later, that circumstance were to lead to a unified liturgy of our two congregations.

Should other congregations decide to introduce our prayerbook, the directorate of our local congregation—seeking no benefit other than that of being of service to the good cause—would certainly be glad to sell the requisite number of books at a price conducive to the introduction of the prayerbook.

This first volume is to be followed, with the help of God, by two further volumes. The next one, which we hope to see completed by the beginning of Ellul (the middle of August), will contain the prayers for New Year and the Day of Atonement. The last volume will contain the prayers for weekdays, half holy days, and, in particular, for domestic devotion. We hope to publish it a year from now.

Leopold Stein, Rabbi

Frankfort o. M., Purim 5620
March 8th, 1860

Joseph von Maier, as we have seen, had published, in 1848, his *Israelitisches Gebet- und Andachtsbuch.* He had done so, as he himself repeatedly stressed, in his individual capacity, neither as the official rabbi of Stuttgart nor as a member of the Wuerttemberg Israelite Supreme

Ecclesiastical Authority. In 1861, however, Maier was charged with the task of publishing a prayerbook in just that latter capacity. The result was basically a new edition of the traditional prayerbook, somewhat abbreviated in its Hebrew section and augmented by German hymns and prayers, but not significantly changed in terms of the doctrines which find expression in the Hebrew liturgy. Knowing from the Preface of his 1848 prayerbook how Maier personally felt about matters liturgical, it is of particular interest to us to see how Maier justified his much more "traditional" prayerbook of 1861. He did so in the Preface to the 1861 edition, which we quote in excerpts.

13) PREFACE TO JOSEPH VON MAIER'S STUTTGART PRAYERBOOK, 1861. (Excerpts.) (*Israelitische Gebetordnung*. Stuttgart.)

Among the most remarkable phenomena in the area of Judaism are the many, often resplendent, synagogues which have been built of late, and for which there have been produced almost as many prayerbooks. If the former give welcome testimony to our reawakened ecclesiastical (*kirchlich*) spirit, the latter prove that, in matters religious, we are still in a state of transition. Particularly in liturgical matters, the views and the needs of the congregations are still rather far apart. This state of affairs is also responsible for the order of prayers which I am publishing herewith.

The better arrangement of the public worship service was one of the main reasons why the local congregation decided to undertake the costly building of a new synagogue, seeing that the old synagogue, on account of its size and whole manner of construction, did not permit the installation of an organ and a choir —the most essential prerequisites for the elevation of the worship service. Now, I would have preferred to be relieved of the task of editing a special prayerbook, and the congregation would have suggested the adoption of one of the existing liturgical collections, if such a step had not appeared to me to be inappropriate to the conditions and the needs of this congregation. The local congregation does not want to separate itself, in its worship, from the other congregations of the country, or from the Synagogue as such. What it desires is *simplicity* and *dignity*. With this, any changes affecting dogma or the transformation of the liturgy were ruled out from the beginning. The present prayerbook differs from the one in use hitherto only in the *omission* of the Talmudic components and of all of the *piyutim,* in the *abbreviation* of some prayers, and in the *inclusion* of German prayers and hymns, and, finally, in a totally new and, in part, metrical *translation*.

Even though these reforms justify themselves, I consider it to be in order to say a few words about them.

Concerning, first of all, the Talmudic passages, *ezehu meqoman*,[27] and *bameh madliqin*[28] and others, they have become antiquated of their own accord. Even before now, they have been recited by only a few, and there cannot be any offense taken by anyone to their total removal. But the same applies to the omission of all of the *piyutim*, to the extent to which the synagogue service for the three festivals ... had still retained them. Science has given its verdict on those additions. They have, in part, artistic, and, in part, scientific or historical value; but none as far as devotion and edification are concerned. At a time when the living Word of God had disappeared from the synagogue, they were, to a certain extent, a substitute for the sermon. But, since, to the joy and refreshment of every truly pious spirit, the sermon has returned to the House of God, the *piyutim* have completely lost any value. Lest they continue to interfere with the dignified recitation of the prayers, and disturb devotion, their total removal has become a holy duty. ...

German prayers and hymns have simply become an irrepressible need if the young generation is to be preserved for the worship service. However hard the school may try to teach Hebrew, with all of the other demands made upon young people nowadays, the school cannot succeed in imparting the kind of knowledge of that language which is necessary if the worship service is to be both interesting and edifying. Apart from that, it seems to me that, if the service, notwithstanding organ and choir, is to be prevented from turning into a dead mechanism, there must be, in addition to the fixed Hebrew prayer, also a variable element. This can only be the German prayer and the German hymn.

It is true that the latter has thus far been unable to acquire its right of domicile in the synagogue, and, in spite of the efforts in that direction of a whole generation, it still appears more or less as a stranger. However, I believe that the guilt is less that of the German hymn than that of two incidental circumstances. In the first place, it was a mistake to issue the German hymns in a separate collection, trying to introduce the latter by the side of the Hebrew prayerbook. On account of this, its use was not only rendered more difficult, since nobody is readily prepared to take two books to the synagogue, but it also appeared, from the very beginning, that the German hymn was a mere unauthorized appendage. A second barrier in the way of the adoption of the German hymn was the tune. The chorale of four parts is far too complicated for the people to make it its own

> with ease. If the German hymn is to come into general use, it must appear as an integral part of the service, and it must be accompanied by a simple tune which can easily be learned. This has happened in the present order of prayers. It incorporates some forty hymns, mostly paraphrases of Psalms, with suitable tunes for one voice, which suffice for the services of the whole year. With the musical talent so frequently found among us, it is to be hoped that the hymns will soon become the property of all, and that, with them, "both young men and maidens, old men and children" will praise the Lord. . . .
>
> In general, I believe that the form to which the congregations in Germany could and should agree would be the following: The sections before *barekhu,* in alternate selections, are to be recited in German, in part as prayers and in part as songs. The sections from *barekhu* through the *Tephillath Shemoneh Esreh* or *Tephillath Shebha'* are to be recited in Hebrew. If, in addition, there be but one—aloud—recitation of the *Tephillah,* and if the Torah be read according to the triennial cycle, then the necessary time will be gained for the sermon—which, after all, has become a generally felt need; and the worship service will, in its totality, become a living adoration of God. . . .
>
> Maier
>
> *Stuttgart, Hanukkah 5621*
> *(December 1861)*

This prayerbook was not only still reprinted for use in Stuttgart some fifty years later (cf. Stuttgart, 1908), but it also formed the basis of the Munich prayerbook of 1876 and its subsequent editions. In his Preface to the 1876 edition of the Munich prayerbook, its editor, Joseph Perles, wrote:

> Invited . . . to work out a program for the intended new order of worship, I was unable and unwilling to increase the already excessive number of prayerbooks by yet another one. Instead, I considered it to be more appropriate to adopt an already existing prayerbook, which would reflect the outlook and the needs of our congregation. As particularly suited to this purpose I regarded the prayerbook of Ecclesiastical Councillor Maier, which has proved its worth in the many Southern German congregations into which it has found its way. It was this prayerbook which, upon my suggestion, was accepted . . . with a few desired modifications and additions.

Joseph Aub, whose 1853 edition of the Mayence liturgy was noted above, was called to the rabbinate of Berlin in 1865. His arrival in the capital coincided with the completion of the building of Berlin's new synagogue. That synagogue, dedicated in 1866, was a highly impressive structure, seating three thousand two hundred persons.[29] The need was apparently felt to have a new liturgy to go with the new synagogue, and, as he explained in the Preface to his 1866 prayerbook, Aub had barely two months in which to prepare it. The liturgy in question is substantially the traditional one—with such changes as are explained in the Preface.

14) PREFACE TO AUB'S PRAYERBOOK FOR THE NEW SYNAGOGUE IN BERLIN, 1866.
(*Gebetbuch ... nach dem Ritus der neuerbauten grossen Synagoge in Berlin.*)

The demand for a prayerbook from which have been removed all the laments for which there is neither cause nor justification at the present time, and which does not contain any petitions or hopes in the granting of which we see no salvation, and the expression of which, with sincerity, is impossible for us—this demand is daily being voiced more loudly and more strongly in most of the Israelite congregations of Germany; and in many of them it has already met with the desired success.

In our congregation, too, wishes and demands have been voiced for many a year, and have led to the resolution that a prayerbook be introduced into the new synagogue—a prayerbook which, cleansed of the above-mentioned laments, petitions and hopes, which disturb devotion, would also do justice to the German element.

The undersigned was charged by the congregational authorities with the task of presenting suggestions and plans for the contents and form of such a new prayerbook. After the examination and approval of the plans, he was commissioned to undertake the editing of this prayerbook. In the motivations we have described there lies the justification for the publication of this prayer-book, which we herewith present, first of all, to the congregation.

It is with great reluctance only that I present this work to the public. For the short period of barely two months, during which this book had to be edited and printed, made it impossible to furnish a solid, or even a merely sufficient, piece of work. On account of the haste, typographical errors naturally crept in, and, particularly in the German section, defects could not be altogether avoided. May the critics, therefore, please judge with clemency.

One could raise the objection that one of the already existing new prayerbooks should have been chosen instead. However, in all of those devotional works there is something to be criticized. In one case we miss the consistent carrying through of a principle, in another there is too much of a blatant difference between the Hebrew text and the German translation. The avoidance of both kinds of error was the aim in editing, and the reason for publishing, the present prayerbook. From the beginning, both the point of view of the congregation and its level of education were decisive in the acceptance and inclusion of the individual prayers. That is why, apart from the original major prayers, which are to be found in all prayerbooks, and which are also not missing in this new one, the prayerbooks have never been identical. Rather has there always been, and still is, a great diversity in this respect, not only between the Portuguese, the Polish, and the German rites, but also within the individual traditions themselves. That is why we must not bemoan nor find fault with the fact that so many new prayerbooks are being published in our time. The newly published prayerbooks are the best testimony to the newly awakened religious spirit. Every one of them contributes to the ennoblement of our worship service, and will serve as a building stone in the rearing of the complete sanctuary of our devotion—once the time has come when our congregations will have come close to one another on the level of their religious education. . . .

Thus may this prayerbook, too, promote devotion, edify the pious souls, and bring celestial blessing into our life.

Dr. Aub

Berlin, August 30th, 1866

Four years later, in 1870, Abraham Geiger was to become Aub's colleague in the Berlin rabbinate, and in that year, too, Geiger was to publish a new edition of his own prayerbook in Berlin. But from 1863 to 1870, Geiger was the rabbi of the Frankfort o. M. Jewish community, where he had taken the place of Leopold Stein, who had resigned from his Frankfort position in 1862. Geiger must have been dissatisfied with Stein's prayerbook in Frankfort, and he prevailed upon the congregation to appoint a commission to authorize the composition of a new prayerbook. The results of the commission's deliberations are summarized in a memoir (*Denkschrift*) which Geiger submitted to the Frankfort congregational authorities in 1869. The principles established in that memoir were so important to Geiger that he reiterated them *verbatim* time and again.[30]

15) ABRAHAM GEIGER'S "DENKSCHRIFT," 1869. (Frankfort o. M.)

To the Worthy Authorities of the Congregation I herewith submit the extensive plan, worked out in twenty-three sessions of the commission, appointed by you, for the composition of a new prayerbook.

The principles which guided the commission in its conclusions, and which the commission applied with conscientious care to the consideration and determination of every single point, are adequately apparent in an examination of the submitted plan. However, it would considerably facilitate and shorten the deliberations if, at the request of the commission, I were briefly to set forth those principles here.

1. The prayerbook, by and large, should retain its customary character. It should continue to express in a precise form its connection with the whole history of Judaism. Consequently, in its essential components, the worship service remains in Hebrew. The traditional Hebrew expression, though here and there not free from a certain Oriental extravagance, is, on the whole, to remain untouched.

2. Nevertheless, particularly on the distinguished days, the service must contain a few *German* prayers and meditations. Furthermore, the Hebrew text must be accompanied by a *German adaptation*. This must not, in rigid fear, force a Hebrew coloration upon the language of our fatherland. Rather should it, with all preservation of the original fervor, appeal to the soul through its accustomed sound.

.3. Special care must be taken that the *duration* of the service be reduced to that degree which facilitates an uninterrupted devotion. Therefore, unnecessary repetitions as well as unessential prayers and those without content must be omitted. Even the heaping up of valuable prayers must be avoided. Rather must their impressiveness be heightened by rotation and by their distribution over various occasions.

4. With all respectful retention of Judaism's historical elements, religious *concepts* which have had a temporal validity, but which have been displaced by *a progressively purer conception,* must not be retained in a one-sided and sharp accentuation. Rather must they be either totally removed or recast into a form which does not contradict the purer conception.

5. Consequently,

(i) *Highly materialistic descriptions of the Deity,* as they occur in the *piyutim,* must be removed;

(ii) The enumeration of the various *angelic* orders and the depiction of their activity cannot be admitted;

(iii) The belief in immortality must not content itself with the one-sided formulation of a *physical resurrection*. It must, instead, be expressed in a manner which also includes the concept of spiritual continuity.

6. Concerning, in particular, *the position of Israel in world history,* this must be strongly articulated in the following direction: Judaism is the religion of truth and of light. Israel received his task, and continues to be the bearer and herald of this doctrine. To this is related his confidence that this doctrine will progressively become the common possession of the entire educated world, thereby enlarging Israel to include all of mankind. Forms of expression which tend to narrow or obscure this lofty thought are unsuitable.

7. Consequently, the *national aspect* of Israel must recede into the background:

(i) The *separation* between Israel and the other peoples, which existed at one time, has no right to be expressed in prayer. Rather ought there to be an expression of the joy that such barriers are increasingly falling.

(ii) The exalted feeling of a noble spiritual vocation must avoid any appearance of *overbearance,* and must shun any side-glances at *"other peoples."*

(iii) The look into the future should arouse the happy hope in the *unification of all mankind,* in truth, in justice, and in peace. However, wholly faded from our consciousness is the belief in the *restoration of a Jewish State in Palestine,* and, correspondingly, in the *building of a temple* in Jerusalem to serve as the point of unification for Israel. The same applies to the belief in the *Ingathering of the Dispersed* and to everything connected with such a restoration of vanished circumstances. The expression of such a hope in prayer, the petition for its realization, would be a blatant untruth.

8. Similarly, that conception, which envisages our worship service as again becoming a *sacrificial service,* is irreconcilable with the whole progress of the times.

Even if it be assumed that, in ancient times, sacrifice was an adequate expression of the adoration of God, sacrifice has long since made way for a more spiritual worship service, and its reintroduction is unthinkable.

Passages which only remotely remind us of ancient human sacrifice, regarded as an abomination by the Judaism of all periods, must be totally removed from the prayerbook.[31]

But *animal sacrifices,* too, no longer have a right to be represented as a desired institution of the future. Just as little *does the memory of them, of the way in which, at one time, they were offered,* contain the least element of religious edification. Of this, too, the prayerbook must remain free.

On the execution of those essential principles, the commission bases the proposals which it has submitted. The commission is convinced that the prayerbook, presented in this form, will, at one and the same time, not be bereft of the suggestions of past tradition, and yet also do justice to the needs of the present.

Most respectfully submitted to the worthy authorities of the congregation,

Dr. Abraham Geiger, Rabbi

Frankfort on the Main, June 8th, 1869

By the time the above principles found their implementation in an actual prayerbook, Geiger had moved from Frankfort to Berlin. The prayerbook was published in Berlin, in 1870, bearing, on its title page, the words: "With the agreement of the directorate of the congregation in Frankfort on the Main."[32]

16) PREFACE TO GEIGER'S PRAYERBOOK, 1870. (*Israelitisches Gebetbuch.* Berlin)

The prayerbook appearing herewith hardly needs to be commended and introduced to the public for which it is meant. The liturgical question has already for years occupied one of the foremost positions in the consideration of the task of adapting the historical form of Judaism to the demands of the present. It is unlikely to lose this favored position for a long time to come. The worship service is the bond which binds the congregation. It is meant to be the expression of religious conviction, as alive in the individual as in the group. It must not deny the connection with the totality of the historical past; yet it must, at the same time, nourish the religious needs of the present. The demands made upon a prayerbook for our time are, therefore, so manifold, and proceed from such divergent points of view, that the publication of a prayerbook which could satisfy *all congregations* simply cannot be undertaken. The divergences between the various congregations, corresponding to the divergent needs felt within them, will not cease for a long time yet.

Perhaps the colorful multiplicity may even increase for a while. But this must not lead us astray; and it must not fill us with the fear of a split. Gradually, the mutual coming together will again take place. In some congregations the questions reach the level of consciousness later than in others. Still, their time comes, too. And the arrangements of congregations which have progressed earlier can then serve as an example for their own improvements. Once the necessity for the one or the other improvement has come to the fore, the need for further reforms will soon be felt, and general unanimity will increasingly come about.

Those are looks into the future. For the immediate present, the prayerbook which we offer here does not claim to meet all the demands. However, it does make its appearance in the confident hope that it will offer guidance to those congregations in which there is an awareness of the task of the present, guidance as to how the newly awakened needs can be satisfied.

The prayerbook has not been modelled according to the theory of an individual. It has its roots in history, and in the expressed invitations of large congregations. It is, therefore, primarily offered to the latter. But, as a new edition of a liturgical arrangement which for sixteen years has already been at home in, and beloved by, many circles, it could also expect the satisfaction of old, and the winning of new, friends.

For many years already, the lack of a well-arranged prayerbook, particularly for New Year and the Day of Atonement, had been felt by the congregation of Frankfort on the Main. Finally, the decision was reached to add this part to the prayerbook for Sabbath and festivals, printed in 1860. An agreement about the manner of execution was reached when men of knowledge and zeal on the board of the congregation themselves seriously undertook to represent this idea. The commission of experts, appointed for this purpose, soon convinced itself that a *complete* work would have to be produced. The daily service and domestic devotions must not be missing. And the services for Sabbath and festivals were also in need of a more convenient arrangement and of a uniform revision. Thus the commission's deliberations were spread over the entire field. Out of the thorough discussions of the commission, there emerged a plan which, according to well-considered guiding principles, showed the necessary respect for the existing practice, removed the contradiction between it and the newly prevailing views, and gave expression to the true religious feelings. The principles were then formulated. They were combined in a memoir, and were approved by the administration already in June 1869, as was the plan of the new prayerbook based upon them, in October of the same year.

[Geiger here quotes *verbatim* the text of the "principles" contained in the *"Denkschrift"* of 1869.]

Just as there was agreement among the members of the commission, and approval on the part of the administration of the congregation, concerning the guiding principles and the plan based upon them, so, too, have the most important German prayers (which are to be recited aloud, and which are considered as part of the public worship service) been determined in common consultations. However, I bear sole responsibility for the German prayers which are recited silently, as well as for the translations, the domestic devotions, and the occasional prayers. Essentially, they follow the edition of the Breslau prayerbook of sixteen years ago. But, in view of the experience gained during that time-span, they have frequently been formulated with greater precision and in a more appropriate form. In this connection, the *Collection of Prayers and Psalms for Israelites,* published in 1847, by Auerbach and Jost, has been particularly useful; and some complete passages have been taken from there almost *verbatim.*

The congregation of Frankfort is important enough to issue its own prayerbook, which is in accord with the views prevalent in its midst. But it may hope, in view of the influence which it exerts, and in view of the homogeneous character which many of the intelligent congregations of South-West Germany share with it, that the liturgical arrangement which it has introduced will also find admission elsewhere.

The prayerbook offers itself no less to the Eastern congregations of our fatherland—particularly in view of the fact that, in essence, it proceeds from the same principles which, sixteen years ago, guided the edition of the Breslau prayerbook. The latter is now out of print. With the attachment which it found in Breslau, and with the positive reception and adoption which it found in many other congregations, the need for a new edition was daily felt to be more urgent. After the plan of this new edition had been made public, many congregations in Germany as well as in America voiced their desire to introduce the new prayerbook after its appearance. In order to facilitate this wider distribution, still another aspect had to be taken into consideration.

The divergences between the so-called *German* rite, prevailing in the South West, and the *Polish* rite, prevailing in the

East of our fatherland, do not, indeed, rest upon any difference of principles. There would be no inherent objection to a compromise between them. However, in the historical evolution of the Jewish worship service, several passages have remained foreign to the German rite, passages which, in the Polish rite, have achieved a standing of respect, having endeared themselves to those accustomed to the Polish rite. The congregations following the German rite would regard it as just as unfounded to be asked to adopt those passages as the congregations following the Polish rite would consider it unjustified to be deprived of those old components, against which there could be no well-founded objection. To give a single example, the German rite does not know of a Memorial Service on the last days of the great festivals, whereas the Polish rite regards this service as a deeply felt need of the heart. For the Day of Atonement, the German rite, at best, has introduced this service after the *Musaph* prayers, whereas, in the Polish rite, it precedes the *Musaph* service. Particularly in the case of the High Holy Days, New Year and the Day of Atonement, the soulful character of which has also been carried over into the excellent prayers customary on those days, there are many divergences between the rites, and a mutual accommodation would be beset by many peculiar difficulties. That is why it seemed in order, as far as the first part of the prayerbook is concerned, to label some passages as belonging solely to the German rite, and others as exclusive components of the Polish rite. But it also seemed in order to publish the second part, containing the services for New Year and the Day of Atonement, in two entirely separate editions. In this way, each of the two rites retained its fundamental character to the extent to which it could be reconciled with the guiding principles.

Thus may this prayerbook begin its journey into the congregations and into the homes with the happy confidence that it will not lack divine blessing. May it be granted the ability to contribute its share to the exaltation of devotion in our synagogues, in order that true piety be aroused and revived in Israel among both young and old!

Geiger

Berlin, July 25th, 1870

Geiger looked upon his prayerbook of 1870 as a revised edition of his Breslau prayerbook of 1854. The revisions lay mainly in a more thoroughgoing application of the Reform principles. The 1870 prayerbook is, therefore, a more "radical" liturgy than its 1854 predecessor. But, while Geiger sat in Frankfort o. M., preparing the new edition of his prayerbook, his old congregation in Breslau had entrusted his successor there, Manuel Joël, with the task of revising Geiger's 1854 prayerbook in a more traditionalist direction. Joël, in 1869, published a leaflet in which he discussed the philosophy guiding him in his revisions.[33] Geiger, at that very moment engaged in a revision of his own prayerbook leading in the opposite direction, gave expression to his annoyance at Joël's undertaking in an article entitled, "Something about Belief and Prayer. In Defense and in Defiance."[34] Joël replied to that attack by writing *In Defense Against Defiance*,[35] and proceeded with the task in hand, leading to the publication of the revised prayerbook in 1872. According to the Preface, Geiger must have given his approval, though, while the Preface does not say so, we may suspect that the approval was given somewhat grudgingly. The major "revision" produced by Joël was the restoration of passages dealing with Zion, Jerusalem, and the sacrifices, which Geiger had deleted. That is to say, Joël would print a "reformed" text of those passages in large print, and the German translation would refer to that "reformed" version. But also, in small print and without translation, Joël would restore the traditional text, for the benefit of those congregants who were uncompromisingly attached to it. Joël's Preface reads, in part, as follows:

17) PREFACE TO JOËL'S PRAYERBOOK, 1872. (*Israelitisches Gebetbuch*. Berlin) (Excerpts.)

> The prayerbook which is herewith presented to the public owes its existence primarily to an event of significance to a single congregation, and its form to a local need. Nevertheless, it does claim to be of use also in wider circles.
>
> The "event" of which we spoke is the erection of a community synagogue, one which, for the first time in the history of the Breslau Jewish community, was built to be representative of the community as a whole. The "need" is the one which arose locally on account of those changed conditions. But the considerations which have been decisive in the editing of this book are liable to apply likewise to the great majority of Jewish communities, at least within our fatherland.
>
> The exposition of those considerations was first of all the task of a larger commission, appointed by order of the committees of the Breslau community. The commission had before it—as a result of the actual conditions in Breslau—two prayerbooks: the unchanged one of the old synagogues (*Siddur* and *Maḥzor*), and the one published almost twenty years ago by

Dr. Geiger, who was then rabbi of Breslau, ... a prayerbook used by an important segment of the community in the hitherto largest synagogue.

After thorough discussions, the commission expressed itself along the following lines, subject to the approval of the appropriate congregational committees:

It would indeed not meet the circumstances and needs currently obtaining in our community to introduce one of the existing prayerbooks, in an unchanged form, into the community synagogue. Rather does an independent procedure seem to be indicated, and a mandate for the editing of a prayerbook. On the other hand, Geiger's prayerbook has wielded such a wholesome influence upon the worthy conduct of the local worship service that it would be praiseworthy if Dr. Geiger were to permit the utilization of his prayerbook in the editing of the new one. In this way, the many parts of it which have proved themselves through years of experience would be preserved for us. After Dr. Geiger had given the desired approval to the board of the Breslau community, the further discussion of the principles governing the new prayerbook was begun, and, after their determination, the undersigned rabbi was entrusted with the editorial work.

Now, the undersigned does not believe that this is the place for an adequate justification of all the details of the work. Rather must he refer those who are interested to the literature on this subject, in general, and to his own little pamphlet, of some years ago, *Toward an Orientation in the Problem of the Cult.* Nevertheless, he does consider it appropriate to explain briefly what is being offered here, and to justify it to those who are in need of such a justification.

One not familiar with liturgical problems may perhaps find the assertion peculiar that a compromise has been reached here which will satisfy the progressive as well as the conservative segments of the community. The expert will not find it to be peculiar. He knows that there is no intention here of either ignoring or of glossing over the existing, widely differing, concepts of religion. On the contrary, after some reflection, he will easily come to the following insight: The difference in the trends of Judaism expresses itself far more in the positions taken about the legal part of religion than in those taken about the dogmatic part. Conversely, it is in the nature of things that the dogmatic part finds far greater expression in the worship service than the legal part. That is why the Jewish worship service is in the fortunate position of being able to clothe itself in a form which does not harshly express the difference of opinions existing elsewhere. It goes without saying that I have in mind only those conservatives who are amenable to the consideration that it was not the entire bulk of the traditional prayers which has received the sanction, or even only the tacit agreement, of the scholars—just as I have in mind only those progressives who are educated enough to value the great importance of that which has historically come to be.

Let us begin with the Hebrew section of the book. Here, above all, we note the pleasing fact that—to the extent to which the changes do not affect questions of principle—even the conservatives do not close their minds to the recognition that the removal of numerous prayers is not only religiously *permitted,* but religiously *commanded*—so that the dignity of the performance may not suffer from the over-abundance of that which has to be recited. At the same time, the omission of a prayer does not imply a value judgment as to its beauty or appropriateness, since even beautiful prayers—*to the extent to which they are not of a fundamental kind*—will have to give way to the possibility of having an appropriate recitation.

As far as the differences in *principle* are concerned, we have dealt with them on the basis of a new point of view which has been approved, already some years ago, by experts belonging to *different* trends.

Years ago already, after inspecting the better known reformed prayerbooks, the undersigned became convinced that, on account of their quite legitimate regard for the divergent opinions prevailing in the larger congregations, those prayerbooks were led to a formulation which satisfied neither the liberals nor the conservatives. The editors of those books were not unaware of this, but they lacked a different procedure. On the other hand, it also happened that, through an unjustified and far too pedestrian evaluation, some prayers which undoubtedly have retained their ability to edify to this day were reckoned among the doubtful prayers. If, however, on the basis of our consideration, we can limit the number of passages which could give rise to a conflict over principles, then the following way is open to the thoughtful:

It is a fact that, as far as the conservative is concerned, there are only two prayers of fundamental importance, to wit:

(1) The Confession of Faith (*Shema*) with its Blessings;
(2) The so-called *Tephillah* proper (The Eighteen Benedictions, the Seven Benedictions, the Nine Benedictions).

Apart from the *Shema,* which offers no ground for differences of opinion,[36] it is also a fact, backed by the most respected authority of the Middle Ages, Maimonides, that the *Tephillah* was not, as at present, recited *twice* during every major portion of a worship service (first in an undertone, and then aloud), but *once* only, in a manner which is still customary, in certain known instances, in all localities. This was by no means the result of being at a loss about what is to be done, but rather the outcome of the experience—which today can be come by at least as easily as it was then—that, at a repeated loud recitation of the *whole,* the congregation can no longer have the attention and the devotion which are mandatory and appropriate. But the prayers giving rise to the differences of opinion are found precisely in that part of the service which is recited silently, where the individual is heard only by his God, and not controlled by his fellow-man. That is why there could be no objection to the retention of the old formulation by the side of the reformed one, which latter corresponds more to our views—provided, of course, that the new formulation does not bear the stamp of arbitrariness, but likewise demonstrates the retention of that which is fundamental.

That is what we have carried out in our prayerbook. The undersigned believes without reservation that he is able to share in the responsibility for it. The possible objections can easily be met. For the most part, they rest upon a faulty conception of what is called "the formulation of the Sages," which must not be changed. What could possibly be the reason that even experts refuse to acknowledge that this phrase was never understood to cover the strict wording of the *Tephillah?!* Indeed, that strict wording cannot be formulated at all, seeing that already the greatest expert in this field, Rabbi D. Abudraham (quoted in *Beth Yoseph* to *Tur Oraḥ Ḥayyim,* chapter 13, end), testifies for his own time that "there was hardly a place where the Eighteen Benedictions were recited in the identical manner, word for word, and where some did not add and others omit." But in this solution, too, there lies the only possibility of avoiding the otherwise inevitable incompleteness and inconsistency. For while, in another procedure, a fair consideration for the views of others necessarily leads to the demand for incompleteness made upon the individual, for his renunciation of the expression which fully satisfies him, in this procedure he is allowed the clearest expression of his own convictions. The prerequisite is his acknowledgment of something which is true even without his acknowledgment, namely the fact that people, standing on the same foundation of faith, nevertheless hold views which do not coincide in all respects, and that, on account of this, without calling into question their spiritual unanimity on other matters, people are entitled to a different formulation of certain convictions.

As far as the wording of the new formulae in all the so-called "*Shemoneh Esreh*" benedictions is concerned, the undersigned, who alone bears responsibility for them, hopes that the true Israelite spirit will not be missed in them. ...

For congregational purposes, I regarded as correct and appropriate the method of Geiger, i.e., to substitute a free paraphrase for a literal translation. On the other hand, as is to be expected, there are so many degrees on the scale between a *free* translation and a *faithful* translation that it is only natural that what appears to be faithful enough to one looks like being too free to another. That is why the undersigned has once more gone through many of the Hebrew prayers, so that he could render their contents in a translation which is free and faithful at one and the same time. ...

What has been said above should suffice to introduce the prayerbook, which, if it is to maintain itself, will have to speak for itself in any case. There only remains the duty of saying a word about the cooperation of the congregation in the editing of this book. As was already mentioned at the beginning, the author, in formulating this book, was responsible to a special commission as well as to both committees of the community. Nevertheless, so far was he from any feeling of constraint that, on the contrary, he found himself greatly supported and advanced by the thoughtful spirit prevailing in those committees. . . .

Joël

Breslau, July 1872

Because of government-imposed restrictions, the Jewish community of Leipzig was of comparatively recent origin. Not until 1847 was a congregation founded there, at which time, too, Adolf Jellinek was elected as preacher. However, long before the establishment of a permanent congregation, the Jews coming to Leipzig for the annual fairs were permitted to hold services. Such services were held by different groups of Jews who congregated on the basis of their particular provenance. Among those temporary services, held during the Leipzig fairs, there was also a branch service of the Hamburg Temple, which was organized as early as 1820 (only two years after the Hamburg Temple's foundation), and which brought to Leipzig such famous preachers as Leopold Zunz and Isaac Noah Mannheimer.[37]

In 1865, that is, eighteen years after the founding of the permanent Leipzig congregation, that congregation issued a collection of German prayers and hymns to supplement the traditional liturgy.[38] Included in that collection was a substitute version for the *Kol Nidré* formula, the text of which we are reproducing elsewhere in these pages. The rabbi of the Leipzig congregation at the time this collection of German prayers and hymns appeared was Abraham Meyer Goldschmidt, who served the Leipzig congregation from 1858 to 1889. In 1874, Goldschmidt published a prayerbook for the Leipzig congregation, containing the liturgy of the High Holy Days, which was to be Volume II of the complete liturgy for the whole year. Volume I, containing the prayers for weekdays, Sabbath and festivals, was published in 1876, and it is for that volume that Goldschmidt wrote his Preface, excerpts of which are quoted below.

Goldschmidt's prayerbook follows the pattern of Joël's, although, theologically, it is slightly more "radical." It is, therefore, all the more curious (or, perhaps, an indication of the editor's diplomatic skill?) to find Goldschmidt discussing minor grammatical points in his Preface, while glossing over the more dogmatic considerations.

18) PREFACE TO THE LEIPZIG PRAYERBOOK, 1876. (*Israelitisches Gebetbuch,* Vol. I. Leipzig.) (Excerpts.)

> The editions of the Israelite prayerbook which have been appearing for about three decades—some of them being most valuable—have made no claim to meeting completely the task presented by science and life to an Israelite prayerbook at the present time. They meant to be *attempts, contributions* to the solution of this problem, which is as important as it is difficult.
>
> None of the editors—least of all the most competent ones—could treat the heritage of our fathers, hallowed through the centuries (and that, after all, is what our prayerbook represents), so objectively that he was able without much ado to remove that which did not seem to correspond to the scientific or aesthetic consciousness of the present, or to make substitutions for it. I, for my part, am not ashamed to admit that I had to endure a not insignificant inner struggle whenever I had to remove a sentence—nay, a single word—from the traditional prayer, and to substitute something else for it. And that, even though an example had been set by men whom I otherwise like to follow.
>
> What has here been said determines the position from which the present edition wants to be judged. It asks for a modest little place among the *attempts* at the solution of a problem which is as important as it is holy, and it hopes to be able to justify such a request.

As far as the *external* arrangement is concerned, it follows, with a few exceptions, the one maintained in the Joël-Geiger prayerbook of 1872, since that seemed to correspond best to the one in use in our services for almost twenty years. Also, as far as the Hebrew text is concerned, I have likewise adopted the method followed by that prayerbook: to print the traditional text by the side of the text designated for the *public* worship service—particularly in the case of the *Tephillah* for weekdays, Sabbath and festivals. No coercion whatsoever is to be applied to the private devotion of the individual. He who finds adequate expression for his religious conviction in the form he has learned to love from his youth, will find that form untouched. We all know from personal experience how hard it is, in the religious realm, to act according to purely theoretical principles. Religion is life; but life goes its own way, not caring about the theories of the scholars—be they ever so ingenious and penetrating.

On the whole, in editing the present prayerbook ... I was guided by the endeavor to retain as much as possible of the connection, not only with the totality of the present, but also with our historical past. That is why the changes which I introduced into the Hebrew text are of a very modest nature. He who is conversant with the relevant literature will need as little justification for my substituting וכל for the hardly intelligible לכל נוצר in the *Yigdal*[39] as he will for the fact, that, in the *'Abhodah* section of the *Tephillah*, the שאותך לבדך ביראה נעבוד, formerly in use universally, has come into its own again. The והבא עלינו שלום, instead of והביאנו, in the prayer introducing the *Shema* of Shaḥarith, is no new formula, but is already found in the *siddur* of R. Amram Gaon (12th century).[40]

The fact that, in the prayer introducing the Priestly Benediction, *barekhenu baberakhah*,[41] I substituted הכתובה בתורה for בתורה הכתובה will not meet with objection on the part of the experts. I hope that they may even welcome it. That I did not go further by substituting the grammatically correct כהני for the form כהנים, which was already criticized by Joseph Kimchi, and that I did not change the *yehi ratzon* into the more simple *amen*—to justify this, I consider to be unnecessary. This is made superfluous by the controversy which has been raging about it for centuries, and which is mentioned in the popular work of Abudraham (ed. Prague, 1784, p. 35b.) At the same time, this controversy proves that discussions about changes which are to be made in the prayerbook are not of quite as recent a date as they are claimed to be by certain quarters, smelling heresy everywhere.

I did not feel called upon to compose new *Hebrew* prayers,

and to incorporate them within the old traditional prayers. This, I believe, would be the task of a commission appointed for such a purpose by a synod—something which will have to happen sooner or later. At such a time, individual works of this kind, composed with taste and expertise, and already in existence, will be of use.

As far as the *German* section of the present prayerbook is concerned, I was unable to follow the paraphrastic method used by some of the newer versions of the prayerbook. Rather did I attempt ... to strive for a translation which would be equally distant from a slavish literal rendering and from a paraphrase, a translation which would render the contents of the text as faithfully as possible. But I was careful to render almost literally the *Biblical* passages contained in the collection of prayers. I do not have the temerity to clothe the Bible in modern garb, to force it, which is exalted above time and space, into the strait-jacket of the fleeting moment. The Bible is entitled to speak its own language. ...

Goldschmidt

Leipzig, New Year's Eve 5637 (September 18th, 1876)

As he had explained at length in the Preface to the 1860 edition of his prayerbook, Leopold Stein had taken a great deal of trouble in getting that prayerbook approved as widely as possible, by both rabbis and laymen, prior to publication. He was, after all, editing the liturgy of Frankfort's Main Synagogue, and that particular setting may have placed restrictions on him to which he would otherwise not have paid attention. Stein left the Frankfort rabbinate in 1862, devoting himself, until his death in 1882, to literature and religious writings. One of the projects to which he devoted himself was the publication of a new edition of the prayerbook, which appeared in the year of his death, 1882. Though not unrelated to Stein's prayerbook of 1860, this new edition is more consistent in applying Stein's Reform point of view, and undoubtedly is far more the work of a single individual and a single mind than was the liturgy he had edited earlier under congregational auspices. The new prayerbook was published in Mannheim; but we have come across no indication that it was actually used by the Jewish congregation of that city. On the face of it, it seems unlikely, seeing that in 1881 (with the Preface dated 1882) M. Steckelmacher published the third edition of Präger's 1855 prayerbook for the specific use of the Mannheim congregation. But, in 1917, Richard Grünfeld adapted Stein's 1882 prayerbook for use by the Augsburg congregation. Nor is it unlikely that, between 1882 and 1917, the prayerbook was used by some other congregations. We quote excerpts from the Preface.

19) PREFACE TO STEIN'S PRAYERBOOK, *1882*. (*Gebetbuch für Israelitische Gemeinden.* Mannheim.) (Excerpts.)

With this volume, containing the prayers for Sabbath, festivals and weekdays, I present to the Synagogue the conclusion of my liturgical labors. Praised be the Lord, the God of my fathers, who has kept me alive, and who has let me reach this time. The labor of a whole lifetime lies before me, a labor of which I hope that it will outlast me, and that it will still establish blessing and edification in later times. For the first time in German Israel does the whole ritual of the Synagogue appear here, edited from a Reform point of view, and assigning the German element its rightful and broad place.

Judaism has here been lifted out of its separated position. It has been inducted into its cosmopolitan calling—without damage to its uniqueness, for the latter consists precisely of its cosmopolitan significance. The labors of my predecessors should not be underestimated. Dr. Philippson[42] has achieved great things in the area of liturgy, even though his labors did not extend to the presentation of the totality of the public worship services of the Synagogue. Geiger has the merit of having been the first in Germany to have edited a Reform prayerbook for all liturgical occasions.[43] But his book suffers from two faults. The German element has been almost completely neglected; and, in the so-called *Ḥag,* the second day of the festivals has been rehabilitated in a manner which no teacher of the Synagogue either can or will follow. Religious truth cannot be bargained with, and the famous word applies to the second days of the festivals: *sint ut sunt, aut non sint,* let them be as they are, or let them not be at all.

As far as Israel's exalted hopes are concerned, we have devoutly retained his holy place for the Messiah, bearer of our ideal future. Thereby we have established the validity of the great promise that, one day, mankind will give concrete expression to its unity in God by a great temple of peoples. That Temple will find its eternal place in Jerusalem. Where else? Not in Berlin, capital of German Protestantism. Not in Rome, center of the pagan world of the past, and of the Catholic world of today. But in Jerusalem, the Holy City, in which all nations and religions have an equal share. . . .

Danzig, on the Baltic Sea, was far removed from Stein's Frankfort, spiritually and culturally as well as geographically. One of the most Eastern outposts of German Judaism, it had as heterogeneous a Jewish community as can be imagined.[44] Yet the cause of liturgical reform found its champions there, too. In fact, it went hand in hand with another ideal, that of the unification of the Danzig Jewish community. The Preface to the 1887 edition of the Danzig prayerbook (a liturgy of a very moderate "Reform" character) spells out the problems and the attempted solutions.

20) PREFACE TO THE DANZIG PRAYERBOOK, *1887*. (*Israelitisches Gebetbuch*. Danzig.)

> To place the appearance of this new prayerbook in the proper light, there is need for a brief description of the conditions obtaining in our community. Peculiar, as perhaps in no second community in Germany, were the associations—for only thus can they be properly described—in which the Israelites of Danzig had hitherto united as a religious community. Originally, there existed congregations of Israelites in the four suburbs, Altschottland, Weinberg, Mattenbuden, and Langfuhr—congregations which were distinct from one another, and to which we have to add the coreligionists who were allowed to live in the city itself. That this was so in the sad days, when our fathers had to live in this scattered manner, can be understood. But it is abnormal that, during the many decades when the Israelites were united within the walls of our city, the five fractions did not unite as a unified whole. It is even more surprising once one bears in mind that the number of members of each single synagogue was not very significant. Nevertheless, the many endeavors to bring about unity, planned by various quarters, including the government authorities, came to grief. Thus the five associations of Israelites lived side by side. Each one had its synagogue, its administration, and its particular institutions. The worship service, the religious school, and the other congregational institutions, could, of course, only suffer on account of such a fragmentation.
>
> It was not a matter of religious differences which constituted the apparently unbridgeable gulf between congregation and congregation. It was not a matter of social differences which prevented the unification of the five members into one great whole. It was only habit, the mother of so many grievances, habit which seeks to justify itself by wrongly invoking the name of piety, habit and the narrow-mindedness which often bars the way to great achievement which were victorious as soon as a unification was attempted. However, experience testifies to the rule that true moral thoughts may be delayed in their execution,

but must finally come to life, after all. That rule found its application in our midst, too. Six years ago, there awoke anew the ideal striving to remove the ills of fragmentation, to organize a strong community life, to build a communal temple, and thereby to cause a new religious life to sprout forth from the ruins. At the suggestion of the undersigned, men of energy and talent came together, men who were serious about this holy cause. They came together for this goodly work of peace, and they refused to be intimidated by the fact that earlier attempts in this direction had come to grief. Rather did they overcome, with patience and devotion, all the doubts which again threatened the newly found union. The efforts were crowned with success. Every one who knows the history of our ancestors realizes that unity and peace alone strengthen the faith and the position of Israel. Every one who remembers the earlier conditions in our community will acknowledge the fact that a thriving religious evolution was hindered by the unstable conditions of those days—and had to be hindered until the united sanctuary of the future was raised upon the one foundation made up of the five stones. Even as in springtime, every day presents glorious blossoms to the light of the sun, so this new era, the springtime of our congregational evolution, was soon to make us glad with a gift which promises blessing.

The old synagogues, witnesses of the earlier division, had to go—however venerable the memories which they aroused. All members of the community were now to be united in a common temple, rejoicing in a worship service which would satisfy our aesthetic sense. This memorial of religious devotion, of joyous sacrificial spirit, and of excellent artistic genius, has now been completed to the glory of God. For the first time, since Israelites have been living in Danzig, the united congregation of all enters the portals of a glorious sanctuary. Surely, we may have the confident hope that, through this work, dedicated to Heaven, the enthusiasm for the ideals of Judaism will gain strength.

Now our community was confronted by the first question: on what prayerbook should the service in the new synagogue be based? The musical accompaniment alone, desired for the elevation of devotion, made it impossible to take over the old prayerbook, with all the many passages contained in it. For their recitation, the time allotted to the worship service would not suffice. Moreover, especially for the festivals, many unessential prayers had hitherto been customary, prayers for the understanding of which such a comprehensive theological knowledge must be presupposed that the like of it can be found among the very fewest only. Those who are sufficiently familiar with our liturgy and with the knowledge of the Law know very well that a not insignificant number of prayers, without binding authority, have, in the course of time, become tied to our liturgy, so that an unburdening of the prayerbook cannot but honor the word of our Sages: "Better a little with devotion than much without devotion." Thus did the undersigned feel moved, at the suggestion of the leading organs of the community, and in agreement with them, to edit a new prayerbook, which would meet the religious needs and the justified wishes of our congregation. Its contents will justify the assertion that the fundamental principles, dear to us Israelites who are loyal to the Law, have been maintained, and that consideration has been given to a dignified and well-ordered worship service, without damage to the prayers sanctified by tradition.

The additional German prayers and hymns, to the introduction of which there is no objection on the part of tradition, are meant to have their elevating effect particularly on Sabbaths and festivals. In the translation, spirit and contents of the prayers have been faithfully rendered. If the individual German words do not always match the original completely, then this is due to the purpose of the translation, which is that the translation itself should be edifying.

The Bible passages contained in this prayerbook have, with a few changes, been taken from the excellent translation of the late Michael Sachs. Some of the poetical and freer translations, and the hymns, have been taken from the prayerbooks edited by Sachs, Joël, Salomon, J. Maier, Perles, and Lewin. In part, they have also been adopted from the prayerbooks introduced in Berlin. The German prayers which are to be recited by the rabbi have not been printed in the text. They are meant to be recited in a variety of forms, thus always elevating the spirit anew. The service for the Ninth of Ab, and for the other fasts and penitential days, remains in the form which had hitherto been customary in our synagogues.

Thus may this new prayerbook bring to our congregation that for which it is intended: the love for the revealed faith of our fathers. May it, with the help of God, arouse within our hearts the mood of devotion which unites man with his Creator.

Rabbi Dr. Werner

Danzig, Ellul 5647—September 1887

Elsewhere in these pages[45] we have described the prayerbook which

Heinemann Vogelstein edited, in 1894, on behalf of the Westphalian congregations. Here, we bring excerpts from its Preface.

21) PREFACE TO VOGELSTEIN'S PRAYERBOOK, 1894. (Excerpts.)
(*Israelitisches Gebetbuch*. Vol. I. Westphalia.)

The prayerbook of which the first part is herewith presented to the public has been edited by me at the behest of the Union of Synagogue Congregations in Westphalia. The motivating principles, adopted by the convention of the congregations held at Bielefeld, in 1892, and agreed to by me before undertaking the commission, are generally those which, for half a century, have been more or less decisively stressed in the reform of the worship service. A careful examination of the available modern prayerbooks has led to the conclusion that, regardless of their advantages, they are unsuitable for the congregations of the Union—partly for reasons of principle, and partly for reasons of expediency. Something may meet the needs of a large congregation which, having different synagogues, supports different forms of the cult, and yet be often unsuitable to the needs and the cherished customs of smaller congregations. A certain amount of freedom and independence had to be allowed the individual congregations within the framework common to all of the congregations of the Union. This was necessary particularly as far as the German part was concerned. Within recent years, the burning desire has made itself felt in many places to have greater justice done to the German element of the public worship service than had been customary thus far. It was not to be restricted to single anthems and hymns, and to the so-called liturgy recited by the preacher. Rather were a number of prayers of the actual Sabbath and festival services to be recited in German. To make this possible, more stress than usual had to be laid on the German translation of the prayers. It was to avoid any overloading and extravagance of expression, being, instead, a free rendering suitable for the warming of the emotions, and for public recitation. It was necessary, furthermore, to insert Hebrew responses also into the German text, so that the transition from one language of prayer to the other could be effected with ease.

To meet a request, which has been voiced several times, I would make the following recommendations to congregations which, in general, retain the Hebrew text of the prayers, but which, for heightened devotion, would like to see more consideration given to German: Particularly suited for recitation in German are, in the service for Sabbath and festivals, *Nishmath;*

the benedictions before and after the *Shema*—both in the morning service and in the evening service; the prayers for taking out and replacing the Torah; the *Kedushah* of the *Musaph* Service; and, on festivals, also the section of the Seven Benedictions following the *Kedushah* for *Shaḥarith*. In all of this, the Hebrew responses inserted in the German text are to be retained.

I have conscientiously tried to apply the principles which have been decisive in the editing of the prayerbook. I have, therefore, not shied away from making appropriate changes also in such prayers as have hitherto remained unchanged: *Yigdal,* the *Kedushah* of the *Musaph* Service, the enumeration of the Thirteen Attributes of God at the taking out of the Torah. On the other hand, I have, out of a feeling of piety, guarded against changing the Hebrew text without compelling reasons, and against petty criticisms. Above all, it was my intention not to admit into the prayers any wish or desire of which we do not seriously seek acceptance and fulfilment. We want to be truthful in everything we say, and most particularly so when, in prayer, we turn to the God of Truth. But I do not believe that I have offended against the principle of truthfulness by retaining, in their old form, the benedictions before the performance of commandments ordained by the scribes: before the recitation of the *Hallel* Psalms, before the kindling of the Hanukkah lights, and before the reading from the Book of Esther. Especially from the liberal point of view, which recognizes the evolution in religious matters, it did not seem right to me to designate as "commanded by God" only those provisions which are contained in the Torah, while withholding this designation from the ordinances of the teachers of Israel who were filled with the spirit of God.

The Union of Synagogue Congregations in Westphalia, at its convention in Dortmund, in May 1893, unanimously adopted the draft of the prayerbook which I submitted, although, admittedly, it was then but in mere outline form. I was honored by the confidence placed in me by being given complete freedom in working out the details, a confidence for which I am expressing my warmest thanks also in this place.

Of the more recent prayerbooks, I have preferably utilized: the prayerbook of the New Synagogue in Berlin, the Frankfort prayerbook of Geiger, and the Breslau prayerbook of Joël. Several hymns have been adopted or adapted from the Munich and Glogau prayerbooks, and from the Prayerbook for Israelite Congregations by Leopold Stein. I am also indebted to the venerable

rabbi, Dr. Wiener of Oppeln, for many a valuable suggestion. . . .
Vogelstein

Stettin, May 1894

The prayerbook of the Hamburg Temple had gone through five editions between 1819 and 1876: there were editions in 1819, 1841, 1845, 1868, and 1876. However, the 1845 edition was merely a reprint of the 1841 edition, as the 1876 edition was but a reprint of the 1868 edition. In terms of contents and arrangement, therefore, there were but three different versions of that prayerbook, those of 1819, 1841, and 1868. Each subsequent edition after 1819 included more material, both in Hebrew and in German, than its predecessor. Moreover, while the Reform theology of successive editions became more pronounced, there also was a marked tendency to move closer, with each edition, to the forms of the traditional service. The editions of 1819, 1841 and 1845 opened, like German books, from left to right. Beginning with the edition of 1868, the prayerbook of the Hamburg Temple opened like a Hebrew book, from right to left. Beginning with that same edition, a marked influence is felt of Geiger's Breslau prayerbook, and of Stein's Frankfort prayerbook.[46] However, through all the five editions between 1819 and 1876, the Hamburg Temple ritual remained wedded to its predilection for adaptations from the Sepharadi ritual, rejecting the Ashkenazi liturgical tradition which one would more reasonably expect in a German congregation in Hamburg. This, however, was changed with the sixth edition of the Hamburg Temple Prayerbook, edited by Paul Rieger, and published in 1904. Although the Reform position was more consistently carried through in the revision of the prayers than before, this edition not only included more Hebrew texts than any previous edition of this historical prayerbook, but it also showed itself receptive to the Ashkenazi liturgical tradition. The Preface to that edition reads as follows:

22) PREFACE TO THE SIXTH EDITION OF THE HAMBURG TEMPLE PRAYERBOOK, 1904.

Not since Mendelssohn's German translation of Holy Scriptures has any book had as enduring an educational influence upon modern Judaism as did the Prayerbook of the venerable Temple Congregation of Hamburg. That congregation is the actual mother congregation of progressive Judaism, and its prayerbook is the pioneer of a purified worship service in the old as well as the new world. The first prayerbook, edited by S. Fränkel and M. J. Bresselau, of blessed memory, is the strong, self-conscious protest against a Judaism petrified in forms and formulae. It is the first sign of life of the awakened recognition that Judaism is the religion of eternal progress and constant development. That consciousness is also alive in the editors of the later revisions of the first edition of the Temple Prayerbook. And the present, sixth, edition of the Prayerbook is proof of the fact that our congregation has energetically progressed along the tried paths.

In the preparatory discussion about the principles of the new revision of our Prayerbook, the directorate entrusted each one of the two preachers, who took part in the discussions, with the composition of a prayerbook. A Prayerbook Commission was constituted which, in addition to the two preachers, consisted of two members of the directorate, two members of the board of representatives, a member of the congregation, and the Cantor. But only one draft for a prayerbook, that of Dr. Rieger, was submitted to that commission, since Dr. Leimdörfer had already previously indicated his agreement with the main principles of Rieger's draft. After lengthy and very thorough deliberations, the submitted draft was accepted with a few unessential changes.

The fundamental thought behind the new revision of our Prayerbook was the sympathetic blending of the Portuguese liturgy, associated with the history of our congregation, and the finest liturgical poetry of the German rite.

Already in the Introduction to the fourth edition of our Prayerbook (1868), reference was made to the fact that "it remained for a future decision" to determine what prayers are to be recited in Hebrew during the worship service, and what prayers in German. Now, the present Prayerbook has undertaken, for the first time, to determine the ritual in this respect. Nevertheless, it always adds the German or Hebrew texts of the prayers, in order to facilitate a possible future change of the worship service.

The Hebrew text corresponds to the wording of the fourth edition. But it avoids some of the linguistic rough edges, overlooked in previous editions. It also removes or softens religious concepts of our liturgical literature which contradict a purified religious feeling. But it does preserve the historical memories of Judaism, even though it substitutes, for the national petitions, liturgical thoughts relating to the universal significance and future of the religion of Israel. The Hebrew text is thus intimately related to the German version of the prayers.

As far as the German part of the worship service is concerned, we have constantly borne in mind the liturgical poems hitherto customary in our congregation. But the present new version of the German prayers seeks a closer relation to the spirit and the contents of those Hebrew prayers for which the German prayers are meant to be a replacement. On the other hand, the prayers in the Appendix have undergone only minor changes.

May the success of this new version of our Prayerbook correspond to the eminent historical significance of the Temple Congregation. But, above all, may the new Prayerbook contribute to the elevation of the religious spirit within our congregation.

The Directorate of the
Israelite Temple Association

Hamburg, July 1903

The abortive attempt to introduce a reformed prayerbook in Baden has been described elsewhere in this book.[47] The draft of the prayerbook, edited by David Mayer, was printed as a manuscript, apparently in 1905, and circulated among the members of the Baden Jewish synod. The prayerbook itself did not contain any preface or introduction. A leaflet containing "Preliminary Remarks about the Prayerbook Published by the Great Baden Supreme Council of the Israelites" was, however, published separately.[48] For reasons stated towards the end of those "Preliminary Remarks," the latter were inserted in some, but not in all, copies of the prayerbook. The following are some excerpts from that interesting publication:

23) PRELIMINARY REMARKS ABOUT THE BADEN PRAYERBOOK, 1905. (Excerpts.)

One of Judaism's most valuable possessions is its prayerbook, which, in its essential components, goes back into the centuries and millennia. Apart from the numerous poetic passages included in it, among them many of the most beautiful Psalms, it is particularly the oldest prayers in prose which are distinguished by a noble simplicity, and by a timeless power and sincerity of expression, giving voice to sentiments which are universally human and ageless. Chapters and verses from the Pentateuch, the Prophets, and the Talmudic writings increase the contents and significance of the collection of prayers.

However, nobody can fail to see that the old Hebrew prayerbook is increasingly losing in esteem, and that it is in danger of falling into disuse among the young generation. The causes of this phenomenon are obvious: too many and too lengthy prayers are repugnant to modern man. Above all, he only wants to pray what he understands, and what corresponds to his sentiments.

One will have to recognize that those convictions and demands are in accord with the best Jewish traditions, . . . and it will be well to return to them.

One can deal with the aversion against excessively extended liturgies by profitably abbreviating prayers which are too long, by avoiding repetitions as far as possible, and by not including too great a number of Psalms in one and the same worship service, distributing them, instead, in accordance with their contents, over different days.

The understanding of the prayers (all of which it would be quite impossible to study in school, nor can they all be properly comprehended by children of school age) can be mediated and facilitated by means of a good German translation, often also by a free paraphrase which, at the same time, takes the place of a commentary.

But the greater the stress which is laid upon comprehension, the greater becomes the necessity of excluding such passages as originated in periods of religious evolution which have been left behind. To this category belong, specifically, the frequent petitions for the restoration of the sacrificial cult, abolished almost two millennia ago, which the Jewish People shared with all the peoples of antiquity. (Footnote refers to Abraham Ibn Daud, Maimonides, and Leviticus Rabbah.) There was, of course, this difference, that the Torah placed the sacrifices into the service of the Only God—a service from which the people constantly sank back into idolatry. Its re-introduction would mean for the Jewish religion, as far as the worship of God is concerned, placing itself to the rear of all existing civilized religions, by the side of cults the mere mention of which, for comparative purposes, would constitute an insult to Judaism. There can be no doubt that, if those petitions were to be granted, a complete schism in Judaism would be the consequence. For the great majority of Israelites in civilized countries would want to have nothing in common with a central sanctuary surrounded by rooms for the placement of oxen etc., in which innocent animals are being slaughtered, and pieces of fat burned—as gratitude for the kind deeds of God, and as atonement for the sins of men—nor with the priests who slaughter, sprinkle blood, offer incense, stir meal-offerings, etc. Happily, those petitions refer to an ideal of the most remote future, the realization of which, according to their own conviction, must not be brought about by the least direct action on the part of those who cherish it. Rather do they hope to promote it by means of piety and virtue. The same applies to the expectation of a Messiah of the Davidic dynasty, which, in contradistinction to the exalted messianic idea as such, is connected with the concept of the rebuilding of the sacrificial temple in the City of David.

The overwhelming majority of those who retain the above prayers do not, in their recitation of them, combine with them any living image. Rather do they regard them as forms, and recite them as a habit. Some people consider this to be harmless, and, therefore, regard a change in the traditional prayers as unnecessary. They overlook the fact that, according to Bible and Talmud, prayer without devotion, and without the agreement of the heart, is worthless, indeed sinful. Moreover, the retention of obsolete passages which are not meant seriously can only redound to the disadvantage of the contents of the other prayers, because, in this way, the spirits become confused, and are finally made indifferent even towards that which continues to be valuable and important. Indeed, the whole of the Jewish religion, and, with it, also morality, become questionable once an ideal is being retained which is repugnant to the modern spirit. For how could one be pious and moral when the ultimate aim which beckons is something which, in his eyes, is impossible, undesirable, and slighted?

Comparable to the passages dealing with the sacrificial cult and the Davidic Messiah are the rest of the obsolete expressions, and certain prayers of Kabbalistic contents. So little do they correspond to pure Judaism that even a Samson Raphael Hirsch, in the prayerbook edited by him with German translation and commentary, has neither translated nor explained them.

The awareness of the defects in the old collection of prayers has led, in the course of the last century, to the publication of new prayerbooks by most of the larger German congregations (Frankfort o. M., Berlin, Breslau, Mannheim, Munich, Nuremberg, Leipzig, Glogau, and others) as well as by whole provinces (Wuerttemberg, Westphalia)—prayerbooks which were then also adopted by numerous other congregations. Those prayerbooks, to a certain extent, all met the existing needs—as is evident from the mere fact of their having maintained themselves in the congregations concerned. In the light of the experience made in the course of the decades, it cannot, however, be denied that they do not completely satisfy. Often, in the striving after brevity in the liturgical material, one has gone too far. For justified omissions, insufficient substitutes were offered. The German translations were often lacking in faithfulness to the spirit of both the German and the Hebrew languages. To this must be added the external mistake, which must not be underestimated, that all of those prayerbooks are both too bulky and too expensive, and, for that reason alone, not popular. They also cannot be used in the schools, a fact which, in the congregations concerned, led to the intolerable situation where one prayerbook is the basis of the public worship service, and another prayerbook is the the basis of religious instruction—of the very instruction which is meant to prepare for the worship service.

Thus, the creation of a prayerbook which was to meet the modern needs, to contain a good German translation, and to be priced as cheaply as possible, was one of the most emphatically voiced desires . . . in the inquiries concerning "The Arrangement of the Worship Service in the Israelite Congregations of the Grand Duchy of Baden," in 1889 and 1897.

The Supreme Council did not rush into the solution of this problem, which it regarded as an inescapable duty. Now, after ten years of conscientious labor, it submits the first part of the prayerbook—for weekdays, Sabbaths, Passover, Pentecost, and Tabernacles—to the judgment of the public. A second volume, for the High Holy Days, and a supplementary volume, for *seliḥoth* and fast-days, are meant to follow.

In the arrangement of the present first volume, the traditional collection of prayers—particularly the Roedelheim edition which is so popular in Germany—was taken as a basis. . . .

The liturgies for the Three Pilgrim Festivals have been incorporated to such an extent that the old *Maḥzor* can be dispensed with. Whatever was somehow valuable in the latter, in terms of *piyutim,* has been retained. In addition, however, the coryphaei of the Spanish-Jewish Golden Age, particularly Judah Halevi and Abraham Ibn Ezra, who are neglected in the Ashkenazi *Maḥzor,* are represented here by some of their most beautiful liturgical compositions. . . . The inclusion of the Memorial Service might be regarded as valuable. . . .

As far as the *adoption* of the new prayerbook is concerned, the Supreme Council will take care, as it has already let it be known, that the work created by it for the maintenance and advancement of true religiosity will not be misused as a means of agitation for party interests. Any kind of compulsion to make the congregations use this prayerbook is absolutely excluded. The synod, which is to meet in 1907 in order to decide about the adoption of the new prayerbook, should establish the same principle as far as the schools are concerned.

In order to prevent any glaring contrast between the present

> prayerbook and the unchanged old prayerbook, these Preliminary Remarks are being printed separately. They are being inserted in some copies of the prayerbook only, and certainly not in those meant for young people. And, regardless of the heavy attacks . . . which have already been directed against the efforts of the Supreme Council, we have confined ourselves here to the indispensable exposition of the proof for the necessity of the changes.
>
> Any objective criticism of the work, from whatever side, will be gratefully received in the interest of its improvement. It is requested that such communications, to the extent to which they are not meant to be submitted to the press, be addressed to the Secretariat of the Great Supreme Council of the Israelites in Karlsruhe. . . .

One of Germany's leading Liberal rabbis was Caesar Seligmann (1860–1950).[49] He was rabbi of the Hamburg Temple from 1889 to 1902, when he was called to the rabbinate of Frankfort o. M. There, in 1910, he published a prayerbook in two volumes, *Israelitisches Gebetbuch*. This work is distinguished by the poetic quality of its German paraphrases and by the manner in which the claims of both tradition and modernity were met. Idelsohn[50] wrote about it that Seligmann "succeeded in breathing into it vitality and a noble inspiration," and considers Seligmann's prayerbook to have been superior to the later *Einheitsgebetbuch* ("Union Prayer Book") of German Liberal Judaism. Seligmann, however, was one of the editors of the latter ritual, and withdrew his own prayerbook once the union ritual appeared in 1929. Volume II, containing the High Holy Day services, had previously appeared in 1904, "printed as manuscript." A third revised edition of Vol. II appeared in 1926, and a second revised edition of Vol. I. in 1928. The two latter editions are marked by an increase in the number of Hebrew prayers. The prayerbook itself contains no Preface. Instead, the reader is told: "The guiding principles, according to which the prayerbook has been edited after detailed committee deliberations, will be published in a special memoir."

That memoir (*Denkschrift*) appeared in 1912.[51] It contained seventy pages. In it, Seligmann begins by telling of a group within the Frankfort congregation who, in 1903, petitioned the board of that congregation for some revisions in the liturgy of the Main Synagogue, a liturgy which had remained unchanged since the days of Geiger, more than thirty years ago. The group had in mind a more modern form of worship which was to be conducted outside of the Main Synagogue, but still within the framework of the over-all Jewish community. Soon thereafter, Seligmann was approached by the lawyer Plotke, a leading member of that group, and asked to work out the desired kind of liturgy.

On March 24th, 1903, Seligmann gave a report, and submitted "theses" concerning "the introduction and formulation of a modern worship service for the High Holy Days" to the Commission of the Department of Worship (*Kommission der Kultus-Sektion*), the report and "theses" being reprinted on pages 22–38 of the memoir.

In giving his report, Seligmann reviews all previous attempts at liturgical reform. The following are excerpts from that report:

24) MEMOIR CONCERNING SELIGMANN'S PRAYERBOOK, 1912. (Excerpts.)

The first attempt at a practical solution is the Hamburg Temple Prayerbook of 1818 (*sic*). In it, the so-called typical prayers, i.e., those which formed the original components of the order of prayers, as well as the Biblical passages, have been retained in Hebrew, while the so-called accessory prayers, i.e., those of later origin, were mainly recited in German. As against this principle, likewise maintained in the 1841 and 1843 (*sic*) editions of that Prayerbook, Geiger argues rather sharply (in his leaflet, *Der Hamburger Tempelstreit,* 1842) that the desire for improvement, contained in the adoption of the German language, suffers a real set-back when it is precisely the most important prayers which are not to be recited in German, whereas the prayers of lesser obligation are to benefit from that language. In this way, the entry of the mother tongue is made to look like an unholy beginning, like something definitely to keep away from the essential prayers, even though one feels compelled to cede the accessory prayers to it. It should be the other way around. Care should be taken that the part of the worship service which is of an obligatory character should also create the deepest impression. Nevertheless, Geiger admits that he can understand the point of view which wants to retain the Hebrew language for those prayers which are deemed to be holy.

Now, it is of special interest for this whole problem that the most recent editions of the Hamburg Temple Prayerbook, reacting to Geiger's critique, and following Geiger's own Breslau edition of the prayerbook, do *not* adopt *German* as the language for the most important prayers, but merely introduce the *Hebrew* version also of the less important prayers, i.e., those of later origin. It was left to the individual to pray the silent prayers either in German or in Hebrew, while the congregational prayer, recited aloud by the cantor, was almost exclusively in Hebrew.

Of the other innovations of the Hamburg Temple, the chorales, borrowed from the Protestant Church, have now been rejected as "un-Jewish" by all German congregations, even by the

Reformgemeinde in Berlin. On the other hand, the stirring songs sung by mixed choirs, the activation of the congregation by means of responses, the original German prayers, infused with modern feeling and only a little too long, and, above all, the uniquely beautiful Memorial Service on the Day of Atonement, have all proved themselves to be excellent, and have been imitated almost everywhere.

As far as the specific question about the proportion of Hebrew and German is concerned, a second attempt at a solution—this time of a theoretical character—was made on a broad scientific basis by the Prayerbook Commission elected by the Rabbinical Conference in Brunswick. In the name of that commission, Ecclesiastical Councillor Maier presented a detailed report at the Rabbinical Conference in Frankfort. The commission deemed the retention of Hebrew advisable for *Barekhu* and its response, for the *Shema,* for the first three and last three benedictions of the *Tephillah,* and for the reading of the Torah. All other components of the liturgy would have to be arranged in German.

Actually, such a far-reaching casting out of the Hebrew has been attempted in no single German congregation. Everywhere, the theory came to grief when confronted by the practical realities. Neither Ecclesiastical Councillor Maier, in his authoritative position in such a progressive congregation as Stuttgart, nor any other member of the commission, nor any other rabbi or congregational board dared to introduce the recommended liturgy in a single synagogue. Geiger expressed the general mood when he said at the Rabbinical Conference: "The report of the commission merely gives us a good advice. . . . For this good and, as I am pleased to admit, well considered advice, I am very grateful to the worthy commission. But its applicability will have to depend upon the individuality of the individual congregations."

At the time of the Rabbinical Conference in Frankfort, there occurred the origin of the Berlin *Reformgemeinde.* Under the unmistakable influence of the Liberal Church movement of the year 1845, which led to the formation of a German-Catholic Church, an attempt was made in Berlin to establish a "Jewish Church," as it is called *verbatim* in a statement by Dr. Stern, the spokesman of that movement. Appeals were sent out into the whole of Germany, and a great synod was to call this "Jewish-German Church" into life. "We want to be sure, first of all," the appeal read, "of the agreement of our German coreligionists, and, together with them, we want to call together a synod for the purpose of establishing that form of Judaism which would correspond to the life of our times and to the feeling of our heart." As a matter of fact, six months after the publication of this appeal, fifty-one larger and smaller congregations had declared their association. But when the Berlin *Reformgemeinde,* relying upon the three to four hundred families who had previously promised their participation, began on its own, *before* the meeting of that projected synod, to establish a German worship service, from which nearly everything characteristic of the historical Jewish worship service had been removed, all of Germany regarded this procedure as a schism. Not a single congregation in Germany joined. The excessively progressive Rabbinical Conference in Frankfort was very cool in its response to the delegation from Berlin, and said very plainly in its official reply (edited by Geiger) that, as a body and as individuals, it could support the *Reformgemeinde* only if the latter were to agree to those principles which the rabbis believe that they would have to follow in a reform of Judaism. Later, Geiger declared that the Berlin Reform had placed itself outside of the totality of Judaism, both of the present and of the past.

And Holdheim himself says, in his *History of the Reformgemeinde* (p. 199), at a time when he was already the rabbi of that congregation: "It cannot be denied that the prayerbook is isolating and estranging us and our efforts to an increasing extent from the Jewish congregations and their endeavors. Missing in the prayerbook is a large part of those points of contact with the total liturgical life of the Jewish congregations in which that life is pulsating. To increase those points of contact—that is our task in the present."

Still under Holdheim, a new edition of the prayerbook of the Jewish *Reformgemeinde* was published in 1885, which, in the words of Levin, in his *Festschrift* on the occasion of the fiftieth anniversary of the *Reformgemeinde* (p. 96), "as to its form, completely follows the traditional prayerbook."[52] The most recent editions, under Levin's influence, have approached the historical pattern even more closely. It is thus to be hoped that, in the matter of its worship service, the Berlin *Reformgemeinde* will again find its connection with the Liberal Judaism of Germany.

Finally, we have to mention the significant practical proposals of Geiger (*Nachgelassene Schriften,* Vol. I, pp. 313f.): The silent prayer of the congregation is best recited in the mother tongue. . . . A different matter is the common prayer at the public worship service, in which the totality appears as such. Here, with all of its history, it cannot cede its rights to the needs of the individual. That is why, particularly in this matter, we have to strive for the proper compromise. . . . The prayers will have to be divided up among the two languages.

Seligmann now proceeds, "with the avoidance of all further theoretical considerations," to the drawing up of his own "theses."

1. The most valuable passages of the liturgy, and those which are most meaningful for our time, shall be recited in German, so that they can be religiously more effective. Those passages include the Psalms, the religiously effective portions of the Torah, of the Prophets, and also the most beautiful portions of the other sacred books which have hitherto not been accepted in our liturgy. The relevant portions of the Torah are to be recited by the rabbi in German *after the Hebrew reading*, according to the manner of the ancient *Targum*. The Prophets and the portions from the rest of the Holy Writings are to be recited according to the manner of our present *Haftaroth*.

Those passages of most valuable contents furthermore include the prayers which most emphatically and characteristically call attention to the essence of the festivals and to their historical significance, e.g., the insertions in the *Musaph* of New Year, the so-called *Malkhuyoth, Zikhronoth* and *Shofaroth,* and the *'Abhodah* on the Day of Atonement. Such prayers are to be recited in a modern German paraphrase.

However, those characteristic prayers to be read aloud, which, on account of their antiquity, or on account of the veneration which they have acquired in the synagogue, or on account of their traditional tune, deserve special attention, such prayers should either be recited in Hebrew only, or in *both* languages. Thus, for example, the *Shema,* the confession of sins, *Abhinu Malkenu, Unethanneh Toqeph*.

2. The prayers which are to be recited silently by the congregation, i.e., the more individualistic prayers, are to be said in German.

3. To meet the requests of the people who desire this new type of service, attention should be given to a more intensive participation of the *rabbi*—but also of the congregation itself. For this purpose, it would be advisable for the *rabbi* to recite the greater part of the German prayers. To facilitate a stronger participation of the congregation, the responses should be set to easy tunes, suitable for congregational singing. The choir is to be merely the vocal leader of the congregation. The Psalms, the taking of the Torah from the Ark, the return of the Torah to the Ark, the inserts for the *Tephillah* of the Holy Days (*zokhrenu leḥayyim,*

etc.), the *Abhinu Malkenu,* and all similar prayers, should, in this manner, be set to tunes for one voice, for congregational singing.

4. Modern German prayers, which express the feeling and the mood of contemporary Jewry, and which serve its religious awakening, should be newly revised. This applies, above all, to the evening services of the Holy Days, and to *Shaḥarith, Musaph* and *Ne'ilah* of Yom Kippur.

5. There is to be a new revision of the Memorial Service on Yom Kippur.

6. Classical choral songs of many parts should be introduced before and after the sermon, and before and after the Memorial Service.

7. A colorful mixture of Hebrew and German seems unharmonious and, therefore, unsuitable. Rather should the worship service be arranged according to the principle whereby the evening service is given a predominantly German character, and the morning service a predominantly Hebrew character.

8. The new worship service should strive as much as possible for a connection with the prayerbook of *Geiger,* which was introduced here more than a generation ago, and which has proved itself since.

9. Of absolute necessity is the retention of Hebrew for *Barekhu, Shema,* the first three and last three benedictions of the *Tephillah,* the responses of the *Kedushah,* the *Kaddish,* and the *Kiddush,* the Torah reading, and for the taking out and the returning of the Torah.

10. Absolutely mandatory is the retention of the second day of *Rosh Hashanah.* The abolition of that day would be of no benefit from the religious point of view. Rather would it be a great loss, the expression of a schism from traditional Judaism.

11. *Yom Kippur* is to be celebrated in the traditional manner; that is to say, without a break. Just as everybody is free to choose a break for himself, so must there be no interference with him who desires to spend the whole day in the House of God.

12. All translated prayers which are recited in German should also be printed in Hebrew, for the benefit of those who feel the need to pray in Hebrew.

The *Denkschrift* (pp. 39–48) now contains a report about the discussions and the decisions of the commission. All "theses" received practically unanimous approval. But the last "thesis," i.e., about printing the Hebrew texts of prayers recited in German only, was rejected.[53] The most important questions concerned:

1. The selection of prayers to be included and excluded. It was decided to avoid any kind of repetition as much as possible. (*Shemoneh Esreh, Kaddish.*)

The abbreviation of the Morning Service by transferring the *Shaḥarith* to an Early Morning Service was considered and warmly advocated by several members of the commission. However, my own view prevailed—that the valuable and meaningful prayers of *Shaḥarith* must not be excluded by transferring them to an Early Morning Service, in which the public does not participate, and which is mainly attended by "*minyan*-men." Such an external clinging to the form, in which the content gets lost, is unworthy of an inner reform of the cult. If there has to be an omission of one part of the Morning Service, it should rather apply to the *Musaph* Service, which undoubtedly is, historically speaking, of much more recent origin. It originated after the cessation of the Temple cult, and is basically nothing else but a repetition of the *Shaḥarith Shemoneh Esreh* with inserts of sacrificial prayers, which have been emended or omitted in all modern prayerbooks. In the ancient sacrificial ritual, the *Musaph* Service was justified, for it was indeed possible to bring an additional sacrifice, a twofold sacrifice of animals for the altar. But to recite the same prayer twice, in rapid succession, that contradicts the very idea of prayer. Nevertheless, the esteem in which this prayer has historically been held would speak against the omission of *Musaph,* particularly in view of the *Musaph Kedushah.* It is also necessary by all means to retain the *Musaph* for Rosh Hashanah and Yom Kippur. It is, therefore, advisable to relegate the *Shaḥarith Shemoneh Esreh* to the silent devotion, in a brief German paraphrase, but to let the *Musaph Shemoneh Esreh* be recited in Hebrew by the cantor.—This suggestion was then adopted as the decision.

For the same reasons, the *Minḥah* Service, which, in essence, is yet another repetition of the *Shemoneh Esreh,* was omitted.

2. Service for weekdays. It was decided to arrange a service for weekdays, for every morning and evening, which was always to take place at the same time, at 7.00 p.m., and at 7.30 a.m. That service was to be worked out according to the same principles as the service for Sabbath and festivals.

The characteristic inserts were to be retained for the termination of the Sabbath, New Moon, *Ḥol Hamo'ed,* Days of Repentance, the morning of Hanukkah, the morning of Purim, and the morning of the Ninth of Ab. On the other hand, the services for the Eves of Purim, Hanukkah, and the Ninth of Ab, were to be worked out as especially solemn services.

3. For the time being, no decision was adopted concerning the service of the second days of the three historical festivals. . . . In the prayerbook, they were not to find direct expression. Should the second day, as it were, abolish itself, if nobody comes to synagogue on that day, then no further consideration is to be given to the second days in the worship service. If, however, it be established that the second day of the festivals is still rooted in the hearts of the participants in the new worship service, then, in later editions, the second day of the festivals is to be distinguished from the first day by means of special Torah portions, *Haftaroth,* and songs. In the meantime, however, before the appearance of a new edition, the service, in this case, is to be identical on the first and second days, and on the seventh and eighth days. An exception is to be made only in the case of *Simḥath Torah,* for which day a special festive liturgy is to be worked out, as well as a special Torah portion and *Haftarah.*[54]

4. Torah Readings. On all Sabbaths and festivals only *one* Torah is to be taken out of the Ark. Since, in most cases, the second Torah Scroll is meant for the reading of sacrificial regulations of the particular day, that decision is merely a logical consequence of the change in the sacrificial prayers. As far as the reading itself is concerned, every Sabbath, as far as possible in accordance with the current portion, a passage of the Torah, chosen by the rabbi, is to be read in Hebrew, followed by the rabbi's translation and explanation. The number of those to be called up depends upon the length of the passage to be read, but is to be, in all cases, a minimum of three. The Hebrew benediction of the one called up is to be retained—if only to compel everybody to learn Hebrew. For the same reason, the benediction and the Hebrew portion of the *bar-mitzvah* are to be retained.

More suitable and effective Torah portions are to be substituted for those which are unsuitable and less impressive.

The same applies to the *Haftaroth* on Sabbaths and festivals. Suitable passages should also be read from the third part of Holy Scripture, the Hagiographa.

It is left to me, as editor of the new prayerbook, to work out a third and fourth volume, containing domestic devotions, and the arrangement and translation of the *Haftaroth* (as well as prayers for special occasions).

The completely unjustifiable habit of many rabbis to quote the first and last verses of the *Haftarah* in Hebrew is to be abolished.

5. The Hebrew text. The Hebrew text of Geiger's prayerbook is to be retained throughout, except that

(a) in the *Kiddush* and in the Torah benediction, the phrase *mikkol ha'ammim,* omited by Geiger, should be restored. Geiger's version was accepted nowhere. It brings an irregularity into the service, particularly in the case of the Torah benediction. And it is objectively unjustified, since the idea of Election does not receive any nuance through that addition which it does not already have.[55]

(b) The *'Alenu* prayer is to be changed by the total omission of *shelo sam* etc., and not, as in Geiger's version, by a new, unaccustomed formulation.[56]

(c) For the Day of Atonement, some very few *piyutim* of beautiful content should be included, possibly from the Sepharadi rite, so that this historical element, too, should not be missing.

(d) If it is fitting for a prayerbook exclusively, or almost exclusively, in Hebrew to be opened from right to left, then the changed character of our new prayerbook should find its immediate expression by being printed from left to right.

6. I am given a completely free hand in the working out of the German translations, and of the new German prayers and songs. The following brief comments may indicate my intentions:

(a) The following perspectives guided me in the translation or paraphrase of the Hebrew prose passages: The German translations should absolutely make the impression of original prayers, since they are, after all, meant for those who do not know Hebrew. To achieve this purpose, it was not only necessary to avoid Hebrew constructions in German, but, in many cases, the whole tenor of the Hebrew prayer had to be given up. Therefore, the German paraphrase is largely to be regarded as an empathizing with, and a free rendering of, the original. Also, as far as the contents are concerned, there are, in several places, great deviations from the original. Not only all phrases and images, but also all thoughts which belong to a world of religious concepts to which we have become strangers, have been replaced by images and thoughts from the world of our religious concepts. As characteristic examples, compare the translation of the first two paragraphs of the *Shema* as well as the paraphrase of the weekday *Shemoneh Esreh*.

(b) In creating new prayers, my ideal was to introduce into

the liturgy, and win the right of domicile in the synagogue for, the new elements and problems arising out of the new conditions and circumstances, the new moods and sentiments, cares and hopes, which have found no expression in the old prayerbook and *Maḥzor*. I have tried to give to those prayers all the religious sincerity and solemn mood, all the verve and artistic expression, of which I was capable—in order to kindle through them a new religious enthusiasm, and to warm, for the holy religion of the fathers, the hearts of those who have become estranged from it. That I have given my best, I may, without false modesty, confess here. How far I have fallen behind my own ideal, that I myself know best. The only German prayer which is not original is the classical prayer for Friday night by M. Joël-Breslau.

(c) In the translation of the poetical passages, I have often wavered as to whether I should prefer the free or the metrical form, the use of rhythm and rhyme or the confinement to an exalted style. In most cases, I have attempted both kinds of rendition, and I have given preference to that kind which, in the given case, appeared to me to be the more suitable one. Passages of heavy thought, like Psalms 90 and 104, do not tolerate confinement by the armour of rhyme and rhythm. Easier passages might stand to gain by a pleasant metrical form. To be quite frank, I did not so much follow definite principles and rules as my own poetic sentiment and feeling for form. . . .

If the Hamburg Temple could claim, with historical justification, to have been the "mother synagogue" of Progressive Judaism, it must nevertheless be recognized that the liturgy of the Hamburg Temple had not been created *ex nihilo*. The services held in Berlin, in the private houses of Jacobson and Beer, had served as a kind of laboratory for what was later to take place in Hamburg. But even the Berlin services were only an extension of something Israel Jacobson had initiated some years before his move to Berlin, in the temple of the school he had founded in Seesen. There, in 1810, Jacobson had dedicated the temple on the school grounds, to the accompaniment of organ music, the singing of German chorales, the ringing of the local church bells, and the introduction of German prayers and the German sermon.[57] Yet it was not until one hundred years later that the liturgy of the Temple of the Jacobson School in Seesen was edited and printed. Entitled *Beth*

Ya'aqobh—Prayers for the Worship Service in the "Temple" of the Jacobson School in Seesen in the Harz, it was edited by A. Strauss, one of the teachers of the school, and published in Seesen, in 1911.[58] Within 205 pages, that prayerbook contains the services for the entire year, including a number of chorales. It has to be pointed out, however, that the prayers to be recited in Hebrew, and there are many of them, are not accompanied by a German translation, German being reserved for the prayers recited in that language. By far the greater part of the Friday night service, for example, is in Hebrew.

As the Preface, about to be reproduced, indicates, for many years prior to 1911 the Hamburg Temple Prayerbook was used at the Seesen Temple. Yet the first edition of that ritual was not published before 1819, and the Seesen Temple was opened in 1810. We have not been able to discover a liturgy, prior to 1911, which was specifically published for the Seesen services. We do not doubt, therefore, that Jacobson himself used the traditional prayerbook for his services at the school Temple, or, rather, that he made a judicious selection from it. This he supplemented by the use of German chorales and hymns, having published such a hymnal in 1810.[59] Interestingly enough, Jacobson's hymnal also included Hebrew translations of German hymns, set to music which was printed from right to left.[60]

25) PREFACE TO PRAYERBOOK OF THE "TEMPLE" AT THE JACOBSON SCHOOL, 1911.

When Israel Jacobson introduced the innovations into the worship service of the synagogue of his school foundation—the "Jacobstempel" which is now one hundred years old—he was undoubtedly thinking about a contemporary reformation of the cult as such, hoping that the example of Seesen would have a beneficial influence upon other Jewish congregations. Still, the service was essentially suited to the needs of youth, for whom that Temple was primarily intended. It was a "youth service" which was instituted here—perhaps for the first time in a Jewish House of God. As such, it has, in the course of time, acquired fixed forms which have now, as it were, become sanctified through a venerable tradition.

The selection of Hebrew and German prayers, made by Herr A. Strauss for the present prayerbook, with a view to our order of service, is based upon the last two editions of the prayerbook of the Hamburg Temple Congregation. The Hamburg Temple Congregation owes its origin to the personal suggestions of Israel Jacobson. Moreover, a former alumnus of the Jacobson School, who later became its director, Dr. Immanuel Wohlwill, had been, before his call to Seesen, in 1838, a member of the directorate of the above-mentioned congregation. He helped to develop it along the Reform ideas of Jacobson. The form of our worship service may primarily be traced back to Wohlwill. It is thus clear why our ritual is, in so many respects, similar to that of Hamburg.

If we now have, nevertheless, decided to give up the Hamburg Prayerbook, which for many years was in the hands of our pupils, it is because we have felt the need for the compilation of those prayers and hymns which correspond to our customary selection, and which meet the needs of our "youth service."

I herewith express my thanks to the honorable Hamburg Temple Congregation for kindly giving us permission to take such German prayers from the Hamburg Prayerbook as we desired. Likewise, I want to mention with gratitude that Herr Strauss was supported by the cooperation of the colleagues Stern and Germer. Herr Stern has especially compiled the chorales, which are almost exclusively translations of the Psalms, and Herr Germer has provided the settings for, or composed, the corresponding tunes—in part traditional, and in part new.

For the present, we have refrained from printing the music.

Dr. N. Friedland
Director of the Jacobson School

Seesen in the Harz, January 1911

Quite different from the development of liturgical reform on the European continent, with its general adherence to the *pattern* of traditional Jewish liturgy even when departing from it in theological nuance, was the liturgy of the Liberal Jewish Synagogue in London—particularly after it began to be edited by the Lithuanian-born and American-trained Rabbi Israel I. Mattuck (1883–1954), who assumed the spiritual leadership of that congregation in 1912. Some of the details of that liturgy have been discussed elsewhere in this book.[61] Here we shall confine ourselves to Volume I of the *Liberal Jewish Prayer Book,* containing the services for weekdays and Sabbath, and edited by Mattuck in 1926. Among other services and prayers, this volume contains fifteen different services for the Sabbath, some of which, with the omission of some specific Sabbath prayers, could be used on weekdays as well. (In the 1937 edition of that prayerbook, the number of those services was increased to twenty-two!) Variety, therefore, is seen to be one of the major characteristics of that liturgy, a variety achieved not only by the use of different materials for different services, but also by arbitrarily changing the sequence of such traditional prayers as have been retained. No service contains the entire Seven Benedictions of the Sabbath, but individual components of it appear here and there, but hardly ever in their traditional sequence. Thus, the Second Service has the fourth of the Seven Benedictions followed by the third.[62] The Ninth Service *begins* with an English version of the *'Alenu,* the traditional concluding prayer.[63] The other characteristics of this prayerbook are spelled out in the Preface, from which we now quote excerpts.

26) PREFACE TO LONDON LIBERAL JEWISH PRAYER BOOK, 1926. (Excerpts.)

In form and content the services and prayers in this book show the ideas of Liberal Judaism. Liberal Judaism in its teaching aims to combine the permanent spiritual values in the Jewish Tradition with modern thought, and to express the spiritual and moral direction of Judaism in a way particularly suitable to the needs of modern Jewish life; this Prayer Book is an attempt to make Jewish public worship conform with this aim. The traditional and the new are combined, forming, we hope, in the case of each service, a unity which shall satisfy the historic feeling and the religious thought of the modern Jewish consciousness.

The new prayers often express more especially the distinctive ideas of Liberal Judaism; and only those traditional prayers have been retained which in themselves or by reinterpretation express ideas which we believe or desires which we feel. When traditional prayers are used, the Hebrew of the original is most often printed with an English paraphrase, which is sometimes like a translation, deviating from literalness only for the sake of ease in reading; at other times, however, the English paraphrases also the meaning of the original, interpreting it so as to accord with our beliefs. In other words, we have here and there read a new meaning into an old prayer, one, however, not unrelated to its original meaning. For some reasons, this procedure is unsatisfactory, it is open to misunderstanding; but it has been adopted only with prayers which are so old that they could not be excluded from Jewish services. . . .

Besides the prayers from the Traditional Services, the historic element in this Prayer Book is further represented by selections from the Bible, Apocrypha, Talmud, and later Jewish writings, especially the Mediaeval Jewish poets. . . .

The use of the Apocrypha, if it needs justification, must find it in the character and quality of the selections used. They sometimes contain ideas which are expressed in no other section of ancient Jewish literature with the same explicitness, and in language that has an attractive quality of its own. Being Jewish in their origin, and showing in many places, we believe, the quality of inspiration, they deserve to be rescued from their long neglect by the Synagogue. ...

A few of the modern prayers have been drawn from non-Jewish sources, and the poems in the Supplement to Vol. I, which are intended for reading as parts of the Services, are mostly by non-Jewish writers.[64] In the second volume there is only one such selection—Shakespeare's Sonnet on the Soul, on page 272. These were all inserted because they were felt to express inspiringly much of our thought and aspiration in a way acceptable to all theists. Poetry, like music, has a place of special value in public worship and in individual prayer. There are, however, very few Jewish poems which in their English translation can be placed among the best poetry with the strongest appeal to the English-speaking Jew; so that most of the poetry in this book comes from non-Jewish writers, who, with a few exceptions, are among the greatest English poets. And the best poetry speaks the language of universal religion. If the use of appropriate non-Jewish writings in a Jewish Prayer Book requires justification other than their intrinsic merit, it would be in the belief which Liberal Jews hold, that Divine inspiration is universal, that, in the words of the prayer on page 42, God inspired the great and good among all the families of the earth; so that their words can help us when we pray.

In form, the Services follow, for the most part, the Traditional Services;[65] especially those for the Holy Days, except that the Musaph (the additional service on the mornings of these days) has been omitted. Only the Day of Atonement has it. This part of the service was so closely associated with the sacrificial system that most Reform and Liberal Jewish congregations have omitted it; and we have followed the general example. ...

A few of the Services for Sabbaths and weekdays do not follow the Traditional form; this is especially the case in Service 12—which has a universalistic character. It was felt that there are times when a Service of this sort has a particular value. In all the Services, however, the Jewish character of the worship is evident. The ideas are always Jewish, and the form is nearly always like that in the Traditional Liturgy. Though there are also prayers which are just theistic, we believe that they add to the Jewish quality of the Services, they do not detract from it; showing that Judaism stands for the teaching of a pure and universal theism.

There are a number of Services for the Sabbaths (some of them can be used at other times), so that no one need be used too often. Prayers are inclined to lose their meaning and inspiring power through frequent repetition. Moreover, variety in the character of the Services held each week seemed desirable to bring out the variety in religious thought.

A word is necessary about the use of Hebrew. Though in the services of the Liberal Jewish Synagogue little Hebrew is used, many of the Traditional prayers have been printed with their Hebrew, so that others who use the Prayer Book could be free to have more or less Hebrew; since, in our view, the language of prayer does not hold any intrinsic merit or power, but draws its value from its appeal to those who pray. This Prayer Book is primarily issued for Jews whose native tongue is English, and who, therefore, wish to say their Jewish prayers in that language.

The distinctive features of this Prayer Book, it will be seen, are related to the principle that present needs have a place in religious teaching and worship. ...

ISRAEL I. MATTUCK

London, October, 1925

As has been noted, Mattuck's prayerbook was published in a revised and enlarged edition in 1937. That second edition has been reprinted in 1952 and in 1957 under the imprint of the Union of Liberal and Progressive Synagogues. It should be pointed out that, within recent years, the ministers of the Union of Liberal and Progressive Synagogues have subjected Mattuck's prayerbook to a thoroughgoing revision, and an altogether new edition of the *Liberal Jewish Prayer Book* is scheduled for publication in 1967. From an experimental edition of the Sabbath services,[66] and from galley proofs graciously made available to this writer, it is evident that the new prayerbook will not depart from Mattuck's theological position. In fact, it is more consistent in revising the Hebrew text of the prayerbook according to Reform principles than Mattuck had been. But it also increases the amount of Hebrew in the prayerbook. Above all, however, while providing a certain amount of variety, it completely departs from Mattucks' arbitrary re-arrangement of the sequence of the prayers, and it adjusts the liturgy of British Liberal Judaism to the pattern of the traditional Jewish prayerbook.

While Mattuck's prayerbook represented a conscious departure from the Jewish liturgical tradition, the very opposite tendency was in evidence, at that time, in German Liberal Judaism. In that country, liturgical experimentation had been going on for more than a hundred years. Many different prayerbooks had been published, based on a variety of outlooks and approaches. The need had long been felt and expressed for a prayerbook which could be used by all German congregations who, in one way or another, had introduced departures from the Orthodox ritual. But it was not until 1929 that such a common prayerbook was published "by order of the Committee on Liberal Worship of the Prussian Union of Jewish Congregations," the prayerbook known as the *Einheitsgebetbuch* ("Union Prayer Book")—although its title page simply called it *Prayerbook for the Whole Year* (*Gebetbuch für das ganze Jahr*). It appeared in two volumes, Volume I containing the services for weekdays, Sabbath and festivals; and Volume II containing the services for the High Holy Days.

The editors of the *Einheitsgebetbuch* were Caesar Seligmann, who has already been mentioned in connection with his own edition of the prayerbook in 1910, Ismar Elbogen (1874–1943), the world-renowned authority on Jewish liturgy and professor at the Liberal rabbinical seminary in Berlin,[67] and the Breslau rabbi, Hermann Vogelstein, a son of the editor of the Westphalian prayerbook of 1894, Heinemann Vogelstein.[68] The prayerbook has been edited in complete accord with Reform principles, yet it tries as much as possible to approximate, in its new Hebrew versions, the very sound and construction of the words which have been displaced. All services are provided with complete Hebrew and German texts, to enable each congregation to select its own proportion of either language. There is, however, an appendix containing additional German prayers (for recitation by the rabbis) and German anthems and hymns.

Political circumstances brought German Jewish life to an end some ten years after the appearance of the *Einheitsgebetbuch*. The latter is, therefore, the last great monument to the striving for Reform, and the liturgical creativity of German Judaism. The Preface to this prayerbook, surveying more than a hundred years of liturgical development from the vantage point of final unification, deserves to be quoted here in full.

27) PREFACE TO THE "EINHEITSGEBETBUCH," 1929.

> This prayerbook, published by order of the Committee on Liberal Worship of the Prussian Union of Jewish Congregations, has its history. For a long time, there have been complaints that nearly every single one of the larger Jewish congregations of Germany has its own prayerbook, even if the latter differs from others in non-essential aspects only. Those prayerbooks were regarded by their own editors as something temporary, as a kind of necessary transition. Abraham Geiger wrote in 1869: "The colorful multiplicity is liable yet to increase for a while. But this must not lead us astray, nor must it fill us with the fear of schism. Slowly, a mutual rapprochement will again come

about . . ., and a general agreement will increasingly take place." Thirty years later, the preface to the Nuremberg Prayerbook (1897) bemoans the "colorful multiplicity of the prayer rites in the German congregations of a progressive tendency." It concludes: "There is an urgent need for the individualism in this sacred area finally to come to an end, for a movement from the present diversity to unity. It is to be hoped that the time is no longer far away when all the congregations of Germany, which glory in the same liberal principles, will rejoice in a common prayerbook and in a common worship service."

The first attempts at a unification of the worship of those congregations which had departed from the Orthodox liturgy go back to the Rabbinical Conferences of 1844–1846. The preparatory work, however, did not exceed the plan which the chairman of the prayerbook revision commission, Leopold Stein, submitted to the Rabbinical Conference in Breslau. After this failure, he tried, in the fifties, to bring about some unification at least for the South-West of Germany, with the result that the Conferences of Rabbis in Wiesbaden, Giessen, and Frankfort o. M. (1854–1856) created the foundation of the "Prayerbook for Israelite Congregations," edited by Leopold Stein. Around the same time (1854), Abraham Geiger had published, in Breslau, his new prayerbook, which, in a number of details, he later revised in Frankfort and in Berlin. Already before that time, new prayerbooks had appeared in Hamburg, Vienna, Prague, Berlin (that of the *Reformgemeinde*), Aachen, and Coblenz. Mannheim, Stuttgart, Brunswick, Berlin, Leipzig, Munich, Augsburg, Nuremberg, Glogau, and other places followed. At the Conference of Rabbis in Cassel,[69] too, where the main topic of debate was the question of worship, the difficulties involved in unification proved to be too great. Again, the result was a referral to committee. The problem was brought no closer to its solution by the two Synods of Leipzig and Augsburg, in 1869 and 1871. Resigned, M. Joël admitted, at the 1887 Conference of Rabbis in Breslau, that there was no longer any difference of opinion about the principal questions, and that the basic prayers were the same everywhere. "The desire for a common prayerbook is perhaps justified."

A first attempt to create a unified prayerbook for a limited area was made by the Union of Synagogue Congregations of Westphalia. Commissioned by that Union, Rabbi Heinemann Vogelstein (Stettin) edited a prayerbook, which, following in the main the pattern of the new prayerbooks of Berlin, Breslau and Frankfort, appeared in the years 1894/96.

An attempt on a large scale to bring the unified prayerbook to realization was made, in 1897, by a member of the Supreme Council of the Israelites in Baden, Dr. David Mayer, in Karlsruhe. Attaching the plan for a unified prayerbook, he invited the larger congregations of Germany to a common settlement of the prayerbook problem. The first volume of this prayerbook appeared in 1905. Its sequel and its introduction (in Baden)[70] came to grief on account of the opposition of the Orthodox and the Zionists. On the other hand, the united Reform congregations of North America were able to create, in 1894, a unified prayerbook, the Union Prayer Book, which has appeared in several revised editions, and which has been introduced in more than three hundred congregations. It represents one of the most important religious possessions of American Jewry.

In Germany, the question of a unified prayerbook became topical again when the economic straits of the post-War period made it impossible for the congregations to reprint their out-of-print prayerbooks. The prayerbook commission, elected by the Union for Liberal Judaism, decided, in 1922, to take, as the basis for the new unified prayerbook which was to be created, the Hebrew text of Geiger's Prayerbook, which—to be sure, in different versions—had been adopted by the large congregations of Berlin, Breslau, Frankfort o. M., and (in Vogelstein's version) in the Westphalian congregations. In order to take into account the individual needs of the various congregations and rabbis, it was decided to remove from the body of the prayerbook all the prayers and liturgies[71] recited by the rabbi, and to publish them either in a special manual or as an appendix. By means of particular rubrics and specific references, ways were to be found of doing justice to the various needs of the congregations.

But this commission, too, proved to be too large and too diversified. That is why, at the main assembly of Liberal Rabbis in Cologne, in 1925, Rabbi C. Seligmann (of Frankfort o. M.) voiced the view that, at first, the large congregations of Berlin, Breslau and Frankfort should find their way to the creation of a common liturgy. This suggestion, supported by Vogelstein (Breslau) and Baeck (Berlin), led to the cooperation of those three congregations. For this purpose, Professor Elbogen, at first commissioned by the Berlin congregation, worked out an elaborate memoir, which, together with a second memoir by Seligmann, became the basis of further work.

After the Committee on Liberal Worship of the Prussian Union of Jewish Congregations was constituted in October 1926, that committee on worship, with the agreement of the previous commission and of those who commissioned it, undertook the further preparation of the unified prayerbook, and charged with it a smaller working committee, consisting of Seligmann, Elbogen and Vogelstein. The overall revision and the German translation were undertaken by Seligmann, the revision of the Hebrew text by Elbogen, and Vogelstein worked together with both of them. In numerous oral consultations, and in written discussions, both questions of principle and of detail were dealt with by these three men in common. Later, famous experts were co-opted, at first for consultation and review of the manuscript, and later also for the galley proofs. In gratitude and in grief we remember the devoted cooperation of Director Dr. Michael Holzmann, whose last worry, before his passing, had to do with the correction of the proofs of this Preface.

Fundamentally new, in conscious departure from the Liberal prayerbooks of the nineteenth century, is the *translation* of the prayers. It aims at being as literal as possible, but also strives to do justice to the different syntax and spirit of the German language as well as to the poetic beauty of the prayers. In this way, the German text, also on its own, should be suitable for prayer.

Since we wanted to assure a wide distribution for the prayerbook, and since the majority of the congregations for whom it is intended desire to maintain their individuality, there could not be any far-reaching innovations in the Hebrew text. Nevertheless, this part, too, has, in many instances, been changed. It is marked by abbreviations as well as by enlargements, by the restoration of old texts, and by the substitution, for unsuitable portions, of those which appeared to be more suitable. The abbreviations are, above all, those based on the principle of avoiding the repetition of one and the same prayer during the same worship service, e.g., *Kaddish, Ashré, Kedushah* (omitted in *hame-ir la-aretz* and in *ubha letziyon,* because it is found in the *Tephillah*). The same applies to the introductory passages of the weekday morning service. The hymn *Yigdal,* which made its appearance in the Polish prayerbook as late as the end of the sixteenth century, has been retained for (Sabbath and) festivals only. The benedictions after *elohai neshamah,* which, according to the provision of the Talmud, are to be recited only on appropriate occasions, have been reduced in number. The congregations are at liberty to relegate to the realm of domestic devotion the first part of the weekday service, up to *barukh she-amar,* and to begin their service with *barukh she-amar*. The *pesuqé dezimra* (Psalms) have been distributed over the various days of the week (or Sabbaths and festivals). *Taḥanun,* originally a *silent* outpouring of the heart, without a fixed form, has been reduced to Psalm 6 with short introductory and concluding formulae. Disturbing extravagances in expression, and the heaping up of synonyms—such as in *ahabhah rabbah, emeth weyatzibh, ya'aleh weyabho,* and also in *nishmath*—have been removed. Among other things, the *Hosha'noth,* too, were largely abbreviated, and, in addition, they have been moved from their unsuitable position at the end of the service to the more suitable position before the taking out of the Torah, or at the beginning of the taking out of the Torah. These examples should illustrate the aim of the abbreviations.

By way of enlargements, we have to mention, above all, a new solemn service for the Eve of Hanukkah, Purim, and the Ninth of Ab, together with the Hebrew and German texts of Esther and Lamentations. Furthermore, we have newly included the most beautiful Psalms, and, particularly for the High Holy Days, several items of the Sepharadi rite. We also recommend to the congregations the introduction of a new Hebrew version of *Kol Nidré,* fitted to the traditional tune and, in part, paralleling the old wording—in addition to the hymns, Psalm 130, and "O Day of God," used by the large congregations.

Older texts have also been restored, as in the weekday *Tephillah,* to the extent to which there were no basic dogmatic reservations, in the confession of sins and the *Abhinu Malkenu* prayer of the High Holy Days, and in many of the alphabetical *piyutim* which have been included.

The Torah and Prophetic portions have been radically revised. In place of the monotonous selections, or of those with little religious contents, new portions have been chosen. For the second day of Passover, the report in Chronicles about Hezekiah's Passover observance has been chosen instead of the Prophetic portion. For the second day of Pentecost, we have adopted the repetition of the Decalogue in Deuteronomy. For the first day of New Year, we offer the congregations a choice between the traditional Torah portion from Genesis, describing the expulsion of Hagar, and the doubtlessly more suitable reading of *Attem Nitzabhim* in Deuteronomy.

The unique character of this new prayerbook, which is not meant for *one* congregation and its needs alone, but for all congregations, made it necessary, to begin with, in the Hebrew part, to preserve a certain freedom. Already Geiger's Prayerbook took into consideration the variations between the South German and the North German *minhag*. The old *Siddur* and *Maḥzor,* too, contain, in many places, the note that this or that prayer is said in many congregations, or that it is omitted, or room is left for two or more possibilities. In this way, too, the extensive rubrics of our prayerbook, carefully noted in the detailed index, are meant to give the congregations an opportunity of conducting their services according to their local traditions and needs, and to retain or to omit this or that prayer. In order to give the congregations the widest possible freedom in the musical arrangement of their services, we have throughout omitted the headings, "Reader" and "Congregation."

This freedom in unity has a heightened meaning for those congregations in which the service includes, in addition to Hebrew, a greater amount of the vernacular. The new way of arranging the contents offers the possibility of either conducting the service entirely in Hebrew or of combining it, to a certain extent, with German prayers and hymns. For this reason, and in order not to compel rabbi and congregation, through fixed German prayers, all the German prayers, to be spoken by the rabbi or read as silent devotion by the congregation, were relegated to the appendix—together with the songs. The only exception is that of the *'Abhodah* on Yom Kippur, where German and Hebrew alternate. But even here, as is stressed in the rubric at the beginning, congregations and functionaries are free either to abbreviate or to use a different German text.

The more extensive German prayers and meditations in the appendix have the function of replacing the sermon in congregations where no sermons are being preached.

In order to recognize the true character of the prayerbook, one must not be influenced by a first impression of the purely Hebrew part. Instead, the German appendix—particularly with the help of the index—must be taken into consideration. It offers the congregations wide possibilities for individual arrangements of the services also with regard to the use of German prayers.

The prayers and hymns of the appendix are, in part, a selection of the passages which seemed to be the most suitable ones in the existing prayerbooks and devotional manuals. In part they are also newly composed prayers and hymns, furnished particularly by Gottschalk (Frankfort), Schönberger (Aachen), Wilde (Magdeburg), and Leonie Meyerhof-Hildeck (Frankfort o. M.)—in addition to those furnished by Seligmann, who was editor-in-chief. The editors know best that it is this part which is in greatest need of improvement. An invitation, addressed to outstanding Jewish poets, asking them to furnish contributions, has remained without any result worth mentioning. Perhaps the completed prayerbook will provide some with the incentive to create, which would be of benefit to a later edition.

It will certainly be an innovation welcomed by many that the prayers are reprinted for every single service. The only exception is that of the *Simḥath Torah* celebration, which is printed immediately preceding the relevant *Shaḥarit* Service of the festivals. Otherwise, there is practically no need at all to leaf through the prayerbook, laboriously seeking the parts of the service which belong together. . . .

A school edition of the prayerbook is scheduled to appear in the near future. It is meant to remove the drawbacks which have hitherto resulted from the use, in our schools, of the old text from which the prayer texts adopted by our synagogues had departed. Furthermore, the publication of a third volume is contemplated, which is meant to include all of the domestic devotions.

The Jewish worship service is far simpler than the size of the prayerbook would lead one to assume. The main prayers are, with minor deviations, the same throughout the year. We have three daily periods of prayer: *Shaḥarith* (the morning prayer), *Minḥah* (the afternoon prayer), *'Arebhith* or *Ma'aribh* (the evening prayer). To this is added the *Musaph* (additional prayer) on Sabbaths, festivals and New Moon, and *Ne'ilah* (concluding prayer) on the Day of Atonement, *Shaḥarith* and *'Arebhith,* morning and evening service, contain the *Shema Yisrael;* all services include the *Tephillah*. The *Shema,* named after its opening word, contains Israel's ancient confession of faith. It is surrounded by hymns which express gratitude for the constant change of day and night, for the revelation given to Israel, and for Israel's redemption from the yoke of Egyptian slavery. The *Tephillah* for weekdays is the prayer of the Eighteen Benedictions (*Shemoneh Esreh*). In essence, it is a petitionary prayer, but the basic form of Jewish prayer is the hymn. That is why this prayer, too, is not only introduced by hymns, but completely made up of them. On Sabbaths and festivals, the *Tephillah* is reduced to seven sections, in such a way that the beginning and the end remain the same, but that the intermediary petitionary prayers are replaced by a single one, *Kedushath Hayom,* the request for the proper consecration of the solemn day. An exception is the *Musaph* of New Year, which contains nine sections, because, on that day, the fundamental ideas of religion are voiced: the praise of God as Lord, Judge, and Redeemer of the world. Unique to the Day of Atonement is the confession of sins. But that adjoins the *Tephillah,* and does not constitute an enlargement of it.

Living piety, throughout the ages, has made additions to this kernel of the prayers, *Shema* and *Tephillah*. Thus, on all days of the year, the *Shema* is preceded by Psalms and introductory morning prayers. The *Tephillah* is followed, on weekdays, by *Taḥanunim* (silent and free prayers for the forgiveness of sins), and, on New Moon, Hanukkah, and the Pilgrim Festivals, by the *Hallel* Psalms. The religious soul has been inexhaustible in creating new poetry for use in worship. Such poems have brought variety and life to the sanctified tradition, and have given the prayerbook its rich contents.

The Jewish worship service, which arose out of the classical religion of the Prophets, is one of Judaism's most significant creations in world history. Founded as a purely spiritual "service of the heart," it spread, already in antiquity, through the greater part of the inhabited world, and it was then carried into the entire world by Israel's daughter religions. Its contents, too, confession of faith, petition and instruction, have been adopted together with their form. The institution of Torah and Prophetic readings as the central part of Sabbath and festival worship—followed, already in most ancient times, by an exposition of the Scriptures—is responsible for making the Bible the common property of educated mankind.

The stock of the prayers is very ancient, composed by the classical religionists, and, therefore, powerful to this day to lend expression to that which moves the heart of those who are children of quite a different age and world. The genius of the Synagogue has never rested; one generation after another has been striving to renew devotion and piety. Every generation has revived the ancient heritage through the expressions of its own time. This prayerbook, too, is presented to the Jewish public as an expression of the faith and the hope, of the humility and the gratitude of *our* age. May it fulfil its mission of stimulating Jewish piety and faithfulness!

Seligmann, Elbogen, Vogelstein

Berlin, Breslau, Frankfort o. M., April 1929

EIGHT

The Eighteen Benedictions

WE HAVE NOTED[1] THAT, WHEN THE ANCIENT RABBIS SPOKE OF "THE Prayer" *par excellence,* they had in mind the so-called Eighteen (really, nineteen) Benedictions. That rubric, together with "The *Shema* and its Blessings," formed the basic component of the original statutory service. With the two exceptions of the Berlin *Reformgemeinde* (Holdheim's congregation) and of the Liberal Jewish Synagogue in London (which used the prayerbook edited by Israel Mattuck), Progressive Judaism in Europe maintained the structure and, to a considerable extent, also the form of the traditional rubrics of the traditional Jewish liturgy —including those of the Eighteen Benedictions. However, in varying degrees, the Liberal and Reform liturgies modified the wording of the traditional prayers in those instances where the traditional formulation seemed to contradict the outlook of Liberal or Reform Judaism.

Chief among the latter are Benediction 10 (the "ingathering of the exiles"), Benediction 11 (prayer for the restoration of a Jewish judicature), Benediction 12 (really a malediction against slanderers and the wicked, originally directed against the Judaeo-Christians and the Roman oppressors), Benediction 14 (for the rebuilding of Jerusalem), Benediction 15 (for the messianic scion of the Davidic dynasty), and Benediction 17 (for the restoration of the sacrificial service.)

In comparison to the six Benedictions mentioned above, the remaining thirteen Benedictions either presented no problems at all, or only problems of a minor character. For example, in Benediction 8, some of the prayerbooks read "who healest the sick," instead of "who healest the sick of Thy people Israel." Again, in Benediction 16, some of the prayerbooks prefer "for Thou hearest the prayer of every mouth" to "for Thou hearest the prayer of Thy people Israel." In both instances, there is an attempt at "universalizing" the traditional prayer, an attempt, however, which is by no means made by all the rituals under consideration.

A few of the prayerbooks also undertook to correct the reference to the Hasmonean Mattathias, in the Hanukkah insert in Benediction 18.[2] The traditional text refers to him as a High Priest. In the light of historical research, some reformed versions of the liturgy speak of him as but an ordinary priest. Similarly, there was some unhappiness with the reference to Haman's end on the gallows, in the insert for Purim;[3] and this was either glossed over in a vernacular paraphrase, or changed in the Hebrew text itself.

In Benediction 1, most rituals retain the word *go-el* (redeemer) in the Hebrew text, and only very few substitute the word *ge-ullah* (redemption).[4] Yet, in the translation, the overwhelming number of the rituals prefer "redemption" to "redeemer." Of the prayerbooks considered here, only the following have a reference to the "redeemer" in their translation: *Göteborg, 1858;*[5] *Stein, 1860; Nuremberg, 1874; Stockholm, 1881; Einheitsgebetbuch, 1929.* The Berlin prayerbook of 1881 (and subsequent editions) solves the problem by making the word *go-el* refer to God Himself, and translates the relevant phrase as follows: "Thou rememberest the piety of the fathers, and remainest their gracious redeemer for all time, for the sake of Thy Name."

As far as the theme of the Resurrection, in Benediction 2, is concerned, the European Liberals and Reformers did not share the strong feelings of their American brethren. (The latter, having made the denial of the Resurrection practically an article of faith, consistently changed the Hebrew text and translated accordingly.) Not a single one of the rituals under consideration here found it necessary to change the Hebrew text, although many of them (but not all!) substituted the concept of Immortality in their vernacular translation or paraphrase. Even Mattuck, who, in his *Liberal Jewish Prayer Book* of 1926, never included the various components of the Eighteen Benedictions in their proper sequence, gave the unchanged Hebrew text of Benediction 2 whenever he included that Benediction at some point of his services. The English paraphrase speaks of "the hope of immortality," but the Hebrew text dealt with the Resurrection. In his Preface, Mattuck explained why he permitted that discrepancy: "We have here and there read a new meaning into an old prayer, one, however, not unrelated to its original meaning. For some reasons, this procedure is unsatisfactory, it is open to misunderstanding; but it has been adopted only with prayers which are so old that they could not be excluded from Jewish services."[6] That rationale was undoubtedly operative in all the other prayerbooks which, in any case, reflected a position not nearly as radical as that of Mattuck. It remains to be pointed out, however, that the 1967 prayerbook of the Union of Liberal and Progressive Synagogues, which is meant to take the place of the Mattuck ritual, and which represents a pronounced attempt to revert to the traditional structure of Jewish prayer, does depart from Mattuck's policy in this particular instance, and removes the references to the Resurrection from the Hebrew text.

Benediction 3 (the Holiness of God) presented no problem in the version meant for silent devotion.[7] On the other hand, some of the prayerbooks were disturbed by the angelology in the public (and responsive) recitation of the Sanctification. They either toned down that angelology, or eliminated it altogether. At the same time, there are rituals which substitute German texts for the connecting links between the Hebrew responses; and, in those German texts, the "angelic choirs" make their re-appearance.[8]

But, as we have noted, the major departures from the traditional text occur in Benedictions 10, 11, 14, 15, and 17. It is to a consideration of those Benedictions that we shall now address ourselves. To enhance the usefulness of that consideration, we give the reformed Hebrew versions in their original. The translations we append are our translations from the Hebrew, and not necessarily the translations or paraphrases of the Hebrew texts printed in the prayerbooks under consideration.

BENEDICTION 10.

Traditional Ashkenazi Version:

תקע בשופר גדול לחרותנו ושא נס לקבץ גליותינו וקבצנו יחד
מארבע כנפות הארץ. ברוך אתה יי מקבץ נדחי עמו ישראל:

Sound the great shofar *for our freedom, and lift up the banner to gather in our exiles, and assemble us together from the four corners of the earth. Praised art Thou, O Lord, who gatherest the dispersed of Thy people Israel.*

Hamburg, 1819: No weekday service.

Hamburg, 1841: German paraphrase of Intermediate Benedictions only.
Sound the call of freedom, and lift up the banner of freedom for all who groan in slavery. Break the yoke, O God, from upon our shoulders wherever it still rests heavily upon us. Praised art Thou, O God, who truly carest for the outcasts of Thy people Israel.

West London Synagogue, 1841: Traditional Sepharadi text, Hebrew and English.

Kirchenrat Maier, 1848: German paraphrase only.
Let the great horn sound for our freedom, and lift up the banner for our redemption. And remove from us, and from all Israel, all oppression and shame, all distress and servitude. Praised art Thou, O Lord, who carest for the outcasts of Israel.

Geiger, 1854:
תקע בשופר גדול לחרותנו והושע יי את-עמך את שארית ישראל בארבע כנפות הארץ. ברוך אתה יי מושיע שארית עמו ישראל:
Sound the great shofar *for our freedom, and save, O Lord, Thy people, the remnant of Israel, in the four corners of the earth. Praised art Thou, O Lord, who savest the remnant of Thy people Israel.*

Göteborg, 1858:
תקע בשופר גדול לחרותנו והושע יי את-עמך ישראל בארבע כנפות הארץ. ברוך אתה יי מושיע עמו ישראל:
Sound the great shofar *for our freedom, and save, O Lord, Thy people Israel in the four corners of the earth. Praised art Thou, O Lord, who savest Thy people Israel.*

Stein, 1860: No weekday service.

Aub (Berlin), 1866:
תקע בשופר גדול לחרותנו ושא נס להושיענו. וקבצנו יחד אליך בארבע כנפות הארץ. ברוך אתה יי מקבץ לשמו שארית עמו ישראל:
Sound the great shofar *for our freedom, and lift up the banner to save us. And gather us together unto Thee in the four corners of the earth. Praised art Thou, O Lord, who gatherest unto Thy Name the remnant of Thy people Israel.*

Hamburg, 1868: Traditional Hebrew text; German based on Hamburg 1841 edition.

Geiger, 1870: As in Geiger's 1854 edition, but omitting, both in Hebrew and in German, "in the four corners of the earth."

Joël, 1872: Traditional Hebrew text given in small print and without translation. In large print:

תקע בשופר גדול לחרותנו וקול דרור וישועה ישמע באהלינו.
ברוך אתה יי משמיע ישועה לשארית ישראל:

Sound the great shofar *for our freedom, and may the sound of liberty and salvation be heard in our tents. Praised art Thou, O Lord, who proclaimest salvation to the remnant of Israel.*

Nuremberg, 1874:

תקע בשופר גדול לחרותנו ושא נס לקבץ גליותינו.
ברוך אתה יי מקבץ נדחי עמו ישראל:

Sound the great shofar *for our freedom, and lift up the banner to gather in our exiles. Praised art Thou, O Lord, who gatherest the dispersed of Thy people Israel.*

Leipzig, 1876: Traditional Hebrew text given in small print and without translation. In large print:

תקע בשופר גדול לחרות כל-העשוקים ושא נס
למיחלים לגאולתך וקול דרור ישמע בארבע כנפות הארץ.
ברוך אתה יי קורא דרור לשבויי כל-הארץ:

Sound the great shofar *for the freedom of all who are oppressed, and lift up the banner for those who hope for Thy redemption; and may the sound of liberty be heard in the four corners of the earth. Praised art Thou, O Lord, who proclaimest liberty to the captives of the whole earth.*

Berlin, 1881:

תקע בשופר גדול לחרותנו ושא נס להושיענו בארבע כנפות
הארץ. ברוך אתה יי מושיע עמו ישראל:

Sound the great shofar *for our freedom, and lift up the banner to save us in the four corners of the earth. Praised art Thou, O Lord, who savest Thy people Israel.*

Stockholm, 1881:

תקע בשופר גדול לחרותנו והושע יי את-עמך בארבע כנפות
הארץ. ברוך אתה יי מושיע עמו ישראל:

Sound the great shofar *for our freedom, and save, O Lord, Thy people Israel in the four corners of the earth. Praised art Thou, O Lord, who savest Thy people Israel.*

Stein, 1882:

תקע בשופר גדול לחרותנו. ושא נס ליחד נפוצותינו. ויעשׂוּ
כל־העמים אגדה אחת לעבדך באמת. ברוך אתה. יי מיחד נפוצות עמו
ישראל:

Sound the great shofar *for our freedom, and lift up the banner to unite our dispersed ones. And may all the peoples form one single band to serve Thee in truth. Praised art Thou, O Lord, who unitest the dispersed ones of Thy people Israel.*

Vogelstein (Westphalia), 1894: As in Geiger's 1854 prayerbook.

Glogau, 189?:

תקע בשופר גדול לחרותנו. ברוך אתה יי מושיע נדחי עמו ישראל.

Sound the great shofar *for our freedom. Praised art Thou, O Lord, who savest the dispersed ones of Thy people Israel.*

Baden, 1905:

תקע בשופר גדול לחרותנו וקול דרור וישועה יִשָּׁמַע באהלינו
והושע את־אחינו הנדחים בארבע כנפות הארץ. ברוך אתה יי
מושיע נדחי עמו ישראל:

Sound the great shofar *for our freedom, and may the sound of liberty and salvation be heard in our tents. And save our brethren who are dispersed in the four corners of the earth. Praised art Thou, O Lord, who savest the dispersed ones of Thy people Israel.*

Danzig, 1905: Traditional Hebrew text. Translation as follows:

May the jubilant call of freedom sound for us all. Raise up the banner of redemption for those who are scattered over all the ends of the earth. Praised art Thou, O Lord, who gatherest around Thyself the banished ones of Israel.

Brunswick, 1906: As in the Berlin prayerbook of 1881.

Seligmann, 1910: German paraphrase of Intermediate Benedictions only.

Danzig, 1924: Hebrew and German as in 1905 edition of Danzig prayer-book.

Seligmann, 1928: Hebrew text as in Geiger's prayerbook of 1870.

Einheitsgebetbuch, 1929:

תקע בשופר גדול לחרותנו ושא נס לקבץ יראיך
בארבע כנפות הארץ. ברוך אתה יי מקבץ עמו ישראל:

Sound the great shofar *for our freedom, and lift up the banner to gather those that fear Thee in the four corners of the earth. Praised art Thou, O Lord, who gatherest Thy people Israel.*

West London Synagogue, 1931: Omitted.

Liberal and Progressive Synagogues (England), 1967:

תקע בשופר גדול לחרותנו, ושא נס לפדות עשוקינו,
וקול דרור יִשָּׁמַע בארבע כנפות הארץ.
ברוך אתה יי פודה עשוקים:

Sound the great shofar *for our freedom, and lift up the banner to redeem those of us who are oppressed; and may the sound of liberty be heard in the four corners of the earth. Praised art Thou, O Lord, who redeemest the oppressed.*

BENEDICTION 11.

Traditional Ashkenazi Version:

השיבה שופטינו כבראשונה ויועצינו כבתחלה והסר ממנו יגון ואנחה
ומלוך עלינו אתה יי לבדך בחסד וברחמים וצדקנו במשפט.
ברוך אתה יי מלך אוהב צדקה ומשפט:

Restore our judges as at first, and our counselors as at the beginning; and remove from us sorrow and sighing. And reign Thou over us, Thou alone, O Lord, in lovingkindness and mercy; and clear us in judgment. Praised art Thou, O Lord, who lovest righteousness and justice.

Hamburg, 1819: No weekday service.

Hamburg, 1841: German paraphrase only:

Grant us a righteous government and a wise administration of law. Remove from us sorrow and sadness. Reign Thou over us. . . .

West London Synagogue, 1841: Traditional Sepharadi version, Hebrew and English.

Kirchenrat Maier, 1848: German paraphrase only.

Fill with Thy spirit—the spirit of wisdom, righteousness and leniency—our king, his counselors, all authorities and all judges of the land; and direct their hearts to the welfare of their sub-

jects. Praised art Thou, O God, who lovest righteousness and justice. Direct our hearts to the respect for superiors and authorities, and to the obedience of laws, that we may live a righteous and honorable life, and that we may act in accordance with Thy will. Praised art Thou, O God, whose will is holy.[9]

Geiger, 1854:

השיבה לנו ששון ישעך ורוח נדיבה תסמכנו והסר ממנו....

Restore to us the joy of Thy salvation, and may a noble spirit sustain us; and remove from us. . . .

Göteborg, 1858:

השיבה לנו ששון ישעך והסר ממנו....

Restore to us the joy of Thy salvation; and remove from us. . . .

Stein, 1860: No weekday service.

Aub (Berlin), 1866:

השיבה שופטי צדק כבראשנה ויועצי שלום כבתחלה והסר....

Restore righteous judges as at first, and counselors of peace as at the beginning; and remove from us. . . .

Hamburg, 1868: Traditional Hebrew text. German translation based on 1841 edition.

Geiger, 1870:

השיבה לנו ששון ישעך ומשפטנו מלפניך יצא והסר....

Restore to us the joy of Thy salvation, and may our judgment come forth from before Thee; and remove from us. . . .

Joël, 1872: Traditional Hebrew text in small print and without translation. In large print:

צדקנו במשפטך ונחנו בעצתך והסר....

Justify us in Thy judgment, and guide us through Thy counsel; and remove from us. . . .

Nuremberg, 1874:

השיבה שופטינו בצדק ויועצינו באמונה והסר....

Restore our judges in righteousness, and our counselors in faithfulness; and remove from us. . . .

Leipzig, 1876: Traditional Hebrew text in small print and without translation. In large print:

הושיבה לנו שופטי צדק ויועצי אמת והסר....

Appoint for us righteous judges and truthful counselors; and remove from us. . . .

Berlin, 1881:

הושיבה שופטי צדק ויועצי שלום והסר....

Appoint righteous judges and counselors of peace; and remove. . . .

Stockholm, 1881: As in the Göteborg prayerbook of 1858.

Stein, 1882: Traditional Hebrew version and corresponding translation.

Vogelstein (Westphalia), 1894: As in Geiger's prayerbook of 1870.

Glogau, 189?:

השיבה שופטי צדק והסר ממנו יגון ואנחה....

Restore righteous judges; and remove from us. . . .

Baden, 1905:

תן לשופטינו צדקתך וליועצינו עצתך והסר....

Give to our judges Thy righteousness, and to our counselors Thy counsel; and remove from us. . . .

Danzig, 1905: Traditional Hebrew text. German reads as follows:
Let righteous judges and advisors rule over us, ...

Brunswick, 1906: As in the Berlin prayerbook of 1881.

Seligmann, 1910: German paraphrase of combined Intermediate Benedictions only.

Danzig, 1924: As in Nuremberg prayerbook of 1874.

Seligmann, 1928: As in Geiger's prayerbook of 1870.

Einheitsgebetbuch, 1929: As in Geiger's prayerbook of 1870.

West London Synagogue, 1931: Omitted.

Liberal and Progressive Synagogues (England), 1967:

על שופטי ארץ שפוך רוחך, והדריכם במשפטי צדקך,
ומלוך עלינו אתה לבדך בחסד וברחמים.
ברוך....

Pour Thy spirit upon the judges of the earth, and guide them in

Thy righteous judgments. And reign Thou alone over us in lovingkindness and mercy. Praised. . . .

BENEDICTION 12.

Traditional Ashkenazi Version:

ולמלשינים אל-תהי תקוה וכל-עושי רשעה כרגע יאבדו
וכל-אויביך מהרה יכרתו והזדים מהרה תעקר ותשבר ותמגר ותכניע
במהרה בימינו. ברוך אתה יי שובר אויבים ומכניע זדים:

And for the slanderers let there be no hope, and all doers of wickedness shall perish as in a moment; and let all Thine enemies be speedily cut off, and the arrogant do Thou speedily uproot and crush, cast down and humble, speedily in our days. Praised art Thou, O Lord, who breakest the enemies and humblest the arrogant.

Hamburg, 1819: No weekday service.

Hamburg, 1841: Omitted.

West London Synagogue, 1841: Omitted.

Kirchenrat Maier, 1848: German paraphrase only.

Terrify the wicked with Thy judgments, and fill the sinners with reverence for Thy righteousness—that sin may vanish from upon the earth, and vice may no longer be encountered. Praised art Thou, O Lord, who punishest evil and vice.

Geiger, 1854:

ולמלשינות אל-תהי תקוה. וכל-הרשעה כרגע תאבד והזדון תכניע
במהרה בימינו. ברוך אתה יי שובר הרשעה ומכניע הזדון:

And for slander let there be no hope, and all wickedness shall perish as in a moment; and do Thou humble arrogance speedily in our days. Praised art Thou, O Lord, who breakest wickedness and humblest arrogance.

Göteborg, 1858: As in Geiger's prayerbook of 1854.

Stein, 1860: No weekday service.

Aub (Berlin), 1866:

ולמלשינות אל-תהי תקוה וכל-הרשעה כלה כעשן תכלה
והזדון תכניע במהרה בימינו. ברוך אתה יי שובר האיבה ומכניע הזדון:

And for slander let there be no hope, and may all wickedness vanish like smoke; and do Thou humble arrogance speedily in our days. Praised art Thou, O Lord, who breakest enmity and humblest arrogance.

Hamburg, 1868: Omitted.

Geiger, 1870:

והתועים אליך ישובו וכל־הרשעה מהרה תאבד
והזדון תכניע בימינו. ברוך אתה יי שובר רשע ומכניע זדון:

And may the erring ones return unto Thee, and may all wickedness perish speedily; and do Thou humble arrogance in our days. Praised art Thou, O Lord, who breakest wickedness and humblest arrogance.

Joël, 1872: Traditional text in small print without translation. In large print:

ולמלשינות אל־תהי תקוה וכל רשעה וזדון תכניע ותשבית.
ברוך אתה יי משבית הרשעה ומכניע זדון:

And for slander let there be no hope, and do Thou humble and destroy all wickedness and arrogance. Praised art Thou, O Lord, who destroyest wickedness and humblest arrogance.

Nuremberg, 1874: Omitted.

Leipzig, 1876: Omitted in the main text meant for public worship, but traditional text is given in small print and without translation.

Berlin, 1881: Omitted.

Stockholm, 1881: Omitted.

Stein, 1882:

ולמלשינים אל־תהי תקוה. והתועים אליך ישובו. שבור מטה
רשע. ומלכות זדון מהרה תעביר מעל פני כל־הארץ.
ברוך אתה יי שובר מטה רשע ומכניע זדון:

And for slanderers let there be no hope. And may the erring ones return unto Thee. Break the staff of wickedness, and cause the kingdom of arrogance to pass away speedily from the face of the earth. Praised art Thou, O Lord, who breakest the staff of wickedness and humblest arrogance.

Vogelstein (Westphalia), 1894: As in Geiger's 1870 prayerbook.

Glogau, 189?:

ולמלשינות אל־תהי תקוה וכל הרשעה כרגע תאבד.
ברוך אתה יי שובר הרשעה ומכניע הזדון:

And for slander let there be no hope, and may all wickedness perish as in a moment. Praised art Thou, O Lord, who breakest wickedness and humblest arrogance.

Baden, 1905:

ולמלשינים אל-תהי תקוה וכל-הרשעה כרגע תאבד
והזדון מהרה תכניע. ברוך אתה יי שובר הרשעה ומכניע הזדון:

And for the slanderers let there be no hope, and let all wickedness perish as in a moment; and do Thou speedily humble arrogance. Praised art Thou, O Lord, who breakest wickedness and humblest arrogance.

Danzig, 1905: As in Aub's Berlin prayerbook of 1866.

Brunswick, 1906: As in Geiger's 1854 prayerbook.

Seligmann, 1910: Paraphrase of combined Intermediate Benedictions only.

Danzig, 1924: As in Aub's Berlin prayerbook of 1866.

Seligmann, 1928: As in Geiger's 1870 prayerbook.

Einheitsgebetbuch, 1929: As in Geiger's 1870 prayerbook.

West London Synagogue, 1931: Omitted.

Liberal and Progressive Synagogues (England), 1967: Omitted.

BENEDICTION 14.

Traditional Ashkenazi Version:

ולירושלים עירך ברחמים תשוב ותשכון בתוכה כאשר דברת,
ובנה אותה בקרוב בימינו בנין עולם, וכסא דוד מהרה לתוכה תכין.
ברוך אתה יי בונה ירושלים:

And to Jerusalem, Thy city, do Thou return in mercy, and do Thou dwell therein as Thou hast spoken. And build it soon in our days as an everlasting building. And speedily set therein the throne of David. Praised art Thou, O Lord, who buildest Jerusalem.

Hamburg, 1819: No weekday service.

Hamburg, 1841: German paraphrase only.

May Thy glory be again enthroned in Thy city of Jerusalem.

Establish and strengthen the seat of truth in an everlasting building, even as Thy word hath promised: "For out of Zion shall go forth instruction, and the word of the Lord from Jerusalem." Praised art Thou, O God, who establishest Jerusalem.

West London Synagogue, 1841: Traditional Sepharadi version, Hebrew and English.

Kirchenrat Maier, 1848: Omitted.

Geiger, 1854:

ולירושלים ברחמים תשוב ותשכון בתוכה כאשר דברת וכסא דוד
מהרה לתוכה תכין. ברוך אתה יי שוכן בירושלים:

And return to Jerusalem in mercy, and dwell therein as Thou hast spoken. And speedily set therein the throne of David. Praised art Thou, O Lord, who dwellest in Jerusalem.

Göteborg, 1858:

ולירושלים ברחמים תשוב ותשכון בתוכה כאשר דברת
וכסאך מהרה לתוכה תכין. ברוך אתה יי כונן ירושלים:

And return to Jerusalem in mercy, and dwell therein as Thou hast spoken. And speedily set Thy throne therein. Praised art Thou, O Lord, who establishest Jerusalem.

Stein, 1860: No weekday service.

Aub (Berlin), 1866:

ולירושלים עירך ברחמים תשוב ותשכון בתוכה כאשר דברת
ובנה אותה לכבוד שמך וכסא דוד מהרה לתוכה תכין. ברוך את יי בונה
ירושלים:

And to Jerusalem, Thy city, do Thou return in mercy, and do Thou dwell therein as Thou hast spoken. And build it to the glory of Thy Name, and speedily set therein the throne of David. Praised art Thou, O Lord, who buildest Jerusalem.

Hamburg, 1868: Traditional Hebrew version. Translation based on 1841 edition.

Geiger, 1870:

וירושלים ברחמים תזכור וצמח ישועה מהרה תצמיח כי לישועתך
קוינו כל־היום. ברוך אתה יי מצמיח קרן ישועה:

And mayest Thou remember Jerusalem in mercy, and speedily cause salvation to sprout forth, because we wait for Thy salvation all the day. Praised art Thou, O Lord, who causest the horn of salvation to flourish.[10]

Joël, 1872:

ועל ירושלים עירך תשוב ותרחם ולזכר עולם חרבותיה תקומם.
ברוך אתה יי זוכר ירושלים וחרבותיה:

And mayest Thou again have mercy on Jerusalem, and raise up her ruins for an eternal remembrance. Praised art Thou, O Lord, who rememberest Jerusalem and her ruins.
(Traditional version appears in small print and without translation.)

Nuremberg, 1874: Traditional Hebrew version, except that "Thy throne" is substituted for "the throne of David."

Leipzig, 1876: As in Joël's prayerbook of 1872.

Berlin, 1881:

ולירושלים עירך רחמים תשיב ותחון אותה כאשר דברת.
ברוך אתה יי הבוחר בירושלים:

And mayest Thou restore mercy to Jerusalem, Thy city, and be gracious unto her as Thou hast spoken. Praised art Thou, O Lord, who choosest Jerusalem.

Stockholm, 1881: As in the Göteborg prayerbook of 1858.

Stein, 1882: As in the Nuremberg prayerbook of 1874.

Vogelstein (Westphalia), 1894: As in Geiger's prayerbook of 1870.

Glogau, 189?:

וירושלים ברחמים תזכור. ברוך אתה יי הבוחר בירושלים:

And mayest Thou remember Jerusalem. Praised art Thou, O Lord, who choosest Jerusalem.[11]

Baden, 1905:

ובנה ירושלים בנין עולם וכסא כבודך לתוכה תכין
ויקרא מקדשך בית תפלה לכל-העמים.
ברוך אתה יי בונה ירושלים:

And build Jerusalem as an everlasting building, and establish therein the throne of Thy glory; and may Thy temple be called a house of prayer for all the peoples. Praised art Thou, O Lord, who buildest Jerusalem.

Danzig, 1905: Traditional Hebrew text. German translation as follows:
Turn to Jerusalem, Thy city, in mercy. Be enthroned in her as Thou hast promised, that she may soon arise again for eternity, and that the messianic throne of peace may firmly be established

within her. Praised art Thou, O Eternal, who rebuildest Jerusalem.

Brunswick, 1906: As in the Berlin prayerbook of 1881.

Seligmann, 1910: Paraphrase of combined Intermediate Benedictions only.

Danzig, 1924: As in the Nuremberg prayerbook of 1874.

Seligmann, 1928: As in Geiger's prayerbook of 1870.

Einheitsgebetbuch, 1929:

ולירושלים עירך רחמים תשיב ותחון אותה כאשר
דברת ובנה אותה בקרוב בימינו בנין עולם.
ברוך אתה יי בונה ירושלים:

And to Jerusalem, Thy city, restore mercy, and be gracious unto her as Thou hast spoken; and build her speedily in our days as an everlasting building. Praised art Thou, O Lord, who buildest Jerusalem.

West London Synagogue, 1931: Omitted.

Liberal and Progressive Synagogues (England), 1967:

ולירושלים עירך ברחמים תפנה. ויהי שלום בשעריה ושלוה בלב יושביה.
ותורתך מציון תצא ודברך מירושלים.
ברוך אתה יי נותן שלום בירושלים ובכל־הארץ:

And mayest Thou turn to Jerusalem in mercy. May peace be within her gates, and tranquility in the heart of her inhabitants. And may Thy Torah go forth from Zion, and Thy word from Jerusalem. Praised art Thou, O Lord, who givest peace in Jerusalem and in all the earth.

BENEDICTION 15.

Traditional Ashkenazi Version:

את־צמח דוד עבדך מהרה תצמיח, וקרנו תרום בישועתך, כי לישועתך
קוינו כל־היום. ברוך אתה יי מצמיח קרן ישועה:

Cause the sprout of David Thy servant to flourish speedily, and let his horn be exalted by Thy salvation, because we wait for Thy salvation all the day. Praised art Thou, O Lord, who causest the horn of salvation to flourish.

Hamburg, 1819: No weekday service.

Hamburg, 1841: German version of traditional text.

West London Synagogue, 1841: Traditional Sepharadi version, Hebrew and English.

Kirchenrat Maier, 1848: Omitted.

Geiger, 1854: Traditional text.

Göteborg, 1858:

את-צמח עבדך משיחך מהרה תצמיח וקרנו תרום....

Cause the sprout of Thy messianic servant to flourish speedily, and let his horn be exalted. . . .

Stein, 1860: No weekday service.

Aub (Berlin), 1866: Traditional text.

Hamburg, 1868: Traditional text.

Geiger, 1870: Combined with Benediction 14.

Joël, 1872: Traditional text in small print without translation. In large print:

את-צמח צדקה תצמיח כאשר דברת וקרננו תרום....

Cause the sprout of righteousness to flourish as Thou hast spoken, and let our horn be exalted. . . .

Nuremberg, 1874:

את-צמח עבדך מהרה תצמיח וקרנו תרום....

Cause the sprout of Thy servant to flourish speedily, and let his horn be exalted. . . .

Leipzig, 1876: Traditional text in small print without translation. In large print:

את-צמח עבדיך מהרה תצמיח וקרננו תרום....

Cause the sprout of Thy servants to flourish speedily, and let our horn be exalted. . . .

Berlin, 1881: As in the Leipzig prayerbook of 1876.

Stockholm, 1881:

את-צמח דוד עבדך משיחך מהרה תצמיח וקרנו תרום....

Cause the sprout of Thy servant David, Thine anointed, to flourish speedily, and let his horn be exalted. . . .[12]

Stein, 1882:

את־צמח ישראל עבדך מהרה תצמיח וקרנו תרום....

Cause the sprout of Israel, Thy servant, to flourish speedily, and let his horn be exalted. . . .

Vogelstein (Westphalia), 1894: As in Geiger's prayerbook of 1870, combining Benedictions 14 and 15.

Glogau, 189?: As in the Leipzig prayerbook of 1876.

Baden, 1905:

את־צמח צדקה מהרה תצמיח וקרננו תרום....

Cause the sprout of righteousness to flourish speedily, and let our horn be exalted. . . .

Danzig, 1905: Traditional Hebrew text. German translation as follows:

Let the salvation of the messianic future sprout speedily, ...

Brunswick, 1906:

את־צמח ישועה תצמיח וקרננו תרום....

Cause the sprout of salvation to flourish speedily, and let our horn be exalted. . . .

Seligmann, 1910: Paraphrase of combined Intermediate Benedictions only.

Danzig, 1924: As in the Nuremberg prayerbook of 1874.

Seligmann, 1928: As in Geiger's prayerbook of 1870, combining Benedictions 14 and 15.

Einheitsgebetbuch, 1929: As in the Brunswick prayerbook of 1906, adding מהרה.

West London Synagogue, 1931: Omitted.

Liberal and Progressive Synagogues (England), 1967:

את־צמח צדקה מהרה תצמיח, וקרן ישועה תרום כנאמך,
כי לישועתך קוינו כל־היום. ברוך אתה....

Cause the sprout of righteousness to flourish speedily, and let the horn of salvation be exalted as Thou hast spoken; for we hope for Thy salvation all the day. Praised art Thou. . . .

BENEDICTION 17.

Traditional Ashkenazi Version:

רצה יי אלהינו בעמך ישראל ובתפלתם. והשב את־העבודה לדביר ביתך, ואשי ישראל ותפלתם באהבה תקבל ברצון, ותהי לרצון תמיד עבודת ישראל עמך. ותחזינה עינינו בשובך לציון ברחמים. ברוך אתה יי המחזיר שכינתו לציון:

Accept, O Lord our God, Thy people Israel and their prayer. And restore the service to the inner sanctuary of Thy house; and receive in love and favor both the fire-offerings of Israel and their prayer. And may the service of Thy people Israel ever be acceptable to Thee. And let our eyes behold Thy return to Zion in mercy. Praised art Thou, O Lord, who restorest Thy divine presence to Zion.

Hamburg, 1819: Traditional version.

Hamburg, 1841:

רצה יי אלהינו בעמך ישראל ובתפלתם (והשב את־העבודה לדביר ביתך. ואשי ישראל ותפלתם באהבה תקבל ברצון) ותהי לרצון תמיד עבודת ישראל עמך: ותחזינה עינינו בשובך לציון ברחמים. ברוך אתה יי שאותך לבדך ביראה נעבוד:

The words we have put in parentheses appear in parentheses and in small print, and remain untranslated. With this equivocation about the restoration of the sacrificial service understood, the Benediction remains substantially the same as in the traditional version, including the plea for God's merciful return to Zion. However, the concluding eulogy, based on that plea, has been changed to "Praised art Thou, O Lord, whom alone we serve in reverence." This wording is actually found in the traditional liturgy, where it is recited during the *musaph* service when the *kohanim* recite the Priestly Benediction.[13] It goes back to the version of this prayer recited by the priests in the Jerusalem Temple, during their daily morning service.[14] Beginning with this edition of the prayerbook of the Hamburg Temple, this version of the concluding eulogy becomes the standard one in Liberal and Reform liturgy, although, here and there, we find reformed rituals which have retained the benediction, "who restorest Thy divine presence to Zion." But those rituals are in the minority. Subsequent reformed prayerbooks are more likely to differ in the number of clauses they retain of the prayer as a whole.

West London Synagogue, 1841: Traditional Sepharadi version, which, in contents, though not in wording, is identical with the Ashkenazi version.

Kirchenrat Maier, 1848:

רצה יי אלהינו בעמך ישראל ובתפלתם ותפלת ישראל
באהבה תקבל ברצון ותהי לרצון תמיד עבודת ישראל עמך.
ברוך אתה יי שאותך לבדך ביראה נעבוד:

All references to the sacrificial service and to God's return to Zion have been excluded.

Aachen, 1853:

רצה יי אלהינו בעמך ישראל ובתפלתם. והשב את העבודה
לדביר ביתך ובתפלתנו (sic) באהבה תקבל ברצון
ותהי לרצון תמיד עבודת ישראל עמך. ותחזינה עינינו בשובך אלינו
ברחמים. ברוך אתה יי שאותך לבדך ביראה נעבוד:

Accept, O Lord our God, Thy people Israel and their prayer. And restore the service to the inner sanctuary of Thy house. And accept our prayer in love and favor; and may the service of Thy people Israel ever be acceptable. And let our eyes behold Thy return unto us in love. Praised art Thou, O Lord, whom alone we serve in reverence.

Geiger, 1854: As in the Hamburg prayerbook of 1841, but omitting all references to restoration of sacrificial service.

Göteborg, 1858: As in Geiger's prayerbook of 1854, but omitting the word ובתפלתם in the first clause.

Stein, 1860: Almost identical with the version of the Hamburg prayerbook of 1841, except that Stein only puts the two words, ואשי ישראל, in parentheses, leaving them untranslated, and, in their place, offers the version, ונדבות ישראל, "and the voluntary offerings of Israel." And Stein uses the traditional concluding eulogy about God's return to Zion.

Aub (Berlin), 1866:

רצה יי אלהינו בעמך ישראל ותפלתם. ותרצה העבודה
בדביר ביתך ורנת ישראל ותפלתם באהבה תקבל ברצון ותהי לרצון תמיד
עבודת ישראל עמך. ותחזינה עינינו...

Accept, O Lord our God, Thy people Israel and their prayer. And be pleased with the service in the inner sanctuary of Thy house; and receive in love and favor the plea of Israel and their prayer . . .

(The rest follows the traditional version.)[15]

Hamburg, 1868:

רצה יי אלהינו בעמך ישראל ותפלתם באהבה תקבל. ותהי לרצון
תמיד עבודת ישראל עמך. ברוך אתה יי שאותך לבדך ביראה נעבוד:

Accept, O Lord our God, Thy people Israel, and receive their prayer in love. And may the service of Thy people Israel ever be acceptable. Praised be Thou, O Lord, whom alone we serve in reverence.[16]

Geiger, 1870: As in the Hamburg prayerbook of 1868.

Joël, 1872: Traditional text in small print and without translation. In large print, the traditional version without the words, "and restore the service to the inner sanctuary of Thy house; and the fire-offerings of Israel."

Nuremberg, 1874: As in the Hamburg prayerbook of 1868.

Leipzig, 1876: As in the Hamburg prayerbook of 1868.

Berlin, 1881: As in the Hamburg prayerbook of 1868, but omitting the word באהבה.

Stockholm, 1881: As in the Göteborg prayerbook of 1858.

Stein, 1882:

רצה יי אלהינו בעמך ישראל ובתפלתם. ונדבותינו באהבה תקבל
ברצון ותהי לרצון תמיד עבודת ישראל עמך. ותחזינה עינינו בשובך לציון
ברחמים. ברוך אתה יי שאותך לבדך ביראה נעבוד:

Accept, O Lord our God, Thy people Israel and their prayer. And receive in love and favor our voluntary offerings; and may the service of Thy people Israel ever be acceptable to Thee. And let our eyes behold Thy return to Zion in mercy. Praised art Thou, O Lord, whom alone we serve in reverence.

Vogelstein (Westphalia), 1894:

רצה יי אלהינו בעמך ישראל. ותפלתם באהבה תקבל
ותהי לרצון תמיד עבודת ישראל עמך: והט לבבנו אליך לעבדך
ביראה. ברוך אתה יי שאותך לבדך ביראה נעבוד:

Basically the version of the Hamburg prayerbook of 1868, but inserting before the concluding eulogy the words, "And incline our hearts to Thee that we may serve Thee in reverence," thus providing a suitable "bridge" to the concluding eulogy.

Glogau, 189?: As in the Hamburg prayerbook of 1868, but omitting the word באהבה.

Baden, 1905:

רצה יי אלהינו בעמך ישראל. ותפלתם באהבה תקבל ברצון ותהי
לרצון תמיד עבודת ישראל עמך. ויחד לבבנו לעבדך ביראה.
ברוך אתה יי שאותך לבדך ביראה נעבוד:

Basically the version of the Hamburg prayerbook of 1868, but, similar to (though not identical with) Vogelstein, inserting a "bridge" to lead into the concluding eulogy: "And unite our hearts that we may serve Thee in reverence."

Danzig, 1905: Traditional Hebrew text. German translation as follows:

Look down with favor, O Eternal our God, upon Thy congregation of Israel, and graciously accept its prayer. Yea, mayest Thou ever be pleased with the adoration of Thy people Israel. May our eyes behold the return of Thy glory in mercy to Zion. Praised art Thou, O Eternal, who causest Thy glory to rise again over Zion.

Brunswick, 1906: As in the Baden prayerbook of 1905, but omitting the word באהבה.

Seligmann, 1910: As in the Hamburg prayerbook of 1868.

Danzig, 1924: Traditional text in small print without translation. In large print, the version of the Hamburg prayerbook of 1868, but adding the word ברצון after ותפלתם באהבה תקבל.

Seligmann, 1928: As in the Hamburg prayerbook of 1868.

Einheitsgebetbuch, 1929: As in the Hamburg prayerbook of 1868, except that the second clause reads: ותפלתם תקבל ברצון.

West London Synagogue, 1931:

רצה יי אלהינו בעמך ישראל. ולתפלתם שעה.
וברחמיך הרבים תחפוץ בנו ותשרה שכינתך על ציון.
ברוך אתה יי המשרה שכינתו על ציון:

Accept, O Lord our God, Thy people Israel, and have regard unto their prayer. And in Thine abundant mercy, deign to regard us graciously, and cause Thy divine presence to rest upon Zion. Praised art Thou, O Lord, who causest Thy divine presence to rest upon Zion.[17]

Seder Tobh Lehodoth (Netherlands) 1964:

The Friday night service includes the version of the *Einheitsgebet-*

buch, but, in the place of the latter's concluding eulogy, it has the traditional "And let our eyes behold . . . ," followed by "Praised art Thou, O Lord, who restorest Thy divine presence to Zion."

The Sabbath morning service has first the complete version of the *Einheitsgebetbuch,* and follows this with "And let our eyes behold . . ." and the concluding eulogy, ". . . who restorest Thy divine presence to Zion." This version thus presents the anomaly of having *two* concluding eulogies.

Liberal and Progressive Synagogues (England), 1967: As in Hamburg prayerbook of 1868.

A number of things will have become clear from this chronologically arranged survey of the changes introduced by various Liberal and Reform rituals in the traditional wording of the Eighteen Benedictions. We note first of all the remarkable attempt made by the majority of the liturgists to depart as little as possible from the traditional wording even in cases where the dogma underlying the traditional formulation has been amended or given up. Next, we note the influence exerted by earlier reformed prayerbooks on those published later. We get the feeling that there was a groping for the most appropriate way of dealing with the problems, of how some versions were "tried out" for a while, only to fall into oblivion later on. We also see how individual editors of prayerbooks have undergone changes. The Geiger of 1870 is, in a way, more "radical" than the Geiger of 1854. The Stein of 1882 is somewhat less "inhibited" and bound by traditional formulations than the Stein who, in 1860, edited the prayerbook "according to the rite of the Main Synagogue in Frankfort o. M." We also recognize that some of the prayerbooks become more "influential" than others, i.e., the changes they introduced find acceptance in a greater number of other prayerbooks. Thus, Geiger's role can be seen as decisive in the whole evolution of European Liberal and Reform liturgy—from having many of his formulations adopted by the liturgy of Swedish Jewry through the influence he exerted on Vogelstein and Seligmann, and, ultimately, on the *Einheitsgebetbuch.* On the other hand, Aub's and Stein's innovations give the appearance of a more idiosyncratic nature, of little appeal elsewhere—though Aub's prayerbook was not altogether without influence on future editions of the Berlin prayerbook, and Stein's 1882 ritual, as revised by Richard Grünfeld, became the 1917/18 prayerbook of the Augsburg Jewish community. Joël's 1872 prayerbook, with its provision, in small print and without translation, of the traditional text for use by the "unreformed" worshipper, and its rather moderate reforms, was reprinted several times for the specific use of other congregations.[18] Its influence on the Leipzig prayerbook of 1876 has been acknowledged by the latter's editor.[19]

Of the prayerbooks considered thus far in this chapter, only the liturgy of the West London Synagogue remained relatively unaffected by the liturgical "experimentation" which marked the evolution of Liberal and Reform liturgy on the European continent. In the Introduction to the first edition of the *Forms of Prayer* of the West London Synagogue, 1841, its editor, D. W. Marks, had written: "We have removed those parts of the service which are deficient in devotional tendency; and we have expunged the few expressions which are known to be the offspring of feelings produced by oppression, and are universally admitted to be foreign to the heart of every true Israelite of our day."[20] Whatever the application of this principle to the rest of the liturgy may have been, as far as the Eighteen Benedictions were concerned, the only departure from the standard Sepharadi rite of this prayer which Marks permitted himself was the omission of Benediction 12, i.e., the malediction against the slanderers and the arrogant. While subsequent editions of this prayerbook also changed the references to the restoration of the sacrificial cult (though not the references to the Return to Zion and the rebuilding of the Temple), the traditional form of the Eighteen Benedictions was otherwise kept intact. Yet when the winds of doctrinal change finally affected the liturgy of the West London Synagogue, in 1931, the impact was so strong that, instead of modifying the traditional wording of the Benedictions concerned, such modification was used only in connection with Benediction 17, while Benedictions 10, 11, 14, and 15 disappeared without a trace! Nor have they been reinstated, in any shape or form, in the volume of *Evening Prayers* which, in 1952, appeared as a supplement to the 1931 prayerbook.[21] This, in a way, is all the more remarkable because, unlike many other reformed rituals, the 1931 edition of the West London Synagogue liturgy did include prayers newly composed in the Hebrew language, or, rather, modern Hebrew translations of newly composed English prayers.[22]

Our treatment of the Eighteen Benedictions in European Liberal and Reform liturgy would be incomplete were we not to include some rather remarkable developments which took place in France and in the Netherlands.

In 1913, the Union Libérale Israélite in Paris published its prayerbook כנפים לארץ—*Des Ailes à la Terre.*[23] In its version of the Eighteen Benedictions,[24] this prayerbook retains Benedictions 1 through 9, omits Benedictions 10 through 17 altogether, and concludes the rubric with the final sentence and eulogy of Benediction 18, followed by the prayer of Mar the son of Rabhina, "O my God, guard my tongue from evil. . . ."

In 1925, the Union Libérale Israélite published a more elaborate prayerbook, תפלות כל השנה—*Rituel des Prières Journalières*. It includes a version of the Eighteen Benedictions[25] which likewise completely omits Benedictions 10 through 15. But Benediction 9 is followed by what amounts to a conflate version of Benedictions 16 and 17. It reads as follows:

> שמע קולנו יי אלהינו חום ורחם עלינו וקבל ברחמים וברצון את-תפלתנו כי אל שומע תפלות ותחנונים אתה. רצה יי אלהינו בעמך ישראל ובתפלתם. ותהי לרצון תמיד עבודת ישראל עמך. ברוך אתה יי שומע תפלה:
>
> *Hear our voice, O Lord our God; spare us and have mercy upon us, and receive our prayer in mercy and favor; for Thou art a God who hearkenest unto prayers and supplications. Accept, O Lord our God, Thy people Israel and their prayer; and may the service of Thy people Israel ever be acceptable. Praised art Thou, O Lord, who hearkenest unto prayer.*

This is followed by the complete traditional text of Benedictions 18 and 19, and the prayer, "O my God, guard my tongue from evil. . . ." It should be noted that, on the Sabbath,[26] the components of Benediction 16 are not united with the new version of Benediction 17. However, even on the Sabbath, Benediction 17 concludes with the ("weekday") eulogy, "Praised art Thou, O Lord, who hearkenest unto prayer."

Yet the Paris prayerbook of 1925 is not quite as "radical" as might appear at first sight. Such Intermediate Benedictions of the Eighteen Benedictions as are included in the service are meant to be recited in an undertone.[27] While this is being done, the more traditionally minded worshipper can find the complete and unabridged text of Benedictions 10 through 17, albeit in Hebrew only, at the end of this prayerbook![28]

In a 1958 photo-offset reprint of *Rituel des Prières Journalières,* reduced in volume but augmented in its Hebrew components, the complete and unchanged Ashkenazi form of the Eighteen Benedictions (including Benediction 12!), together with a French translation, is given as the sole version of this prayer.[29]

The Liberal Jews of the Netherlands have made an interesting contribution to the wording of Benedictions 17 and 18 of the Eighteen Benedictions. In a number of booklets containing services for various occasions, which began to appear in the thirties of this century,[30] and some of which still appeared in the fifties,[31] Benediction 17 takes the following form:

> רצה יי אלהינו בעמך ישראל ובתפלתם ורחם על ציון ויעבדוך עבדיך בירושלים. ברוך אתה יי שאותך לבדך ביראה נעבוד:
>
> *Accept, O Lord our God, Thy people Israel and their prayer.*

Have mercy upon Zion; and may Thy servants worship Thee in Jerusalem. Praised art Thou, O Lord, whom alone we serve in reverence.

Benediction 18 reads as follows:

מודים אנחנו לך יי אלהינו ואלהי אבותינו על כל הטובות החסד
והרחמים שעשית עמנו ועם אבותינו על חיינו המסורים בידך ועל
נשמותינו הפקודות לך ואם אמרנו מטה רגלנו חסדך יי יסעדנו.
ברוך אתה יי הטוב שמך ולך נאה להודות:

We give thanks unto Thee, O Lord our God, and God of our fathers, for all the goodness, the lovingkindness and the mercy, which Thou hast done for us and for our fathers, for our lives which are committed unto Thy hand, and for our souls which are in Thy charge. And if we were to say, "Our foot slippeth," Thy mercy, O Lord, would sustain us. Praised art Thou, O Lord, whose Name is All-good, and unto whom it is fitting to give thanks.

These versions of Benedictions 17 and 18 are not only shorter than the traditional Ashkenazi versions, but they distinctly echo the wording of Benedictions 17 and 18 in the old Palestinian rite, as discovered in the Cairo Genizah.[32] The old Palestinian version reads:

רצה י״י אלהינו ושכון בציון
ויעבדוך עבדיך בירושלים.
ברוך אתה י״י שאותך ביראה נעבד.

מודים אנחנו לך אתה הוא י״י אלהינו ואלהי אבותינו על כל הטובות
החסד והרחמים שגמלתנו ושעשית עמנו ועם אבותינו מלפנינו,
ואם אמרנו מטה רגלנו חסדך י״י יסעדנו.
ברוך אתה י״י הטוב לך להודות:

Rabbi Dr. Jacob Soetendorp of Amsterdam has offered the following explanation for those traces of the old Palestinian rite in the liturgy of Dutch Liberal Jews:[33] The founder of the Liberal Jewish movement in the Netherlands was a Mr. L. Levisson, owner of one of the most important printing plants in Holland, who had in his possession a very good collection of prayerbooks and of the old Hebrew types of the famous printing press of Athias and of Proops. Mr. Levisson would on occasion use those types for some of his prayerbooks. Moreover, one of his closest assistants in this enterprise was a Mr. Raphael Isaiah Spitz, a great scholar in the field of liturgy. Levisson and Spitz decided to incorporate parts of the old Carpentras rite in their prayerbooks, and they also knew all about the nearly forgotten Palestinian rite.

We may add to Dr. Soetendorp's interesting description that, in view of Schechter's publication of the Genizah texts in 1898, it was, of course, not difficult to have them available in the nineteen-thirties. But it is one thing to have texts available. It is quite another, again, to utilize them for actual worship purposes. Dr. Soetendorp's reference to the "delight of the collector, the experimenter and the inventor," which marked the activities of Messrs. Levisson and Spitz, would, however, explain their utilization of this ancient material in twentieth-century Liberal Jewish worship. It also explains, at least in part, why, in the new 1964 edition of the Dutch prayerbook, *Seder Tobh Lehodoth,* the Palestinian versions have been abandoned in favor of a return to more conventional texts.

This, however, is not yet the end of that story. While Liberal Judaism in the Netherlands has turned away from the liturgical experiments of Messrs. Levisson and Spitz, the Liberal Jews of Switzerland have published a prayerbook for Sabbath Eve, in which Benedictions 17 and 18 appear in the form they had earlier been given in the liturgical publications of Liberal Judaism in the Netherlands.[34] There is, moreover, no secret about it, the Swiss editors having stated the fact of their having made use of the Amsterdam plates.[35]

NINE

Reform of the Musaph Service

THE MUSAPH (LIT. "ADDITIONAL") SERVICE IN THE TRADITIONAL LITURGY[1] follows the reading of Torah and Prophets on the mornings of Sabbath and festivals, and is meant to take the place of the additional sacrifices brought in the Jerusalem Temple on those occasions. It contains the first three and last three of the Seven Benedictions (which are also part of the Morning Service) as well as the benediction dealing with the "holiness of the day," praising God who sanctifies the Sabbath and/or the festivals. That much the *Musaph* prayer has in common with the *Shaḥarith* prayer. But the distinguishing feature of the *Musaph* Service is that, after the third of the Seven Benedictions, mention is made of the "additional sacrifice" which was brought in the Temple, followed by an appropriate quotation from Numbers chapters 28 and 29, in which the sacrifices of the particular day are specified. This quotation from the Bible is surrounded by a framework of prayers which refer to the divine institution of the sacrificial cult and to the hope for its restoration, and, particularly on the festivals, also to the fact that "on account of our sins, we were exiled from our land," and are thus unable to bring the sacrifices to which we are obligated.

Now, there may be a great diversity of opinions in Reform Jewish ranks on any number of topics. There is disagreement about the relative amounts of Hebrew and the vernacular in any given service. There is no unanimity as to whether Zion and Jerusalem should figure in the liturgy or not, or whether the prayers should refer to a personal Messiah, or merely to a "de-personalized" Redemption. But it may be safe to assert that there is one subject on which all Liberal and Reform Jews do agree: they do not look forward to, and they do not pray for, the restoration of the sacrificial cult. One would, therefore, expect that, from its very beginning, Reform Judaism had done away with the *Musaph* Service. Such, however, was not the case.

On the whole, it would be true to say that liturgies designed for, what we have called, "Reform from within," and they account for the majority of European rituals, have retained the *Musaph* Service (although not in an unchanged form), whereas liturgies designed for independent Reform congregations have abolished it. Such a statement must, however, be qualified by noting that the Hamburg Temple Prayerbook (in all of its editions) does have a *Musaph* Service, and so did the *Forms of Prayer* of the West London Synagogue until the more recent editions of that liturgy.[2] But today, no *Musaph* Service is included in the liturgies of the Reform Synagogues of Great Britain and of the English Union of Liberal and Progressive Synagogues. Nor does *Musaph* form a part of the rituals of either the French *Union Libérale Israélite* or the Dutch *Verbond van Liberaal Religieuze Joden in Nederland.* In pre-World War II Germany, the Berlin *Reformgemeinde* had no *Musaph;* but all other reformed rituals for congregational worship did, as did the prayerbooks of official Swedish Judaism (which were based on the German models) as well as the congregation of St. Gallen in Switzerland, which had adopted the Nuremberg Prayerbook. In other words, the majority of the prayerbooks under consideration in this volume had provisions for the *Musaph* Service.

There were several reasons for this, as will become apparent when we trace the discussions which took place about the *Musaph* Service in the forties of the last century. There was, above all, one very practical reason. The *Shaḥarith service* in the average German synagogue was not too well attended. It was only when the Torah was taken from the Ark that the majority of the worshippers assembled, and that the chief cantor and the choir made their appearance. That was the beginning of the "main service," as Aub called it in his Preface to the

1853 edition of the Mayence liturgy.[3] That "main service" consisted of Torah and *Haftarah* readings, the sermon, some German prayers, and – – –*Musaph*. Even Seligmann, who, in 1910, edited a prayerbook reflecting a pronounced Reform point of view, was aware of the realities of the situation,[4] and, wishing to avoid meaningless repetition, he sacrificed the Seven Benedictions of the *Shaḥarith* Service (for which he substituted a brief German prayer for silent devotion) to the retention of the Seven Benedictions of *Musaph*.

The services held in Berlin under Israel Jacobson's guidance, in 1815 and 1816, included the *Musaph* prayers in their unchanged Hebrew form.[5] But the prayerbook which came out of those services, *Die Deutsche Synagoge* (1817/18), omitted the *Musaph* on Sabbath and festivals, retaining it for the High Holy Days only.[6] Interestingly enough, in the two cases where *Die Deutsche Synagoge* did retain the *Musaph*, it also retained the traditional prayer which declares, "on account of our sins, we were exiled from our land, ... and we are unable to fulfil our obligations in Thy chosen house." But it omitted the continuation of that prayer which voices the request for the restoration of the sacrificial service.

But when the Hamburg Prayerbook was published, in 1819, it featured a *Musaph* Service for all the occasions called for by tradition. It changed the mention of the sacrificial service from a future hope into a reminiscence of the past, but, unlike the *Deutsche Synagoge*, one editor of which became a preacher of the Hamburg Temple, the Hamburg Prayerbook did not abolish the *Musaph* Service. It retained it, moreover, in all subsequent editions.

Yet, with the growing self-consciousness of the advocates of religious reform, it was not too long before the problem of *Musaph* came up for discussion among the leaders of the new movement. At the Brunswick Rabbinical Conference, in 1844, Kirchenrat Maier, of Stuttgart, asked for the appointment of a Commission on Liturgy, a commission which, among other things, would have to rule on the question, whether the *Musaph* Services were to be retained.[7] Such a commission was appointed, consisting of Herzfeld, Bodenheimer, Holdheim, and Salomon, with Maier as chairman.[8]

The following year, 1845, at the Rabbinical Conference in Frankfort o. M., Maier brought in the lengthy report of the Commission on Liturgy.[9] About the problem of *Musaph*, he said the following:

> We are further from making a decision in the case of the *tephilloth musaphim*. According to the principles which the Commission has established in connection with the doctrine of the Messiah, there seems to be no room in the new liturgy for those additional prayers. For, if we eliminate the passages dealing with the restoration of the nationality, of the Temple, and of

> the sacrifices, we are left with only the first three and the last three benedictions, together with one other passage, all of which already occur in the *tephillath shaḥarith,* and which, if recited once more, would be a tiring repetition. As against this, we have to bear in mind that, on the High Holy Days, we cannot very well do without those prayers. Thus, if they were to be omitted on Sabbath and festivals, a disturbing unevenness in worship would result. The Commission, therefore, is divided on this matter.[10]

A protracted discussion, spread over two sessions, ensued, in which all aspects of the "*Musaph* Problem" were dealt with.[11] One of the protagonists of having *Musaph* altogether abolished was Salomon, a preacher of the Hamburg Temple, the prayerbook of which, as we have noted, included the *Musaph* Service. There were the usual comments about sacrifices being an outgrown stage in the evolution of religion, and the inevitable references to Maimonides, who saw sacrifices as a divine concession to the contemporary mode of worship. There were those who upheld the symbolical significance of the sacrifices, and those who championed their mystical significance. Among the latter was Abraham Adler, whose words deserve to be quoted in full, if only because of his reputation as a "radical reformer."[12]

> One of the previous speakers has asserted that the idea of sacrifice had disappeared from contemporary consciousness, and has, therefore, become obsolete. Why, then, the mention of sacrifices in our prayers?—That is not right. The idea of sacrifice must be an eternally true one, since we cannot and must not assume that, throughout the millennia, Judaism has retained a lie. There is a confusion between the idea itself and the form in which that idea was outwardly expressed. The idea of sacrifice is one of devotion, of the union of the finite individual with the Infinite, the submersion of the transitory in the eternal Source. As long as man himself still stood on the level of externality, he was in need of the external act, through which alone he achieved self-consciousness. However, contrary to what another speaker has mentioned, sacrifice, in Judaism, was not of a symbolical, but of a mystical nature: the one who brought the sacrifice was, through the sacrificial act, conscious of his relation to God. The view of Maimonides, according to which the sacrificial cult was only an accommodation to the paganism from which the people could not altogether free itself, and which, therefore, had to be retained, is undoubtedly an erroneous one. How else could we account for the fact that the sacrificial laws were laid down to the last minutia?! Only when Judaism tran-

> scended the level of externality, did sacrifice become something abstractly external, and only then did the Prophets begin to fulminate against it. The idea then created for itself a new and more appropriate form, that of prayer. In that sense we must understand the Talmudic passage, *tephilloth keneged temidin tiqqenu* (the sacrifices found their counterpart in the prayers). We cannot, therefore, become indifferent to the sacrificial cult, since, in it, we possess the original form of devotion. I, therefore, demand the retention of those liturgical passages which refer to the sacrificial cult—as a reminiscence. On the other hand, the prayers for its restoration, about which we cannot be serious, are to be omitted. As for the *Musaph* Service itself, it is to be retained, seeing that, on festive days, the Torah requires a special sacrifice, in addition to the daily one.[13]

There is no indication that Adler's theoretical position was universally shared. But what Adler had said about the actual liturgical practice did become the official policy of the Conference. The final stages of the discussion took the following form:

> Shall the petitions for the restoration of the sacrificial cult be removed from our prayers?
>
> Unanimously affirmed.
>
> Shall a reminiscence of the sacrifices be included in our prayers? [Geiger objects to the formulation of the question, since it has no practical significance. The President, Leopold Stein, asserts that the question is indeed of practical significance. Geiger retorts that, if this were so, then sacrifices would also have to be mentioned in our daily services, according to the principle that the prayers were ordained as a counterpart to the sacrifices.]
>
> Majority vote in the affirmative.
>
> Shall the *musaphim* be retained?
>
> Decisive majority in the affirmative.[14]

And so, the working out of an appropriate *Musaph* Service became the task of a new Commission on Liturgy, consisting of Stein as chairman, and Salomon, Geiger, Maier and Herzfeld.[15]

By the time the third Rabbinical Conference met in Breslau, in 1846, Stein had worked out a "Plan of the New Prayerbook for the Public Worship Service of the Israelites,"[16] including his own proposals as well as the objections of some of his fellow-members on the commission. Concerning the *Musaph* Service, Stein's "Plan" has this to say:

> The contents of the silent *Musaph* devotion might be the following:
>
> (a) God, in the past, ordained the sacrifices, and particularly for this festival;

(b) God has destroyed the Temple, and, as a consequence, He has abolished the sacrificial cult;
(c) Our spirit surrenders to God; it soars, without mediation, towards the spirit of God;
(d) Passages from the Prophets about the substitution of the heart's surrender for the sacrifices;
(e) Prayer for the restoration of the Temple in Jerusalem, where all nations will worship God in spirit.

Geiger wants the silent *Musaph* devotion to be strictly *me'en hayyom* (i.e., dealing with the festival itself, and not with the sacrifices). Herzfeld remarks to (e): "It would be better to have the petition that, one day, all nations, converted to God, will unite to build a Temple in Jerusalem."[17]

Stein's "Plan," "printed as manuscript," was submitted to the rabbis who attended the Rabbinical Conference in Breslau, in 1846, and it was on the basis of that "Plan" that Stein presented to the Breslau Rabbinical Conference the report of the Commission on Liturgy.[18] The report indicated that there were a number of items on which the commission could reach no unanimous decision. One of them was: the composition of the silent *Musaph* devotions.[19] Geiger, who presided over that Conference, cut off any further discussion by saying that, in view of the fact that the members of the commission were unable to reach any agreement among themselves, it was unlikely that the Conference as a whole would be able to do so immediately, particularly since the "Plan" had been circulated among the members of the Conference only one day previously, and, in some cases, on the day of the commission's report itself. And Holdheim felt that enough time had already been spent during the last Conference on the discussion of matters liturgical. It would, therefore, be better to elect a commission to examine the "Plan," so that only the really important matters would be brought to the floor of the Conference for debate.[20]

Such an "examining commission" was duly elected. It consisted of Einhorn as chairman, and of S. Adler, Wechsler, Holdheim, and Philippson.[21] Whether that "examining commission" ever met, we do not know. The Breslau Conference was the last of the great gatherings of the German rabbis. In later years, there were meetings of rabbis on a more limited and regional basis. But the annual meetings of all the progressive rabbis of Germany had come to an end with the Breslau Conference. There was no follow-up, and there was to be no common prayerbook for another eighty years or so, and there was no settlement of the "*Musaph* Problem."

Stein, however, persevered. What could not be achieved on a national scheme, he tried to accomplish on a regional basis; and, at a meeting of rabbis from the South of Germany, held on October 19th–

22nd, 1857, in Frankfort o. M., Stein obtained general, if not universal, approval of a number of revised prayer texts, among them also the *Musaph* Service.[22] We shall examine the latter and its influence upon subsequent reformed rituals after first looking at some attempts to deal with the *Musaph* Service in prayerbooks published prior to that 1857 meeting.

First, however, a word of explanation is in order about the arrangement of the rest of this chapter. Since most European liturgies included a *Musaph* Service, it is, of course, not possible to reproduce all of them within these pages. We shall confine ourselves to giving examples of the major *types* of *Musaph* adaptations, a procedure which is suggested by the fact that so many of the new versions differ from one another by only a word or two. Also, we shall treat the Sabbath *Musaph* and the festival *Musaph* under separate headings, for it occasionally happened that a prayerbook not differing too much from other prayerbooks in its treatment of the one *Musaph* had an original contribution to make in its treatment of the other.

It should also be borne in mind that the re-writing of the *Musaph* prayers was one of the rather few instances in the history of European Liberal and Reform liturgy where the modern prayerbooks made a creative contribution *in Hebrew*. To be able to appreciate the nature of the Hebraic innovations, it will be necessary for us to compare them with the traditional prototypes. For purposes of comparison, we, therefore, give the traditional text before proceeding to a consideration of the reformed versions. Moreover, since the prayerbook of the Hamburg Temple based its *Musaph* on that of the Sepharadi tradition, the latter is given here as well in the case of the *Musaph* for Sabbath, which differs markedly from the Ashkenazi version. (In the case of the festivals, the Ashkenazi and Sepharadi versions of the *Musaph* are more closely related, thus obviating the necessity of quoting both of them here.)

The translations given here are our translations of the Hebrew texts. They do not necessarily match the translations or paraphrases given in the prayerbooks themselves. Also, since translations of the traditional liturgy are readily available, only the Hebrew text of the traditional liturgy will be quoted here, while translations will be given of all the reformed versions.

Finally, it should be borne in mind that, in this chapter, we are dealing with the *specific* insert for *Musaph,* and not with the entire prayer of the Seven Benedictions of which the *Musaph* Service is composed. It is understood, therefore, that, in all cases, we have the first three and the last three benedictions of the Seven Benedictions. In addition, it is understood that the *Musaph* for the Sabbath, in the prayerbooks under consideration here, includes *yismehu* and *elohenu welohé abhothenu retzeh,*[23] while the *Musaph* for the festivals includes *attah bheḥartanu* and *watiten lanu*[24] as well as *wehassi-enu.*[25]

I. THE SABBATH MUSAPH

(1) *The traditional Ashkenazi version.*

תכנת שבת רצית קרבנותיה. צוית פרושיה עם סדורי נסכיה. מענגיה
לעולם כבוד ינחלו. טועמיה חיים זכו. וגם האוהבים דבריה גדלה בחרו.
אז מסיני נצטוו עליה. ותצונו יי אלהינו להקריב בה קרבן מוסף שבת
כראוי: יהי רצון מלפניך יי אלהינו ואלהי אבותינו שתעלנו בשמחה
לארצנו ותטענו בגבולנו. ושם נעשה לפניך את קרבנות חובותינו.
תמידים כסדרם ומוספים כהלכתם. ואת־מוסף יום השבת הזה נעשה
ונקריב לפניך באהבה כמצות רצונך כמו שכתבת עלינו בתורתך על־ידי
משה עבדך מפי כבודך כאמור: וביום השבת שני־כבשים בני־שנה
תמימים ושני עשרנים סלת מנחה בלולה בשמן ונסכו: עלת שבת
בשבתו על־עלת התמיד ונסכה:

(2) *The traditional Sepharadi version.*

למשה צוית על הר סיני מצות שבת זכור ושמור. ובו צויתנו יי אלהינו
להקריב בו קרבן מוסף שבת כראוי: יהי רצון מלפניך יי אלהינו ואלהי
אבותינו שתעלנו בשמחה לארצנו ותטענו בגבולנו. ושם נעשה לפניך את
קרבנות חובותינו. תמידין כסדרן ומוספין כהלכתן: את־מוסף יום השבת
הזה נעשה ונקריב לפניך באהבה. כמצות רצונך. כמו שכתבת עלינו
בתורתך על ידי משה עבדך כאמור. וביום השבת שני־כבשים בני־שנה...:

(3) *HAMBURG, 1819.*

למשה צוית בהר סיני מצות שבת זכור ושמור. ובו צויתנו יי אלהינו
להקריב בה קרבן מוסף שבת כראוי. ובכן יהי רצון מלפניך יי אלהינו
ואלהי אבותינו שתקבל ברחמים וברצון ארשת שפתינו במקום קרבנות
חובותינו. תמידים כסדרם ומוספים כהלכתם. ואת מוסף יום השבת הזה
כמצות רצונך. כמו שכתבת עלינו בתורתך על ידי משה עבדך:

To Moses Thou didst command at Mount Sinai the commandment of the Sabbath: "Remember!" and "Observe!" And there Thou didst command us, O Lord our God, to offer thereon the additional sacrifice of the Sabbath in its proper form. May it thus be Thy will, O Lord our God and God of our fathers, to accept in mercy and with favor the expression of our lips in place of our obligatory sacrifices—the continual offerings according to their order, and the additional sacrifices according to their rule, and the additional sacrifice of this Sabbath day according to the command of Thy will, even as Thou hast written for us in Thy Torah, by the hands of Thy servant Moses.

This version of the *Musaph* remained substantially the same in all the subsequent editions of the prayerbook of the Hamburg Temple. Such changes as were introduced in later editions were of a stylistic nature only, removing some of the ambiguities of the 1819 edition.

(4) *MAYENCE, 1853.*
This prayerbook retains the complete traditional Hebrew text, for reasons explained by its editor, Joseph Aub, in his Preface.[26] The German version, however, is to the following effect:

> *O God, Thou hast blessed and sanctified the Sabbath, and, at Mount Sinai, Thou hast commanded us to remember this day, and to celebrate it with rest and consecration. Even as our fathers in days of old brought one sacrifice more on the Sabbath than they did on weekdays, so our own devotions are increased on this day, as we gather in Thy sanctuary. Here we find edification in Thy Word. Here we worship Thee, and acknowledge that Thou, to Whom the Sabbath testifieth, art the Creator and Ruler of the world. O Heavenly Father, let Thy grace reign over us, and accept our prayer as an acceptable sacrifice. Grant holy enlightenment to our soul, and blessed rest to our heart.*

A similar text, if somewhat closer in its relation to the Hebrew original, was used in the Mannheim Prayerbook of 1855.

(5) *GEIGER, 1854.*

> תכנת שבת צוית פרושיה מענגיה לעולם כבוד ינחלו. טועמיה חיים זכו. וגם האוהבים דבריה גדלה בחרו. אז מסיני נצטוו עליה. ואת מוסף יום השבת הזה נעשה לפניך באהבה כמצות רצונך כמו שכתבת עלינו בתורתך על־ידי משה עבדך מפי כבודך:
>
> *Thou hast instituted the Sabbath and commanded its specific obligations. They that find delight in it shall inherit glory for ever. They that taste it merit life, while such as love its teachings have chosen greatness. Already from Sinai they were commanded concerning it. And the* Musaph *Service*[27] *of this Sabbath day we are holding before Thee in love, according to the commandment of Thy will, even as Thou hast written for us in Thy Torah through Thy servant Moses, by the mouth of Thy glory.*

In the 1870 edition of his prayerbook, Geiger omitted this paragraph altogether, as did Seligmann later, in 1910 and 1928, restricting the actual contents of the *Musaph* to the remaining two paragraphs, *yismeḥu* and *elohenu welohé abhothenu retzeh.*

(6) *CONFERENCE OF RABBIS, 1857.*
The rabbis of Southern Germany, called together by Stein, in Frankfort o. M., in 1857, adopted by majority vote, though not unanimously, the following version of the *Musaph*.[28] The dots before this new version indicate that, up to that point, the traditional version was to be followed, just as the "etc." at the end shows that the prayer was to conclude with the full text of the sacrificial law in Numbers 28: 9–10.

...אז מסיני נצטוו עליה: לכן גם אנו מוסיפים תפלתנו ביום המנוח הזה: יהי רצון מלפניך יי אלהינו ואלהי אבותינו שתכין לבבנו ולבב כל בני האדם אליך, לא ירעו ולא ישחיתו בכל הר קדשך ושבתה הארץ שבת ליי: וארשת שפתינו אל תמנע יי אלהינו, ותפלת מוסף יום השבת הזה תקבל ממנו באהבה כמו שקבלת מאבותינו ברצון את קרבן מוספם אשר הקריבו לפניך כמו שכתבת וכו׳:

... Already from Sinai they were commanded concerning it. Therefore, we, too, are adding to our prayer on this day of rest. May it be Thy will, O Lord our God and God of our fathers, to direct our heart and the heart of all the sons of man unto Thee. May they not hurt nor destroy in all Thy holy mountain; and may the earth keep a Sabbath unto the Lord. And do not refuse, O Lord our God, the expression of our lips; and accept from us in love the Musaph *prayer of this Sabbath day, as Thou didst receive, with favor, the* Musaph *sacrifice which our fathers brought before Thee, according to the commandment of Thy will, even as Thou hast written etc.*

In this particular form, the *Musaph* prayer was adopted nowhere, not even by Stein himself in his 1860 and 1882 editions of the prayerbook. But many of the prayerbooks appearing after the 1857 Conference, and not only in Southern Germany, bear some traces of that 1857 text.

(7) *STEIN, 1860.*

...ותצוה (ותצונו) יי אלהינו להקריב בה קרבן מוסף שבת כראוי: יהי רצון מלפני יי אלהינו ואלהי אבותינו שתקבל מאתנו היום את־תפלת מוספנו ברחמים כאשר רצית בקרבן מוסף יום השבת הזה אשר הקריבו לפניך אבותינו באהבה כמצות רצונך כמו שכתבת בתורתך על־ידי משה עבדך מפי כבודך כאמור: וביום השבת שני־כבשים...:

... and Thou hast commanded to bring thereon the additional sacrifice of the Sabbath in its proper form. May it be Thy will, O Lord our God and God of our fathers to accept this day from us, in mercy, our Musaph *prayer, as Thou didst find pleasure in the* Musaph *sacrifice of this Sabbath day which our fathers brought before Thee in love, according to the commandant of Thy will, even as Thou hast written in Thy Torah through*

Thy servant Moses, by the mouth of Thy glory: "And on the Sabbath day, two he-lambs etc."

Note that, while retaining the full sacrificial text, Stein made it quite clear, by means of minor verbal changes, that the sacrificial commandment was addressed to "our fathers," and not to us. While, no doubt, for the benefit of the more "traditionalist" members, Stein has retained the word *wattetzawwenu* ("And Thou hast commanded us"), that word, together with the rest of the traditional version, appears in small print only.

Aub's Berlin prayerbook of 1866 follows Stein's Hebrew text, although its German version is identical with that of the Mayence prayerbook of 1853. Also related to Stein's text, but omitting the Biblical passage concerning the sacrifices, are the *Musaph* versions of the Göteborg prayerbook of 1858 and of the Nuremberg prayerbook of 1874. The former, of course, antedating Stein's prayerbook by two years, was not based on Stein's text itself, but, obviously, on the prototype used by Stein, the version produced by the Conference of Rabbis in 1857.

(8) *JOËL, 1872.*

...אז מסיני נצטוו עליה: יהי רצון מלפניך יי אלהינו ואלהי אבותינו שתכין לבנו לשמור שבתותיך ותביא ברכה בארצנו ושלוה בגבולנו למען יהיה לבנו פתוח לעבודתך: ותערב עליך ארשת שפתינו במקום מוסף יום השבת הזה שהקריבו לפניך אבותינו כמצות רצונך כמו שכתבת עלינו בתורתך על־ידי משה עבדך מפי כבודך:

... Already from Sinai they were commanded concerning it. May it be Thy will, O Lord our God and God of our fathers, to direct our hearts to keep Thy Sabbaths, and to bring blessing to our land and tranquility to our borders, that our heart may be open to the service of Thee. And may the expression of our lips be acceptable unto Thee in place of the Musaph *sacrifice which our fathers brought before Thee on this Sabbath day, according to the commandment of Thy will, even as Thou hast written for us in Thy Torah through Thy servant Moses, by the mouth of Thy glory.*

In small print, Joël also retains the traditional version, but leaves it untranslated. Joël's version was also adopted by the Munich prayerbooks of 1876 and 1891.

(9) *LEIPZIG, 1876.*

תכנת שבת רצית בקדושתו מענגיו לעולם כבוד ינחלו. טוֹעמיו חיים זכו. וגם האוהבים דבריו גדלה בחרו. אז מסיני נצטוו עליו: ותצונו יי אלהינו לשמור את־יום השבת ולקדשו כראוי:

Thou hast instituted the Sabbath, and hast found pleasure in its sanctification. They that delight in it shall inherit glory for ever, they that taste it merit life, while such as love its teachings have chosen greatness. Already from Sinai they were commanded concerning it. And Thou hast commanded us, O Lord our God, to observe the Sabbath day, and to hallow it as is fitting.

It will be observed that the Hebrew word, *shabbath,* is here treated as a masculine noun, marking a departure from the grammar of the traditional text which employs feminine forms. While, in rare instances, the word *shabbath* has been treated as a masculine noun, the far more usual way is to consider it as feminine.[29] Why Goldschmidt, the editor of the Leipzig prayerbook, whose predilection for grammatical niceties is evident from his Preface,[30] should have chosen those unusual forms, is not altogether clear.

Of greater importance, however, is the fact that, in this version, any reminiscence of, or connection with, the sacrificial cult of the past has been removed. Instead, the Sabbath commandment referred to in the text of the prayer is clearly understood to be that of Exodus 20: 8ff. and Deuteronomy 5: 12ff. Those texts, and also Leviticus 23: 3, from now on make their appearance in the reformed versions of the *Musaph.*

(10) *BERLIN, NEUE SYNAGOGE, 1881.*

תקנת [31] שבת רצית קדושיה צוית פקודיה. מענגיה לעולם כבוד ינחלו. טועמיה חיים זכו. וגם האוהבים דבריה גדלה בחרו. אז מסיני נצטוו עליה כמו שכתוב בתורתך על־ידי משה עבדך מפי כבודך כאמור: זכור את־יום השבת לקדשו. ששת ימים תעבד ועשית כל־מלאכתך. ויום השביעי שבת ליי אלהיך:

Thou hast ordained the Sabbath, and found pleasure in its sanctification. Thou hast commanded its precepts. They that delight in it shall inherit glory for ever, they that taste it merit life, while they that love its teachings have chosen greatness. Already from Sinai they were commanded concerning it, as it is written in Thy Torah through Thy servant Moses, by the mouth of Thy glory, saying: "Remember the Sabbath day, to keep it holy. Six days shalt thou labor and do all thy work. But the seventh day is the Sabbath unto the Lord thy God."

This version was retained by later editions of the Berlin prayerbook, and also adopted by the Stockholm prayerbook of 1930. The Brunswick prayerbook of 1906 also has it, but here the letter *kaph* is restored in *tikkanta.*

(11) *STEIN, 1882.*

...אז מסיני נצטוו עליה. יהי רצון מלפניך יי אלהינו ואלהי אבותינו שתקבל מאתנו את־תפלת מוספנו ברחמים ביום השבת הזה אשר צויתנו לקדש אותו כמו שכתבת בתורתך על־ידי משה עבדך מפי כבודך כאמור: ששת ימים תעשה מלאכה. וביום השביעי שבת שבתון מקרא קדש. כל־מלאכה לא תעשו. שבת היא ליי בכל משבתיכם:

. . . Already from Sinai they were commanded concerning it. May it be Thy will, O Lord our God and God of our fathers, to accept from us, in mercy, our Musaph *prayer on this Sabbath day, which Thou hast commanded us to sanctify, even as Thou hast written in Thy Torah through Thy servant Moses, by the mouth of Thy glory, saying: "Six days shall work be done; but on the seventh day is a Sabbath of solemn rest, a holy convocation; ye shall do no manner of work; it is a Sabbath unto the Lord in all your habitations."*

A very similar version, but considerably abbreviating the alphabetical acrostic, *tikkanta,* with its references to the sacrificial cult, retained by Stein, is found in Vogelstein's 1894 edition of the prayerbook, and in the 1905 prayerbook of Baden.

(12) *EINHEITSGEBETBUCH, 1929.*

תקנת שבת רצית קדושיה. מענגיה לעולם כבוד ינחלו. טועמיה חיים זכו. וגם האוהבים דבריה גדלה בחרו. אז מסיני נצטוו עליה. ככתוב בתורתך: זכור את־יום השבת לקדשו. ששת ימים תעבד ועשית כל־מלאכתך ויום השביעי שבת ליי אלהיך:

Thou hast ordained the Sabbath, and found pleasure in its sanctification. They that delight in it shall inherit glory for ever, they that taste it merit life, while they that love its teachings have chosen greatness. Already from Sinai they were commanded concerning it, as it is written in Thy Torah: "Remember the Sabbath day, to keep it holy. Six days shalt thou labor and do all thy work; but the seventh day is the Sabbath unto the Lord thy God."

II. THE FESTIVAL MUSAPH

(1) *The traditional Ashkenazi version.*

ומפני חטאינו גלינו מארצנו ונתרחקנו מעל אדמתנו. ואין אנחנו יכולים לעלות ולראות ולהשתחוות לפניך ולעשות חובותינו בבית בחירתך בבית הגדול והקדוש שנקרא שמך עליו מפני היד שנשתלחה במקדשך: יהי רצון מלפניך יי אלהינו ואלהי אבותינו מלך רחמן שתשוב ותרחם עלינו ועל מקדשך ברחמיך הרבים ותבנהו מהרה ותגדל כבודו: אבינו מלכנו. גלה כבוד מלכותך עלינו מהרה והופע והנשא עלינו לעיני כל־חי.

וקרב פזורינו מבין הגוים ונפוצותינו כנס מירכתי ארץ. והביאנו לציון
עירך ברנה ולירושלים בית מקדשך בשמחת עולם. ושם נעשה לפניך
את-קרבנות חובותינו תמידים כסדרם ומוספים כהלכתם: ואת-מוסף
יום חג... הזה נעשה ונקריב לפניך באהבה כמצות רצונך כמו שכתבת
עלינו בתורתך על-ידי משה עבדך מפי כבודך כאמור:
(פסוקים ע״ד הקרבנות מספר במדבר פרקים כ״ח וכ״ט.)
אלהינו ואלהי אבותינו מלך רחמן רחם עלינו טוב ומטיב הדרש-לנו. שובה
אלינו (בנוסח הספרדי: עלינו) בהמון רחמיך בגלל אבות שעשו רצונך.
בנה ביתך כבתחלה וכונן מקדשך על-מכונו. והראנו בבנינו ושמחנו
בתקונו. והשב כהנים לעבודתם ולוים לשירם ולזמרם והשב ישראל
לנויהם. ושם נעלה ונראה ונשתחוה לפניך בשלש פעמי רגלינו. ככתוב
בתורתך. שלוש פעמים בשנה יראה כל-זכורך את-פני יי אלהיך במקום
אשר יבחר בחג המצות ובחג השבעות ובחג הסכות ולא יראה את-פני
יי ריקם: איש כמתנת ידו כברכת יי אלהיך אשר נתן-לך:

(2) *HAMBURG, 1819.*

ומפני חטאינו גלינו מארצנו ונתרחקנו מעל אדמתנו. ואין אנחנו
יכולים לעשות חובותינו בבית בחירתך. בבית הגדול והקדוש שנקרא
שמך עליו מפני היד השלוחה במקדשך: יהי רצון מלפניך יי אלהינו
ואלהי אבותינו שתקבל ברחמים וברצון ארשת שפתינו במקום קרבנות
חובותינו. תמידים כסדרם ומוספים כהלכתם. ובמקום מוספי יום חג...
הזה. באהבה כמצות רצונך. כמו שכתבת עלינו בתורתך על ידי משה
עבדך מפי כבודך: ובכן יהי רצון מלפניך יי אלהינו ואלהי אבותינו.
מלך רחמן שתשוב ותרחם עלינו ועל מקדשך ברחמיך הרבים. ותבנהו
מהרה ותגדל כבודו. אבינו מלכנו. גלה כבוד מלכותך עלינו מהרה והופע
והנשא עלינו לעיני כל חי: אלהינו ואלהי אבותינו. מלך רחמן רחם עלינו.
טוב ומטיב הדרש לנו. שובה עלינו בהמון רחמיך בגלל אבות שעשו
רצונך. שבענו מברכותיך. ושמחנו במועדיך. בהשתחות לפניך בשלש
פעמי רגלינו. ככתוב בתורתך. שלש פעמים בשנה יראה כל-זכורך את פני
יי אלהיך במקום אשר יבחר בחג המצות ובחג השבעות ובחג הסכות
ולא יראה את-פני יי ריקם: איש כמתנת ידו כברכת יי אלהיך אשר
נתן לך:

And on account of our sins we were exiled from our land, and removed from our soil; and we are unable to fulfil our obligations in Thy chosen house, that great and holy temple which was called by Thy Name, because of the hand that hath been stretched out against Thy sanctuary. May it be Thy will, O Lord our God and God of our fathers, to accept the expression of our lips in place of our obligatory sacrifices, the continual offerings according to their order, and the Musaph *sacrifices according to their rule—and in place of the* Musaph *sacrifices of this feast of . . ., in love, according to the commandment of Thy will, as Thou hast written for us in Thy Torah through Thy servant Moses, by the mouth of Thy glory. May it therefore be Thy will,*

O Lord our God and God of our fathers, merciful King, that Thou mayest again, in Thine abundant compassion, have mercy upon us and upon Thy sanctuary. Rebuild it speedily, and magnify its glory. Our Father, our King, reveal the glory of Thy kingdom upon us speedily, shine forth and be Thou exalted upon us in the sight of all the living. Our God and God of our fathers, merciful King, have mercy upon us, O Thou Who art good and doest good, let Thyself be sought of us. Return unto us in the abundance of Thy mercy, for the sake of the fathers who did Thy will. Satisfy us with Thy blessings, and cause us to rejoice in Thy festive seasons, as we worship Thee on our three pilgrim festivals; even as it is written in Thy Torah: "Three times in the year shall all thy males appear before the Lord thy God, in the place which He shall choose, on the feast of unleavened bread, and on the feast of weeks, and on the feast of tabernacles; and they shall not appear before the Lord empty. Every man shall bring according as he is able, according to the blessing of the Lord thy God which He hath given thee."

This version remains basically the same in all subsequent editions of this liturgy, except for some stylistic improvements of a minor character. The 1904 edition, however, omits the request that God have mercy upon His sanctuary, that He rebuild it and magnify its glory. That edition also adds the hope that "we may return unto Thee with a whole heart," concluding the prayer as follows:

אלהינו ואלהי אבותינו מלך רחמן רחם עלינו. טוב ומטיב הדרש לנו.
שובה אלינו בהמון רחמיך. בגלל אבות שעשו רצונך : ונשוב אליך בלבב
שלם. ונשתחוה לפניך בשלוש פעמי רגלינו. ככתוב בתורתך. שלוש
פעמים בשנה... :

The version of the Hamburg Temple Prayerbook served as the pattern for several other prayerbooks for more than a hundred years. While there are variations among them, the variations are of a minor character. What all the versions have in common is the tendency to abbreviate the traditional version, without introducing any new elements, and the removal of the petition for the restoration of the sacrificial cult. They differ from one another in the retention or omission of the introductory clause, "on account of our sins we were exiled, etc.," in the presence or absence of the plea for God's mercy on the Temple, where "Temple" is frequently explained to be "a house of prayer for all peoples," and in the presence or absence of the relevant Scripture verses from Numbers 28 and 29—with or without the specific mention of the sacrifices. In detail, a comparison of the various prayerbooks in this category looks as follows:

	"On account of our sins"	Mercy on the Temple	Numbers verses with sacrifices	Numbers verses without sacrifices
GEIGER, 1854[32]	x	x		x
GEIGER, 1870[33]		x		x
NUREMBERG, 1874	x	x		
LEIPZIG, 1876[34]		x		x
STOCKHOLM, 1907	x	x	x	
SELIGMANN, 1928		x		
EINHEITSGEBET-BUCH, 1929		x		x

(3) *MAYENCE, 1853.*
The same reasons which induced Aub to retain the traditional Hebrew text of the *Musaph* for Sabbath, while departing from it completely in his German paraphrase, also applied in the case of the *Musaph* for the festivals. The paraphrase of the latter is as follows:

On account of their sins, our ancestors were driven out of their land, and removed from their country. Thus they became unable to make pilgrimages to Thy great and holy Temple, to worship Thee there, and to offer sacrifices. For the sanctuary was destroyed.

O God, merciful King, mayest Thou have mercy upon us and upon our sanctuary, that Thy Temple may be built in glory, and Thy kingdom extend over the whole earth. Thus will the whole earth become a Temple for Thy worship. And even as, in the days of old, Thou didst accept in grace the daily sacrifices and the festival offerings, so do Thou now hearken to our prayer on this feast of. . . . For we direct our prayers unto Thee, as our fathers directed their sacrifices in ancient days, even as was ordained in Thy commandment, given through Moses:

[Here follow the relevant verses from Numbers 28 and 29, omitting the mention of the sacrifices—except in the case of the verses dealing with the Sabbath.]

O Holy One of Israel! Merciful King! Have mercy upon us! Thou Who art All-Good and doest good, let Thyself be entreated by us, and turn unto us in the abundance of Thy mercy, for the sake of the fathers who did Thy will. Build Thy Temple according to Thy promise, so that Thy sanctuary may be made secure through faith in Thee, and that, in the words of the Prophet, it may be called a house of prayer for all men. May Israel and all mankind know Thee and worship Thee, and may they say: "Come ye, and let us go up to the mountain of the Lord, to the house of the God of Jacob, that He may teach us of His ways, and that we may walk in His paths. For out of Zion goeth forth instruction, and the word of the Lord from Jerusalem,"—even as, in days of yore, our fathers went up to Jerusalem on this festival, according to Thy commandment: "Three times in the year. . . ."

(4) *CONFERENCE OF RABBIS, 1857.*[35]

ומפני חטאינו גלה יקרנו ונטל כבוד מבית חיינו, עטרת תפארתנו הסרת וקרן ישראל לעפר השפלת: יהי רצון מלפניך יי אלהינו ואלהי אבותינו, מלך רחמן שתשוב ותרחם עלינו ועל מקדשך ברחמיך הרבים: אורו תחדש, כבודו תגדל, וביתך בית תפלה לכל העמים יקרא: אבינו מלכנו גלה כבוד מלכותך עלינו מהרה, וביתך בית תפלה לכל העמים יקרא אבינו מלכנו גלה כבוד מלכותך עלינו מהרה, והופע והנשא עלינו לעיני כל חי: בשמך תרום קרננו וראו כל אפסי ארץ את ישועת אלהינו, וזבחי תודה נקריב לך ברנה ובשמחת עולם: וארשת שפתינו אל תמנע יי אלהינו, ואת תפלת מוסף יום... הזה תקבל ממנו ברחמים כמו שקבלת מאבותינו ברצון את קרבן מוספם (קרבנות מוספיהם) אשר הקריבו לפניך באהבה כמצות רצונך, כמו שכתבת בתורתך וכו׳:

...בגלל אבות שעשו רצונך, הכן לבב בניהם לעבודתך, ובקול רנה המון חוגג נבוא בשלש פעמי רגלינו להראות ולהשתחוות לפניך ונדבות פינו ומתנות ידינו תהיינה לרצון לפניך יי אלהינו ככתוב בתורתך שלוש פעמים וכו׳:

And on account of our sins, our splendor was exiled, and the glory was taken away from the house of our life. The diadem of our glory Thou didst remove, and the horn of Israel Thou didst bring low to the dust. May it be Thy will, O Lord our God and God of our fathers, O merciful King, to be merciful unto us again and unto Thy sanctuary, in Thy manifold mercies. Renew its light; magnify its glory; and may Thy house be called a house of prayer for all peoples. Our Father, our King, reveal the glory of Thy kingdom upon us speedily; shine forth and be exalted above us in the sight of all the living. Exalt our horn in Thy Name, so that all the ends of the earth may see the salvation of our God. Then shall we offer unto Thee the sacrifices of thanksgiving in jubilation and in everlasting joy. And do not refuse, O Lord our God, the expression of our lips, and the Musaph *prayer of this . . . day do Thou accept from us in mercy, even as Thou didst receive with favor the* Musaph *sacrifice which our fathers brought before Thee in love, according to the commandment of Thy will, as Thou hast written in Thy Torah. . . .* [The prayer now continues according to the traditional version, including the verses dealing with the sacrifices.]

> . . . *for the sake of the fathers who did Thy will, direct the heart of their children unto Thy service; and with the joyful sound of a multitude keeping holyday will we come, on our three pilgrim festivals, to appear before Thee, and to worship Thee, O Lord our God, even as it is written in Thy Torah: "Three times in the year. . . ."*

Like the proposed *Musaph* for the Sabbath adopted by this Conference, the *Musaph* for the festivals was also adopted by majority vote only, and not unanimously. There is, in fact, not a single prayerbook which includes this version in an unchanged form, although there are several prayerbooks which clearly show its influence. Thus, the Göteborg prayerbook of 1858, while considerably abbreviating the wording and removing the Numbers verses, and, on the other hand, restoring the first four words of the traditional version, represents, in substance, this 1857 text. Stein, in his 1860 edition of the prayerbook, follows the 1857 version much more closely, including the verses dealing with the sacrifices. He even restores the reference to the rebuilding of the Temple in the concluding sentence, thus:

> אלהינו ואלהי אבותינו מלך רחמן רחם עלינו טוב ומטיב הדרש לנו שובה אלינו בהמון רחמיך בגלל אבות שעשו רצונך בנה ביתך כבתחלה וכונן מקדשך על-מכונו והראנו בבנינו ושמחנו בתקונו. והכן לבב כל-בני-ישראל לעבודתך. ובקול רנה ותודה נבוא ונשתחוה לפניך בשלש פעמי רגלינו. ככתוב בתורתך שלוש פעמים בשנה...

However, in the 1882 edition of the prayerbook, Stein, while still retaining the Numbers verses about the festivals, omits the verses which actually mention the sacrifices. In the concluding sentence, the petition for the rebuilding of the Temple is now omitted.

(5) *AUB, BERLIN, 1866.*

> ומפני חטאיהם גלו אבותינו מארצם ונתרחקו מעל אדמתם ולא היו יכולים עוד לעלות ולראות ולהשתחוות לפניך ולעשות חובותיהם בבית בחירתך בבית הגדול והקדוש שנקרא שמך עליו מפני היד השלוחה במקדשך: יהי רצון מלפניך יי אליהנו ואלהי אבותינו מלך רחמן שתשוב ותרחם עלינו ועל מקדשך ברחמיך הרבים ותגדל כבודו לתפארתך. אבינו מלכנו גלה כבוד מלכותך עלינו מהרה והופע והנשא עלינו לעיני כל חי וקרבנו לעבדך באמת וראו כל־אפסי־ארץ את ישועת אלהינו ונודה לשמך ברנה ובשמחת עולם וקבל ברחמים וברצון ארשת שפתינו כקרבנות שהקריבו לפניך אבותינו תמידים כסדרם ומוספים כהלכתם כמו שכתבת בתורתך על-ידי משה עבדך מפי כבודך כאמור :
>
> (The verses from Numbers 28 and 29, including the sacrifices.)
>
> אלהינו ואלהי אבותינו מלך רחמן רחם עלינו טוב ומטיב הדרש לנו שובה

אליונ בהמון רחמיך בגלל אבות שעשו רצונך בנה ביתך בית תפלה
לכל העמים וכונן בכל הארץ מקדשך לעבודתך והראנו חסדך ושמחנו
במועדיך ונראה ונשתחוה לפניך בשלש פעמי רגלינו ככתוב בתורתך
שלוש פעמים בשנה...:

This is, in essence, a Hebrew version of the German paraphrase of the *Musaph* which Aub had included in his 1853 edition of the Mayence prayerbook, even as that 1853 paraphrase now appears as the German translation of the 1866 Hebrew version. (The sacrificial verses included in the Hebrew text remain untranslated.) Aub's changes in the Hebrew text, to the effect that it was on account of *their* sins that *our fathers* were exiled from *their* land etc., had an influence on some of the modern prayerbooks which were published in later years, as we shall have occasion to see.

(6) *JOËL, 1872.*

ומפני חטאינו גלינו מארצנו ונתרחקנו מעל אדמתנו ולא יכלנו לעלות
ולראות ולהשתחוות לפניך ולעשות חובותינו בבית בחירתך בבית הגדול
והקדוש שנקרא שמך עליו מפני היד שנשתלחה במקדשך: ומעת ההיא
כבה זהרנו וסר עדינו מעלינו. יהי רצון מלפניך יי אלהינו ואלהי אבותינו
מלך רחמן שתשוב ותרחם עלינו ועל מקדשך ברחמיך הרבים: חדש רוח
נכון בקרבנו לעבדך בלבב שלם ואז ברצונך תרום קרננו וכל-יושבי תבל
יתנו יקר לשמנו: אבינו מלכנו גלה כבוד מלכותך עלינו מהרה. והופע
והנשא עלינו לעיני כל-חי. ושים אהבה ואחוה בקרב פזורינו עד-ירכתי
ארץ: אנא תן ברכה בארצנו ושלום בגבולנו למען יהיה לבנו פתוח
לעבודתך: שמח ישראל עמך וקבל ברצון ניב שפתינו במקום מוסף יום...
הזה שהקריבו לפניך אבותינו כמצות רצונך כמו שכתבת עלינו בתורתך
על-ידי משה עבדך מפי כבודך: ובתורתך כתוב לאמר:

(Verses from Numbers 28 and 29, omitting those dealing with sacrifices.)

אלהינו ואלהי אבותינו מלך רחמן רחם עלינו טוב ומטיב הדרש לנו שובה
אלינו בהמון רחמיך בגלל אבות שעשו רצונך תושיע בניהם וכונן מקדשך
בקרבם לראות ולהשתחוות לפניך בלבב שלם ככתוב בתורתך שלוש
פעמים בשנה...:

And on account of our sins we were exiled from our land, and removed from our soil, and we were (sic) *unable to go up, and appear, and worship before Thee, and to fulfil our obligations in Thy chosen house, the great and holy Temple which was called by Thy Name, because of the hand which had been stretched out against it. And from that time on, our splendor was extinguished, and our ornament departed from upon us. May it be Thy will, O Lord our God and God of our fathers, merciful King, that Thou mayest again have mercy upon us and upon Thy sanctuary, in Thy great mercy. Renew a steadfast spirit within us, that we may serve Thee with a whole heart. And then, in Thy favor, raise up our horn, that all the dwellers of the earth may give honor unto our name. Our Father, our King, reveal the glory of Thy kingdom upon us speedily. Shine forth and be Thou exalted over us in the sight of all the living. Give love and brotherhood to our scattered ones, to the farthest parts of the earth. O give blessing to our land, and peace to our borders, so that our heart may be open to the service of Thee. Make Israel, Thy people, happy, and accept with favor the fruit of our lips in place of the* Musaph *sacrifice of this . . . day, which our fathers brought before Thee according to the commandment of Thy will, as Thou hast written for us in Thy Torah through Thy servant Moses, by the mouth of Thy glory. And in Thy Torah it is written, saying:*

[Here follow the relevant verses from Numbers 28 and 29, without mention of the sacrifices.]

Our God and God of our fathers, merciful King, have mercy upon us, O Thou Who art good and doest good let Thyself be sought of us. Return unto us in the multitude of Thy mercies. For the sake of the fathers who did Thy will, save their children, establish Thy sanctuary in their midst, so that they may appear and worship before Thee with a perfect heart, even as it is written in Thy Torah: "Three times in the year. . . ."

Joël also retains the traditional version, but in small print and without translation. Joël's version was adopted by the Munich prayerbooks of 1876 and 1891.

(7) *BERLIN, NEUE SYNAGOGE, 1881.*

אבותינו גלו מארצם ונתרחקו מעל אדמתם אכן אתה אל מסתתר אלהי ישראל מושיע. זריתנו בארצות לקדש את-שמך בעולם ממזרח שמש עד מבואו: יהי רצון מלפניך יי אלהינו ואלהי אבותינו מלך רחמן שתרחם עלינו ועל מקדשך ברחמים הרבים. ותרם קרן ישראל ותגדל כבודו. אבינו מלכנו גלה כבוד מלכותך עלינו מהרה והופע והנשא עלינו לעיני כל-חי ולך תעלה קדשה מירכתי הארץ. חקי רצונך נשמור דבר יום ביומו ואת-חקת יום... הזה נעשה לפניך באהבה כמצות רצונך כמו שכתבת עלינו בתורתך על-ידי משה עבדך מפי כבודך כאמור:

(The festival verses from Numbers 28 and 29, without mention of sacrifices.)

אלהינו ואלהי אבותינו מלך רחמן... בגלל אבות שעשו רצונך בנה ביתך בית תפלה לכל-העמים וכונן בכל-הארץ מקדשך לעבודתך והראנו חסדך ושמחנו במועדיך ונראה ונשתחוה לפניך בשלש פעמי רגלינו ככתוב בתורתך שלוש פעמים בשנה...:

Our fathers were exiled from their land, and removed from their soil. Verily Thou art a God that hidest Thyself, O God of Israel, the Savior! Thou hast scattered us in the lands, to sanctify Thy Name in the world, from the rising of the sun unto the going down thereof. May it be Thy will, O Lord our God and God of our fathers, that Thou mayest again have mercy upon us and upon Thy sanctuary, in Thy great mercies. Raise up the horn of Israel, and magnify its glory. Our Father, our King, reveal the glory of Thy kingdom upon us speedily. Shine forth and be Thou exalted over us in the sight of all the living. Then shall the proclamation of Thy holiness rise up unto Thee from the uttermost parts of the earth. And we shall keep the statutes of Thy will, according to the requirements of every single day; and the statute of this . . . day we shall perform before Thee in love, according to the commandment of Thy will, even as Thou hast written for us in Thy Torah through Thy servant Moses, by the mouth of Thy glory, as it is said:

[Here follow the festival verses from Numbers 28 and 29, without mention of the sacrifices.]

Our God and God of our fathers, merciful King, . . . For the sake of the fathers who did Thy will, build Thy Temple as a house of prayer for all the peoples, and establish Thy sanctuary for Thy service in the whole earth. Show us Thy kindness, and rejoice us in Thy festive seasons. And we shall appear and worship before Thee on our three pilgrim festivals, as it is written in Thy Torah: "Three times in the year . . . ."

This version was retained in subsequent editions of this prayerbook, and also adopted by the Brunswick prayerbook of 1906. The same version is found in the Stockholm prayerbook of 1930, although, there, the first seven words of the traditional text have been restored, replacing the first six words of the present version.

As for the 1881 Berlin version, it will be noted that all references to the sacrificial cult, even by way of historical reminiscence, have disappeared; and so has the notion, still given currency by Aub's prayerbook of 1866, that our fathers' exile was "on account of their sins." Instead, the *Musaph* prayer, in full awareness of Israel's geographical diffusion, develops the theme of the Mission of Israel.

(8) *GLOGAU, 1892(?).*

יהי רצון מלפניך יי אלהינו ואלהי אבותינו מלך רחמן שתשוב ותרחם עלינו. אבינו מלכנו גלה כבוד מלכותך עלינו מהרה והופע והנשא עלינו לעיני כל־חי ואת יום חג... הזה נקדיש לפניך באהבה כמצות רצונך כמו שכתבת עלינו בתורתך על ידי משך עבדך מפי כבודך כאמור : אלהינו ואלהי אבותינו מלך רחמן... (בנוסח של הסידור של ברלין משנת 1881):

May it be Thy will, O Lord our God and God of our fathers, that Thou mayest again have mercy upon us. Our Father, our King, reveal the glory of Thy kingdom upon us speedily. Shine forth and be exalted over us in the sight of all the living. And this festive day of . . . we shall sanctify before Thee in love, according to the commandment of Thy will, even as Thou hast written for us in Thy Torah through Thy servant Moses, by the mouth of Thy glory, as it is said. Our God and God of our fathers, merciful King, have mercy upon us, . . . [the rest of this prayer as in the Berlin prayerbook of 1881].

This version, one of the briefest we have encountered, includes no Scripture verses, thereby making the retention of the word *ka-amur* somewhat anomalous.

(9) *VOGELSTEIN, 1894.*

יהי רצון מלפניך יי אלהינו ואלהי אבותינו שתרחם עליו ברחמיך הרבים. ותרם קרן ישראל ותגדל כבודו: אבינו מלכנו גלה כבוד מלכותך עלינו מהרה והופע והנשא עלינו לעיני כל־חי: יערב (*sic*) עליך עתירתנו. ואת־תפילת מוסף יום... הזה תקבל ברצון והאר עינינו כי מיחלים אנחנו לך: ובתורתך כתוב לאמר: (פסוקים מספר במדבר פרקים כ״ח וכ״ט, בלי הזכרת הקרבנות). אלהינו ואלהי אבותינו מלך רחמן... (בנוסח של סידור ברלין משנת 1881):

May it be Thy will, O Lord our God and God of our fathers, to have mercy upon us in Thy manifold mercies. Lift up the horn of Israel, and magnify its honor. Our Father, our King, reveal the glory of Thy kingdom upon us speedily. Shine forth and be Thou exalted over us in the sight of all the living. May our prayer be pleasing unto Thee, and accept with favor the Musaph *prayer of this . . . day. Enlighten our eyes, for in Thee do we hope. And in Thy Torah it is written:*

[Here follow the verses from Numbers 28 and 29, without mention of sacrifices.]

Our God and God of our fathers, merciful King . . . [as in the Berlin prayerbook of 1881].

(10) *BADEN, 1905.*

ומפני עצת קדשך גלו אבותינו מארצם ונתרחקו מעל אדמתם ונתפזרו בין העמים בכל ירכתי ארץ. ואתה ברב חסדיך לא־מאסתם ולא־געלתם להפר בריתך אתם כי הושעתם ואת בניהם מכל צר והיית עזרם ומגינם תמיד למען יספרו שמך ממזרח שמש עד מבואו. יהי רצון מלפניך יי אלהינו ואלהי אבותינו שתוסיף תרחם עלינו ברחמיך הרבים ותרם קרן ישראל ותגדל כבודו: אבינו מלכנו גלה ...לעיני כל־חי ויראו כל אפסי־ ארץ את ישועת אלהינו. אז נשיר לך שיר חדש בקול רנה ותודה

ובשמחת עולם. ותערב עליך עתירתנו יי אלהינו ביום חג... הזה שצויתנו לקדש אותו כמו שכתבת עלינו בתורתך על-ידי משה עבדך מפי כבודך כאמור : (פסוקים מספר במדבר, פרקים כ"ח וכ"ט, בלי הזכרת הקרבנות.) אלהינו ואלהי אבותינו מלך רחמן... בגלל אבות שעשו רצונך בנה ביתך בית תפלה לכל העמים וכונן מקדשך בתוכינו ושמחנו במועדיך וזכנו לשמח נפש האביונים ולהתנדב לך בשמחה מאשר חוננתנו. ובכן נעלה ונראה ונשתחוה לפניך בשלש פעמי רגלינו ככתוב בתורתך שלוש פעמים בשנה... :

And on account of Thy holy plan, our fathers were exiled from their land, and removed from their soil, and they were scattered among the peoples in all the farthest parts of the earth. But Thou, in the abundance of Thy lovingkindness, didst not reject them nor abhor them, to break Thy covenant with them; but Thou didst save them and their children from every oppressor. Thou hast been their help and their shield at all times, that they may declare Thy Name from the rising of the sun unto the going down thereof. May it be Thy will, O Lord our God and God of our fathers, that Thou mayest continue to have mercy upon us in Thy manifold mercies, and that Thou mayest lift up the horn of Israel, and magnify its glory. Our Father, our King, reveal . . . in the sight of all the living, that all the ends of the earth may see the salvation of our God. Then shall we sing unto Thee a new song, in the voice of jubilation and thanksgiving, and in everlasting joy. And may our prayer on this festive day of . . . be pleasing unto Thee, which Thou hast commanded us to sanctify, according to what Thou hast written for us in Thy Torah through Thy servant Moses, by the mouth of Thy glory, as it is said: [The relevant verses from Numbers 28 and 29, without mention of the sacrifices.]

Our God and God of our fathers, merciful King, . . . for the sake of the fathers who did Thy will, build Thy Temple as a house of prayer for all the peoples, and establish Thy sanctuary in our midst. Make us joyful on Thy festive seasons, and make us worthy to rejoice the soul of the poor by offering unto Thee from that which Thou hast graciously bestowed upon us. Thus shall we go up and appear and worship before Thee on our three pilgrim festivals, as it is written in Thy Torah: "Three times in the year. . . ."

As the experimentation with various new versions of the *Musaph* went on, one becomes aware of a significant theological change, beginning with Geiger's 1870 prayerbook. It will be recalled that the Rabbinical Conferences of the eighteen-forties had accepted, as one of the reasons for the retention of the *Musaph* Service, the religious need of preserving reminiscences of the ancient sacrificial cult. Prayers for its restoration were, of course, to be excluded; but the *Musaph* prayer itself was to be represented as very adequately taking the place of the ancient sacrifices. Some of the early reformed prayerbooks did, in fact, word the *Musaph* Service accordingly. Most of the later prayerbooks did not. The following table will help to clarify the change which occurred:

	Musaph Prayer seen as substitute.	*Musaph* Prayer *not* viewed as sacrifice substitute.
HAMBURG, 1819.	x	
HAMBURG, 1841.	x	
MAYENCE, 1853.	x	
GEIGER, 1854.	x	
GÖTEBORG, 1858.	x	
STEIN, 1860.	x	
AUB, 1866.	x	
HAMBURG, 1868.	x	
GEIGER, 1870.		x
JOËL, 1872.	x	
NUREMBERG, 1874.	x	
LEIPZIG, 1876.		x
BERLIN, 1881.		x
STEIN, 1882.		x
GLOGAU, 1892(?).		x
VOGELSTEIN, 1894.		x
BADEN, 1905.		x
STOCKHOLM, 1907.	x	
SELIGMANN, 1928.		x
EINHEITSGEBETBUCH, 1929.		x
STOCKHOLM, 1930.		x

In view of the fact that Geiger's ideological opposition to "sacrificial thinking" seems to have prevailed in the long run, it would follow that the theoretical basis of the Liberal or Reform *Musaph* Service had disappeared altogether. If the prayerbooks nevertheless continued to include a *Musaph* Service, then the reason for that could solely have been the very "practical" one: that the congregations for whose edification the prayerbooks were published continued to regard the *Musaph* Service as their "main service" (*Hauptgottesdienst*)—in just the way in which Aub had stated the case in his Preface to the 1853 edition of the Mayence prayerbook.

Seen from the perspective of the Liberal or Reform Jew, who is accustomed to a different liturgical procedure, this would make the old European reformed *Musaph* Services a matter which is of historical interest only. It should, however, not be overlooked that the very retention of the *Musaph* Service afforded the European Reformers an opportunity for liturgical creativity—*in Hebrew*. Moreover, some of the versions they produced, such as that of the 1905 Baden Prayerbook, contain elements of more than mere historical interest, which remain among the potential materials upon which future liturgists of Reform Judaism may very well look as a source of enrichment for their own services.

TEN

Reform Benedictions for Rabbinic Ordinances

AS THE PUBLICATIONS אור נגה, נוגה הצדק (1818) and חרב נוקמת נקם ברית (1819) show, the early Reformers were at first convinced that the changes they had introduced could be justified on the basis of the Talmud and the Codes. Unlike the West London Synagogue of British Jews, which, in the forties of the nineteenth century, had adopted a pronounced anti-Talmudic stance,[1] the first Reformers on the European continent regarded their reforms as being within the framework of Rabbinic Judaism. The next few generations, however, were no longer so sure.[2] Still, with the exception of Holdheim and his Berlin *Reformgemeinde,* and of the Frankfort "Friends of Reform," who consciously rejected "Rabbinism," there was, even then, no official break with Tradition. Proof texts from Talmud and Codes continued to figure in Reform apologetics, and structure and contents of the worship service were still very much those of the traditional Synagogue.

Nevertheless, the Reform liturgy of those days indicates that the absolute claim to authority which had been made on behalf of Rabbinic ordinances was rejected by the Reformers. This can be seen in certain minor and subtle changes which many of the Reformers introduced into the benedictions (*berakhoth*) preceding the performance of non-Pentateuchal commandments. Tradition ordains the formula, "Praised art Thou, O Lord our God, Sovereign of the universe, Who hast sanctified us by Thy commandments, and commanded us to . . .," for the performance of ritual observances; and Tradition does not distinguish in this context between observances derived from the Pentateuch and observances ordained by the Rabbis. Thus, the same formula is used in connection with the eating of unleavened bread on Passover, and the blowing of the *shofar* on New Year, both of which are "Biblical," and with the recitation of the *Hallel* Psalms (Psalms 113–118), the reading of the Book of Esther on Purim, and the kindling of the Hanukkah lights, all of which are "Rabbinical." It is true, the Talmud itself (b. *Shabbath* 23a) already raises a question about the legitimacy of using this formula in connection with the Hanukkah lights, since the Maccabean festival could obviously not have been ordained in the Pentateuch. But the Talmud finds a justification for the use of this formula by insisting that all ordinances of duly established authorities have the backing of the Torah.[3] Nevertheless, this problem continued to bother the apologetes of Rabbinic Judaism throughout the centuries. Judah Halevi, Maimonides, David Nieto, and many others, all had to address themselves to this problem.[4]

It is instructive for our purposes to see how the Karaite liturgy dealt with this problem. Of course, Hanukkah, being a post-Biblical festival, does not exist for that sect at all. For the Biblical festivals, the *Hallel* Psalms are included in the Karaite liturgy, but they are not preceded by a benediction.[5] The Psalms themselves are Biblical; the practice to recite those particular Psalms on a given festival is not understood by the Karaites to be a Biblical commandment. A similar logic is evident in the reading of the Book of Esther on Purim. The Book of Esther is, of course, a Biblical book, and the feast of Purim, though not Pentateuchal, is of Biblical origin. But the reading of the Book of Esther on Purim is not recognized by the Karaites as a Biblical commandment. It is, however, preceded by two benedictions which are obvious adaptations of similar Rabbinic benedictions. They are:

ברוך אתה ה׳ אלהינו מלך העולם אשר עשה נסים וגבורות אותות
ונפלאות עם אבותינו בימים ההם ובזמן הזה : אמן :

Praised art Thou, O Lord our God, Sovereign of the universe, who hast wrought miracles and mighty deeds, signs and wonders, for our fathers in those days, and at this time. Amen.

And:

ברוך אתה ה׳ אלהינו מלך העולם אשר החינו וקימנו והגיענו לזמן הזה לקרא מגלת אסתר : אמן :

Praised art Thou, O Lord our God, Sovereign of the universe, who hast kept us alive, sustained us, and brought us to this season, to read the Scroll of Esther. Amen.

The two benedictions correspond to the second and third benedictions of the Rabbinic Tradition. The first Rabbinic benediction, however, which states that God has commanded the reading of the Scroll of Esther, has been omitted. Instead, mention of that reading has been added to what corresponds (without that addition) to the third benediction of the Tradition. (Isaac M. Wise, in the United States, had adopted the identical procedure, in his *Minhag America,* in connection with the kindling of the Hanukkah lights and with the *Megillah* reading.)[7]

We shall find that, without achieving Karaite consistency, the European Liberal and Reform liturgists were moving in the same direction with respect to the benedictions preceding the recitation of the *Hallel* Psalms, the reading of the Scroll of Esther, and the kindling of the Hanukkah lights. That is, they were moving in the same direction from the forties of the nineteenth century until the early part of the twentieth century. However, at the beginning of the twentieth century, a re-appraisal of Rabbinic Judaism took place, which also found its repercussion in the wording of the benedictions under consideration.

In the second volume of *Die Deutsche Synagoge,* edited by E. Kley and C. S. Günsburg, and published in Berlin, in 1818, we find the *Hallel* Psalms preceded, on page 44, by the traditional benediction. Though it is here printed in German only, the direction, given on page 28, indicates that this is part of that section of the service which is conducted in Hebrew. Since *Die Deutsche Synagoge* contains no services for the eve of the Sabbath, or for weekdays, we cannot tell how the matter of the Hanukkah lights and the *Megillah* reading was handled.

A year later, in 1819, the first edition of the Hamburg Prayerbook appeared.[8] This volume confines itself to the services of Sabbaths, festivals, and holy days. Hanukkah and Purim services are, therefore, not included. But the *Hallel* Psalms are included for the festivals, and they are preceded by the traditional benediction, the text of which is given, on page 80[x], both in Hebrew and in German.

By the time of the second edition of the Hamburg Prayerbook, in 1841, a change had taken place. On page 104, the traditional Hebrew benediction for the *Hallel* still appears. But it is printed in small type, and in parentheses. Moreover, it remains untranslated. The same procedure is followed with the first benediction for the Hanukkah lights, on page 416, and for the reading of the Book of Esther, on page 417. Services for those two occasions were included in the second edition of the Hamburg Prayerbook, and remained in all later editions.

That this way of handling the benedictions indicated a wavering on the part of the editors was already noted and criticized at the time by Abraham Geiger.[9] Apparently, the editors took Geiger's criticism to heart, for, in the 1868 edition of the Hamburg Prayerbook, the formula praising God for *commanding* the observance has been omitted in connection with the *Hallel* (page 141), the Hanukkah lights (page 384), and the reading of the Book of Esther (page 392).

In the meantime, the prayerbook of the West London Synagogue of British Jews had appeared, in 1841. As one would expect, this prayerbook omits the benediction before the *Hallel* (page 87), before the kindling of the Hanukkah lights (page 96), and before the reading of the Book of Esther (page 103). The second and third Rabbinic benedictions have been retained for the latter two.

In 1848, Kirchenrath Joseph von Maier of Stuttgart published his *Israelitisches Gebet- und Andachtsbuch*. He, too, omits the benediction before the *Hallel* (page 367). For Hanukkah and Purim, he offers a German paraphrase of the second and third benedictions, omitting the first benediction altogether (pages 426 and 429). It should be noted, however, that, as he states in his Preface, Maier published this prayerbook in his individual capacity. When, in 1861, he published the *Israelitische Gebetordnung*, "by order of the Royal Wuerttemberg Supreme Ecclesiastical Authority," i.e., for all the Jews of the kingdom, the traditional benediction for the *Hallel* was included, in Hebrew and in German (pp. 284f.), as were the benedictions for Hanukkah (pp. 386f.) and Purim (pp. 392f.).

The Aachen prayerbook of 1853[10] prints the traditional Hebrew benediction for the recitation of the *Hallel*, on page 123. However, instead of a literal German translation, it offers the following paraphrase: "Praised art Thou, O Lord our God, Sovereign of the universe, who hast sanctified us through Thy commandments. It is Thy will that we sing our songs of praise to Thee." Perhaps the editors felt that, while, in ordaining the recitation of the *Hallel*, the Rabbis were indeed acting according to the will of God, in a general kind of way, that recitation still did not rate the description of "commandment." We suspect, though, that the subtlety of the distinction may have been lost on many a worshipper. It is in the nature of the Aachen prayerbook that no rubrics appear for the kindling of the Hanukkah lights and the reading of the *Megillah*.

Abraham Geiger published his first prayerbook in 1854.[11] He retains the traditional Hebrew benediction for the *Hallel* (page 107), but, in German, he paraphrases it as follows: "Praised art Thou, O God. We recognize the duty of bringing unto Thee this day even more especial thanks and praise." He also retains the traditional Hanukkah benedictions in Hebrew (page 141), but he renders the first one, in his German translation, as: "Praised art Thou, O God, in whose honor and praise we celebrate this Feast of Dedication, and illuminate the temple." The same applies to the benedictions preceding the reading of the *Megillah* (page 142), of which the first one is rendered into German as: "Praised art Thou, O God, in whose honor and praise we celebrate this Feast of Purim, and read the document of its origin." Geiger, however, seems to have had some scruples even about ascribing "Biblical" ceremonies to a direct "commandment" from God. In connection with the *lulabh* on Tabernacles, he likewise retains the traditional Hebrew benediction (page 186), but translates it as: "Praised art Thou, O God, in whose honor and praise we take the festival bouquet this day."

Geiger adopted the identical procedure in the 1870 edition of his prayerbook,[12] and so did Manuel Joël, in his 1872 revision of Geiger's 1854 edition of the prayerbook.[13]

The 1858 edition of the prayerbook in Göteborg, Sweden,[14] omits the benediction before the *Hallel*. We are also told that, in those days, the Swedish congregations omitted the first benediction for Hanukkah and Purim.[15]

In 1860, Leopold Stein published his first edition of the prayerbook.[16] On page 188, he gives the traditional benediction for the *Hallel*, both in Hebrew and in German. Since there is no provision in this book for weekday services, we cannot tell what Stein's practice was at that time with regard to the kindling of the Hanukkah lights and the reading of the Book of Esther.

Joseph Aub edited the liturgy for the Great Synagogue of Berlin, in 1866.[17] He retains the traditional *Hallel* benediction, both in Hebrew and in German (Vol. I, p. 188), and adopts the same procedure with regard to the Hanukkah and *Megillah* benedictions (Vol. I, pp. 264–265). In all of these instances, Aub has no reservations about saying, "Thou hast commanded us."

Likewise, the Nuremberg prayerbook of 1874[18] retains the traditional benedictions for all three occasions, in Hebrew and in German, as do the subsequent editions of that prayerbook. On the other hand, the Leipzig prayerbook of 1876[19] follows the arrangement of Geiger and Joël in this, as in other matters. So does the Berlin prayerbook of 1881.[20] The traditional *Hallel* benediction is retained in Hebrew (page 187), but the German translation renders it as follows: "Praised art Thou, O Eternal our God, Sovereign of the universe, who hast sanctified us through Thy commandments, and for whose glorification we intone the *Hallel*." All three Purim benedictions appear in their traditional Hebrew form (page 326), but, instead of a translation, the prayerbook offers a paraphrase, in which there is no mention of the "commandment." The Hanukkah benedictions (page 327) are treated in the same way.

A revolutionary change is introduced by Leopold Stein, in his 1882 edition of the prayerbook.[21] Stein actually changes the wording of the traditional Hebrew benedictions—in a way which makes the Hebrew correspond to the kind of German paraphrase introduced by Geiger. Thus, his benediction for the *Hallel* (page 94) reads as follows:

ברוך אתה ה׳ אלהינו מלך העולם אשר לכבוד שמו הגדול
אנו קוראים את־ההלל:

This would mean: "Praised art Thou, O Lord our God, Sovereign of the universe, in honor of whose great Name we recite the *Hallel*." Actually, however, the translation which Stein offers for this benediction does not correspond at all to his Hebrew version. It is, in fact, the translation of the *traditional* Hebrew version of which Stein does not print the original! In that translation, he speaks, of God's making it our *duty* to intone songs of praise. One wonders why Stein is guilty of this inconsistency. He seems to have been aware of this difficulty himself, for, in a footnote to this translation, he refers the reader to the Preface. Alas, there is nothing in the Preface which could shed any light on this difficulty. Apparently, Stein forgot about it when he came to write that Preface.

Stein is more consistent in his treatment of the Hanukkah and Purim benedictions. For the former, he gives the following version (page 205):

ברוך אתה ה׳ אלהינו מלך העולם אשר לזכרון שמו הגדול
אנו מדליקים נר שלחנוכה:

He translates it as follows: "Praised art Thou, O Eternal our God, Sovereign of the universe, in glorification of whose great Name we annually kindle the lights of this Feast of Dedication."

Similarly, the first benediction before the reading of the *Megillah* is given this form (page 215):

ברוך אתה ה׳ אלהינו מלך העולם אשר לזכרון שמו הגדול
אנו קוראים את־המגלה:

This is translated as: "Praised art Thou, O Eternal our God, Sovereign of the universe, in glorification of whose great Name we read the sacred tale from the Book of Esther."

That Stein clearly meant to distinguish between "Biblical" commandments and "Rabbinic" ordinances is indicated by the fact that he retained the traditional benediction, both in Hebrew and in German, for the *lulabh* (page 94). It is no less obvious that Stein himself had undergone a change of mind since he published his first prayerbook in 1860, where, as we have seen, he had retained the traditional *Hallel* benediction. Nor was the retention, at that time, a matter of oversight or expediency.

Preparatory to editing his own 1860 prayerbook, Stein had published, in 1855, a survey of all the reformed rituals which had appeared until then.[22] In that survey he also mentioned the prayerbook of the West London Synagogue, mistakenly called by him, "West End Synagogue." He wrote at that time:

> That congregation has taken the decisive step of severing itself from Rabbinic Judaism. It has done so with sharp demarkations, and with a consistency appropriate to the English national character, by adhering in life and cult, only to the Mosaic Law in its pristine purity. . . . All prayers have been retained in Hebrew, their form and contents changed only to the extent to which a recognition of the Talmud was implied. That is why all those benedictions have been excluded in which the ceremonies are made to appear as having been commanded by God, when, in reality, they are merely a Rabbinic ordinance; e.g., the kindling of the Hanukkah lights.

Stein concludes his evaluation of the liturgy of the West London Synagogue by saying:

> That particular congregation in London, in the manner of the Karaites, has entered and maintained the clearly defined ground of a sect. Our endeavor, on the other hand, is not to remove Tradition, which we understand as the eternally living spirit of the Synagogue, but merely to purify its contents. That is why the changes introduced in London contain little which would recommend them for imitation.[23]

While it is true that Stein's prayerbook of 1882 does not have the full "Karaite" tendencies of the liturgy of the West London Synagogue, it is no less true that, in the particular instances of *Hallel,* Hanukkah and Purim benedictions, he follows the same kind of "Karaite" reasoning, if not the same practice, as the London Reformers. On the other hand, we need not assume that Stein was actually influenced by the London example. He merely carried over into the Hebrew section of his prayerbook an outlook to which the German Reformers had given expression, in the German section of their prayerbooks, since 1841. Yet such was the conservative character of European Liberal and Reform Judaism that Stein found no imitators in this respect. It was rather the pattern set by Geiger which was to prevail throughout the nineteenth century.

The Glogau prayerbook of 1892(?) keeps *Hallel,* Purim and Hanukkah benedictions in their traditional Hebrew form. But it follows the pattern of the time by introducing subtle changes into the translation. Thus, the *Hallel* benediction praises God "who hast made us worthy to intone the *Hallel.*" (". . .*und uns gewürdigt hast, das Hallel anzustimmen.*")[24] The first Purim benediction becomes: "Praise be to Thee, O God! Following the ordinances of the pious sages, whom Thou hast enlightened with Thy spirit, we now read the Book of Esther."[25] Similarly, the first Hanukkah benediction reads: "Praise be to Thee, O God! Following the ordinances of the pious sages, whom Thou hast enlightened with Thy spirit, we now kindle the Hanukkah light."[26] It remains to be pointed out that, in the case of the *lulabh,*[27] the Glogau prayerbook, while retaining the Hebrew benediction, offers neither German translation nor paraphrase.

When Heinemann Vogelstein, in 1894, published the prayerbook for the Jewish congregations of Westphalia,[28] he retained the traditional Hebrew *Hallel* benediction (page 288), rendering it, in German, as: "Praised art Thou, O Eternal our God, Sovereign of the universe, who hast sanctified us through Thy commandments, and in whose honor and praise we intone the *Hallel* Psalms." All the traditional Hanukkah benedictions have also been retained in Hebrew (page 496), though the translation follows that of Geiger. The Hebrew text of the *Megillah* benedictions (page 498) has likewise been left unchanged, but the first one is rendered into German as: "Praised art Thou, O God, in whose honor and praise we celebrate this Feast of Purim and, in devotion, read the story of the Esther Scroll." Vogelstein also follows Geiger in the paraphrasing of the *lulabh* benediction (page 412).

The prayerbook for the Jewish congregations of Baden, published by David Mayer in 1905, but never officially adopted for use,[29] retains the traditional Hebrew benedictions for *Hallel* (page 208), the Hanukkah lights (page 474), and the *Megillah* (page 478). It paraphrases the *Hallel* benediction in German as: "Praise and thanks be to Thee, O God! For our sanctification Thou hast given us Thy commandments. For our edification and perfection Thou desirest of us that we acknowledge Thee in Thy greatness and grace! Amen." The paraphrase of the Hanukkah benediction is: "In praise of the eternal Sovereign of the universe, whose grace was wonderfully extended over our fathers, and preserved Israel at this time from threatened destruction, we kindle the light of dedication." Similarly, the paraphrase of the *Megillah* benediction reads: "In praise of the eternal Sovereign of the universe, whose grace was wonderfully extended over our fathers, and preserved Israel at this time from threatened destruction, we read the Esther Scroll."

The Brunswick prayerbook of 1906[30] largely follows the Berlin prayerbook of 1881. However, it does have some emphases of its own. The traditional *Hallel* benediction is given in Hebrew (page 217), and is translated as follows: "Praised art Thou, O Eternal our God, Sovereign of the universe, who hast sanctified us through Thy commandments, and hast made us worthy (*und uns gewürdigt hat*) of reading the *Hallel.*" The traditional Hebrew Hanukkah benedictions are given on page 270. But, instead of a translation, they are paraphrased in German, the paraphrase making no mention of a "commandment." The same applies to the *Megillah* benedictions on page 273.

The Stockholm prayerbook of 1907[31] has the traditional Hebrew *Hallel* benediction, but makes no mention of the "commandment" in the Swedish paraphrase. Since it contains no weekday evening services, the question of Hanukkah and Purim benedictions does not arise.

Caesar Seligmann, in his 1910 prayerbook,[32] gives the traditional Hebrew benediction for *Hallel* on page 148. He translates it as follows: "O Eternal, our God, who rulest over men and nations, to Thee we bring in gratitude our jubilant song of praise." He also gives the traditional Hebrew benedictions for Hanukkah (page 259) and Purim (pp. 291f.), but makes no mention of the "commandment" in his German paraphrases. The same procedure is adopted in the 1928 edition of this prayerbook (pp. 148f., 307, and 334). Here, however, the *Hallel* benediction (pp. 148f.) is paraphrased as follows: "O Eternal, our God, Sovereign of the universe, who hast called us to Thy holy service, we do homage unto Thee with festive songs of praise."

The 1925 prayerbook of the Union Libérale Israélite in Paris[33] omits the benediction for the *Hallel* Psalms (page 91). It has the traditional Hebrew benedictions for the Hanukkah lights (page 214), which it translates as: "Praised art Thou, O Lord our God, Sovereign of the universe, who hast sanctified us through Thy commandments. In kindling these lights of Hanukkah, we offer unto Thee the homage of our hearts." (Page 213.) A similar text is used in connection with the *Megillah* blessings (pp. 215f.).

In 1929, the *Einheitsgebetbuch* ("Union Prayer Book") of the German Liberal congregations[34] not only gives the traditional Hebrew text of the benedictions for *Hallel*, Hanukkah lights, and *Megillah* reading (pp. 36f., 490f., and 510f.), but it also provides a literal German translation of those benedictions. The idea of "divine commandment" as applied to Rabbinic ordinances was thereby re-introduced into the liturgy of Liberal Judaism.

Two years later, in 1931, the *Einheitsgebetbuch* was followed in this respect by the sixth edition of the prayerbook of the West London Synagogue.[35] While it does not restore the *Hallel* benediction, this edition of the West London Synagogue prayerbook has definitely broken with the "Karaite" tendencies in the congregation's background by offering the traditional Hebrew benedictions, with a literal English translation, for both Hanukkah lights (page 45) and the *Megillah* reading (page 44).

We may now summarize our findings by saying that the earliest generation of Reformers (apart from those in England) did not yet make any distinctions between Biblical commandments and Rabbinic ordinances when it came to the recitation of benedictions. By 1841, the Hamburg Reformers began to feel uneasy about this problem, and wavered in the method of dealing with it. It was left to Geiger to see, and to point out, the full implications. But when Geiger himself was faced with the practical task of editing a prayerbook, he, too, compromised. He left the Hebrew unchanged, and merely indicated by his German paraphrases that he did not consider the Rabbinic ordinances to be "divine commandments." But Geiger went further than this. As is shown by his treatment of the benediction for the *lulabh,* he was also reluctant to ascribe this "Biblical" ceremony to an express divine commandment. Geiger was no Karaite. Unlike the English Reformers, he could not ascribe Biblical ceremonies to divine revelation, and Rabbinic ceremonies to the mere invention of men. Ceremonies were ceremonies. Only the monotheistic idea and the Moral Law could truly be linked with revelation. Ceremonies are valuable, even essential. But they are not divinely "commanded."

Geiger's way of handling the problem was adopted by the majority of European Liberal and Reform liturgies. Only very few of them entirely omitted the benediction praising God for commanding the ceremony. And only one man, Leopold Stein, saw fit to change the Hebrew wording of the traditional benedictions. Why Geiger and his followers should have left the Hebrew text unchanged, is easy to see. Those men, Liberals though they were, had to produce liturgies which would be acceptable to entire Jewish communities, and not just for declared Reform congregations, as was the case in the Anglo-Saxon world. Congregants of a traditionalist frame of mind might not object to German paraphrases. But they would have been strongly opposed to any tampering with the traditional Hebrew wording of well-known benedictions.

Besides, Geiger might well have adopted the rationale which Aub expressed in his Preface to the prayerbook of Mayence, in 1853.[36] In that prayerbook, Aub had given a very free paraphrase of the *Musaph,* omitting any reference to the restoration of the sacrificial cult. Yet he had left the traditional Hebrew text of the *Musaph* completely unchanged. Anticipating criticism on that score, Aub said in his Preface:

> To the possible objection, why we did not also change the Hebrew text accordingly, we would reply that worship is not the occasion to do violence to the conscience of those worshippers who regard those former elements, highlighted in the old prayer, as essential. It is, moreover, that group among our brethren in faith which prefers to pray in Hebrew, while it is the other, larger, group, accepting a more spiritual-religious concept of the messianic doctrine, which prefers to pray silently in German.

What Aub had said about the *Musaph* no doubt applied to the "divine commandment" of Rabbinic ordinances as well; and most German reformed rituals made provisions accordingly.

This, however, does not yet account for the re-introduction of the traditional benediction, in its literal German or English translation, into the *Einheitsgebetbuch* of 1929, and into the 1931 edition of the prayer-book of the West London Synagogue. Here, another factor must also be considered. A new appreciation of Rabbinic Judaism had come about in Reform Jewish circles. We may clarify it in the following way:

Orthodox Judaism would not distinguish, in the matter of benedictions, between ceremonies of Biblical and those of Rabbinic origin. The latter, being part of the Oral Torah, are as much included in revelation as are the former. An early generation of Reformers, particularly in England, restricted the concept of revelation to the Written Torah, denying the divine sanction of Rabbinic ordinances. A later generation of Reformers (e.g., Geiger) restricted the concept of revelation still further by excluding the so-called "ceremonial law" from its domain. It could as little regard a Biblical ceremony as divinely "commanded" as it could so regard a Rabbinic ceremony. While this group of Reformers maintained the Hebrew text of the benedictions unchanged (for "practical reasons"), it paraphrased it in a manner which excluded the notion of "commandment" as far as both Biblical and Rabbinical ceremonies were concerned. But if that generation was able to obliterate the distinction between Biblical and Rabbinic observances, in a *negative* kind of way, a still later generation, abiding by that obliteration of the distinction, found it possible to give a *positive* evaluation to that obliteration.

Wrote Morris Joseph (1848–1930), a Senior Minister of the West London Synagogue in the early part of the twentieth century:

> The whole body of Tradition, then, . . . is invested with authority. In other words, new conditions call for new interpretations and new ordinances, and these are sacred. They form part and parcel of the true, because the living Judaism. . . . Moreover, all such later teachings may be regarded as having added to the stream of the Divine revelation which took its rise in the inspired writings of the Bible. For God has never been without His messengers.[37]

Similarly, Israel Abrahams (1858–1925), one of the founding members and mentors of the (more radical) Liberal Jewish Synagogue in London, begins a popular pamphlet which he wrote for the Liberal Jewish movement[38] by discussing the traditional benediction for the Hanukkah lights. He notes that, although Hanukkah is clearly not Biblical, the benediction ascribes the custom of lighting Hanukkah lights to a divine commandment. Abrahams continues:

> Am I blaming the Rabbis for imagining a Divine sanction for non-Biblical ceremonies? Far from it. I admit, I proclaim, their competence; and as it was because of what they did that Jewish tradition became a real, living thing, I applaud their action. For what is the inference to be drawn from it? The inference that historical Judaism assumed, and rightly assumed, the power and

> privilege of describing certain ceremonies as *sanctified,* as expressing Israel's response to the Will and Love of God, solely or chiefly because the Jewish consciousness felt that those observances were necessary and valuable aids to the religious life. And this is precisely the principle on which we shall act.[39]

Morris Joseph and Israel Abrahams express the same idea. The positive approach to the Rabbinic Tradition is a corollary of the Reform doctrine of "progressive revelation." It is the final step in the rejection of Fundamentalism. Reform Judaism is free not to accept everything in the Bible as eternally binding. But it is also free *not* to reject everything in the Talmud. Indeed, the Talmud, no less than the Bible, is evidence of God's revelation, and of man's response to it, a response which often takes the form of "laws and commandments"—of *mitzvoth.* The same process is at work in the Bible as well as in the Talmud.

Morris Joseph, who died in 1930, still had a hand in the preparation of the sixth edition of the prayerbook of the West London Synagogue, an edition which, as we have seen, restored the traditional benedictions for Hanukkah and Purim. Israel Abrahams, who died in 1925, still had a share in the compilation of the *Liberal Jewish Prayer Book,* which appeared in 1926, under the editorship of Israel I. Mattuck.[40] But the very Hanukkah benediction which Abrahams had so successfully used in his popular pamphlet failed to be admitted into this prayerbook. Nor is there a benediction for the *Hallel;* and Purim is altogether excluded. All of this still applies to the 1957 edition of the *Liberal Jewish Prayer Book.*

On the other hand, the prayerbook published by the Dutch Liberal Jews, in 1964,[41] includes all the traditional Hebrew benedictions: for the *Hallel* (page 149), for the Hanukkah lights (page 250), and for the reading of the Book of Esther (p. 254). Not a single one of them, however, is accompanied by a translation or a paraphrase.

A year later, in a volume meant to take the place of the festival liturgy of the West London Synagogue,[42] the Reform Jews of England have restored the traditional *Hallel* benediction, both in Hebrew and in English (page 38). They have even reverted to the traditional formulation of the *lulabh* benediction (*loc. cit.*), after having substituted, as an anti-Rabbinic gesture in 1842, practically the whole verse of Leviticus 23: 40 for the two simple Rabbinic terms, *netilath lulabh.*[43]

The more recent liturgical publications of European Liberal and Reform Judaism thus show that the quasi-Karaite stage in its development has now been generally outgrown. A more sophisticated view of revelation has brought about a renewed willingness to use the Rabbinic formulation of the benedictions even for post-Biblical ordinances.

ELEVEN

Zion and Jerusalem

THE PRESENCE OF THE MANY PLEAS FOR THE RESTORATION OF ZION AND for the Return to Jerusalem, in the traditional liturgy, was one of the main motivations for the liturgical reform of the nineteenth century. Such pleas no longer "rang true" when uttered by the "German of the Mosaic Persuasion," who had no wish to be uprooted from his German fatherland. As early as 1812, David Friedländer had reacted negatively to prayers for the Return:

> As long as the Jews were, if not actually persecuted, at least regarded as strangers and treated as such, as long as they nowhere formed an integral part of a state, as long as they were not only made to feel—but were actually told—that they were only tolerated and that they really belonged to Palestine, so long was there neither cause nor reason to change the contents and the

> language of the prayers. Among both rulers and ruled, one and the same idea had struck root. Among the former, that the Jews were still hoping for a Messiah, that, because of this, they had no fatherland in Europe, and that, consequently, they could have no love and loyalty. Among the latter, tradition, commandments, and oppression maintained the identical thoughts and expectations. . . . How could anyone think of changing the prayer formulae? Whence the cause? And thus they remained unchanged.[1]

Friedländer wrote that in the year when the Jews of Prussia achieved their Emancipation. In the light of the changed circumstances, he felt the need to change and to abrogate the prayers which no longer adequately reflected the desires of the Prussian Jews:

> Indeed, it requires no special mental effort, only rectitude of soul, for the religious Israelite to say to himself: "Here I stand before God. I pray for blessing and success for my king, for my fellow-citizens, for myself and for my family—and not for a return to Jerusalem, not for a restoration of the Temple and the sacrifices. Such wishes I do not have in my heart. Their fulfilment would not make me happy. My mouth shall not utter them."[2]

Friedländer's radical program was not put into effect immediately. Neither the reformed services which were held a few years later in Berlin nor the Hamburg Temple Prayerbook of 1819 saw fit to do away completely with the references to Zion and Jerusalem. The elimination of such prayers was a gradual process in the history of European Liberal and Reform liturgies, nor was it a process which led in one direction only. Yet, until the post-World War II editions of the prayerbook, the sentiments voiced by Friedländer in 1812 dominated the thinking of the editors of Reform and Liberal liturgies in Europe. There were disagreements. But the disagreements were about details and about formulations, and not about the principle.

Typical of the level on which the problem was debated is a controversy between Abraham Geiger (1810–1874) and Manuel Joël (1826–1890) which we shall now consider in some greater detail.

In 1854, Geiger had edited a prayerbook for the use of the Breslau community, in which, among other changes, the references to Jerusalem had been altered (though not completely abolished). As Geiger stated in his Preface:

> Jerusalem and Zion are places from which instruction went forth, and to which holy memories are attached. But, as a whole, they are to be celebrated more as a spiritual idea—as the nur-

> sery of the Kingdom of God—than as a certain geographical locale connected with a special divine providence for all times.[3]

Manuel Joël became Geiger's successor as rabbi of the Breslau community, in 1864. In 1872, Joël published a revised version of Geiger's prayerbook,[4] the revisions all being in the direction of greater faithfulness to the traditional text and the traditional doctrines. The groundwork for those revisions was laid by Joël in a pamphlet entitled, *Toward an Orientation in the Problem of the Cult.*[5] On the question of Zion and Jerusalem, Joël expressed himself as follows:

> There has never been any argument about the fact that Jerusalem has to be mentioned in the prayerbook. If one has but the slightest idea of the essence of worship, he will declare a Jewish prayerbook, from which Jerusalem is missing, to be resting upon faulty liturgical principles. If the historical past is to find its place in the worship service, and *nobody* denies this, then Jerusalem and Palestine occupy the most important place in that past. That is why they will always remain a precious and indelible memory in the Jewish heart. It would be tantamount to a self-denial were we to forget the place where David sang his Psalms, and where the Prophets spoke their words which have sounded down through the millennia. Jew, Christian and Muslim regard the cradle of religion with like veneration, and they are unwilling to consider Jerusalem as an indifferent city. That is why we shall remember her in our prayer. We shall ask of the Lord that He lift her up out of her present sad condition. In this way, too, the prayers for the restoration of Jerusalem from her lamentable circumstances are harmless. The difference in principle only begins where we give expression in prayer to the wish for a *personal return*. Modern consciousness is unable to make this wish its own; and it is this point against which protest is made.[6]

Joël's *Orientation* was fiercely attacked by Geiger, in an article entitled, "Something about Belief and Prayer. In Defense and in Defiance."[7]

> About Jerusalem I can only repeat what I said, fifteen years ago, in the Preface to my prayerbook: "Jerusalem and Zion are places from which instruction went forth . . ." On that basis, too, the changes in my prayerbook have been made. What goes beyond that is evil. Dr. J., in his desire for concessions and their theoretical justification, seeks, here too, to go a little beyond that. He thinks that the Jew, the Christian and the Muslim look upon Jerusalem, also today, as the cradle of religion, and that they are unwilling to consider her as an indifferent city. That

is why, according to him, we shall not only remember her in our prayer, but we shall also ask of the Lord "that He lift her up out of her present sad condition. In this way, too, the prayers for the restoration of Jerusalem from her lamentable circumstances are harmless." *Here* is the parting of the ways. As far as we are concerned—and I speak in the name of the majority with the same right in which Dr. J. does so—as far as we are concerned, the Jerusalem of today is not the cradle of religion. It is for us an entirely indifferent city. It is nothing more than a venerable ruin, a decayed knight's castle—just as, for us, the Athens of today is not at all the ancient one, bathed in spiritual splendor. We regret that the city has sunk so low, that her inhabitants live in deep misery. But far more do we commiserate with the many hundred of thousands of co-religionists in Eastern Europe whose abundant capacities are atrophying on account of oppression, poverty, and the lack of all opportunity of an education for free men. We commiserate with them all the more because highly talented and assiduous people are perishing here, people who could be active to their own joy and the advantage of the world. We could feel impelled to intercede on their behalf, because we may, after all, expect from the future an improvement of their condition, for their good and ours, and because we also arouse ourselves to an active and productive help. On the other hand, the commiseration with Jerusalem and with the misery of her inhabitants is vain, a mere romantic phrase. It is the inexorable fate of places like that, which sun themselves in the faded splendor of an ancient sanctity, to become a sickly burden to themselves and to the world as a whole, as long as they let themselves be blinded by that false glimmer, and as long as they do not embark upon an altogether new and sober existence. Around those "holy tombs" there gather only idlers, fanatics, and the admirers of stupidity. To pray for them is of no use, a *tephillath shaw*. Indeed, such a prayer for a new splendor of those places is a veritable suicide, a blasphemy of God. Their power would lead to the ruin of all. It would always be misused for the presumptuous desire to wield a spiritual and ecclesiastical rule over all the adherents of that religion. In order to retain the old splendor, it would try to impose an obedient subordination upon the rest of the world, interfering with every free development. The ancient Rome of the Republic and the Caesars, with art amateurs making their pilgrimages to the remains of classical antiquity, that ancient Rome does not impose upon the world an oppressive yoke. Her power is gone. But the Rome of the rock of

> St. Peter's, with her ecclesiastical nimbus, that Rome will not cease—until her splendor has completely faded, and her power has been completely broken—to forge fetters for the world, endangering its progress. *A Jerusalem with a mighty Jewish population would be the tyrant's strong castle of Judaism, the Jewish Rome.*

Joël replied to Geiger's attack by publishing a supplement to his *Orientation,* entitled, *In Defense Against Defiance.*[8] He did not, however, comment on Geiger's stand on the Jerusalem question. Joël's prayerbook of 1872 restored a number of the Zion and Jerusalem passages which Geiger had deleted in 1854. On the other hand, publishing a new edition of his own prayerbook, in 1870,[9] Geiger was even more radical in the deletion of Zion and Jerusalem passages than he had been in 1854.

If Geiger could not wax enthusiastic about the mere memory of Jerusalem, and if even Joël fought for no more than the prayer to have God lift up Jerusalem "out of her present sad condition," a much more positive note was struck by Leopold Stein, who, in the Preface to his 1882 edition of the prayerbook,[10] had this to say on the subject:

> As far as Israel's exalted hopes are concerned, we have devoutly retained his holy place for the Messiah, bearer of our ideal future. Thereby we have established the validity of the great promise that, one day, mankind will give concrete expression to its unity in God by a great temple of peoples. That Temple will find its eternal place in Jerusalem. Where else? Not in Berlin, capital of German Protestantism. Not in Rome, center of the pagan world of the past, and of the Catholic world of today. But in Jerusalem, the Holy City, in which all nations and religions have an equal share.[11]

The positions of Geiger and of Stein represent the extreme poles between which the Reform endeavor to come to terms with Zion and Jerusalem moved in the liturgical sphere. It was only in the liturgy of the West London Synagogue that we find the curious phenomenon of a Reform liturgy which not only contains prayers for the rebuilding of Jerusalem, but also prayers for the Return to Palestine ("and speedily lead us securely to our land"),[12] and even for the restoration of the sacrificial cult ("restore the service to the oracle of thine house; so that the burnt-offerings of Israel, and their prayers, may be speedily accepted by thee with love and favour").[13] Yet, in succeeding editions of that liturgy, the word "speedily" was omitted both in Hebrew and in English, and the restoration of the sacrifices no longer figured in the petition for God's return to Zion. In the sixth edition (1931), all remaining petitions for the rebuilding of Jerusalem, and for the Return to Zion (both God's and Israel's) have been omitted. One suspects that what was originally at stake for the London Reformers was not so much a deeply-felt need to leave England for Palestine, but a strict adherence to what were, after all, *Biblical* doctrines and promises.[14] Since the establishment of the State of Israel, in 1948, a further change has taken place in the liturgy of the West London Synagogue. A "Prayer for the Land of Israel" is now inserted after the Prayer for the Royal Family. It reads as follows:

> *O God and God of our fathers, we ask thy blessing upon the land of Israel. May her leaders and counsellors be guided by thy wisdom and strengthened by thy help. May the people of Israel proclaim the message of righteousness and peace to all mankind, so that out of Zion may go forth the law and thy word from Jerusalem. Amen.*[15]

A more elaborate prayer for the State of Israel has been included in the English translation of the German *Einheitsgebetbuch* Vol. II, which was published by Rabbi Jakob J. Kokotek for the London New Liberal Jewish Congregation, in 1962.[16] It reads, in part, as follows:

> . . . *Countless generations of our people have turned to Thee in hopeful prayer for the restoration of our ancestral land, for the redemption of the oppressed and the salvation of the homeless of our people. We, O Lord of redemption, are permitted to see this hope and dream of our sages, poets and people, come true. Deserts have been swept away, ruins have been rebuilt, and out of desolation and oblivion rises again on the holy soil of Zion the Nation of Israel. . . .*[17]

Rather curious is the prayer for the State of Israel in the 1964 edition of the prayerbook of the Dutch Liberal congregations.[18] It is an unchanged reprint of the "Prayer for the Welfare of the State" in the prayerbook of the Jerusalem Reform congregation[19]—down to the peculiarities of the spelling adopted by that Jerusalem congregation.[20] Yet the prayer in the Jerusalem Reform prayerbook is itself but an adaptation of the "Prayer for Our Country" (in this case, the United States) in the *Sabbath Prayer Book* of the Reconstructionists.[21] In other words, a prayer originally composed by American Jews for their own country, i.e., the United States, was adapted by the Israeli Reform Jews to their own use by making "our country" refer more directly to the State of Israel and its needs. This prayer was then taken over, in an unchanged form (that is, unchanged in Hebrew, the Dutch paraphrase being somewhat less "Zionistic"), by the Liberal Jews of Holland to express their sentiments about the State of Israel.

The major changes which Liberal and Reform liturgies introduced in connection with the prayers for Zion and Jerusalem were, of course, in the relevant benedictions of the Eighteen Benedictions. With those changes we are dealing elsewhere.[22] Here we want to illustrate liturgical reform in connection with the two benedictions preceding the *Shema* in the morning service, with the Torah Service, and with the liturgy of the Ninth of Ab.

First, however, we give the relevant phrases in the two morning benedictions as they occur in the various traditional rites. The great divergences between the traditional rites in this respect will easily be seen. The early Reformers made much of them. The differences within the *traditional* rites themselves served as a good excuse for the further modifications introduced by Reform Judaism.

For example, A. M. Goldschmidt, who edited the Leipzig prayerbook of 1876,[23] defends his change of the messianic petition in the second benediction before the *Shema* by claiming, in his Preface:

> The *vehabhé 'alenu shalom* ("and bring up on us peace from the four corners of the earth"), in the prayer introducing the *Shema* of *Shaharith*, is no new formula, but is already found in the *siddur* of R. Amram Gaon (12th century).

[What Goldschmidt fails to tell his reader, however, is that Amram goes on to say, "and lead us speedily upright to our land,"—a phrase which Goldschmidt did not include!]

Similarly, much was made in nineteenth-century Reform apologetics of the fact that Saadia Gaon was opposed to the inclusion of the phrase, "cause a new light to shine upon Zion," in the first benediction before the *Shema*. One suspects, however, that the Reformers opposed that phrase for reasons quite different from those adduced by Saadia. The latter, of course, was not opposed at all to the idea of "the new light upon Zion." He merely had *halakhic* objections, as we shall have occasion to see, to the inclusion of this petition in that particular benediction. At any rate, the changes listed in the following pages will tell their own story.

The petition for the "messianic light" included in the first benediction before the *Shema*[24] reads as follows in the traditional *Ashkenazi* rite:

> אור חדש על ציון תאיר. ונזכה כלנו מהרה לאורו:
>
> Cause a new light to shine upon Zion, and may we all be worthy speedily to behold its brightness.

The traditional *Sepharadi* rite does not have this petition at all, nor do the *Siddur Rav Saadia Gaon*, the *Tikhlal* (Yemenite Rite), and the *Minhag Italiani*.

Rav Amram Gaon was obviously familiar with that petition, although he did not include it in his prayerbook. Instead, he quotes Saadia Gaon to the following effect:

> And thus said Rav Saadia Gaon, of blessed memory: He who concludes with "cause a new light to shine upon Zion etc." errs; because the Sages did not ordain this benediction with reference to the future light of the messianic days, but with reference to the light which shines every day—just as we say the benediction, "Who bringest on the evening twilight," in the evening service. But if someone does recite that phrase, then he has uttered the Name of God in vain.[25]

The prayer for the "Return," which is inserted in the second benediction before the *Shema,* has several variants in the different traditional rites. We list six of them to indicate the range.

1) *Seder Rav Amram:*[26]

הבא עלינו ברכה ושלום מארבע כנפות הארץ,
והוליכנו מהרה קוממיות לארצנו:

Bring us blessing and peace from the four corners of the earth, and lead us speedily upright to our land.

2) *Siddur Rav Saadia Gaon:*[27]

והביא לנו ישועה ושלום מארבע כנפות הארץ
והוליכנו מהרה קוממיות לארצנו:

And bring us salvation and peace from the four corners of the earth, and lead us speedily upright to our land.

3) *Sepharadi Rite:*[28]

מהר והבא עלינו ברכה ושלום מהרה מארבע כנפות
כל־הארץ. ושבור על הגוים מעל צוארינו.
והוליכנו מהרה קוממיות לארצנו:

O hasten and bring upon us speedily blessing and peace from the four corners of all the earth; and break the yoke of the nations from off our necks; and lead us speedily upright to our land.

4) *Tikhlal* (Yemenite):[29]

והבא עלינו ברכה ושלום מארבע כנפות הארץ
והוליכנו מהרה קוממיות לארצנו:

And bring upon us blessing and peace from the four corners of the earth, and lead us speedily upright to our land.

5) *Ashkenazi Rite:*[30]

והביאנו לשלום מארבע כנפות הארץ
ותוליכנו קוממיות לארצנו:

And bring us in peace from the four corners of the earth, and lead us upright to our land.

6) *Minhag Italiani:*[31]

והבא עלינו ברכה ושלום מהרה מארבע כנפות הארץ
והוליכנו מהרה קוממיות לארצנו:

And bring us blessing and peace speedily from the four corners of the earth, and lead us speedily upright to our land.

After noting the varieties in the traditional rites, we shall now look at the way the two petitionary inserts in the benedictions before the *Shema* have been handled in a representative sampling of European Liberal and Reform prayerbooks.[32]

Deutsche Synagoge (Berlin) 1817:
(p. 11) *Or ḥadash* meant to be recited in Hebrew. Literal German translation.
(p. 12) *Ahabhah Rabbah* meant to be recited in Hebrew, presumably in the traditional version; but German translation omits *ve-habhi-enu.*

Hamburg, 1819:
(p. 35) *Or ḥadash* omitted.
(p. 36) מהר והבא עלינו ברכה ושלום מארבע כנפות הארץ
(Tr. "Bring to us Thy blessing in all parts of the earth.")

Hamburg, 1841:
(p. 58) *Or ḥadash* in small print and parentheses, but left untranslated.
(p. 59) *Maher* as in 1819 edition.

West London Synagogue, 1841:
(p. 14) *Or ḥadash* omitted.
(p. 13) *Maher* as in Sepharadi prototype, but omitting, in both Hebrew and English, the phrase, "and break the yoke etc."

Kirchenrat Maier, 1848:
(p. 14) *Or ḥadash* omitted.
(p. 15) *Maher* as in Hamburg 1819 edition. German paraphrase.

Aachen, 1853:
(p. 76) *Or ḥadash* in Hebrew text, but left untranslated.
(p. 77) Complete Ashkenazi text, but German paraphrase omits "and lead us upright to our land."

Geiger, 1854:
(p. 33) *Or ḥadash* in Hebrew text. Translation reads: "Let the light

of the spirit, the sun of truth and salvation, rise over all of us, that we may rejoice in it, in clarity and sincerity."
(p. 34) *Vehabhi-enu* omitted.

Göteborg, 1858:
(p. 36) *Or ḥadash* included and translated.
(p. 37) *Vehabhi-enu* omitted.

Stein, 1860:
(p. 166) *Or ḥadash* included and translated.
(p. 168) *Vehabhi-enu* in small print and parentheses, left untranslated.

Aub (Berlin), 1866:
(p. 45) *Or ḥadash* omitted.
(p. 46) *Vehabhi-enu* omitted.

Hamburg, 1868:
(p. 98) *Or ḥadash* omitted.
(p. 99) *Maher* as in 1819 edition, but not included in German paraphrase.

Geiger, 1870:
(p. 10) *Or ḥadash* omitted.
(p. 11) *Vehabhi-enu* omitted.

Joël, 1872:
(p. 41) *Or ḥadash* included, and translated as: "O God, let a new light shine also for Zion, and may that light also brighten our path."
(p. 42) והבא עלינו שלום מארבע כנפות הארץ, and corresponding German paraphrase.

Leipzig, 1876:
(p. 41) *Or ḥadash* and corresponding German translation included.
(p. 42) *Vehabhé* as in Joël's 1872 prayerbook.

Berlin, 1881:
(p. 41) *Or ḥadash* omitted.
(p. 42) *Vehabhi-enu* omitted.

Stockholm, 1881 (Vol. III):
(p. 75) *Or ḥadash* and translation included.
(p. 76) *Vehabhi-enu* omitted.

Stein, 1882:
(p. 78) *Or ḥadash* and translation included.
(p. 78) *Vehabhi-enu* omitted.

Vogelstein (Westphalia), 1894:
(p. 56) *Or ḥadash* omitted.
(p. 56) *Vehabhi-enu* omitted.

Glogau, 1892(?):
(p. 31) *Or ḥadash* omitted.
(p. 31) *Vehabhi-enu* omitted.

Hamburg, 1904:
(p. 75) *Or ḥadash* omitted.
(p. 76) *Maher* of earlier Hamburg editions omitted.

Baden, 1905:
(p. 82) *Or ḥadash* omitted.
(p. 84) *Vehabhi-enu* omitted.

Brunswick, 1906:
(p. 37) *Or ḥadash* omitted.
(p. 37) *Vehabhi-enu* omitted.

Stockholm, 1907:
(p. 72) *Or ḥadash* and translation included.
(p. 74) *Vehabhi-enu* omitted.

Seligmann, 1910:
(p. 42) German paraphrase only, omitting reference to *or ḥadash*.
(p. 43) German paraphrase only, omitting reference to *vehabhi-enu*.

Nuremberg, 1914:
(p. 30) *Or ḥadash* omitted.
(p. 30) *Vehabhi-enu* omitted.

Danzig, 1924: (Vol. II):
(p. 106) *Or ḥadash* and translation included.
(p. 108) *Vehabhi-enu* included, and translated as: "Bring us peace in all the ends of the earth, and grant us freedom in all lands."

Paris, 1925:
(p. 152) *Or ḥadash* included, and translated as: "Spread a new light over the world, and Thy all-pervading peace in our hearts."
(p. 51) *Vehabhi-enu* omitted.

Seligmann, 1928:
(p. 53) *Or ḥadash* omitted.
(p. 53) *Vehabhi-enu* omitted.

Einheitsgebetbuch, 1929:
(p. 16) *Or ḥadash* omitted.
(p. 16) *Vehabhi-enu* omitted.

Stockholm, 1930:
(p. 70) *Or ḥadash* and translation included.
(p. 70) *Vehabhi-enu* omitted.

West London Synagogue, 1931:
(p. 19) *Or ḥadash* omitted.
(p. 19) *Maher* (of earlier editions which increasingly modified the Sepharadi version) omitted.

Seder Tobh Lehodoth (Netherlands), 1964:
(p. 58) *Or ḥadash* and translation included.
(p. 59) *Vehabhi-enu* included, but Dutch paraphrase speaks about the unity of the Jewish People.

Just as there was no uniformity in Liberal and Reform liturgies, but interesting and instructive variations, in the matter of the messianic petitions included in the benedictions before the *Shema,* so was there a wide range of multiple choices in connection with another part of the worship service where the Ashkenazi Rite (though not the Sepharadi one) makes mention of Zion and Jerusalem. We are referring to the Scripture verses and prayers included in the ritual accompanying the taking of the Scroll from the Ark.[33] Among them the following are included:

אב הרחמים היטיבה ברצונך את-ציון תבנה חומות ירושלים: כי בך לבד בטחנו מלך אל רם ונשא אדון עולמים:

Father of mercies, do good in Thy favor unto Zion; build the walls of Jerusalem. For in Thee alone do we trust, O King, high and exalted God, Lord of eternity.

כי מציון תצא תורה ודבר-ה׳ מירושלם:

For out of Zion shall go forth the Torah,
and the word of the Lord from Jerusalem. (Isaiah 2:3b.)

The recitation of the customary prayers and verses constituting the "Torah Service" cannot be traced back further than the thirteenth century.[34] There are also great divergences among the various rites. Not surprisingly, therefore, the Reformers did not feel particularly bound by this rubric. Several substitutions (e.g., Psalm 24, as in the prayer-book of the Hamburg Temple) were provided. Nevertheless, many Liberal and Reform rituals continued to adhere to the traditional form and structure in this respect—introducing, however, minor modifications. A sampling of the latter is provided here. It may serve as an indication of how various Reform liturgists related to the concepts of "Zion" and "Jerusalem."

The verse from Isaiah chapter 2, when seen within its context, permits of a future translation only. "For out of Zion *shall* go forth the Torah. . . ." The two Jewish Bible translations readily available to most of the editors of reformed prayerbooks, that of Moses Mendelssohn and his disciples, and the translation edited by Zunz, do, as a matter of fact, render it thus. Yet many of the new prayerbooks have a tendency to use either the present or the past tense. The former would indicate the understanding of "Zion" as a "spiritual idea." The latter makes of "Zion" a historical reminiscence. But there were also exceptions.

Incidentally, we may note that *Torah* is almost universally rendered as "Teaching" (German: *Lehre*). The preference of *Lehre* over *Gesetz* (i.e., "Law") as a translation of *Torah* was one of the characteristics of early Reform liturgy as well as of Reform homiletics, polemics and theology.

In the following listing, the letters A.H. will stand for *Abh Haraḥamim* ("Father of mercies, do good in Thy favor unto Zion etc."), and the letters K.M. for *Ki mitziyon* ("For out of Zion shall go forth etc.").

West London Synagogue, 1841:
(p. 69) Contains both A.H. and K.M. ("For out of Zion shall the law go forth . . .")
This is remarkable in view of the fact that this ritual mostly follows the Sepharadi Rite, which does not include the two passages in question.

Aachen, 1853:
(p. 145) Includes both A.H. and K.M. (For out of Zion *goeth forth* the Teaching, . . .)

Geiger, 1854:
(p. 113) No A.H. Includes K.M. (The Teaching *which went forth* from Zion . . . .)

Stein, 1860:
(pp. 199f.) Includes both A.H. and K.M. (For out of Zion *goeth forth* the Teaching . . . .)

Aub (Berlin), 1866:
(p. 196) No A.H. Includes K.M. (For out of Zion *goeth forth* the Teaching . . . .)

Geiger, 1870:
(p. 103) Same as in Geiger's 1854 edition.

Joël, 1872:
(p. 141) Same as in Geiger's 1854 edition.

Berlin, 1881:
(p. 123) No A.H. Includes K.M. (For out of Zion *goeth forth* the Teaching . . . .)

Stockholm, 1881 (Vol. III):
(p. 109) Includes A.H., but omits phrase about "build the walls of Jerusalem." Whole passage is left untranslated. K.M. is included without translation.

Stein, 1882:
(p. 104) Includes A.H. with translation, and K.M. (For out of Zion *goeth forth* the Teaching . . . .)

Vogelstein (Westphalia), 1894:
(p. 186) No A.H. Includes K.M. (For out of Zion the Teaching *hath gone forth* . . . .)

Glogau, 189?:
(p. 105) No A.H. Includes K.M. (Out of Zion *goeth forth* the Teaching . . . .)

Baden, 1905:
(p. 218) No A.H. Includes K.M. (Mayest Thou, O Lord, at all times guide the bearers of the Teaching *which was proclaimed in Zion,* and of the Word of God *which went forth* from Jerusalem.)

Brunswick, 1906:
(p. 146) No A.H. Includes K.M. (from Zion *goeth forth* the Teaching . . . .)

Seligmann, 1910:
(p. 53) No A.H. Includes K.M. (For out of Zion *went forth* . . . .)

Nuremberg, 1914:
(p. 173) No A.H. Includes K.M. (Thus doth the Teaching *come out* of Zion . . . .)

Paris, 1925:
(p. 74) No A.H. Includes K.M. ("C'est de Sion que *sort* la Loi . . . .")

Einheitsgebetbuch, 1929:
(pp. 216ff.) No A.H. Includes K.M. (Out of Zion *goeth forth* the Teaching . . . .)

West London Synagogue, 1931:
(p. 24) Includes A.H., omitting *tibhneh ḥomoth yerushalayim,* and corresponding translation. K.M. is included as part of complete Isaiah 2:2–3. (For out of Zion *shall go forth* the law . . . .)

Seder Tobh Lehodoth (Netherlands), 1964:
(pp. 72f.) Includes A.H. and translation. Includes K.M. (For out of Zion *shall go forth* the Teaching . . . .)

If so many of the Liberal and Reform prayerbooks reflect a certain uneasiness about a single verse from the second chapter of the Book of Isaiah, we would expect that the Reform liturgists really faced a problem when it came to the Ninth of Ab. American Reform Judaism was ultimately to solve that problem by ignoring that day of the Jewish calendar. Not so the European Reformers who, by and large, labored for a "Reform from within." That is why, notwithstanding Geiger's extremely negative views on the subject of Zion, neither Geiger himself nor the vast majority of the other European Liberal and Reform liturgists did away with the services for the Ninth of Ab. Not only did many of them retain the appropriate Torah and Haftarah readings, but they also invested the Eve of the Ninth of Ab with a special solemnity, and called for a sermon as part of that service. The practice of reading the Book of Lamentations was continued, and even some selections from the more literary *kinoth* (elegies) were included in the services. Of course, the tendency of the various Liberal and Reform Ninth of Ab services was to stress the *universal* Kingdom of God. But, in the very nature of the case, "Zion" and "Jerusalem" became the symbols of Jewish historical continuity.

A representative sampling of Ninth of Ab services follows:

Hamburg, 1841:
(pp. 418f.) The Eve of Tish'ah BeAbh service calls for the reading

of the Book of Lamentations. An abbreviated text and translation of אלי ציון[35] is given.

Berlin (Gebetbuch der Genossenschaft für Reform im Judenthum), 1848:

This, the most radical congregation on the European continent, did not make provision for a special Ninth of Ab service. But the prayerbook (on pp. 161–163) did include a lengthy German prayer to be recited by the reader on the "Celebration in Memory of the Destruction of Jerusalem." On account of its daring attempt to transpose the whole concept of the Ninth of Ab, we give it here in full:

> *We remember today the day on which Jerusalem fell through the mighty hand of the foe, on which Judah ceased to be a people of the Lord, its sons and daughters being exiled and scattered over all the parts of the earth. We remember that today, after almost two millennia; and we praise Thee, O God, because we are still united to proclaim Thy holy Name which Thou didst reveal unto our fathers.*
>
> *Wondrously, O Lord, hast Thou guided the destiny of the people whom Thou hast called that the holiness of Thine infinite being may be known among the sons of man. Lamenting, the exiles wandered away, lamenting over Jerusalem, which lay in ruins, over the Temple, consumed by the greedy flames, and over the people whose name was to be blotted out among the nations of the earth. Year after year they mourned the fall of the Temple, and unceasingly they longed for the holy city. In days of heavy oppression, they constantly hoped that Thou wouldst again restore them to the Promised Land, raise up again the kingdom of Judah, mightier than before, and rebuild Thy Temple in Jerusalem to the honor of Thy Name and to the glory of Thy people.*
>
> *Thou didst hear their laments, but Thou didst not silence them. Thou didst hearken unto their plea, but Thou didst not grant it. Thou didst know their hope, but Thou didst not fulfil it. Yet it was not because Thou wast angry with them that Thou didst scatter them, but because Thou hast chosen them for Thy service didst Thou send them out to the peoples of the earth. Not because Thy punishment extends into the millennia didst Thou keep their remote descendants far from the land of their ancestors, but because Thy work is to be accomplished everywhere. Not because Thou wouldst chastise them for backsliding from Thy holy Teaching did they have to bear persecutions and oppressions, but in order that they might bear witness to the*

insuperable power of Thy truth did they have to confess Thy Name, under severe suffering, in the face of their despisers.

A great and holy task hast Thou placed in our hand, O God; for Thou didst want us to carry through the world, in silence, the light of the knowledge of Thee—until the coming of the time when the eyes of the peoples will be opened by Thy light. It was Thy will that we not ask, "What have I sinned that such heavy burden bends me to the ground?," but that we bear in humility what Thou hast decreed for us—until the hatred of the peoples vanish before the sunny glance of the love we are to proclaim in Thy Name.

We mourn not, O God, for the fallen Temple, for Thou wilt now erect Thy Temple in the hearts of all earth's children. Thou wilt erect it on the heights of the earth, so that all the peoples will unite to worship Thee. We mourn not the fall of Jerusalem, Thy holy city, for all the cities whither Thou didst send us are to be consecrated unto Thee through the worship of Thy Name. We mourn not for the ruined kingdom of Israel, and for Judah which Thou hast destroyed, for Thou hast set Thine eye upon all mankind, so that it may become Thy possession even as Israel was of old. And we mourn not for the humiliation, which was the price we had to pay, for we know that we bore it for Thy Name's sake. Now, in Thy mercy, Thou hast taken from our shoulders the burden of oppression which crushed our fathers. Here, on the soil of a new homeland, Thou hast restored to us the fatherland which we have lost for ever in the land of our fathers; and Thou hast given us a full and unlimited portion in the freedom of this great and free nation to which we belong. Thou, O Lord, wilt ever increase on earth the might of the kingdom of Thy love, that we may rejoice in it together with all our brethren, and that, united, we may labor towards the completion of the great task to which Thou hast called Thy whole mankind.[36]

Abraham Geiger undoubtedly shared much of the sentiment expressed in the above prayer; but, editing a prayerbook for use by a whole Jewish community, he showed himself more attentive to the mood and traditional forms of the Ninth of Ab. His liturgical treatment of that day follows.

Geiger, 1854:
(pp. 144-147) Eve of Tish'ah Be'Abh.
First two chapters of Lamentations.

[37] בליל זה יבכיון.
[38] שומרון קול תתן.
[39] עד אנה בכיה בציון. (First line only.)
[40] תרחם ציון כאשר אמרת.

The complete Hebrew text of *teraḥem* is given, but, instead of a literal translation, Geiger paraphrased it as follows:

> Enough of lamenting for Zion and Jerusalem! God buildeth the indestructible walls of the eternal Jerusalem—of the Jerusalem which proclaimeth the mercy of God to all. The glory of God will become manifest in her; and the blessing of God and comfort and joy will flow over all. Thanksgiving and praise will dwell there. Amen.

Geiger, 1854:
(pp. 148–156) Tish'ah Be'Abh Morning.
Last three chapters of Lamentations.
[41] ציון הלא תשאלי.
[42] שאלי שרופה.
[43] אלי ציון.
[44] שומרון קול תתן.
[45] עד אנה בכיה בציון. (First line only.)
[46] תרחם ציון. (With German paraphrase as in the evening service.)

By 1870, when he published the second edition of his prayerbook, Geiger had gone further in bringing the contents of the liturgy into accord with his religious orientation. The Ninth of Ab services have now been considerably shortened.

Geiger, 1870:
(pp. 141–143) Eve of Tish'ah Be'Abh Service.
First two chapters of Lamentations.
שומרון קול תתן.
תמהר ישועה. (i.e., תרחם ציון with omission of first seven words. Translation as in 1854 edition.)
(pp. 144–151) Tish'ah Be'Abh Morning Service.
Last three chapters of Lamentations.
ציון הלא תשאלי.
שאלי שרופה.

Stein, 1882:
(pp. 273–284) Tish'ah Be'Abh Eve Service.
German prayer:
O Lord, our God and God of our fathers! In a solemn evening hour we are gathered here to pay due tribute to the memory of

the sad fates of our fathers. For tomorrow is a day which seems to be one of a particularly hard fate for Israel. On it, the Holy Temple and the Holy City .were twice destroyed. Twice was Israel expelled from the Promised Land of its ancestors, and thrust into captivity and distress, into the hatred of the nations. Like unto those who mourn for father and mother, they sat on the ground, for they had lost their fatherland and their freedom. A future covered by darkness stood before them like a night without stars, in which a darkly veiled sky threatens to bring on terrifying storms. Yet it terminated, that ghastly night. The bright morning of a better time dawned. Painful memories and glad hopes together animate us in this hour. . . .

First chapter of Lamentations.

אלי ציון.
שומרון קול תתן.
שאלי שרופה.

Lamentations 3:1–40; 5:19–22.

Vogelstein (Westphalia), 1894:

(pp. 501–503) Tish'ah Be'Abh Eve Service.

German Hymn, "O Holy City, we remember thee."

First two chapters of Lamentations.

בליל זה יבכיון. (First line only.)

תמהר ישועה. (As in Geiger's 1870 prayerbook, but with a new translation, as follows:)

The thought of God's help, which Israel did not lack even in difficult and painful times, and which smoothed and brightened his path of thorns, that thought fills us on this night of meaningful remembrance with faithful trust and hopeful confidence. . . . Walking in the light of God's Teaching, diligently laboring for the welfare of mankind, and promoting everything good and noble, we honor best the memory of Zion and Jerusalem—of those sites whence the Word of the Lord had gone forth. Thus do we contribute building stones to the sublime temple of mankind, from the pinnacles of which there waves as a shining sign the banner of the knowledge of God and the love of man. . . .

(pp. 504–508) Tish'ah Be'Abh Morning Service.

Last three chapters of Lamentations.

ציון הלא תשאלי.
תמהר ישועה.

Einheitsgebetbuch, 1929:

(pp. 556–574) Tish'ah Be'Abh Eve.

First two chapters of Lamentations.

ציון הלא תשאלי.
אלי ציון.
תרחם ציון. (With *literal* translation.)

(pp. 582–602) Tish'ah Be'Abh Morning.
Last three chapters of Lamentations.
שומרון קול תתן.
שאלי שרופה.
תרחם ציון.

This prayerbook also offers a number of German hymns, prayers and meditations for inclusion in the Ninth of Abh services.

Our description of the variety of Ninth of Abh services in European Liberal and Reform congregations would not be complete were we not also to draw attention to Volume V of the *Forms of Prayer* of the West London Synagogue. Published in 1843, it is subtitled, "Prayers for Various Occasions." A glance at its Table of Contents alone is highly instructive:

Evening Service for the Ninth of Ab.
Morning Service for the Ninth of Ab.
Afternoon Service for the Ninth of Ab.
Morning Service for the Fast of Gedaliah.
Morning Service for the Tenth Day of Tebeth.
Morning Service for the Seventeenth Day of Tammuz.
Service for Circumcision.
Redemption of the First Born.
Service for Naming a Girl.
Burial Service.
Prayer for Mourners.
Prayer said by the Minister on the Sabbath after a Funeral.

It is clear, therefore, that all the "historical" fasts have been retained by that congregation to the extent of finding specific liturgical expression. The Ninth of Abh services, containing Torah and Haftarah readings and the Book of Lamentations, omit all but two of the traditional *kinoth*. In place of the latter, and quite in character with the *tendenz* of that synagogue in the period of its foundation, the Ninth of Abh liturgy relies heavily on the Biblical Book of Psalms. The following Psalms are included: 74; 76; 78; 137; and 130.

Towards the middle of the twentieth century (and probably for a considerable time before then), this volume of the prayerbook of the West London Synagogue was no longer in use, and no further editions of it appeared. But the Book of Lamentations continues to be read at that synagogue on Tish'ah Be'Abh Eve.

The role of Zion and Jerusalem in the liturgy of European Liberal and Reform Judaism can thus be seen to have been a fluctuating one. Nor was it solely determined by purely dogmatic considerations. Political circumstances and the position of the Jew in Western society had something to do with it as well. The easy optimism of a David Friedländer in 1812, the year of the Emancipation of the Jews in Prussia, was not necessarily the mood of the liturgists in the late twenties of the present century. Also, the creation of the State of Israel, in 1948, has left its impact on those Liberal and Reform prayerbooks in Europe which appeared after that date. But, whatever the changing role of Zion and Jerusalem in Liberal and Reform liturgy, the omission of prayers for the restoration of the sacrificial cult, and for the ingathering of *all* Jews in the land of the fathers, has remained a constant element in that liturgy—one which testifies to the honesty before God of the worshipper, and to the "rectitude of soul" which Friedländer had demanded in 1812. [47]

TWELVE

The Problem of "Particularism" in the 'Alenu Prayer

THE 'ALENU,[1] A PRAYER WHICH MAY HAVE ORIGINATED ALREADY IN Temple days,[2] was used by the third-century Babylonian Amora, Rabh, as the introductory prayer for the *malkhuyoth* section of the New Year *Musaph* Service.[3] Since around 1300, it also figures, in all rites, as the concluding prayer of all daily services—although only the Ashkenazi rite uses *both* paragraphs of the *'Alenu* for that purpose.[4]

When both paragraphs are taken together, they represent a combination of the "particularist" and the "universalist" dimensions of Judaism. In the first paragraph, the Lord of the Universe is praised "because He hath not made us like the nations of the lands, and hath not placed us like the families of the earth; since He hath not assigned unto us a portion as unto them, nor a lot as unto all their multitude."

שלא עשנו כגויי הארצות ולא שמנו כמשפחות האדמה.
שלא שם חלקנו כהם וגורלנו ככל-המונם :

If the first paragraph thus expresses the unique character of Israel, the second paragraph gives voice to the hope that the world may speedily be perfected under the kingdom of the Almighty,[5] and that all the children of man will call upon God, Who will be King over all the earth. "On that day shall the Lord be One, and His Name One."

While the prayer, as a whole, thus kept the balance between "particularism" and "universalism," the form in which the "particularism" was expressed has generally been found to be disturbing by the liturgists of Liberal and Reform Judaism. As Abraham Geiger expressed it, in his *Denkschrift* of 1869, "the separation between Israel and the other peoples, which existed at one time, has no right to be expressed in prayer. Rather ought there to be an expression of the joy that such barriers are increasingly falling." Drawing the extreme logical conclusion of this sentiment, several Reform rites have indeed omitted the "invidious comparison" from the *'Alenu* prayer altogether, thereby making the first paragraph a prayer of praise to God for the creation of heaven and earth, and completely eradicating the element of "particularism."[6]

But even the editors of prayerbooks of a decidedly "conservative" outlook found it difficult, in the nineteenth and twentieth centuries, to perpetuate the outspoken form of "particularism" which found its expression in the first paragraph of the *'Alenu*. While they did not alter the Hebrew text, they indicated, in a vernacular translation or paraphrase, that the significance of Israel's not being like other peoples lay in the fact that those other peoples were idolaters. Thus, the *Israelitische Gebetordnung,* published, in 1861, by Kirchenrat Joseph von Maier, and officially adopted by the Supreme Ecclesiastical Authority of the Jews of Wuerttemberg, a modernized but very "conservative" prayerbook, retains the traditional Hebrew text of *'Alenu,* but translates it as follows:

> It is our duty to praise the Lord of all, and to proclaim the greatness of the Creator, for not having made us like unto the heathens nor similar to the tribes sunk in superstition. But He hath given us a different destiny, and a portion other than the lot of that multitude. (Page 97.)

That version was later adopted in the *Israelitische Gebetordnung,* edited by Joseph Perles, Munich, 1876, and reprinted in the second edition of 1891. Similarly, the official prayerbook of Conservative Judaism in the United States translates the traditional *'Alenu* text as follows: ". . . for He hath not made us like the pagans of other lands, nor placed us like the heathen tribes of the earth."[7]

This approach to the translation of that prayer has, on occasion, been criticized as being too "apologetic" and something less than completely honest. Actually, the *original* version of the *'Alenu* prayer completely justifies this kind of translation. On account of censorship,[8] the original version is no longer in use among the Ashkenazim, but the Sepharadim have retained it. It reads:

> ...שלא עשנו כגויי הארצות. ולא שמנו כמשפחות האדמה : שלא שם חלקנו כהם. וגורלנו ככל-המונם : שהם משתחוים להבל וריק. ומתפללים אל-אל לא יושיע : ואנחנו...
>
> . . . since He did not make us like the nations of other countries, nor place us like other families of the earth; neither did He appoint our portion like theirs, nor our lot like that of their multitude, who worship vain and worthless things, and make supplication to a god that cannot save. But we bow down. . . . [9]

From this original version of the prayer it can clearly be seen that the contrast between Israel and the other peoples was motivated by the consideration that "they bow down to vain and worthless things; but *we* bow down to the King of Kings." The meaning of "nations of other countries" and "families of the earth" is, therefore, quite definitely that of "pagans" and "heathen tribes," and the "modernized" translations we have mentioned are thus quite justified.

The majority of European Liberal and Reform liturgies have, however, neither eliminated the "particularism" completely nor sought refuge in contrasting Israel with the *pagan* nations. A sizable number does retain the traditional Hebrew text (in its censored Ashkenazi form), but the translation (or paraphrase) stresses the fact that Israel has been saved from *paganism*—rather than made different from the *pagans*. (Just as, in the case of the twelfth of the Eighteen Benedictions, many Liberal and Reform liturgies prefer to pray for the destruction of *wickedness,* rather than for the destruction of the *wicked.*)[10]

Other Liberal and Reform prayerbooks, however, go one step further. Instead of expressing negatively that Jews are not pagans, they state positively what the "plus" of Judaism is. The first paragraph of the *'Alenu* thus praises God for the Election and the Mission of Israel, for the Covenant, and for the possession of the Torah. Often, too, this changed emphasis finds expression in an emended version of the traditional Hebrew text. It should be borne in mind that, with all its eagerness to remove liturgical formulations which the non-Jew might find offensive, classical Reform Judaism, perhaps even more than Orthodoxy, stressed the doctrine of the Mission of Israel as the sole *raison d'être* of Jewish survival.[11] The original *intent* of *'Alenu,* if not necessarily its traditional formulation, was, therefore, something with which Liberal and Reform liturgy could not so easily dispense.

The following pages will show how a representative number of European Liberal and Reform prayerbooks have handled the problem of "particularism" in the *'Alenu* prayer. The English translations we append are *not* those of the Hebrew texts we quote, but our English rendition of the vernacular translations or paraphrases which the prayerbooks under consideration offer of the Hebrew texts they print.

1) *DIE DEUTSCHE SYNAGOGE (Berlin), 1817.*
'Alenu is not used as a concluding prayer, but only as part of the New Year *Musaph* Service. The Hebrew text is not printed, but a rubric indicates that the traditional Hebrew text is to be recited.
Translation: . . . Who hath not placed us like unto the other tribes of the earth. Not such is our portion, not like the lot of their multitude.

2) *HAMBURG, 1819.*
Not used as concluding prayer, but only as part of the New Year *Musaph* Service. Traditional Hebrew text.
Translation: He hath not made us like unto many of the peoples of the earth, and hath not commingled us with the heathen tribes. Our destiny is not like unto theirs, nor our portion like unto that of their great multitude.

3) *HAMBURG, 1841.*
Not used as a concluding prayer, but only as part of the New Year *Musaph* Service. Traditional Hebrew text.
Translation: . . . that He did not let us become like unto the peoples of the lands, and that He did not make us like unto those tribes of the earth; that He did not make our portion equal unto theirs, nor our destiny like unto that of their great multitude.

4) *WEST LONDON SYNAGOGUE, 1841.*
אשר בחר־בנו מכל־העמים. ונתן לנו את־תורתו.
Translation: Who hath chosen us from amongst all people and hath given us His Law.

5) *KIRCHENRAT MAIER, 1848.*
German only. . . . that He hath redeemed us from the darkness of unbelief and superstition, and hath revealed unto us His enlightening Word.

6) *AACHEN, 1853.*
Traditional Hebrew text.
Translation: . . . that Thou hast redeemed us from the darkness of all false belief and superstition, and enlightened

us with the light of Thy revelation. Not before wood and stone, wrought by the hand of man, and not before silver and gold, refined by the smelter's fire, but before Thee, the King of Kings, the All-Holy, do we bow down.

7) *GEIGER, 1854.*

שנגלה לאבותינו והודיעם את־רצונו וכרת אתם את־בריתו והנחילנו תורתו.

In the German paraphrase of this prayer, there is no mention of the Covenant.

8) *GÖTEBORG, 1858.*

Hebrew text as in Geiger's 1854 prayerbook, but a translation of that text is furnished.

The Stockholm prayerbook of 1881 follows the 1858 Göteborg liturgy in this.

9) *SAALSCHÜTZ (Königsberg), 1859.*

German only. . . . that He hath not let us be like the pagans, and that He hath given us a lot different from that of their large multitude.

A footnote to this passage reads as follows:

Two thirds of mankind, as is known, still belong to paganism. Israelites, Christians, and Mohammedans together represent only one third of the inhabitants of the earth.[12]

10) *STEIN, 1860.*

German only. . . . Who hath called us to His service, and, in grace, hath redeemed us from the heathen errors; Who hath given us truth as an inheritance, and destined us to proclaim His Name among mankind.

11) *AUB (Berlin), 1866.*

Traditional Hebrew text.

Translation: . . . Who hath not let us sink into the idolatry of heathen peoples, but hath called us to revere Him and to proclaim His holy Name.

12) *HAMBURG, 1868.*

From this edition on, *'Alenu* is used as a concluding prayer.

Traditional Hebrew text.

Translation: . . . that He hath guarded us from heathen error, and called us to proclaim His holy Name.

13) *GEIGER, 1870.*

ששם חלקנו ליחד את־שמו וקרבנו לעבודתו.

Translation: We, who acknowledge His Unity and are called to dedicate ourselves to His Name and to His service, we, in particular, are obligated to praise the Lord of the Universe, and to proclaim the greatness of the world's Creator. . . .

14) *JOËL, 1872.*

Hebrew text as in Geiger's 1854 edition of the prayerbook.

Translation: He hath revealed Himself to our fathers, and hath made known His will unto them. He hath made the eternal covenant with them; and unto us He hath given the holy teaching as an inheritance.

15) *NUREMBERG, 1874.*

German version only. No reference to the Election of Israel.

16) *LEIPZIG, 1876.*

שבראנו לכבודו והבדילנו מן התועים ונתן לנו תורת אמת.

Translation: . . . Who hath called us to glorify Him, Who hath preserved us from the madness of idolatry, and Who hath given us the Teaching of truth.

17) *BERLIN (Neue Synagoge), 1881.*

ששם חלקנו לעבדו באמת בכל־משפחות האדמה.

Translation: Dedicated to Thy service, we confess Thy Unity. In ancient days Thou hast called us to proclaim Thy holy Name unto all mankind.

18) *STEIN, 1882.*

As in Stein's 1860 edition of the prayerbook.

19) *GLOGAU, 1892(?).*

Hebrew text omits all references, positive or negative, to the distinction between Israel and other peoples. However, the German "translation" reads as follows:

O Lord of all! We thank Thee that Thou didst lead our fathers out of the desert of paganism into Thy bright pastures of truth. We know that Thou alone art God. . . .

20) *VOGELSTEIN (Westphalia), 1894.*

שנגלה לאבותינו והודיעם את־רצונו ושם חלקנו ליחד את־שמו וקרבנו לעבודתו.

Translation: He hath revealed Himself unto our fathers, and hath made His will known unto them. He hath called us to confess the Unity of His Name, and to dedicate ourselves to His service.

Note that Vogelstein has used a combination of Geiger's version of 1854 and that of 1870.

21) *HAMBURG, 1904.*
Traditional Hebrew text.
Translation: He hath revealed Himself unto our fathers, that we may proclaim His unity unto mankind.

22) *BADEN, 1905.*

ששם חלקנו ליחד את־שמו וגורלנו לעבדו באמת.

Translation: . . . that He hath chosen us for His service, and hath called us to proclaim His Name among mankind.

23) *DANZIG, 1905.*
Traditional Hebrew text.
Translation: He hath freed us from the error of heathenism, and hath exalted us above the tribes which knew not God and His Law.

24) *BRUNSWICK, 1906.*
Hebrew and German as in the prayerbook of the Berlin New Synagogue, 1881.

25) *STOCKHOLM, 1907.*
Hebrew and Swedish texts omit all references, positive or negative, to the Covenant and the Election of Israel.

26) *SELIGMANN, 1910.*
Hebrew text as in the Baden prayerbook of 1905.
Translation: . . . that He hath, in ancient days, led our fathers from the night of superstition to the bright regions of His truth.

27) *NUREMBERG, 1914.*
Hebrew text, omitted from 1874 edition, is supplied; but neither Hebrew nor German texts make any reference to the Election of Israel and the Covenant.

28) *DANZIG, 1924.*

ששם חלקנו לעבדו באמת מכל־משפחות האדמה.

Translation: He hath called us, before all the tribes of the earth, to serve Him in truth.

Note: Except for *mikkol,* instead of *bekhol,* the Hebrew is that of the prayerbook of the Berlin New Synagogue, 1881. But the *mem* is no accident or printer's error. The translation makes it clear that a "*mem* of comparison" is intended here.

29) *PARIS, 1925.*
Traditional Hebrew text.
Translation: . . . Who hath called us to the knowledge of truth, and consecrated us to His service.

30) *MATTUCK (London), 1926.*
English only, and not in all services.
He was the guide of our fathers throughout the ages; and He will lead mankind unto the time when the knowledge of Him and obedience to His law shall fill the hearts of all men.[13]

31) *SELIGMANN, 1928.*
Hebrew and German texts as in his 1910 edition of the prayerbook.

32) *EINHEITSGEBETBUCH, 1929.*
שבחר־בנו ליחד את־שמו וקרבנו לעבודתו.
Translation: . . . that He hath made us worthy to confess His Unity, and hath called us to His service.

33) *STOCKHOLM, 1930.*
Hebrew and Swedish texts as in the 1907 edition of the Stockholm prayerbook.

34) *WEST LONDON SYNAGOGUE, 1931.*
Reference to the Election of Israel, contained in earlier editions of this liturgy, now omitted from both the Hebrew and the English texts.

35) *SEDER TOBH LEHODOTH (Holland), 1964.*
Hebrew text and Dutch translation of the *Einheitsgebetbuch* version of 1929.

36) *UNION OF LIBERAL & PROGRESSIVE SYNAGOGUES (England), 1967.*
שהוא שם חלקנו ליחד את־שמו, וגורלנו להמליך מלכותו:
. . . for he chose us to make known his unity, and called us to proclaim him King.
(Translation and spelling of the prayerbook.)

Our investigation of the way in which the various European Liberal and Reform prayerbooks dealt with the problem of "particularism" in the *'Alenu* prayer thus leads to the conclusion that, while a few of the prayerbooks retained the traditional Hebrew text and translated it literally, and while a few others removed the "offending" clauses from both the Hebrew and the vernacular texts without providing a substitute version, the majority of the prayerbooks under consideration adopted another solution. They maintained the balance of the *'Alenu* prayer by emphasizing "particularism" in the first paragraph, and "universalism" in the second. But, whereas the traditional version stated the "particularism" in negative terms, the reformed prayerbooks stated it positively.

THIRTEEN

New Liturgical Creations

WHEN THE EARLY REFORMERS UNDERTOOK THE ABBREVIATION OF THE traditional liturgy, they were undoubtedly motivated by their knowledge of the modern man's span of attention. The traditional services were simply too long to enable the worshipper to concentrate on everything that was being recited, and a lack of decorum was the inevitable consequence. But, in reducing the number of prayers, the Reformers were not only thinking of the number of traditional prayers which could be recited with devotion and decorum. For them, it was not merely a matter of *traditional* prayers. The modern age, too, was entitled to its share of liturgical creations; and, in reducing the number of traditional prayers selected for recitation, the Reformers were also bearing in mind that the time allocated for worship would have to include prayers reflecting their own needs and concerns, over and above the prayers which they had taken over from the traditional liturgy. In this, they showed themselves faithful to the teachings of the Talmud on the subject of prayer. Rabbi Eliezer had warned against making prayer a matter of routine.[1] In explaining the meaning of "routine," some later Rabbis, Rabbah and Rabh Joseph, had defined it as the prayer of him "who is unable to say something new in it."[2]

Even so, the earliest reformed rituals, *Die Deutsche Synagoge* of 1817/18, and the Hamburg Temple Prayer Books of 1819 and 1841, did not actually contain any newly written prayers. The element of the "new" was found in the sermon, on the one hand, and in the German hymns and chorales, inserted in various parts of the services, on the other. But already in 1842 we find new liturgical creations making their appearance in reformed prayerbooks. The amount of space devoted to new prayers always depended on the degree of faithfulness to which a given ritual adhered to the traditional format; and most of the reformed rituals of Germany adhered rather closely to that format. On the other hand, prayerbooks which followed the traditional format far less closely, such as the prayerbook of the Berlin *Reformgemeinde,* or the *Liberal Jewish Prayer Book,* edited by Israel I. Mattuck in London, were able to incorporate new liturgical creations to a far greater extent.

It was in America, and not in Europe, that the serious attempt was first made to strike a balance between the old and the new. David Einhorn's prayerbook, *'Olath Tamid* (Baltimore, 1856/8), was the first ritual to combine the old and the new in about equal proportions, and it was followed in this by the American *Union Prayer Book.* The influence of the latter is clearly discernible in Caesar Seligmann's 1910 prayerbook, although Seligmann was more given to the paraphrasing of the traditional prayers in a modern vein than to creating prayers *de novo.* Only in the 1967 prayerbook of the Union of Liberal and Progressive Synagogues, in England, do we find the inclusion of the old and of the new in equal proportions.

The following pages can offer no more than a few samples of the type of prayer newly created by Liberal and Reform Judaism. There is no attempt here to include all, or even most, of the new prayerbooks. Nor, in the case of each ritual cited here, can we do more than quote one or two characteristic new prayers. But enough will be quoted to show that the reform of the liturgy was more than a mere matter of abbreviation. It was, in part, a pruning of the old, in order to make room for the new.

(1) *Forms of Prayer used in the West London Synagogue of British Jews,* ed. D. W. Marks. Vol. II. (Prayers for the Festivals.) London, 1842, page 76.

This ritual, while including a *Musaph* Service, does not contain the traditional prayers for rain and for dew, which are recited on Tabernacles and Passover respectively. Instead, this liturgy provides an entirely new prayer, in Hebrew and in English, which is meant to be said after the *Musaph* Benedictions. Note the reference to the restoration of Jerusalem.

ברכת מועדי השנה:

אנא יי אלהים בורא שמים ויוסד ארץ. נותן שמש לאור יומם. חקות ירח וכוכבים לאור לילה. גבול שמת לים. על הרוח ועל הגשם צוית. תשב רוחך יזלו מים. השמים יערפו טל בדברך. ושלג וברד ימטירו באמרתך: זמן ומועד לכלם קצבת בעומק תבונתך. ואת כל זאת לטוב לנו עשית כי טוב ומטיב אתה: על כן יי אלהינו. המכסה שמים בעבים המכין לארץ מטר. לפניך נפיל תחנתנו. להשפיע ברכותיך במועד השנה הזה: חום ורחם על פני האדמה. נא תן טל השמים ומטר הארץ בעתם. ונתנה הארץ יבולה ועץ השדה יתן פריו: ואחינו בני ישראל הנפוצים ימה וקדמה. צפנה ונגבה. אשר הם רחוקים ממנו ולבם קרוב אלינו. לקרא כלם בשם יי ולעבדו שכם אחד. פקוד נא אותם בחסדך הגדול לברך מועדיהם כפי אדמתם. וזכור נא ברחמיך ירושלים עיר הקדש אשר נכספה נפשנו לראות בכבודו הראשון ובתפארת גדלו כימי קדם: שלח לנו שנת טובה וברכה שנת שבע וחיים. כי תשביע העולם כלו מטובך ותמלא ידינו מברכותיך: ברוך אתה יי. מברך מועדי השנה:

THE BLESSING FOR THE SEASONS.

O Lord God, thou hast created the heavens and laid the foundations of the earth; thou hast given the sun for a light by day, and the ordinances of the moon and of the stars for a light by night. A boundary hast thou fixed to the seas, the rain and the wind obey thy behests, the heavens distil dew at thy word, and the snow and the hail descend at thy bidding. In the depths of thy wisdom thou hast established for all these a time and a season; all this hast thou done for our benefit, for thou art gracious and beneficent. Therefore we supplicate thee, O Lord our God, who coverest the heavens with clouds and preparest rain for the earth, to pour out thy blessing upon this season of the year. O have compassion upon the face of the ground, and bestow upon us rain and dew in their season; so that the earth may yield her increase, and the tree of the field shoot forth its fruit. And do thou, O Lord, in thy great mercy remember all our brethren, who are scattered east, west, north and south, but who, though distant, unite with us in proclaiming the name of God, and in serving him with one accord; and bless the seasons according to the climes where thy people are dispersed. Remember also Jerusalem, the holy city, on which our eyes anxiously wait, and which we hope to behold in all its former glory and ancient splendour. O grant unto us all a happy and blessed year, a year of life and plenty; for thou, O Lord, satisfiest thy whole earth with thy goodness, and fillest our hands with thy blessings. Blessed art thou, O Lord, who blessest the seasons of the year!

Subsequent editions of this prayerbook[3] offer a greatly improved Hebrew version, in which the grammatical mistakes are also corrected, but the themes remain the same. However, in the 1965 edition of this volume, undertaken by The Assembly of Ministers of The Reform Synagogues of Great Britain, the reference to Jerusalem has been omitted. This, of course, reflects a further step in Reform Jewish thinking, which the founders of the West London Synagogue of British Jews had not yet taken. The irony of the situation lies in the fact that the Hebrew portion of the 1965 volume was printed in the State of Israel![4] The phrase, "bless the seasons according to the climes where thy people are dispersed," represents a delicate handling of one of the problems which agitated the early Reformers: whether *Europeans* should pray for rain and for dew at just the times set for those prayers by the *Babylonian* codifiers of the liturgy?[5] In the course of this chapter, we shall come across other attempts to deal with that problem.

(2) *Israelitisches Gebet- und Andachtsbuch*, ed. Joseph von Maier. Stuttgart, 1848, page 38.

The brief prayer to be quoted is the introductory prayer of the daily evening service. In the traditional liturgy, this prayer consists of two Scripture verses, Psalm 78: 38, and Psalm 20: 10, and reads as follows:

And He being merciful, forgiveth iniquity, and destroyeth not: yea, many a time He turneth His anger away, and doth not stir up all His wrath. Save, Lord: may the King answer us on the day when we call.

Maier's lengthy paraphrase, which follows below, is typical of the way in which he handled traditional prayers in general, in his 1848 edition of the prayerbook:

He is a merciful and gracious God, who forgiveth sin and destroyeth not. On this day, too, we have experienced in manifold ways His merciful grace; for He hath not dealt with us according to our sins, nor requited us according to our transgressions. But He hath satisfied us with all good; He hath granted us life and health, sustenance and raiment. He hath saved our souls from destruction, and He hath crowned our life with love and with mercy.

(3) *Gebetbuch der Genossenschaft für Reform im Judenthum*. Part I. Berlin, 1848, pp. 66f.

After giving a German paraphrase of the *elohai neshamah* prayer,[6] this prayerbook develops the theme still further by including the following prayer:

> *Father of all the world! In the abundance of Thy grace Thou hast created man in Thine own image. Thou hast endowed him with spirit of Thine own spirit, and hast sent a ray of Thine eternal life into his soul. Thou lookest upon him, and Thou watchest over him, that he may keep and guard his divine portion within him. But Thou, in Thy wisdom, hast also appointed us as guardians of our own soul, that we may faithfully preserve it, and keep it pure from the dust of the earth to which we are attached with our being, pure from the stain of passion and sin which darken our soul. Ours is the task of leading our soul to the well of knowledge, from which it will ever drink renewed thirst for Thy truth. Ours is the task of strengthening our soul to reach worthy and firm decisions, of encouraging it to perform the right deed, and of arming it with constancy for the struggle against the vicissitudes of life. Teach us, O God, to protect fittingly Thine own portion which Thou hast lent unto us, that we may follow Thy example in truth, even as Thou hast created us in Thine own image. Amen.*

(4) *Israelitisches Gebetbuch,* ed. Abraham Geiger. Breslau, 1854, pp. 239f.

This prayer, to be recited by the rabbi before the open Ark, is meant to take the place of the Prayer for Dew on the first day of Passover:

> *O Lord, my God! Thy children are approaching Thy throne. With confidence they look up unto Thee, but not without concern. A plea is hovering on every tongue. O may the words of their mouth and the longing of their heart find acceptance before Thee, my God and my Redeemer! A harsh winter has passed over us. Its storms have not only bent the leaf of the tree, but, alas, many a head, too, was forced to bow under it. The poor man sighed deeply under the burden of want. (The rough hand of winter is not yet gone from us altogether; yet we trust in Thy goodness. Thou wilt again send us the bright ray of the sun, and there will again be light unto all Thy children, in their habitations. The air of spring will refresh our body and our soul. Thy dew will revive us.) O Lord, if we did not submit unto Thee in joyful confidence, what hope would there remain for us? Make us glad, O Lord, according to the days wherein Thou hast afflicted us. Our strength is vanity when Thou removest Thy hand from us. Send us a mild and happy spring, and a vigorous and blissful summer! The farmer scattereth his*

seed over the earth; O let it sprout to provide ample nourishment for Thy creatures! Refresh the earth, and water it in its right season. Thy brook is full of blessing; O may it flow towards us! Thou hast given the earth unto the children of men, so that they may dress it and keep it. Thou wilt also open the womb of the earth, so that its produce may give nourishment to man. May the earth be the peaceful soil upon which will reign freedom and law, justice and mutual respect. Thus may every man unfold his noble powers, and prepare himself worthily to become a citizen of the Kingdom of Heaven. Thus let the spring and the summer come unto us for a blessing, and not for a curse; for satiation, and not for scarcity; for life, and not for death. O Lord, Thy love is without end, and Thy mercy is inexhaustible. Praised be Thy Name in eternity! Amen.

שאתה הוא יי אלהינו משיב הרוח ומוריד הטל :
לברכה ולא לקללה (אמן) : לשבע ולא לרזון (אמן) :
לחיים ולא למות (אמן) :

(5) *Gebetbuch für Israelitische Gemeinden*, ed. Leopold Stein. Frankfort o. M., 1860, page 88.

This prayer is said aloud after the silent recitation of the Seven Benedictions on the eve of the festivals:

And the Lord spoke unto Moses: speak unto the children of Israel, and say unto them: The festivals of the Lord, which ye shall proclaim to be holy convocations, even these are My *festivals.*

O Lord our God, Thou dost call them Thy *festivals! For the freedom which they celebrate is* Thy *gift, O Shield and Redeemer of Israel!—The law of which they admonish us is the emanation of* Thy *holy will, O Teacher and Guide of Israel!—The joy which they afford us is a ray of* Thy *fatherly graciousness and faithfulness, refreshing all!*

Bestow upon us, then, through the blessing of Thy festivals, those threefold gifts:—freedom from earthly cares, knowledge and insight into Thy holy will, and gladness and joy in the celebration of Thy holy service. Praised art Thou, O Lord, who sanctifiest Israel through the celebration of Thy festivals. Amen.

(6) *Israelitische Gebetordnung*, ed. Joseph von Maier. Vol. I. Stuttgart, 1861, pp. 306f.

Maier's 1848 prayerbook was published as the work of an individual. But, as an official of the Wuerttemberg Supreme Ecclesiastical Authority, Maier was also charged with the publication of a prayerbook which could be used by all the Jews in the kingdom. While, by the standards of those days, the 1848 prayerbook was rather "radical," the 1861 ritual was basically the traditional *siddur* with very minor changes. However, the *piyutim* were abolished, and, in their place, a number of German hymns and German prayers were introduced. Among the latter, there is this introductory prayer for the service on the Eve of Pentecost:

> *Lord, God and Father! With joyful hearts we have appeared in Thy presence, to thank Thee for the grace and the faithfulness which Thou hast shown unto our fathers and unto us. When darkness covered the earth, and thick darkness the nations, when error and delusion kept mankind captive, then didst Thou choose our fathers, in order to reveal unto them the truth of Thy teaching, and to have them spread throughout the earth the knowledge of Thy being and of Thy will. Thou hast made Israel a kingdom of priests, walking in light and in right, and having light and right go forth from them unto all the dwellers on earth. O Father of Light! Our fathers have faithfully complied with their mission. Like the apple of their eye, they have guarded the teaching which Thou hast given unto them. They did not cast away from them the torch of Thy light even when it became a consuming fire over their heads. Pure and unblemished they have passed on this teaching into our hands. Be with us, that we, too, may walk in this light, in all endeavors for the good, in righteousness and in truth. In happiness and in peace, let us not forget that our priestly task will not be completed until the time when the word of Thy promise will have been fulfilled: "The Lord shall be king over all the earth; on that day the Lord shall be One, and His Name One." Amen.*

(7) *Israelitisches Gebetbuch,* ed. Bernhard Friedmann. Mannheim, 1868, pp. 264f.

The traditional liturgy of the Ashkenazi rite includes a prayer for the martyrs after the Torah reading on the Sabbath before Pentecost, and on the Sabbath before the Ninth of Abh.[7] Originating in the Rhineland, at the time of the Crusades, this prayer asks God to remember the martyrs, and to avenge the blood of the innocent. The Mannheim prayerbook gives the traditional Hebrew text which speaks about remembrance, but it omits the part of the prayer calling for vengeance. The German paraphrase, which accompanies the abbreviated Hebrew text, is an interesting illustration of the manner in which a generation of Jews, but recently emancipated, reacted to the components of the liturgy in which the experiences of martyrdom found their literary repercussions:

> *Father of mercies, who dwellest on high! In the depth of Thy love, graciously remember those devoted ones, the righteous and*

the guiltless, the holy congregations who laid down their lives for the sanctification of Thy Name. Beloved of Thee in their lives, they are not separated from Thee even in death. They were swifter than eagles, and stronger than lions, to do the will of their Master and the desire of their Rock. Remember them for salvation, O God, together with all the noble ones who sacrificed themselves on earth in the cause of truth.—The times have become brighter, the thoughts clearer, and the sentiments more humane. The dungeon and the stake no longer await the Israelite who would live and die in faithfulness to Thy divine commandment. Thanks and praise be to Thee, O Master of the Universe and Guide of the Times! At every moment, our fathers *had to be prepared to cast away freedom and life, in order not to reject their faith; and they were happy to die for the Torah if they were not allowed to live for it. But a more favorable fate smiles* upon us. *In the brightest sunshine of the century, we can be Israelites; we can bring the pure faith in Thee to its realization and glory in the midst of the meeting of minds, in the council of the citizens, in the full flow of science and art, of industry and education. O that this fortune may not deprive us of that which misfortune was unable to wrest from our fathers!—O Lord, let the memory of those heroes of faith, strong in conviction and undaunted by death, kindle within our spirits and our hearts a renewed and sacrificial devotion to our faith. May we live for that for which they died. May we preserve in life the loyalty which they sealed with their death. May we vigorously and joyously, gladly and freely acknowledge Thy truth before all the world. May we observe Thy commandments of righteousness, love and holiness. Amen.*

(8) *Gebetbuch für Israelitische Gemeinden,* ed. Leopold Stein. Mannheim, 1882, Vol. I, pp. 483f.

In addition to increasing the number of German prayers for synagogue worship over those contained in the 1860 edition of his prayerbook, Stein paid much attention, in the 1882 edition, to domestic devotions. This volume contains a German Passover *Haggadah* as well as some fine German adaptations of the traditional Sabbath table hymns. Also included in this volume is a ceremony marking the re-appearance of (leavened) bread on the Jewish table, after a week of *matzoth*. Stein, who was a very vocal opponent of the "second day" of the festivals, quite naturally scheduled the ceremony of the "Welcoming of the Bread" at the termination of the Seventh Day of Passover:

Bread, bread, be welcome, cherished and beloved bread!

We, the children of men, learn the value of all good things only through being deprived of them. That is why we have to miss our customary daily bread for a whole week in the year, in order that we may value and appreciate its high worth. And we do that on the festival which inaugurates the most beautiful season of the year, the season which brings in a new year of fertility. That is why Pesach is the festival of the bread and of the wine, the two most glorious gifts of our Mother Earth for her dear children. Judaism neither deifies the things of visible creation nor does it endow them with a symbolical divine meaning. Nevertheless, it honors with gratitude the highest gifts of Nature by ordaining specific benedictions for both of them.

For the Wine

Praised by Thou, O Eternal, our God,
Who hast created the fruit of the vine.

ברוך אתה יי אלהינו מלך העולם
בורא פרי הגפן :

For Bread

Who causest bread to sprout from the earth. המוציא לחם מן הארץ:

How great is the goodness of God, who causes the blade of grass to grow, from which we obtain bread! Centuries, perhaps millennia, had gone by ere man obtained bread from the blade of grass—bread, the staff supporting the heart. Behold it, behold it with amazement, that field of grain—bowing like a pious congregation before God, the Heavenly Giver of Bread. The cultivation of the soil has founded families, communities, yea, mankind itself. Honor the bread which has taught men to live together, "and the movable tent became peaceful and firm huts."

And so we praise thee again, O cherished and beloved bread. Beholding thee, we laud God, the holy Guide of the human race. Looking upon the bread, we celebrate Judaism, we celebrate our cherished ancestral doctrine, which so simply and so reasonably brings the highest truths close to our thinking mind and to our feeling heart. Rise, then, and lift up your hearts in prayer:

Praised be Thou, O Eternal our God,
Who causest bread to sprout
from the earth. Amen. Amen.

ברוך אתה יי אלהינו
מלך העולם המוציא לחם
מן הארץ :

(9) *Gebetbuch,* (ed. David Mayer). Baden, 1905.

(a) Page 8.

One of the benedictions, included in the traditional daily morning service, and recited by the Orthodox Jew after answering nature's call, is so explicit in its reference to anatomical and physiological details[8] that most editors of reformed prayerbooks were too embarrassed to include it.

The Baden prayerbook, however, recognizing the significance of having a prayer dealing with man's body in juxtaposition to a prayer dealing with man's soul, did not omit that benediction. Instead, the prayer was rewritten in a way which could not give offense to anyone:

> ברוך אתה יי אלהינו מלך העולם אשר יצר את־האדם בחכמה וברא בו פלאות אין מספר והרבה רפואות להחלימו ולהחיותו. גלוי וידוע לפני כסא כבודך שאם תעלים עיניך ממנו אף רגע אחד אי־אפשר להתקים ולעמוד לפניך: ברוך אתה יי רופא כל־בשר ומפליא לעשות:
>
> *Praised art Thou, O Lord our God, Sovereign of the Universe, who hast formed man in wisdom, and hast created innumerable wonders within him; and Thou hast multiplied the remedies wherewith to heal him and to keep him alive. It is known before the throne of Thy glory that, wert Thou to hide Thine eyes from him for but a moment, he could no longer exist and stand before Thee. Praised art Thou, O Lord, physician of all flesh, who doest wondrously.*

(b) Page 383.

The prayer upon leaving the *sukkah* on Shemini 'Atzereth is of late Kabbalistic origin. It reads, in the traditional version:

> May it be Thy will, O Lord our God and God of our fathers, that, just as I have fulfilled the commandment and have dwelt in this *sukkah,* I may be worthy next year to dwell in the *sukkah* made from the skin of Leviathan.[9]

It is not surprising that Liberal and Reform liturgies, in their total rejection of Kabbalistic accretions, have also eliminated this "Prayer upon Leaving the *Sukkah.*" Not so the Baden prayerbook! It offers, on page 382, a reformed Hebrew version: "May it be Thy will, O Lord our God and God of our fathers, that, just as I have fulfilled the commandment and have dwelt in this *sukkah,* I may always be worthy to dwell in the tabernacle of Thy peace. Amen." But the Baden prayerbook also offers a more elaborate German prayer for that occasion. It reads as follows:

> *God and Father! With joy and with gratitude we have entered the tabernacle at the beginning of the feast. And now that we have to leave it again, we are filled with sincere thanks for the blessing which hath gone forth from this room. In an intimate circle we have enjoyed the peace of this lovely festival, and we have refreshed ourselves with Thy rich gifts, even as we have acquired a new and strengthened confidence in Thy care. May Thy grace, O Lord, accompany us also through the inclement*

time of winter, and make our dwelling a tabernacle of peace all the days of our life! Amen.

(10) *Israelitisches Gebetbuch,* ed. Caesar Seligmann. Frankfort o. M., 1910.

Seligmann's contribution, as has already been noted, lay in the re-creation of traditional prayers by means of paraphrases, rather than in the writing of entirely new prayers, although his liturgical work contains some of the latter as well. His was a truly poetic German style, which is not easy to render into English. However, the following renditions, while not doing justice to Seligmann's mastery of the German language, may at least convey to the English reader some idea of what Seligmann was trying to do.

(a) Pages 6–9. (From the *Shema.*)[10]

Hear, O Israel, God is our Lord, God is unique!
Thou shalt love the Lord thy God with a whole heart and a whole soul. These words thou shalt write into thy soul. Teach them diligently unto thy children, so that they never let go of them. For they are Israel's most precious treasure of faith, a holy inheritance. They shall accompany thee, as a true guide, upon all the paths of thy life. With them thou shalt greet each new morning, and they shall be thy last thought at the waning eve. With indelible script thou shalt write them upon the tablets of thy heart.

If ye will hearken unto My commandments, to love the Eternal your God, and to serve Him with a whole heart and a whole soul, then I will give peace unto your soul and joyous success in your labors, that ye may rejoice in God's radiant blessing. But beware, and be ye not enticed to forsake your God! For then the punishment of God would come upon you. The sky would be darkened for you, and the earth would withhold its blessings from you. And ye would walk upon the blessed earth with discord in your heart, and with remorse in your soul. Therefore ye shall write My words with indelible script upon the tablets of your heart, etc., etc.

(b) Pages 12–14. (The first three of the Eighteen Benedictions.)[11]

O Eternal, our God and God of our fathers! Among all peoples, our ancestors were the first to know Thee in Thy creative greatness and in the abundance of Thy love. And even as they, in piety and in faith, lifted up their souls unto Thee, so do we pray unto Thee, in humility and in confidence, O Thou merciful Shield of our fathers!

We are deeply moved, O Almighty, by the thought of our dependence upon Thee. Thou callest men to life, and leadest them unto death. But, out of death, Thou causest new life to sprout forth. As Thy breath reviveth the wintery field, causing the verdure of a new spring, so dost Thou revive the dead to enjoy a radiant light. All the hope and all the comfort of man's ephemeral life lie in looking up unto Thee. Thou dost extend a supporting arm to the stumbling; Thou dost send healing to the sick, comfort to the mourners, courage to them that are bowed down. Thou redeemest the soul of them that sleep in the dust. Thy mercy is watching over them, and Thou wilt not suffer their spirit to vanish in the dust.

Surrounded by the barriers of finitude, we are unable to know Thine incomprehensible and exalted ways. Only one thing do we know: In Thee do all moral feelings and thoughts have the ground of their being. Thou art the Source and the Guarantor of morality! Thou art the All-Holy! Thus did our pious ones praise Thee. Thus, too, would we worship Thee, O holy God of our fathers!

(11) *Liberal Jewish Prayer Book,* ed. Israel I. Mattuck. Vol. I. London, 1926. Pages 58–60.

Reader:
In the pursuit of our daily tasks, we are often under the domination of desires and needs which tend to obscure the higher purpose of life for which man is fitted by his spiritual endowment. Though the body is holy when dedicated to the service of God, it holds desires which become unholy passions if uncontrolled; and even its ordinary demands, because they are physical, may through excess so absorb our being as to shut out spiritual endeavor.
Congregation:
Deliver us, O God, from unworthy desires and ambitions.
Reader:
But in the power and beauty of the universe, which reveal the presence of God; in the works of men, which show righteousness or beauty; in the strivings and sacrifices for high ends, in all influences that open the soul towards the perfection of the ideal, our hearts can find an impulse to exercise their divine life.
Congregation:
We praise thee, our Father, for thy guidance.
Reader:
We are not in ourselves strong enough for the demands laid

upon us by the divine nature of man. Truth is difficult, righteousness exacting. Weakness and temptation threaten to spoil our lives, withholding them from the pursuit and attainment of the best that is possible for man.
Congregation:
Help us, O God, against our weakness.
Reader:
When the soul meditates upon the greatness of God and his transcendent power, it bows before him in awe and trembling. But trust overcomes fear, giving rest from all terrors; and the soul strives, with yearning and faith, to unite with him, who is our heavenly Father.
Congregation:
Send out thy light and truth, let them lead us and let them bring us to thy holy hill.
Reader:
With the knowledge of God's sustaining care comes strength. Though we are far from the full realisation of his presence, and our hold upon his leading is weak and inconstant, yet the very desire to know him makes us strong and the yearning for him fills our soul with the light of his grace.
Choir:
Rejoice in the Lord ye righteous, and give thanks unto his holy name.

(12) *Einheitsgebetbuch,* 1929.

This "Union Prayer Book" of German Liberal Judaism offers, in its main part, the traditional Hebrew services in an abbreviated form and with such emendations of the text as are necessitated by a Reform approach to traditional dogma. However, in an Appendix of 124 pages, a number of German prayers are provided, some of which were meant to supplement the Hebrew services, while others were designed to be used as substitutes for traditional prayers.

(a) Appendix, page 34. (Prayer after the reading of the Torah).

O Lord our God, the voice of the Torah hath spoken to us again. But in its voice we hear Thee. Thou hast again revealed Thyself unto us, Thou hast again enriched us through Thy Word. With our whole heart we thank Thee. With our whole heart we entreat Thee: speak Thou unto us whenever we are in need of Thee; answer us whenever we call upon Thee. Amen.

(b) Appendix, page 104. (To take the place of the traditional Prayer for Rain.)

Heavenly Father! The season of the festivals is approaching its conclusion. Soon our labors will call us again, and the cares of winter are drawing nigh. All too many will suffer from cold and from hunger. Oh, let this time pass by mildly. Open the hearts of men that they may gladly assist their brothers and their sisters in the time of need. But let us also enjoy the benefits of winter, and let us be thankful for its gifts. Let us joyfully participate in the destiny of all of our Jewish brethren, but also to do our share for the welfare of all mankind.
O Lord, let the time of winter come upon us
for a blessing, and not for a curse;
for satiation, and not for hunger;
for life, and not for death. Amen.

(13) *Forms of Prayer for Jewish Worship*. West London Synagogue. Vol. I. 6th Edition. 1931.

This prayerbook contains a number of newly created opening prayers, both in Hebrew and in English, of which the former are evidently translations of the latter. Moreover, while the Sabbath Morning Service of this prayerbook contains all three traditional paragraphs of the *Shema*, only the first paragraph is recited in unison by the congregation. The remaining two paragraphs are said silently, while six English prayers and meditations are provided for those who prefer them to the readings from Deuteronomy and Numbers. We quote one example of each type of prayer.

(a) Page 13. (Opening Prayer.)

אלהינו היה אתנו במשך השבוע הבא: למדנו לעשות את־רצונך בלב שלם. שלא נזלזל בצרכי נפשנו. ושלא נהיה קרירי רוח לצרכי אחרים: סעדנו במעשינו ובכל משלח ידינו וישמשו לנו אמצעים לחיי טהר ויפי: תמכנו־נא שנגדע להכיר במאור שבתורתנו. לקים ביתר שאת את־החובות הגדולות שדתנו מטלת עלינו. ונעבוד בעד קדוש שמך ותקון העולם במלכות שדי: אמן:

Be with us, O God, during the coming week. Teach us to do thy will, and make us brave in performing it. Help us to overcome our failings, our forgetfulness of thee, our indifference to the needs of others, our heedlessness of the claims of our souls. Help us in our daily work, so that in very truth we may live by it, making it the source of our ennoblement, the instrument of the higher life. Help us to be better Israelites, to realise the splendour of our religious heritage, and to fulfil more faithfully the high responsibilities it lays upon us. For so shall we work for thy greater glory and for the establishment of thy Kingdom on earth. Amen.

(b) Pages 37f. (Optional meditation during the silent recitation of the *Shema.*)

There have been times, O God, when I have been disloyal to thee in thought. My faith in thee has wavered: my conviction of thy goodness, of thy rectitude, of thy very existence, has been shaken. The struggle of life was too fierce; its bitterness was more than I could bear. My plans and my hopes foundered; everything went against me; there seemed no chance of help, of redress, anywhere. And I said, There is no justice in this life of ours. Sometimes suffering—my own, but still more poignantly the suffering of others—filled me with doubts. Why, I cried, does God so sorely afflict his own children? Where is his compassion? Where his power? Thou hadst almost ceased to exist for me then. I lost touch of thy hand, which would have guided and soothed me, had I but looked for it more steadily, sought for it more diligently.

I dared to judge thee, O righteous Judge; I set my mind above thine, O God of infinite wisdom. I saw but one side of the truth. I saw only the shadows which now and again darken the way; I forgot the sunbeams which as often illumine it. I forgot that the world in which thou hast placed us is beautiful, that Nature has a smiling face for us on many a day, that the sting of the life-struggle is a spur to a higher nature, that human goodness is a sure token of thy goodness, O gracious Creator. My heart was haughty, and I exercised myself in things too hard for me.

Pardon this my sin—my presumption, my blindness. But help me, too, O God. Help me to see life more steadily, with something of thy calm and all-embracing gaze. Help me to see that order rules in all the seeming chaos of human life, love in all its defeats and tribulations. For thy mercies never fail; never does thy heart cease to feel the woe of thy children, O heavenly Father. Amen.

(14) *The Service of the Heart.* London, Union of Liberal and Progressive Synagogues, 1967.

This prayerbook provides a number of different services for each occasion. Some of the services include more traditional texts than others. But even in services where modern prayers have been substituted for traditional texts, the traditional sequence of ideas has been adopted, a far-reaching departure from the *Liberal Jewish Prayer Book* of Israel I. Mattuck, the immediate predecessor of the present volume. The following prayer (pp. 142f.) takes the place of the two traditional benedictions before the *Shema* of the morning service:

> *We thank You, O God, for this new day; for morning sun and evening star; for flowering of tree and flowing of tide; for life-giving rains and cooling breeze; for the earth's patient turning, the seasons' alternation, the cycle of growth and decay, of life and death. When our eyes behold the beauty and grandeur of Your world, we see the wisdom, power and goodness of its Creator.*
>
> *We awake and, behold! a new day. "Lord, renew us unto life." Teach us to recognise Your dominion over Creation, that we may thank You for all Your gifts, and dedicate all our powers to Your service.*
>
> *O God, the guide and inspiration of all humanity, we thank You for teaching us the laws of life, and we rejoice that You have given us the power to choose how we shall live. Though You are One, You have spoken in a thousand tongues for all to hear. We give thanks for the sages and teachers of all mankind, who have brought many to a deeper understanding of You and Your will.*
>
> *Humbly and gratefully, we recall that foremost among them were the lawgivers and prophets, the psalmists and sages of Israel. Joyfully we remember that from the very dawn of Israel's life, Your children have turned towards You, as flowers seek the sun. Help us, O Lord, to maintain our precious heritage. Teach us also to treasure the knowledge that we are all Your children, and that all truth is sacred.*
>
> *May the teachings of our fathers live on in our minds, and their passion for righteousness retain its power to move our hearts.*
>
> *Help us, O Lord our God, so to live, that our daily conduct may reveal the beauty of our faith, and that the house of Israel may continue to give witness to Your truth among all men.*

FOURTEEN

Kaddish and Memorial Services

WHILE THE KADDISH PRAYER, IN ITS SEVERAL VERSIONS,[1] GOES BACK TO the period of the Talmud, the custom of having the mourners recite it at the end of the service, for a period of eleven months after bereavement, is of comparatively recent origin. The custom originated in Germany at the time of the persecutions which accompanied the crusades. Eleazar of Worms, writing around 1200, is still very indefinite about the custom. Isaac Or Zaru'a, in 1220, reports that, in Bohemia and along the Rhine, orphans recite the Kaddish at the conclusion of the services, whereas that custom had not been adopted in France. As for the Kaddish recited by the orphan on the anniversary of his parents' deaths, Jacob Moellin, in the fifteenth century, seems to be the first to record it. But, after that, both kinds of Kaddish custom spread very rapidly throughout the Jewish world.[2]

The Kaddish is, of course, an eschatological prayer. Its reference to the establishment of the Kingdom of God would be understood by the learned to refer to the time when, among other eschatological happenings, the dead will be resurrected. However, apart from the version of the Kaddish recited at the graveside after a burial, which specifically mentions the resurrection and life eternal,[3] no other forms of the Kaddish make any explicit references to the dead. That includes the form of the Kaddish customarily recited by the mourners.[4] The so-called Mourners' Kaddish, in its actual wording, is a doxology addressed to God, which, when recited by the bereaved, is meant to dramatize the theme of "The Lord hath given, and the Lord hath taken away; praised be the Name of the Lord." That, at any rate, would be the ideal. In practice, however, helped along by folklore and superstition, the Mourners' Kaddish was increasingly understood as the kind of prayer which the living offer up *on behalf of the dead*—somewhat analogous to the Roman Catholic Mass for the Dead. Like the latter, it was believed to be actually efficacious; so that the view quite naturally gained ground that the more times Kaddish would be recited, the more assured would be the salvation (or the rescue from hell) of the departed on whose behalf the Kaddish was said. As a consequence, seeing that nobody wants to be deficient in filial devotion and piety, the traditional service was to witness a veritable proliferation of Kaddish recitations.

That the liturgical reform of the nineteenth century drastically reduced the number of recitations of the Mourners' Kaddish almost goes without saying. That was in line with abbreviating the liturgy as a whole, and omitting repetitions. But what about the Kaddish itself? What did Reform do to divest the Kaddish of its superstitious associations, and of the notion that the Kaddish was a prayer which the living offer on behalf of the dead? Theoretically, a radical Reform movement might have done away with the Kaddish altogether, just as it had eliminated a number of customs and ceremonies which, in the mind of the people, had given rise to superstitious notions. But, in practice, Reform Judaism did nothing of the kind with the Kaddish. On the contrary, it provided an Introduction to the Kaddish, and it added a paragraph to the Kaddish, in such a way that henceforth the Kaddish would express in its actual wording the meaning which people had read into it all along. Reform Judaism made the Kaddish a "prayer for the dead." The Hamburg Temple Prayerbook of 1819 was the first to do so.

Stating that "this prayer is recited only when mourners are present at the Temple," that prayerbook offers the following text:

כל ישראל יש להם חלק לעולם הבא. שנאמר ועמך כלם צדיקים. לעולם
יירשו ארץ: אשרי מי שעמלו בתורה. ועשה נחת רוח ליוצרו. גדל בשם
טוב. ונפטר בשם טוב מן העולם: ועליו אמר שלמה בחכמתו. טוב שם
משמן טוב ויום המות מיום הולדו: למוד תורה הרבה. ויתנו לך שכר

הרבה. ודע מתן שכרם של צדיקים לעתיד לבא:
יתגדל ויתקדש שמיה רבא. דהוא עתיד לחדתא עלמא. ולאחאה מתיא.
וימליך מלכותיה בחייכון וביומיכון וגו׳:
אמן, יהא שמה רבא וגו׳:
יתברך וישתבח וגו׳:
על ישראל. ועל צדיקיא. ועל כל מן דאתפטר מן עלמא הדין ברעותיה
דאלהא. יהא להון שלמא רבא. וחולקא טבא לחיי עלמא דאתי. וחסדא
ורחמי. מן קדם מאריה שמיא וארעא. ואמרו אמן:
יהא שלמא רבא וגו׳:
עשה שלום במרומיו וגו׳:[5]

All Israel have a share in the world-to-come, as it is said, "And thy people shall be all righteous; they shall inherit the land for ever." [6]

Happy is he whose labor was in the Torah, and who has given pleasure to his Creator. He grew up with a good name, and departed the world with a good name. And it is about him that Solomon said in his wisdom: "A good name is better than precious oil, and the day of death than the day of one's birth." [7]

Study much Torah, and they will give you much reward; and know that the giving of the reward to the righteous is in the world-to-come.[8]

Magnified and sanctified be the great Name of Him Who will renew the world and revive the dead. May He establish His kingdom during your life and during your days, etc.
Amen. May His great Name be blessed etc.
Blessed, praised, glorified etc.
May there be to Israel, and to the righteous, and to all who have departed from this world by the will of God, abundant peace, and a good portion in the life of the world-to-come, and grace and mercy from the Master of heaven and earth; and say ye, Amen.

May there be abundant peace etc.

He who maketh peace in His high places, etc.

Before we trace the influence of this unprecendented form of the Kaddish upon the further development of European Liberal and Reform liturgy, something ought to be said about the sources whence form, wording and ideas of this Kaddish were derived. For, while this version of the Kaddish had been without precedent in liturgical history, it was constructed out of materials contributed by both the Ashkenazi and the Sepharadi rites.

First, we must note the *Hashkabhah* prayer of the Sepharadi rite. This is a prayer recited for the repose of the departed as part of the Burial Service, in the house of the mourner, and on occasions when someone commemorating the anniversary of a death is called to the Torah.[9] The *Hashkabhah* prayer, which asks for celestial respose to be granted to the departed, is preceded by a number of Scripture verses which vary in accordance with the departed person's standing in the community, and which are different in the cases of men and of women. Unlike the passages introducing the Hamburg Kaddish, which are all taken from Rabbinic literature, the verses preceding the *Hashkabhah* are all from the Bible. But, apart from the fact that Ecclesiastes 7:1 happens to occur in both rituals, it is important to realize that the custom of reciting suitable passages before the "prayer for the dead" comes from the Sepharadi rite. Moreover, the *Hashkabhah* prayer itself contains the kind of ideas (and some of the words) which the Hamburg Reformers inserted into the Kaddish. Quoting the text of the *Hashkabhah* in Hebrew only, we underline the words which found their way into the Hamburg Kaddish.

מנוחה נכונה בישיבה עליונה. תחת כנפי השכינה. במעלת קדושים
וטהורים : כזהר הרקיע מאירים ומזהירים. וחלוץ עצמים. וכפרת **אשמים**.
והרחקת פשע. והקרבת ישע. וחמלה וחנינה. מלפני שוכן מענה. **וחלקא
טבא לחיי העולם הבא.** שם תהא מנת ומחיצת וישיבת נפש השם הטוב
(פלוני) רוח יי תניחנו בגן עדן. **דאתפטר מן עלמא הדין. כרעות אלהא
מרא שמיא וארעא** : המלך ברחמיו יחס ויחמל עליו : וילוה אליו השלום.
ועל משכבו יהיה שלום. כדכתיב. יבא שלום ינוחו על־משכבותם. הלך
נכחו : הוא וכל־בני ישראל השכבים עמו בכלל הרחמים והסליחות.
וכן יהי רצון ונאמר אמן :

We may note in passing that, apart from the vocabulary which the *Hashkabhah* of the Sepharadi rite furnished for the Hamburg Kaddish, the *Hashkabhah* itself—although in a simplified form, and made to apply to *all* the departed rather than to individuals—found its way into many a reformed ritual (including the Hamburg Temple Prayerbook) as a part of the Memorial Service.

A second source of the Hamburg Kaddish is to be found in the traditional Burial Kaddish, which begins as follows:[10]

יתגדל ויתקדש שמה רבא בעלמא דהוא עתיד לחדתא, ולאחיאה מתיא,
ולאסקא יתהון לחיי עלמא, ולמבנא קרתא דירושלם ולשכללא היכלה
בגוה, ולמעקר פלחנא נכראה בן ארעא, ולאתבא פלחנא דשמיא לאתרה.
וימלוך קדשא בריך הוא במלכותה ויקרה בחייכון וביומיכון וגו׳ :

Finally, as far as the structure of the Kaddish insert is concerned, the prototype is to be found in the traditional *Kaddish DeRabbanan,* which is recited after the study of passages from Rabbinic literature.[11]

על **ישראל** ועל רבנן ועל תלמידיהון, ועל כל תלמידי תלמידיהון, ועל כל
מן דעסקין באוריתא, די באתרא הדן ודי בכל אתר ואתר, **יהא** להון ולכון
שלמא רבא, חנא וחסדא ורחמין, וחיין אריכין, ומזוני רויחי, ופרקנא
מן קדם אבוהון **דבשמיא וארעא,** ואמרו אמן :

There is undoubtedly a peculiar irony in the fact that the Hamburg Reformers turned this traditional prayer, which asked for spiritual grace and material welfare to be granted to the living scholars of Israel, into a prayer requesting celestial bliss for the dead. It should be borne in mind, however, that, by the side of this explicit Mourners' Kaddish, the Hamburg Temple Prayerbook also retained other forms of the Kaddish, the "Half Kaddish" and the "Full Kaddish," in different sections of the service, thereby retaining the pure doxological character of the traditional Kaddish. In this, the Hamburg Temple Prayerbook was followed by other German reformed editions of the prayerbook. It was only in the liturgy of American Reform Judaism that the Kaddish was lost as a doxology, when the single recitation of the Kaddish, at the conclusion of the service, was given the character of a Mourners' Kaddish by the adoption of the Hamburg insert, "May there be to Israel, and to the righteous, and to all who have departed." Altogether, it may be said that the Hamburg version of the Mourner's Kaddish exerted a greater influence on American Reform liturgy than on the development of European Liberal and Reform liturgy. In European countries outside of Germany, the Kaddish insert does not seem to have been adopted at all; i.e., in England, France, Holland, and Sweden. In Germany itself, some rituals, of which we shall consider a number of examples below, did adopt the Hamburg Kaddish; others used it only as part of the Memorial Service. What caught on much more was the idea of an Introduction to the Kaddish, usually in the vernacular, and not necessarily in the form of the Rabbinic passages selected by the 1819 edition of the Hamburg Temple Prayerbook. Thus, without changing the text of the Kaddish itself, it was possible to give expression to the mood of an explicit mourners' prayer.

Moreover, the Hamburg Temple Prayerbook, which retained the text of its 1819 version of the Mourners' Kaddish, although it introduced some changes in the introductory passages, in subsequent editions, remained alone in utilizing the phrases from the Burial Kaddish for the beginning of the Mourners' Kaddish. It was followed in this by the Aachen prayerbook of 1853; but the Aachen prayerbook used the Hamburg Mourners' Kaddish as a Burial Kaddish only,[12] and not for the conclusion of other services. At a time when Reform Judaism was beginning to tone down the traditional dogma of the Resurrection, few Reformers may have felt called upon to introduce specific references to that dogma into the traditional version of the Mourners' Kaddish which did not contain them. However, Kirchenrat Joseph von Maier, in the prayerbook for private devotion, which he published in 1848, did adopt the Hamburg Kaddish, complete with introductory passages and insert.[13] However, Maier provides two separate German meditations, one to be said by mourners in the year of bereavement, and one to be said by those observing the anniversary of a death, which were meant to be read silently while the cantor recited the Rabbinic passages of the Introduction—a procedure which was later adopted by other rituals as well. Also, in his German version of the Mourners' Kaddish, Maier paraphrases the reference to the resurrection of the dead in terms of spiritual immortality.

Geiger, in his 1854 edition of the prayerbook, leaves the traditional Mourners' Kaddish unchanged, and provides no Introduction to it. However, the Hamburg introductory passages to the Kaddish are used in the Memorial Service,[14] while the Kaddish there remains without the Hamburg insert.

Stein's 1860 edition of the prayerbook contains the Hamburg introductory passages to the Kaddish, omitting only the first part of the last passage, for which Proverbs 12:28 and 23:18 are substituted. Stein follows Maier in providing silent German meditations while those passages are being read aloud. The special mourners' insert in the Kaddish is adopted.[15]

After Stein had adopted and amended the Hamburg version of 1819 and 1841, the 1868 edition of the Hamburg Temple Prayerbook, in its turn, adopted the introductory passages as amended by Stein, retaining, however, the 1819 version of the opening words of the Kaddish itself.[16]

Two years later, in 1870, Geiger followed Stein in the choice of introductory passages and in the inclusion of the Kaddish insert, both at the conclusion of the Sabbath Eve and at the conclusion of the Sabbath Morning Service[17]—representing a departure from his own 1854 ritual.

On the other hand, the prayerbook of the Berlin New Synagogue, published in 1881, adopted the Kaddish insert for the Memorial Service only.[18] Its regular Introduction to the Mourners' Kaddish on Sabbaths and festivals consists of Psalm 36:8–10,[19] one of the introductory passages of the Sepharadi *Hashkabhah*. This remained in all subsequent editions of the Berlin prayerbook.

In his 1882 edition of the prayerbook, Stein reprinted his 1860 version—with one interesting change. The opening words now read:

כל ישראל. כל-צדיקי וחסידי העולם. יש להם חלק לעולם הבא.

All Israel, all the righteous and the pious of the world, have a share in the world-to-come.[20]

Vogelstein, in 1894, follows Geiger's 1870 version.[21] But Stein's 1882 attempt at "universalizing" the franchise of candidates for the world-to-come, in the Introduction to the Kaddish, is pushed beyond the logical limits in Seligmann's 1910 edition of the prayerbook. For Sabbaths and festivals, Seligmann has a German Introduction to the Mourners' Kaddish, which bears no resemblance to the tradition initiated in Hamburg. The Kaddish itself has the Hamburg insert. But for the conclusion of the weekday services, both evening and morning[22] Seligmann takes over Stein's introductory passages, omitting the last, and changing the first to read as follows:

חסידי אמות העולם יש להם חלק לעולם הבא:

> The pious of the nations of the world have a share in the world-to-come.

Now, it is obvious that, if the pious of *all* peoples have such a share, the pious Israelites would automatically be included in that definition; and, in his 1912 *Denkschrift,* Seligmann makes the point that it is self-evident (*selbstverständlich*) that he means Jews to be included. Unfortunately, language occasionally imposes its own logic; and, in Rabbinic Hebrew *ḥasidé ummoth ha'olam* never includes Jews, but specifically the pious among the Gentiles. The concept is based on *Tosephta Sanhedrin* 13:2, where, however, the noun used is *tzaddikim* rather than *ḥasidim*. However, the *Tosephta* passage is popularly quoted in the very phraseology which Seligmann uses to introduce the Kaddish.[23] Thus, any Jew familiar with Rabbinic literature who reads Seligmann's Introduction to the Kaddish can only conclude that there is no room for Jews in the world-to-come!

While the above is not directly relevant to the theme of the Kaddish, we found it necessary to pay some attention to it, if only to alert future liturgists of Reform Judaism to the danger inherent in over-stating one's universalism. We now revert to the fate of the Hamburg Kaddish.

The *Einheitsgebetbuch* of 1929, which on purpose and by design reflects the more prevalent liturgical forms of German Liberal Judaism, provides, in its Appendix, a number of German Introductions to the Kaddish, none of them, however, based on the Hamburg passages. The Hamburg Kaddish insert is regularly printed whenever the Mourners' Kaddish is called for, but it is separated from the rest of the text, and marked, "In some congregations." Of the two Memorial Services contained in that volume, one includes the Kaddish insert, and the other does not. It may thus be seen that, with some notable exceptions, including Stein, Geiger, and Seligmann, European Liberal and Reform liturgy—unlike the Reform liturgy of America—failed to follow the Hamburg example in making the text of the Mourners' Kaddish conform to the popular understanding of that prayer. This much, though, can be said for the influence of the Hamburg Temple in the matter of the Kaddish: the recitation of suitable introductory prayers or meditations in the vernacular became the standard procedure in practically all non-Orthodox synagogues in the Old World as well as in the New.

And Hamburg's example was followed also in another matter connected with the departed, the Memorial Service. The history of the

Memorial Service in the traditional synagogue is complicated, and the reports frequently seem confused and contradictory. A helpful sifting of the sources has been undertaken by Solomon B. Freehof, who traces the institution of the Memorial Service back to the times of the Crusades.[24] But, regardless of the involved history of the institution, the texts included in the traditional Ashkenazi Memorial Service (on the Day of Atonement, according to the German rite, and also on the last days of the three Pilgrim Festivals, according to the Polish rite) were very few and simple. They consisted of the *yizkor* prayer,[25] recited silently by the survivors in memory of the departed, and including the promise of a donation to be made on behalf of the repose of the departed, the *el malé raḥamim* prayer, of similar contents, but recited aloud by the cantor,[26] and the *abh haraḥamim* prayer,[27] commemorating the victims of the Crusades. Whatever else is printed, even in Orthodox prayerbooks today, as part of the Memorial Service, by way of Psalms and other readings, already represents the influence of the Reform movement in Judaism. Thus, the late Chief Rabbi Joseph H. Hertz, who reprints the Memorial Service arranged by Chief Rabbi Hermann Adler (in which *yizkor* is preceded by a number of verses from the Psalms and Ecclesiastes, and followed by a newly composed prayer), says in a note:

> It has for several centuries been customary to commemorate the dead on the last day of Festivals, and especially on the Day of Atonement. In recent generations, such prayers have become an important feature of the Festival Service.[28]

What the Orthodox Chief Rabbi so coyly covers by the phrase, "in recent generations," is, of course, the liturgical endeavor of nascent Reform Judaism. Writing about the development of the modern form of the Memorial Service, as distinct from the few traditional prayers we have mentioned above, Max Joseph[29] correctly saw its origin in the German congregations using a reformed liturgy. But when Joseph also ascribed the introduction of the first modern Memorial Service to Kirchenrat Maier, in Stuttgart and other congregations of Wuerttemberg, "around the middle of the nineteenth-century," he was dating the beginning of the new form of the Memorial Service some decades too late. It was, in fact, the Hamburg Temple Prayerbook of 1819 which, as far as we have been able to ascertain, was the first prayerbook to contain a specific "Memorial Service" (*Todten-Feyer*) for the Day of Atonement.[30]

The Memorial Service of that prayerbook begins with a German hymn. This is followed by a rather lengthy prayer, which is really more of a philosophical argument "demonstrating" immortality than an actual "prayer." We are quoting a few excerpts from it here:

Great Spirit, whose ways are beyond searching out! Ruler over life and death! Thou didst call forth the infinite universe out of nothing. Thine almighty word did adorn it with magnificence and beauty. Thy breath breathed into it living beings of innumerable shapes; and man towers supreme above all. Thou hast created him in Thine own image, and Thou hast given him the power of command over the work of Thy hands. Thou didst kindle within him the divine spark of reason, so that he might recognize Thy might and greatness in all creation. Yet, in Thy wise providence, it hath pleased Thee to apportion a finite time unto all Thy creatures; and thus didst Thou set a limit also for man. ... But Thou, Almighty, hast not created Thy works in order to give them over to destruction. Nothing is destroyed. Nothing will be lost which was created by Thy creative hand. Everything dies in order to be newly formed: not a mote of dust will lose its being, seeing that Thy creative breath hath formed it. How, then, should man, the masterpiece of all creatures, be annihilated by death? How wouldst Thou, who only createst, but destroyest nothing, destroy the spirit living in man, which is a part of Thine own being? No! Thou raisest the spirit unto Thyself, and only the fragile shell which contained the divine spark, only the body which is mortal, rests in the lap of the earth, and will turn into the dust out of which it was created.... .

Through death, a purer and better life begins for us in the blissful abodes of peace. No cover of earth limits the pure spirit. ... Death is a gate which leads from darkness into pure light, ... where the soul, saturated by pure joy, will cast its glance into eternity, and will acknowledge more deeply and more ardently the perfection of the Eternal, and proclaim Thy praise in the choir of the spirits, O Thou Unsearchable One! ...

This is followed (in Hebrew) by Psalm 144: 3, 4; Psalm 90: 6, 3; Deuteronomy 32: 29; Psalm 49: 18; Psalm 37: 37; and Psalm 34: 23.

After this, there is, for silent devotion, a German adaptation (and elaboration) of the traditional *yizkor* prayer:

Of thee, O my beloved father (my beloved mother), I think in this solemn hour, and of the love, the care, and the fidelity with which thou didst guide me as long as thou wast with me on earth. Thou didst depart from me, and leave me behind; but I remember the teachings which thou gavest me, and my heart is deeply touched, and beats loudly and warmly towards thine immortal spirit, which dwells aloft with its Heavenly Father. O that the Almighty may have received thy soul into His fatherly protection, united with those who live forever, basking in the glory of the divine greatness and majesty, and hovering over me until my spirit, too, will be associated with thine, and meet, in the kingdom of purest light, those who wandered virtuously on this earth, and who were so dear and beloved to me. And Thou, O Heavenly Father, think Thou of the pious gift which I vow to the benefit of this house, and devote to the dear memory of the departed. O that the willing sacrifices of my mouth may be acceptable unto Thee.

A similar prayer is provided on behalf of other departed relatives.

After those silent meditations, the service continues with an abbreviated form of the Sepharadi *Hashkabhah* in Hebrew, including the preliminary Scripture verses. This is followed by the Introduction to the Mourners' Kaddish and the Mourners' Kaddish itself, in the form initiated by this prayerbook. The service concludes with another German hymn.

In the 1841 edition of the Hamburg Temple Prayerbook, the Memorial Service is even more elaborate. But the same pattern prevails—not only in subsequent editions of the Hamburg Temple Prayerbook, but in all reformed rituals published after that time. There are variations in detail. Some continue to make reference to the donations vowed on behalf of the departed, others omit any reference of that kind. Some versions of the Memorial Service have the survivors address the departed in the second person, others let the survivors speak to God about the departed. Such matters could be of profound theological import, and a difference in nuance could represent important dogmatic divergences. Yet the over-all impression one gains is that the liturgists producing those prayers and meditations were far less concerned with theological niceties than they were with comforting the mourners, and turning the Memorial Service into a didactic occasion for the contemplation of life, death, and immortality.

As the inclusion of Memorial Services even in modern Orthodox prayerbooks (where, however, they are never quite as elaborate as in the reformed rituals) shows, this innovation of Reform Judaism, first introduced in the Hamburg Temple, was an immediate success. A. Wiener, the rabbi of Oppeln and, by the standards of those days, something of a religious radical, remained largely unheeded when, in a criticism of Geiger's version of the Memorial Service, he urged:

> It is not at all fitting for us to speak, in our prayers, about the ways and the manner of immortality as though we were intimates and confidants of God, completely initiated into that obscure mystery. ... Such confident assertions about the Here-

> after, especially when voiced in a sceptical age like ours, often achieve the very opposite effect from the one intended. Our statements about it must be very modest and very cautious. Our expressions must be carefully chosen. . . . Particularly with regard to that kind of prayer, we cannot urgently enough recommend the words of Ecclesiastes 5: 1. ("Be not rash with thy mouth, and let not thy heart be hasty to utter a word before God; for God is in heaven, and thou upon earth; therefore let thy words be few.")[31]

Perhaps the modern type of Memorial Service became so popular because, in many cases, one's attachment to the memory of his parents may be stronger than his devotion to Judaism, and will certainly outlast it. At any rate, experience has shown that the Memorial Service will bring people into the synagogue who worship on no other occasions throughout the year. Max Joseph, writing in 1928, may have been a little premature in his apprehensions; but, when one surveys the Reform liturgy for Memorial Services, and delves into its motivations, the words of Max Joseph could well have a sobering effect. He wrote:

> The intention to arouse religiosity and devotion to Judaism by means of the feelings of filial piety is bound to miss the mark to the extent to which the contemporary generation is no longer able to look back upon parents who were pious and permeated by their Judaism.[32]

FIFTEEN

New Versions of Kol Nidré

KOL NIDRÉ IS THE NAME BY WHICH THE SERVICE OF ATONEMENT EVE IS traditionally known. It comes from a legal formula which is recited before the actual beginning of the service proper, a formula, moreover, which, in terms of Jewish law, is no more closely linked to the Day of Atonement than to any other occasion of the Jewish calendar. It is an aspect of the rather complicated subject of the annulment of vows, something which, under certain restricted circumstances, is a possibility in the legislation of both Torah and Talmud. At any time during the year, a Jew may present himself before a *beth din* (a rabbinical court) of three, express regret for vows he has hastily and unthinkingly made, and obtain the required annulment. Of course, this possibility exists only in the case of vows a man makes to God. The formula of annulment is not effective in the case of legal contracts and promises governing a man's relation with his fellowmen. It is reasonably clear why Jews should be particularly interested in "turning over a new leaf" in their dealings with God before the onset of the New Year, traditionally understood as the Day of Judgment. That is why some traditional prayerbooks to this day provide an "Order of the Annulment of Vows" as the item immediately preceding the afternoon service of New Year's Eve.[1]

It is far less obvious why this legal procedure, involving an individual and a court of three, should have found its way into the service of Atonement Eve, as a formula applying to the whole congregation. We first hear about it in the ninth century, and, at that, mainly in the form of violent objections raised by Babylonian Geonim against that practice.[2] That is to say, the Geonim were not opposed to the possibility of having one's private vows annulled, along the channels provided by Talmudic legislation. They did, however, oppose the inclusion of that legal machinery within the service marking the beginning of the Day of Atonement. Rabbinic opposition was to no avail; and the custom of reciting the legal formula at the beginning of the Atonement Eve service was, in the course of time, adopted by all the various rites—some using the formula in Hebrew, which seems to have been the original form, others, and that includes the majority, in Aramaic.

At first, the formula was used in a retroactive sense. Annulment was expressed for the vows made "between the last Day of Atonement and this Day of Atonement." In the twelfth century, the formula was changed by Rabbenu Tam, and henceforth in the majority of rites the annulment is made to refer to the vows which will be made "from this Day of Atonement until the next Day of Atonement."

As we have noted, the formula annulling "all vows" (*Kol Nidré*) is effective within the strictly religious realm only. It means to annul those vows and promises which a man may hastily and unthinkingly make to God, and of the full implications of which he would not be aware at the time of making them. But this restricted application of the formula did not prevent anti-Semites, throughout the centuries, from utilizing the *Kol Nidré* formula as a spring-board for attacks on the trustworthiness of the Jew. The formula also played its part in keeping on the books of various countries the special and degrading "Jewish Oath" (*More Judaico*), in which Jews had to declare that the particular testimony or legal transaction in which they were engaged would not be voided by the recitation of the *Kol Nidré* formula.[4]

But the *Kol Nidré,* once having established itself, and in the face of original Rabbinic opposition at that, was not to be that easily dislodged. Moreover, Jewish folklore had woven around it heart-rending tales of secret Marrano Atonement services in the days of the Spanish Inquisition—notwithstanding the fact that the custom of reciting the formula on Atonement Eve is some centuries older than that. Above all, it was the haunting melody to which the formula was sung (although it is of comparatively recent origin, and is unknown to the Spanish and Portuguese Jews)[5] which caused the formula to be regarded as the indispensable "mood setter" for the Atonement Eve service. As with so many other parts of Jewish liturgy, the meaning which the worshipper brought to the words, and read into them, was so much more significant than the actual, literal meaning of the words themselves.

Yet the abolition of the *Kol Nidré* was one of the first items to which the modernist rabbis of Germany addressed themselves once they had managed to get together for their first conference. The seventh session of the First Rabbinical Conference, held in Brunswick, in 1844, was devoted to a discussion of the steps to be taken in order to induce the various German governments to abolish the special "Jewish Oath." It was—significantly—as part of that discussion that the consideration of *Kol Nidré* came up. Various speakers felt that, although this was based on a misunderstanding and a misrepresentation of that formula, the fact remained that *Kol Nidré* did give rise to the mistrust with which the courts looked upon the oath of a Jew, and to the elaborate and distasteful ceremony to which they subjected Jews who had to make an oath as part of common legal proceedings. This did not sit well with the Jewish religious leaders at the dawn of Emancipation. They, therefore, decided that *Kol Nidré* had to go.[6]

The following *verbatim* translation of the last part of the minutes of that session may be of interest, not only for the context in which the *Kol Nidré* problem was discussed in 1844, but also as an indication of what the process of liturgical reform entailed for rabbis serving the total Jewish community, rather than specific Reform congregations. This is how the minutes read:

> The discussion is declared concluded. The question is now asked:
>
> 1) Should the Conference declare that the oath of a Jew, invoking the Name of God, is binding without any further ceremony?
>
> Unanimous response: Yes!
>
> 2) Does the Conference declare that *Kol Nidré* is unessential? And will the members of the Conference, in their spheres of jurisdiction, work for its abolition, already in time for next Yom Kippur?
>
> Yes!
>
> Bodenheimer notes that he could not obligate himself to abolish this liturgical piece in his synagogue already in time for next Yom Kippur; and that merely on account of the fact that he had already submitted a "*Synagogen-Ordnung*" to the govern-

ment, in which no mention was made of this piece. It would, therefore, be inconsistent were he to make this abolition already at this time. Incidentally, he considers the *Kol Nidré* to be absolutely unessential. Indeed, five *Geonim* voted against its introduction in the first place.
Rabbi Goldmann: He is afraid that he will not be able to make any headway with this matter in his congregation.[7]

While some members of the Rabbinical Conference of 1844 anticipated difficulties with their congregations in connection with the abolition of *Kol Nidré,* some rabbis and congregations had already dropped the *Kol Nidré* long before the rabbis met in conference. The Berlin prayerbook of 1817 (*Die Deutsche Synagoge*) had omitted *Kol Nidré,* and substituted for it a lengthy Hebrew passage which we shall consider later in this chapter. The Hamburg Temple prayerbooks of 1819 and 1841 had made no provision for *Kol Nidré* at all. But of perhaps even greater interest—because it is so unexpected—is the fact that, on at least one occasion, *Kol Nidré* was omitted by Samson Raphael Hirsch, the founder of Neo-Orthodoxy and leader of the "counter-reformation."

Writing in 1863, Joseph Aub stated that "Rabbi Hirsch of Frankfort o. M., while he was still chief rabbi of Oldenburg, did away with the *Kol Nidré*" ("*. . . dem Kol Nidre seinen Abschied schrieb*".)[8] Aub made that statement as part of a polemic against Marcus Lehmann, the Orthodox preacher of Mayence and editor of *Der Israelit.* Lehmann had attacked Aub for abolishing the *Kol Nidré,* and, in his reply, Aub listed various authorities who had declared themselves against the *Kol Nidré.* Samson Raphael Hirsch figures in that list as someone "in whom the preacher Lehmann will certainly recognize his own master."

The late Kurt Wilhelm, Chief Rabbi of Sweden, gave new currency to this report, in an article written in 1957. "As District Rabbi in Oldenburg, he (Hirsch) had compromised with reformist tendencies, and had done away with the *Kol Nidrei.*"[9]

On the other hand, a latter-day descendant of Hirsch, living in the United States today, has the tradition that "Hirsch in fact did omit *Kol Nidré* once as a *hora-ath sha'ah* (emergency measure in Jewish law) in 1843, while rabbi in Emden (not Oldenburg), as a demonstration against the local acceptance of *Kol Nidré* as an absolution from formal pledges and commitments."[10]

If that family tradition is correct, it would show that Hirsch omitted the *Kol Nidré* at least twice, once in Emden and once in Oldenburg; for there is a local tradition in Oldenburg that it was there that Hirsch "abolished the *Kol Nidré.*" Leo Trepp, who, before the second World War, was himself Landesrabbiner of Oldenburg, reports in a recent book[11] that he was told by some of his older members that Samson

Raphael Hirsch abolished the *Kol Nidré* while in Oldenburg. Trepp, in looking for the reason why an ultra-traditionalist like Hirsch should have done a thing like that, ventures the opinion that it may have been connected with the contemporary fight against the "Jewish Oath."

Whether it was a case of *hora-ath sha'ah* (emergency measure), or whether it was meant as a more permanent arrangement, whether it happened in Emden or in Oldenburg, or whether it happened in both places, whether, finally, it was Hirsch's contribution to the fight against the "Jewish Oath," or whether it was his fight against a *Jewish* misunderstanding of the *Kol Nidré,* one thing seems to be certain: Samson Raphael Hirsch was involved in this problem. And this fact alone warrants the amount of space we have given the reports about him. For, if even an ultra-traditionalist like Hirsch had his problem with *Kol Nidré,* quite a different perspective and dimension are added to the Reform endeavors in this direction.

For the Reformers, however, it was not only a question of doing away with *Kol Nidré*. It was also a case of providing a substitution for it. One of the rabbis who provided a substitution, one, moreover, which found wide acceptance on both sides of the Atlantic, was Leopold Stein.[12] While ministering to the Franconian congregations of Burgkundstadt and Altenkundstadt, Stein published, in 1840 (i.e., four years before the Brunswick Conference), a volume of German prayers and hymns to supplement, and to take the place of, some of the traditional rubrics of the High Holy Day services. The title of the work is:

חזוק הבית
Gebete und Gesänge
zum Gebrauche bei der öffentlichen Andacht
der Israeliten.
Oder:
Bausteine zur Auferbauung eines veredelten Synagogengottesdienstes.
Erste Lieferung: *Neujahr und Versöhnungstag.*
Herausgegeben von *Leopold Stein.*
Erlangen, 1840.

On pages 81–84 of this book, Stein gives his substitution for the *Kol Nidré*. It is the anthem, "O Tag des Herrn!" ("O Day of the Lord"), which has remained a part of Reform liturgy ever since. The hymn, "O come, day of God," in the American *Union Prayer Book,* Newly Revised, Vol. II, page 127, is an adaptation of this—though Stein's original is three times as long.[13]

Interesting—and characteristic of the whole Reform approach to *Kol*

Nidré—is Stein's "footnote," which he appends to his anthem. It reads as follows:

> This is not the place in which to deal with the value of the original *Kol Nidré* formula, and to justify those—including the author—who have ordered its removal. That much, though, is certain, and cannot be denied by anyone: that the formula is by no means suited to introduce the holiest of all days, and that it would have been more suitable for any occasion but that of the eve of the exalted Day of Atonement. It almost seems that there has been an awareness of this incongruity. That is why, partly consciously, and partly unconsciously, a tune has been fitted to this uninspiring text—a tune which indeed did not fit the text, but which, to a high degree, was in consonance with the solemnity of the day it is meant to introduce. Whoever has once visited a synagogue on Atonement Eve will remember the deep devotion and the sincerity with which all those assembled listened to the first song of that evening. This most certainly cannot be ascribed to the uninspiring text, but solely and alone to the warm and pious spirit which breathes and lives in the tune. To forego this noble tune, which has so very much endeared itself to our coreligionists—that made me feel uncomfortable about the abolition of the above-mentioned formula. The holy day would be lacking its long accustomed solemn introduction. I found no rest until I had satisfied my feeling in this respect. I, therefore, requested my cantor, Herr J. M. Ochs of Altenkundtsadt, to provide me with the simple musical setting of the *Kol Nidré*. This he soon produced, omitting all of the traditional embellishments. I then sought to feel myself into the tune, and to clothe in words the pious feeling of the original composer. In the musical setting before me I found the expression of a threefold feeling: at first, an anxiety at the approach of the solemn day; then a daring rising towards the Divine Pardoner; and, finally, a sincere plea before the throne of the All-Merciful One. The words came into my mouth of their own accord. In this way the first stanza of this song came to be. I now submit it to the considerate judgment as to whether my limited ability has achieved the right thing or not. Later on, I composed two further stanzas to follow the first one. In the second stanza, I tried to express the idea of reconciliation with our fellow-men; and, in the third stanza, reconciliation with our own selves, that is to say, the sanctification of our soul through the transcendence of our sensual nature. Through its use in my synagogues, the whole has produced a deep impression and a most

> ardent feeling, which, I trust, will yet be heightened when the text is in the hands of all the worshippers who will, from year to year, make it more and more their very own. For we now have *'eth liphrotz we'eth libhnoth,* a time not only for tearing down, but also for building up. The modern and newly introduced institutions, animated by the spirit of our religion, will, with the help of God, one day become the dear and cherished possession of our grandchildren and great-grandchildren; and pious custom will not withhold its sanctifying power in days to come, even as in the days of old.[14]

In 1844, Leopold Stein became rabbi of Frankfort o. M., where, in 1860, he published a prayerbook. Some time between 1844 and 1860, and probably much closer to the earlier date, Stein published another leaflet of German prayers and hymns. There is in existence a leaflet, entitled

> *Deutsche Gebete und Gesänge für Neujahr und Versöhnungstag.* Zum Gebrauche beim öffentlichen Gottesdienste in der Haupt-synagoge zu Frankfurt am Main.

This leaflet was published in Frankfort, but it bears no indication either of the name of the author or of the year of publication. However, the leaflet is partly identical in contents with Stein's *Ḥizzuq Habayith* of 1840; and, on pp. 17f., it contains, as an introductory hymn for Atonement Eve, Stein's anthem, "O Tag des Herrn!"—without the author's name, and without any footnote. It stands to reason that Stein was the author of this prayer leaflet, and that it must have been published shortly after Stein had moved to Frankfort o. M. In this leaflet, "O Tag des Herrn!" is preceded by Psalm 103, in Hebrew and German.

The omission of the traditional *Kol Nidré* formula not only became universal in all European Liberal and Reform rituals, but many congregations, which otherwise followed the traditional liturgy, followed suit in this respect. To take the place of *Kol Nidré,* some congregations introduced Psalm 103, others Psalm 130, and still others Stein's "O Day of the Lord." Nor was it uncommon for a prayerbook to offer a combination of some of those texts.

There were a number of rabbis, however, who made attempts at creating a Hebrew formula which would take the place (and completely change the meaning) of *Kol Nidré,* while fitting the tune of the original formula, and, in most cases, retaining the first two words. Often such a new version of *Kol Nidré* was provided as an addition to Psalm 130 or Stein's "O Day of the Lord," or as an alternative to the latter.

The following pages will present the texts which have been available to us. We give the Hebrew as we found it. The English translation is based on that Hebrew text, and does not necessarily correspond to the German versions which accompanied the Hebrew formula in the prayerbooks we have consulted, which, in many cases, was a paraphrase rather than a translation.

BERLIN, 1817. (*Die Deutsche Synagoge,* ed. E. Kley and C. S. Günsburg.)

עדה קדושה דורשי אלהים גרים ותושבים! אתם הנצבים פה בית תפלה לפני אלהי צבאות! הכונו, התקדשו, הטהרו ליום גדול ונורא, כי ביום הזה יכפר עליכם לטהר אתכם.

The congregation responds:

ונסלח לכל עדת בני ישראל ולגר הגר בתוכם, כי לכל העם בשגגה.

אנוש, אנוש, יצר לבו רע מנעוריו, לפתח חטאת רובץ; בדרכיו כושל, קלו אשוריו למעד, שובו, שובו, הנחמו! מכל חטאתיכם לפני ה׳ תטהרו.

ונסלח וגו׳

שימו לבבכם על מעשיכם, חפשו דרכיכם, קחו עמכם דברים, קומו ושובו עד ה׳ אלהיכם; רחצו, הזכו, הטיבו לפני עליון שפכו שיח, כי ביום הזה יכפר עליכם לטהר אתכם, מכל חטאתיכם לפני ה׳ תטהרו.

ונסלח וגו׳

Holy congregation, seekers of God, strangers and sojourners! You who are standing here in the house of prayer before the Lord of hosts! Prepare yourselves, sanctify yourselves, purify yourselves for the great and awesome day. For on this day shall atonement be made for you, to cleanse you.

(The congregation responds:)
And all the congregation of the children of Israel shall be forgiven, and the stranger that sojourneth among them; for in respect of all the people it was done unwittingly.

Man, O man! The imagination of his heart is evil from his youth. Sin coucheth at the door. Man stumbles in his ways. How easily do his steps slide! Turn ye, turn ye, repent yourselves! From all your sins before the Lord shall ye be clean.

(The congregation responds:)
And all the congregation . . . .

Pay attention to your deeds, search your ways! Take with you words, arise, and return unto the Lord your God! Wash you, make you clean, do the good, pour forth your prayer before the Most High. For on this day shall atonement be made for you, to cleanse you; from all your sins before the Lord shall ye be clean.

(The congregation responds:)
And all the congregation . . . .

The fact that, in 1817, the compilers of a liturgy which aimed at introducing more German into the Jewish worship service should have written a new prayer in Hebrew, to introduce the Day of Atonement, is not without historical interest. Moreover, in this case, the Hebrew, being a concatenation of Biblical phrases, seems to have been composed before the German translation, and not *vice versa*—as happened later in that century with an introductory prayer for Atonement Eve which is so "un-Hebraic" that it can only be understood as a literal translation from the German original. The prayer to which we are referring does not occur in any of the Liberal and Reform prayerbooks we have been able to consult. But it is printed in a minister's handbook, published in 1891, and must obviously have been used in some non-Orthodox congregations as a substitute for *Kol Nidré*. The poverty of its Hebrew style and its excessive length prevent its inclusion here.[15] We mention it in this connection for two reasons. First, because the Hebrew of the 1817 *Deutsche Synagoge* is so superior to that of the later composition. Second, and above all, because this later prayer was obviously influenced by the contents and structure of the *Kol Nidré* substitute of *Die Deutsche Synagoge*. And that, moreover, was the only trace of an influence which we have been able to discover. All the other *Kol Nidré* substitutes we have seen do not follow the pattern of the 1817 prayer, but are more conscious imitations of the original *Kol Nidré* formula. The first such endeavor seems to have been Geiger's, in 1854.

GEIGER, 1854. (*Israelitisches Gebetbuch.* Breslau.)

כל-פְּשָׁעַי וּפשעי הקהל הזה ופשעי כל-עמך ישראל מחם והעבירם מנגד עיניך וטהר לבנו מיום כפורים זה עד יום כפורים הבא עלינו לטובה לבנו נשבר רוחנו נדכאה מעשים אין אתנו בצדקתך נשעננו נא רחום אל תעזבנו כי עפר אנחנו כעונותינו נא אל תגמל:

All my transgressions, and the transgressions of this congregation, and the transgressions of all Thy people Israel—blot them out and make them to pass away from before Thine eyes; and purify our hearts from this Day of Atonement unto the next Day of Atonement, may it come to us for good. Our heart is broken, our spirit is humbled, we have no works. We rely on Thy love alone. O Merciful One, do not forsake us, for we are but dust. Requite us not according to our iniquities.

In the 1870 edition of his prayerbook, Geiger no longer retained his 1854 text, but included Stein's "O Tag des Herrn!" instead.

LEIPZIG, 1865.[16]

כל-סתרי רעיונות ותעלומות לבבנו לפניך ערוכות הן וגלויות: ידעת מזמותינו ומחשבותינו העולות על נפשותינו מיום כפורים זה עד יום כפורים הבא עלינו לטובה: אנא רחום. עמוד לנו. טהר לבבנו: חטאים ופשעים השרש מקרבנו. וכפר נא משובתנו: פשעינו כחטאים וזדונות כשגגות:

All the secret desires and hidden thoughts of our heart are spread out and revealed before Thee. Thou knowest the devices and thoughts which enter our mind from this Day of Atonement unto the next Day of Atonement, may it come to us for good. O Merciful One, stand by us. Purify us. Uproot the sins and transgressions from among us, and grant atonement for our backsliding. May our transgressions be regarded as mere failings, and our presumptuous sins as unwitting errors.

Nine years later, in 1874, this prayer, which first appeared in a leaflet containing German prayers and hymns to supplement the traditional liturgy, was included in Vol. II of the permanent Leipzig prayerbook, edited by A. M. Goldschmidt.

HANNOVER, 1870.[17]

א.

כל נדרי בני ישראל אשר המה נדרים לך מלכנו לשמר את דברי תורתך ועדותך ולבלתי סור מן המצוה ימין ושמאל מיום כפורים זה עד יום כפורים הבא עלינו לטובה. כלם יעלו ויבאו ויגיעו ויראו לפניך לרחמים ותן בלבם לאהבה וליראה את שמך הגדול והנורא ולא יבושו לעולם:

ב.

כל נדרי בני ישראל אשר המה נדרים לך אבינו ללכת בדרכי הצדקה והחסד והרחמים ולבלתי אמץ את לבבם מאחיהם מיום כפורים זה עד יום כפורים הבא עלינו לטובה כלם יעלו ויבאו ויגיעו ויראו לפניך לרחמים וכף את יצרם והכנע את ערפם לתת יד לפשעים נגדם ומחטאתם יטהרו:

ג.

כל נדרי בני ישראל אשר המה נדרים לך אדוננו בנשאם עיניהם אליך היושבי בשמים לשוב אליך בכל לבבם ובכל נפשם מיום כפורים זה עד יום כפורים הבא עלינו לטובה כלם יעלו ויבאו ויגיעו ויראו לפניך לרחמים וחדש רוח נכון בקרבם למען יסורו מדרכם הרעה ואל ישובו לכסלם:

(1)

All the vows of the children of Israel which they vow unto Thee, O our King, to keep the words of Thy Torah and Thy testimonies, not to depart from the commandments either to the right or to the left, from this Day of Atonement unto the next Day of Atonement, may it come to us for good, yea, may all of them ascend and come and be accepted before Thee for mercy. And put it in their heart to love and to fear Thy great and awesome Name; and may they never be put to shame.

(2)

All the vows of the children of Israel which they vow unto Thee, O our Father, to walk in the ways of justice and loving-kindness and mercy, and not to harden their heart against their brothers, from this Day of Atonement unto the next Day of Atonement, may it come to us for good, yea, may all of them ascend and come and be accepted before Thee for mercy. And bend their inclination, and subdue their stiff-neckedness, so that they may stretch out a hand to those who transgress against them. And may they be cleansed from their sin.

(3)

All the vows of the children of Israel which they vow unto Thee, O our Lord, lifting up their eyes unto Thee, O Thou that dwellest in the heavens, to return unto Thee with all their heart and with all their soul, from this Day of Atonement unto the next Day of Atonement, may it come to us for good, yea, may all of them ascend and come and be accepted before Thee for mercy. And renew a steadfast spirit within them, that they may depart from their evil way, and not return unto their folly.

The three different texts were undoubtedly due to the fact that the traditional custom of reciting the *Kol Nidré* three times was followed in Hannover—with this additional innovation: that each repetition introduced a new element. There is no indication of who the author of this version was. The Hannover rabbi at that time was Samuel Meyer,[18] who, if he did not write this *Kol Nidré* version himself, must, at any rate, have sanctioned its introduction in Hannover. Our inability to identify the author of this version with any precision is all the more regrettable because, with the exception of Joël's 1872 *Kol Nidré* text, all subsequent *Kol Nidré* texts in European Liberal and Reform prayerbooks until the *Einheitsgebetbuch* of 1929 are adaptations of the phraseology used Hannover, in 1870.

JOËL, 1872. (*Israelitisches Gebetbuch*. Breslau.)

כל פִּשְׁעֵי וחטאי עמך בית־ישראל נא כפר עליהם ותאמר סלחתי
ודברך זה יסעד ויבטח לבנו מיום כפורים זה עד יום כפורים הבא עלינו

לטובה: כלנו שבים אליך. כלנו עומדים לפניך. מתנחמים. מתודים.
נכנעים ונדכאים. לא בגאוה ולא בגדל לבב: נא אל תטשנו. נא אל
תכלימנו. נא אל תשיבנו ריקם מלפניך:

All the transgressions and sins of Thy people, the house of Israel—O do Thou make atonement for them, and say, "I have forgiven." And this Thy word will support and make sure our hearts from this Day of Atonement unto the next Day of Atonement, may it come to us for good. All of us are returning unto Thee. All of us are standing before Thee, repenting, confessing, subdued and humbled—not in pride, and not in haughtiness of heart. O do not cast us away; do not shame us; and do not turn us away empty from Thy presence.

This version was retained in all later editions of Joël's prayerbook. It seems clear that Joël wanted both to retain and to improve upon the opening words of Geiger's 1854 version. Geiger had begun his version with the words, *kol pesha'ai* ("all my transgressions"). In an attempt to make the words more closely resemble the sound of *Kol Nidré,* Joël had changed that to *kol pish'é* ("all the transgressions of"). In doing so, however, he had to string together two nouns connected by a *waw conjunctive,* both of them being in the construct state—not a very acceptable syntax in Hebrew grammar.

MUNICH, 1899. (*Israelitische Gebetordnung.* 2nd edition.)

כל נדרי בני ישראל אשר המה נדרים לך אבינו בנשאם עיניהם אליך
הישבי בשמים לשוב אליך בכל לבבם ובכל נפשם מיום כפורים זה עד
יום כפורים הבא עלינו לטובה כלם יעלו ויבאו ויגיעו יידאו לפניך
לרחמים וחדש רוח נכון בקרבם למען יסורו מדרכם הרעה ואל ישובו
לכסלם:

All the vows of the children of Israel which they vow unto Thee, O our Father, lifting up their eyes unto Thee, O Thou that dwellest in the heavens, to return unto Thee with all their heart and with all their soul, from this Day of Atonement unto the next Day of Atonement, may it come to us for good, yea, may all of them ascend and come and be accepted before Thee for mercy. And renew a steadfast spirit within them, that they may depart from their evil way, and not return unto their folly.

HAMBURG, 1904. (*Gebetbuch herausgegeben vom Israelitischen Tempelverband in Hamburg.* 6th edition.)

כל נדרי בני ישראל אשר המה נודרים לך אבינו. לשוב אליך בכל-
לבבם. ללכת בדרכי תורתך באורח צדקה ומשפט. מיום כפורים זה עד
יום כפורים הבא עלינו לטובה. כלם יעלו ויבאו ויגיעו ויראו וירצו
וישמעו מלפניך ברחמים וכף נא את-יצרם. ותן בלבבם לאהבה וליראה
את-שמך הגדול והנורא:

All the vows of the children of Israel which they vow unto Thee, O our Father, to return unto Thee with all their heart and with all their soul, to walk in the ways of Thy Torah, on the path of righteousness and justice, from this Day of Atonement unto the next Day of Atonement, may it come to us for good, yea, may all of them ascend and come and be accepted and heard before Thee in mercy. And bend their inclination. And put it in their heart to love and to fear Thy great and awesome Name.

This sixth edition of the prayerbook of the Hamburg Temple, edited by Paul Rieger,[19] was the first edition of that particular liturgy to include any form of the *Kol Nidré*. The text used here is a composite of phrases taken from the three different Hannover versions, but the synonyms of *ya'alu weyabho-u* have been increased here—on the analogy of the traditional *ya'aleh weyabho* prayer.[20]

BEUTHEN O.-S., 1906.
In 1906, the Beuthen congregation published a collection of German prayers and hymns to supplement the traditional prayerbook.[21] On page 15, the three *Kol Nidré* formulae of Hannover, in Hebrew and German, are reprinted for use in place of the traditional *Kol Nidré*.

DANZIG, 1924. (Israelitisches Gebetbuch für die Neue Synagoge in Danzig. 3rd edition.)
This prayerbook uses the *Kol Nidré* version of the Munich ritual of 1899.

EINHEITSGEBETBUCH, 1929.

כל-נדרי בני ישראל אשר נדרו לך היום יי אלהינו ואלהי אבותינו באמת ובתמים—קולנו אנא שמע-נא. ודויינו ותחנונינו קבל ברצון. מיום כפרים זה עד יום כפרים הבא עלינו לטובה: אלהינו לך הטאנו הרע בעיניך עשינו. סלח-נא מחל-נא עבר-נא על פשע חנון ורחום ומרבה לסלח:

אליך נשואות עינינו. בטחוננו בך תלינו. עשה עמנו כאשר דברת:

All the vows of the children of Israel which they have vowed unto Thee this day, O Lord our God and God of our fathers, are made in truth and with sincerity. O hearken unto our voice, and accept with favor our confessions and our supplications, from this Day of Atonement unto the next Day of Atonement, may it come to us for good. O our God, we have sinned before Thee, and we have done what is evil in Thy sight. O forgive us, pardon us, pass over our transgression, O Thou who art gracious and merciful and ever forgiving. Our eyes are lifted up unto Thee, our trust we have placed in Thee. Do with us as Thou hast promised.

STOCKHOLM, 1931. (*Bönbok . . .*, Vol. II.)
Kol Nidré text as in the Munich ritual of 1899. Earlier editions of the Swedish prayerbook had substituted Psalm 103 for the *Kol Nidré*. This edition retains Psalm 103 as a silent devotion before the *Kol Nidré*.

HOLLAND, 1964. (*Seder Tobh Lehodoth,* Vol. II.)
Text as in the Munich edition of 1899, to which the last line of the *Einheitsgebetbuch* version has been added.

An earlier text used by the Dutch Liberal congregations was that of the *Einheitsgebetbuch* a photo-offset edition of which was issued by the Dutch congregations in 1960.

Such, then, have been the major examples of the new versions of *Kol Nidré* which have been introduced in the liturgy of European Liberal and Reform Judaism. What they all share with the traditional *Kol Nidré* formula is the sentence, "from this Day of Atonement unto the next Day of Atonement, may it come to us for good." Yet it is precisely that sentence which, as we have noted, goes back to the change introduced by Rabbenu Tam in the twelfth century, earlier versions of the *Kol Nidré* formula having referred to the period between "the last Day of Atonement and this Day of Atonement." Apart from this echo of Rabbenu Tam's wording, however, and, possibly, the first two words, *Kol Nidré,* those modern versions have no connection with the traditional formula at all. For one thing, the new versions are all in Hebrew, whereas, in most rites, the traditional formula was in Aramaic. For another, and this is by far more important, the traditional text was a legal formula, while the new versions are all *prayers*. And, when it comes to what those prayers have to say, we find that, in many instances, they say the very opposite of what the old formula implied. The latter had requested the annulment of vows. The new prayers ask for the divine acceptance of the vows.

There is, of course, one very strong connection between the traditional *Kol Nidré* formula and the new versions. That connection is the tune! All of the modern *Kol Nidré* versions have been written for the express purpose of providing suitable words for the traditional tune, which was, by all means, to be retained. And the interpretation of the meaning of the tune, which Leopold Stein had so eloquently given in his "footnote" of 1840, is an interpretation which fits the newer Hebrew versions no less than Stein's "O Tag des Herrn!" Both represent attempts to capture the mood of the occasion in words appropriate to the opening of the most solemn evening service of the year.

EPILOGUE

The various prayerbooks, which we have considered under the general heading of "The Liturgy of European Liberal and Reform Judaism," by no means represent a unified point of view—as the reader will have had ample opportunity to discover. In fact, were we to produce a "composite portrait" of the entirety of Liberal and Reform rites discussed in this volume, we would undoubtedly end up with the complete traditional Ashkenazi rite—minus some of the more recondite *piyutim,* and enriched by a number of prayers in the vernacular as well as by some borrowings from the Sepharadi rite.

It will have been noticed that one reformed prayerbook abolished something which another reformed prayerbook retained, and that textual alterations, introduced by some, fell short of acceptance by others. For example, while none of the editors of the prayerbooks we have examined looked forward to the restoration of the sacrificial cult, the absence of that expectation manifested itself in any number of different ways. Some rituals, for example, went as far as to abolish the *Musaph* Service altogether. Others introduced some slight verbal changes, which made such prayers express historical memories rather than pleas for the future. Still others retained the complete traditional text (in Hebrew), confining their departures from traditional teachings to paraphrases in the vernacular. Similar variations have been found in connection with the traditional prayers for the Return to Zion and the Coming of the (personal) Messiah. The prayers reflecting traditional doctrines of the Hereafter are another instance, although, with certain notable exceptions, the substitution of Immortality for Resurrection—axiomatic in American Reform rituals—was confined, in Europe, to the vernacular translation, while the Hebrew text retained its traditional formulation. Angelology, too, likewise consistently eliminated in American Reform rituals, met with different treatments at the hands of various European liturgists. On the whole, there was a recognizable tendency to de-emphasize this aspect of the traditional liturgy. Yet, at the same time, there were reformed prayerbooks which, in newly composed prayers and anthems in the vernacular, did not shrink from mentioning the heavenly choirs. Finally, while all the prayerbooks, which we have considered in this volume, are predicated on the legitimacy of prayer in the vernacular, the ratio of Hebrew to vernacular fluctuates widely—from an all-German service (with two or three Hebrew sentences and a Hebrew Torah reading) in the Berlin *Reformgemeinde,* and a predominantly English service in the Liberal Jewish Synagogue of London, through the practically all-Hebrew service of the average German Liberal Synagogue.

If, in the light of all this, we were to search for that which *all* the European Liberal and Reform rituals had in common, we would find that it was primarily the conviction that every generation has the right to introduce changes into the liturgical material inherited from the past. Students of the history of the liturgy tend to take that right for granted. That, after all, is how it had always been. Yet it was precisely that right which was at issue in the nineteenth century. And, in this connection, it made no difference whether the contemplated (or accomplished) change was of a major or of a minor character. The early Berlin and Hamburg Reformers were as fiercely attacked for changing from the Ashkenazi to the Sepharadi pronunciation of Hebrew as, some fifty years later, Geiger was attacked for deviating from the traditional formulations of the Chosen People concept. The abolition of the *piyutim* (themselves of rather doubtful standing in terms of Rabbinic law) was considered, by the opposition, as no less serious than, say, the change from the annual to the triennial cycle of Torah readings. Now, as we have seen, there was no unanimity among the various Liberal and Reform rituals as to the precise nature of the changes which were to be introduced (and that, in part, accounts for the very large number of prayerbooks which we had to consider), but all of them came into existence because the men who edited them, and the circles for which they were intended, did agree on the principle *that* change was possible, necessary, *and* legitimate.

A Jewish worship service which had become all *qebha'*—fixed, routine, traditional—was in need of a new infusion of *kawwanah*—of the spontaneous, the relevant, and the new. Reform Judaism set out to meet that need. In doing so, it merely continued a process which had been going on for millennia. The last major liturgical reform had taken place some three centuries before, under the influence of the Safed mystics, who had added many a new element to the traditional worship service.[1] Nineteenth-century liturgical reform, however, differed in one important respect from earlier liturgical reforms. The latter had always taken the form of additions. Nineteenth-century liturgical reform, on the other hand, did not only add. It also *omitted*. The omissions, even more than the additions, gave rise to the protracted controversies which have not yet altogether died down. There were two major motivations for those omissions. One was the desire to curtail the duration of the worship service so that, from its beginning to its end, people could concentrate on their devotions. It was, in other words, an attempt to put into practice a principle of the *Shulḥan 'Arukh* itself: "Better a few supplications with devotion than many without devotion."[2]

But the second motivation was far more controversial. The Reformers omitted some traditional prayers not only because they wanted to curtail the time spent in worship, but also because those prayers expressed beliefs which the Reformers no longer held, and voiced petitions which found no echo in their hearts. Prayer, they held, requires absolute honesty. Now, the German Jew, but recently emancipated, and still in the state of exhilaration induced by that Emancipation, did not really feel himself to be "in exile," and could not *honestly* entreat the Almighty to lead him speedily to the Land of Israel. Here, then, was the kind of question which led to an answer in the giving of which nineteenth-century liturgical reform differed from all previous liturgical reforms. Should the prayerbook *reflect* the beliefs and convictions of the Jews, or should the prayerbook *dictate* those beliefs and convictions? Is the *siddur* a mirror of the Jewish soul, or is it normative? For a long time, of course, the *siddur* had been both. In addition to its more obvious functions, it had also served as the religious catechism and theological vade mecum of the average Jew. The inclusion in the *siddur* of the Maimonidean Thirteen Principles of the Faith, in both prose and poetry, was, therefore, quite in character. Moreover, for many a century, the tenets and beliefs expressed in, and inculcated by, the *siddur* found their confirmation the moment a Jew stepped out of the synagogue into his hostile environment. There was, during all that time, little need for liturgical changes based on dogmatic considerations.

But the times were different now, or, at least, they seemed to be—for a while. Reform Judaism wanted the *siddur* to be a reflection of what the Jew actually believed, and an expression of what he honestly and sincerely desired. It did not want an earlier reflection of Jewish existence and faith to dictate to the nineteenth-century Jew the tenets of his own faith. That, too, was an aspect of making the modern Jewish worship service expressive of true *kawwanah*. From the hindsight of historical perspective, it is easy for us to criticize those early Reformers. The dialectics of *qebha'* and *kawwanah* are an on-going process; and what is required, at any given time, is the striking of a balance between the two, rather than an over-emphasis of the one or the other. From this perspective, then, it is possible to argue that some of the Reformers—though by no means all of them—did not sufficiently value the element of *qebha'*. Their zeal for *kawwanah* and relevance was such that the sense of historical continuity tended to atrophy. Yet, that, too, had been one of the functions of the traditional *siddur*. It had bound the generations one to another. Its very concreteness of imagery made possible a constant re-living of historical moments—both of victory and of defeat, of laughter and of tears. And, if and when the fortunes of Jewish life changed, recourse could always be had to the *siddur*, in which the repercussions of a precedent or of a close parallel were bound to be found. For the *siddur*, in spite of its structure fixed by tradition, by no means reflected a doctrinal consistency or an evenness of mood. Too many generations had had a hand in shaping it, and too many historical events, of different kinds, had inspired the liturgical creations of those many generations. The *siddur* sings of both the weeping "by the rivers of Babylon" (Psalm 137), and the laughter "when the Lord restored the captivity of Zion" (Pslam 126). There were times, sometimes whole generations, when circumstances called for the emphasis to be laid on one mood. Other times called for expressions of the other mood. But the *siddur* contained them both, and, containing both, it managed to combine past, present, and future, accompanying the Jew on his strange and lonely path through history—always, and under all circumstances, having something appropriate to say to him. The Reformers of the nineteenth century frequently failed to see that dimension of the *siddur*, and, failing to see it, they deprived themselves and their children of some of the inner strength which comes from an awareness of historical continuity.

Yet such a judgment is possible only from the vantage-point of hindsight. The early Reformers themselves were too pre-occupied, and most understandably so, with other things to be side-tracked by such considerations. The revolution (not evolution) which had marked their external circumstances, their entry into the life of full citizenship after centuries of pariah existence, their discovery—as participants—of the world of Western civilization, that revolution had to find its counterpart in the religious realm, that is, if religion, *Jewish* religion, was to retain its hold upon them at all. It had to be revolution, not evolution, for the established guardians of the Tradition had refused, for a very long time, to make such adjustments to the new and unprecedented scene as the Tradition itself might have authorized. And it was that revolution which left its imprint upon the new liturgy. For the moment, the present was more important than the past. The present represented the new *kawwanah*.

The present, moreover, stood under the two signs of Universalism and of Rationalism. The spread of both of them had brought about those conditions which enabled the Jew to step out of the Ghetto, and to get himself accepted as a full member of Western society. Their further spread would ultimately bring about the Messianic Age—that, and not the coming of a latter-day scion of the Davidic dynasty who would lead all the Jews back to the Land of Israel, and ascend the throne of Jerusalem. But, if Universalism and Rationalism were the great concern of the moment, then, of necessity, they were ingredients of that new *kawwanah* which now entered the prayerbook. Many of the liturgical additions, and also many of the changes and the omissions were inspired by them.

Sometimes, indeed, one gets the impression—and not only from the liturgical efforts of the early nineteenth century—that the Reformers took their Universalism so seriously, that they were so certain of living at the threshhold of the time when the house of Israel's God would be "called a house of prayer for all the peoples," that consideration for the feelings of those "peoples" interfered with the intimacy that had marked Israel's conversation with his God. Some Reformers became reluctant to thank God for the lovingkindnesses He has bestowed upon Israel. They preferred to speak about the lovingkindnesses which He has bestowed upon *all* His creatures. And, where mention of Israel was unavoidable, they hastened to add that the God Who has had dealings with Israel has also dealt with others. Of course, the contributors to the traditional *siddur* would never have denied that. They, too, had occasionally voiced lofty "universalistic" sentiments. But, apparently, they did not feel the need to carry their Universalism on their sleeve—least of all when standing in prayer before God. The liturgies of Liberal and Reform Judaism tended to be far more apologetic about this, and many of the intimate conversations between Israel and God, and many of the reminiscences about events in family history, were now turned into programmatic declarations of a lofty Universalism, designed, one occasionally suspects, not only for the ear of God.

If nineteenth-century Universalism (which, in some of its other manifestations, also dissolved the individual human being into Man, and the individual human soul into Absolute Spirit) led to a de-emphasis of God's particular concern for His "peculiar people," nineteenth-century Rationalism, for its part, encouraged an approach to documents (any documents) which searched for the literal truth of what was being stated in them. And, if what was stated was found not to be literally true, it was considered not to be true at all. Within the Rationalist universe of discourse, one had to be very careful about what one said; and particularly so about what one said about God. One certainly did not talk about Him in anthropomorphic and anthropopathetic terms!

The traditional Jewish prayerbook did not have a chance when confronted by that kind of Rationalism. The imagery of the *siddur,* its poetry, and its emotive language stand condemned before the bar of Rationalism—of the kind of Rationalism, at any rate, which would insist on reading poetry as prose, the Bible as a textbook on geology, and the *siddur* as a philosophical dissertation. But that was exactly the kind of Rationalism with which the early Reformers (and some, but not all, of their later successors) approached the language of the *siddur.* Radical changes in liturgy were the inevitable result. Prayer, it was argued, demands absolute honesty; and the corollary was understood to imply that the prayerbook can contain only such statements as are factually correct, literally true, and historically verifiable. In applying this principle to the revision of the liturgy, the European Reformers (with the possible exception of the Liberal Jews of England) never went to the extreme lengths to which their American brethren had gone. But, by 1842, they had already gone far enough to encounter the following criticism from the pen of M. Löwengard:[3]

> It is undoubtedly a great thought which has guided the Liturgical Commission (of the Hamburg Temple, in producing the second edition of the Hamburg Temple Prayerbook): "Not to recite before God words with the meaning of which the mind and the heart of the worshipper are not equally filled." But, if we look more closely, are not *all* the expressions we use about God's essence, His attributes, and His relation to the world and to man, with or without criticism, in scientific dissertations or in prayer and song, are they not all only metaphorical? Is it not so that they do not even *approximately* express the truth? . . . "For as the heavens are higher than the earth, so are My ways higher than your ways, etc." (Isaiah 55:9.) If we follow this thought through consistently, we come to the conclusion which the Rabbis have already clearly expressed in their beautiful

> translation—although it is somewhat out of context—of the opening words of Psalm 65: *lekha dumiyah tehillah*—silent adoration is the most glorious praise of God.[4] But should we, to be thus consistent, close our lips and our houses of God forever? Yet, if we can, and if we must—impelled by religious feeling—regard it as justified to approach God with such words as are incapable of adequately expressing . . . the infinite, then this "religio-poetical" license must not be confined within pedantically narrow limits. Obstinate rigorism, however honorable the religious and moral principles which give rise to it, would soon lead us to the limit of everything positive.[5]

Löwengard was ahead of his time. In 1842, Orthodox and Reformer had at least this much in common: they both took the words of the *siddur* in their most literal sense—the former by way of affirmation, the latter by way of rejection. Neither side was able to see—what Löwengard so clearly saw—that the language of prayer is the language of poetry.

If, in the nineteenth century, both traditionalists and modernists had understood this simple and fundamental fact, the whole history of European Liberal and Reform Judaism would have run a different course. There still would have been enough scope for disagreements. There still would have been arguments, and even fierce controversies, about the length of the worship service, about the place of the vernacular, about musical accompaniment, and even about those statements in the traditional liturgy (such as the petitions for the restoration of the sacrificial cult, describing its concrete details in full) which simply do not lend themselves to poetical interpretation. But several of the chapters of this book would not have had to be written.

Yet those chapters were written. They were written because, in the ninteenth century, the poetical nature of the language of prayer was not understood. Perhaps, in the nineteenth century, it could not have been understood: Nor is it for us to criticize the men of the nineteenth century for not understanding it. We should rather praise them for what they did accomplish. Given the circumstances—and the limitations—of their day, they did succeed in breathing new life into the synagogue, and in bringing a new *kawwanah* to the liturgy—a *kawwanah* which, of necessity, had to reflect their joyous espousal of Universalism and their enthusiastic commitment to Rationalism.

But, if it be the law of liturgical development that one generation's *kawwanah* becomes the *qebha'* inheritance of the next, and in our Chapter Two we have demonstrated that law historically, then it must follow that the particular formulation which the nineteenth century had bestowed upon *kawwanah* has by now turned into the *qebha'* of the Liberal and Reform worship service. Some of our European congregations have appreciated that fact sooner than others, and have tried to meet the need of a new infusion of *kawwanah* which would reflect the concerns of our age. And that new *kawwanah* may even, on occasion, salvage something of what an earlier generation had jettisoned as unwelcome *qebha'*. For the battle-field assumes a different aspect after the battle has been won; and the obstacles of yesteryear may be viewed as things of beauty today. And although, particularly in Europe, there are still occasional skirmishes, reminiscent of the nineteenth century, the major battles have been won. It is thus that the future developments of European (and perhaps not only European) Liberal and Reform Liturgy may well take into account the words spoken, some forty years ago, by Hermann Vogelstein:

> If, in the early period of Liberalism, it was a question of fighting against the preponderance of forms, which threatened to kill the soul of religion, and to make room for free development, today we are able to face with complete freedom the problem of the religious language of forms. The unconditional and uncritical submission to the form is unfree; but equally unfree is its unconditional rejection.[6]

NOTES

INTRODUCTION

1) For full bibliographical details, see the Bibliography at the end of this volume.

2) Der israelitische Oberrath von Mecklenburg-Schwerin, *Den öffentlichen Cultus betreffende Differenzpunkte zwischen den verschiedenen religiösen Partheien.* Schwerin, 1850.

CHAPTER ONE

1) This prayerbook was evidently introduced in some other congregations as well. Thus, a report appearing in *Der Israelit des neunzehnten Jahrhunderts,* Vol. III (1842), p. 153, indicates that the village congregations of Witterschlick, Poppelsdorf and Beuel (in the district of Bonn) had adopted the Hamburg Temple Prayerbook.

2) This prayerbook was also adopted by the (short-lived) radical Reform congregation in Pesth, Hungary. See Samuel Holdheim, *Geschichte der Entstehung und Entwickelung der jüdischen Reformgemeinde in Berlin*. Berlin, 1857, p. 79.

3) In 1881, this prayerbook was introduced in the synagogue of St. Gallen, Switzerland, where it is still in use today. One of the reasons inducing the St. Gallen rabbi, Engelbert, to recommend Levin's ritual in preference to those of Geiger and Stein was the former's relative brevity. The St. Gallen congregation had previously used—in this order—Maier's 1848 prayerbook and Aub's 1866 prayerbook. For the interesting story of the choice of a suitable ritual for St. Gallen, see Lothar Rothschild, *Im Strom der Zeit*. St. Gallen, 1963, pp. 57–61.

4) This prayerbook was an outgrowth of Aub's 1866 prayerbook. In accordance with decisions reached by the Berlin community in 1870 and 1871, Aub's ritual was submitted for revision to a commission consisting of Rabbis Aub, Geiger, Rudolf Ungerleider, Professor M. Lazarus, and several members of the congregational authorities. Cf. Marcus Blatt, *Zur Einführung der Gebetbücher der neuen Synagoge in Berlin im isr. Gotteshause zu Troppau*. Berlin, 1884, p. 6. The last-named work also indicates that the 1881 Berlin prayerbook was adopted in Troppau, in 1884. The German translation of this Berlin prayerbook, although undoubtedly of a later edition of it, is also the basis of the German prayers in a Jewish soldiers' prayerbook, published, in 1914, by the Union of German Jews: *Feldgebetbuch für die jüdischen Mannschaften des Heeres*. Berlin, H. Itzkowski, 1914. This contains 23 pages of Hebrew prayers (abbreviated, but doctrinally Orthodox) and 29 pages of German (including selected Psalms and folksongs). The German text is throughout based on that of the German translation of the Berlin New Synagogue. The editor of this soldiers' prayerbook, not named in the prayerbook itself, was Leo Baeck. Cf. Walter Breslauer, "Der Verband der Deutschen Juden," in *Bulletin des Leo Baeck Instituts,* No. 28, Tel-Aviv, 1964, p. 377.

5) In 1926, Heinrich Stern reported that there were five Liberal synagogues in Berlin, using three different prayerbooks, which differ from one another in the greater or lesser introduction of German into the worship service. See Heinrich Stern, "Die Entwicklung des Deutschen Liberalen Judentums," in *International Conference of Liberal Jews*. London, 1926, p. 46. In addition to the prayerbooks of the New Synagogue and that of the Fasanenstrasse Synagogue, there must obviously have been yet a third Berlin prayerbook which we have been unable to locate. The prayerbook of the Fasanenstrasse Synagogue itself makes provision for the differing rite of two other Berlin synagogues. Thus, on page 325, in the *Musaph* for the Festivals, the prayerbook indicates that, while in the Fasanenstrasse, the *Kedushah* is sung in Hebrew only, a German version with Hebrew responses is sung in the synagogues in the Lindenstrasse and the Lützowstrasse. The major difference between the prayerbook of the New Synagogue and that of the Fasanenstrasse Synagogue is simply that in the latter slightly more German was used than in the former—both synagogues having most of the service in Hebrew. In terms of the prayerbooks themselves, this was merely a typographical difference. Both prayerbooks contain both the Hebrew and the German texts, printing, on the top half of the page, the language in which a given prayer was recited in the particular synagogue, and, on the bottom half, either the German translation or the Hebrew original.

CHAPTER TWO

1) See Ismar Elbogen, *Der jüdische Gottesdienst in seiner geschichtlichen Entwicklung.*[4] Hildesheim, Georg Olms, 1962; Joseph Heinemann, *Prayer in the Period of the Tanna'im and the Amora'im* (Hebrew). Jerusalem, Magnes Press, 1964; Zvi Karl, *Meḥqarim betoledoth hatephillah.* Tel-Aviv, Twersky, 1950; A. Z. Idelsohn, *Jewish Liturgy and its Development.* New York, Holt, 1932.

2) See, for example, b. *Berakhoth* 11b.

3) B. *Berakhoth* 16b, 17a.

4) Abraham J. Heschel, *Man's Quest for God.* New York, Scribner's, 1954. See especially pp. 64ff.

5) See Rashi to b. *Berakhoth* 11b, s.v. *wa'abhodah.*

6) Cf. *Seder Rav Amram,* ed. Frumkin. Vol. I, p. 192.

7) Philip Birnbaum, ed., *Daily Prayer Book.* New York, Hebrew Publishing Co., 1949, pp. 683f. Note that, though this prayerbook is supposed to be "translated and annotated," this passage and similar ones remain untranslated. No simple translation could ever do justice to them.

8) See Ibn Ezra's commentary on Ecclesiastes 5:1. Cf. also the collection of traditional objections to the *piyutim* in A. A. Wolff, *Die Stimmen der ältesten glaubwürdigsten Rabbinen über die Pijutim.* Leipzig, 1857.

9) W. Gunther Plaut, *The Rise of Reform Judaism.* New York, WUPJ, 1963, p. 184.

10) Birnbaum, *op. cit.,* p. 377.

CHAPTER THREE

1) David Philipson, *The Reform Movement in Judaism.* New York, Macmillan, 1907, pp. 78f.; and cf. the sources listed there.

2) Caesar Seligmann, "Zum hundertjährigen Geburtstag Abraham Geigers," in *Liberales Judentum,* Vol. II (1910), pp. 97–104.

3) *Protokolle und Aktenstücke der zweiten Rabbiner-Versammlung.* Frankfort o. M., 1845, pp. 180ff.

4) *Protocolle der ersten Rabbiner-Versammlung.* Brunswick, 1844, p. 42.

5) See about him in *Jüdisches Lexikon,* Vol. V, p. 1220.

6) Cf. the Introduction to Vogelstein's prayerbook, pp. 183 f, below.

7) See below, pp. 106 ff.

8) A. Berliner, *Das Gebetbuch des Dr. Vogelstein beurtheilt*. Berlin, Itzkowski, 1894.

9) Berliner, *op. cit.*, p. 1.

10) A. Lewertoff, ed., *50 Gutachten über das neue "westfälische Gebetbuch" von Rabbiner Dr. Vogelstein*. Höxter a/W., 1895.

11) *Freie Vereinigung für die Interessen des Orthodoxen Judentums*. About that organization, see Hermann Schwab, *The History of Orthodox Jewry in Germany*. London, n.d., pp. 89, 101–105, 111, 132.

12) *Gutachtensammlung, das Vogelstein'sche Gebetbuch betreffend*, herausgegeben vom Ausschuss des Verbandes der Synagogen-Gemeinden Westfalens. 1896.

13) *Op. cit.*, p. 18.

14) *Op. cit.*, p. 19.

15) *Op. cit.*, p. 11

16) *Op. cit.*, p. 9.

17) Adolf Lewin, *Geschichte der badischen Juden*. Karlsruhe, 1909, p. 453.

18) Lewin, *op. cit.*, pp. 462f.

19) *Ibid.*, p. 465.

20) Ismar Elbogen, *Der jüdische Gottesdienst in seiner geschichtlichen Entwicklung*.[4] Hildesheim, Georg Olms, 1962, p. 430. See also the Introduction to the *Einheitsgebetbuch* of 1929, p. xiii. A copy of the Baden prayerbook in the possession of this writer bears the editor's autograph, dated "August 1906."

21) Lewin, *op. cit.*, p. 474.

22) *Der Israelit,* January 3rd, 1907, pp. 7f.

23) Lewin, *op. cit.*, p. 475. Some hitherto unpublished comments by Orthodox authorities on the Baden prayerbook are now printed in Max Sinasohn, *Adass Jisroel Berlin*. Jerusalem, 1966, pp. 139–152.

24) Lewin, *op. cit.*, pp. 475–479.

25) *Ibid.*, p. 480.

26) Quoted in Lewin, *op. cit.*, p. 483.

27) *Israelitisches Gebetbuch*. Im Auftrage des Verbandes der Synagogen-Gemeinden Westfalens bearbeitet von Dr. Vogelstein, Rabbiner in Stettin. Part I. 1894.

28) *Israelitisches Gebetbuch für Schule und Haus*. Im Auftrage ... von Dr. Vogelstein .... Bielefeld, 1896.

CHAPTER FOUR

1) Cf. Henrik Wolff, "Liberal Judaism in Sweden," in *International Conference of Liberal Jews*. London, 1926, pp. 68–70.

2) For a convenient survey, see Ludwig Philippson's article, "Geschichte der deutschen Rabbinerversammlungen," in *Allgemeine Zeitung des Judenthums*, Vol. XLVIII (1884), pp. 213ff., 229ff., 245ff., 261ff., 277ff., and 293ff.

3) Cf. W. Gunther Plaut, *The Rise of Reform Judaism*. New York, WUPJ, 1963, pp. 85–90.

4) *Second Conference of the World Union for Progressive Judaism*. London, 1930, p. 149.

5) Cf. A. Harkavy, *Liqquté Qadmoniyoth*. Vol. II. St. Petersburg, 1903, p. 158.

6) Cf. P. Selvin Goldberg, *Karaite Liturgy and its Relation to Synagogue Worship*. Manchester University Press, 1957.

7) Cf. Jakob J. Petuchowski, "Karaite Tendencies in an Early Reform Haggadah," in *HUCA*, Vol. XXXI (1960), pp. 223–249.

8) A. A. Wolff, *Die Stimmen der ältesten glaubwürdigsten Rabbinen über die Pijutim*. Leipzig, 1857.

9) Cf. *J. E.*, Vol. XII, pp. 551f., art. "Wolff, Abraham Alexander."

10) A. A. Wolff, *op. cit.*, p. 8.

11) The identification of that author with Leon da Modena, widely accepted since Isaac S. Reggio published the *Kol Sakhal* in 1852, has been denied by Ellis Rivkin, in *Leon Da Modena and the Kol Sakhal*. Cincinnati, HUC Press, 1952.

12) Isaac S. Reggio, ed., *Beḥinath haQabbalah*. Göritzia, 1852, p. 40.

13) *Op. cit.*, p. 43.

14) Cf., for example, Abraham Geiger, *Leon da Modena*. Breslau, 1856.

15) Jakob J. Petuchowski, *The Theology of Haham David Nieto*. New York, Bloch, 1954, pp. 32–48.

16) Jakob J. Petuchowski, "Karaite Tendencies in an Early Reform Haggadah," in *HUCA*, Vol. XXXI (1960), p. 225.

17) Lou H. Silberman, *American Impact—Judaism in the United States in the Nineteenth Century*. Syracuse University, The B. G. Rudolph Lectures in Judaic Studies, 1964.

18) Cf. Graetz, *Geschichte* ..., Vol. XI[2], pp. 218f.; and Elbogen, *Der jüdische Gottesdienst*, p. 398.

19) Aaron Moses Isaac ben Abraham (Graanboom), *Sepher Melitz Yosher*. Amsterdam, 5569.

20) The "thirty divisions of the Book of Psalms" must refer to a specific lectionary, probably aiming at a complete reading of the entire Book of Psalms once every month—as against other lectionaries in which the entire Book of Psalms is read through once every week.

21) Graanboom, *op. cit.*, p. 2a.

22) *Op. cit.*, p. 2b.

23) *Ibid.*

24) Graanboom, *op. cit.*, p. 3a.

25) *Op. cit.*, p. 3b.

26) *Op. cit.*, p. 4a.

27) *Op. cit.*, p. 5a.

28) *Op. cit.*, p. 6a.

29) Graetz, *op. cit.*, p. 218.

30) Cf. *Jüdisches Lexikon,* Vol. I, p. 292, art. "Amsterdam."

31) In a private communication to the author, dated February 7th, 1966.

32) Cf. Philip Birnbaum, ed., *Daily Prayer Book*. New York, Hebrew Publishing Company, 1949, pp. 237–283.

33) Pp. 1–25.

34) Cf. Birnbaum, *op. cit.*, pp. 11–47, 299–415.

35) Pp. 25–64.

36) Seckel I. Fränkel, *Schutzschrift des zu Hamburg erschienenen Israelitischen Gebetbuchs*. Hamburg, 1819.

37) See below, pp. 267 f.

38) A bibliography of all the relevant writings which had appeared until then is given in *Der Orient*, Vol. III (1842), pp. 231f. An evaluation of that literature is found in *Literaturblatt des Orients*, 1842, pp. 186ff. See also Edward M. Maline, *Controversies over the Hamburg Prayer Book*. (Unpublished M. A. Thesis in the Hebrew Union College Library.) 1963.

39) For the Judaeo-German text of that "Proclamation," see *Theologische Gutachten über das Gebetbuch nach dem Gebrauche des Neuen Israelitischen Tempelvereins in Hamburg*. Hamburg, 1842, pp. 14f.

40) Z. Frankel in *Der Orient,* Vol. III (1842), pp. 53ff., 61ff., and 71ff.

41) Abraham Geiger, *Der Hamburger Tempelstreit, eine Zeitfrage.* Breslau, 1842.

42) Geiger, *op. cit.,* pp. 74–80.

43) Samuel Holdheim, *Verketzerung und Gewissensfreiheit. Ein zweites Votum.* Schwerin, 1842, p. iv.

44) About him, cf. *J. E.,* Vol. VIII, p. 194, art. "Löwengard, Max."

45) M. Loewengard, *Auch einige Worte über das neue Gebetbuch im Hamburger Tempel.* Tübingen, 1842, pp. 14f.

46) See below, pp. 137–139.

47) Caesar Seligmann, "Hundertzwanzig Jahre Hamburger Tempel," in Bruno Italiener, ed., *Festschrift zum hundertzwanzigjährigen Bestehen des Israelitischen Tempels in Hamburg.* Hamburg, 1937, p. 13.

48) Cf. David Philipson, *The Reform Movement in Judaism.* New York, Macmillan, 1907, pp. 317–368; and Plaut, *op. cit.,* pp. 55–61.

49) See above, pp. 1–21.

50) *Gebetbuch.* Verlag der Jüdischen Reform-Gemeinde, n.d. [A note on page 2 states that this liturgy was compiled between the years 1925–1932.]

51) Immanuel Heinrich Ritter, *Die jüdische Reformgemeinde zu Berlin.* (Part IV of Ritter's *Geschichte der jüdischen Reformation,* ed. S. Samuel.) Berlin, 1902, pp. 65f.

52) Cf. Samuel Holdheim, *Geschichte der Entstehung und Entwickelung der jüdischen Reformgemeinde in Berlin.* Berlin, 1857, pp. 153–155.

53) Cf. *Gebetbuch der jüdischen Reformgemeinde zu Berlin.* New edition. Berlin, 1885, p. 20.

54) Cf. the prayerbook mentioned in Note 50, above, p. 6.

55) Samuel Holdheim, *Geschichte der Entstehung* etc., pp. 195f.

56) *Gebetbuch der jüdischen Reformgemeinde in Berlin.* Jubiläumsausgabe. Berlin, 1895, p. 39.

57) *Gebetbuch.* Berlin, Verlag der Jüdischen Reform-Gemeinde, n.d. (probably 1933), pp. 6–11.

58) Cf. Birnbaum, *op. cit.,* p. 3.

59) Cf. *op. cit.,* p. 51.

60) This is an approximate translation, trying to preserve the rhythm of the original. The first stanza, with slight variations, appears first in *Israelitisches Ge-*

betbuch, ed. Caesar Seligmann. Vol. I. Frankfort o. M., 1910, p. 17. See also *Einheitsgebetbuch,* 1929, Appendix, p. 12. The second stanza may be original.

61) Cf. Birnbaum, *op. cit.,* p. 71.

62) Cf. *op. cit.,* p. 15.

63) Cf. *op. cit.,* p. 657. (From the New Year liturgy.)

64) Cf. *op. cit.,* p. 351.

65) Cf. *op. cit.,* p. 413.

66) Cf. *op. cit.,* pp. 413ff.

67) Cf. *op. cit.,* p. 361.

68) Cf. *op. cit.,* p. 369.

69) Cf. *op. cit.,* p. 389.

70) Cf. *op. cit.,* p. 363.

71) Cf. *op. cit.,* pp. 343ff.

72) Cf. *op. cit.,* pp. 365ff.

73) Adapted from Psalm 19.

74) Cf. Birnbaum, *op. cit.,* p. 389.

75) Cf. *op. cit.,* p. 423.

76) Cf. Philipson, *op. cit.,* pp. 122–146; and Plaut, *op. cit.,* pp. 47f., 136f.

77) For a detailed analysis of the liturgy of the West London Synagogue, see Sefton D. Temkin, *The Liturgy of the West London Synagogue.* (Unpublished Ph.D. Minor Thesis in the Hebrew Union College Library.) 1963.

78) *Forms of Prayer used in the West London Synagogue of British Jews,* ed. D. W. Marks. Vol. I. London, 1841, pp. 74f.

79) *Op. cit.,* p. 74.

80) Cf. Birnbaum, *op. cit.,* p. 273.

81) *Forms of Prayer ...,* Vol. I., p. 75.

82) *Op. cit.,* p. 1. This should be compared with the version of the Kaddish used in the Sepharadi liturgy, on which it is based. Cf. Moses Gaster, ed., *The Book of Prayer and Order of Service according to the Custom of the Spanish and Portuguese Jews.* Vol. I. Oxford University Press, 1949, p. 55.

83) Cf., e.g., the 3rd edition of Volume III. London, 1885, p. 2.

84) *Forms of Prayer* .... Vol. I., London, 1841, p. 13.

85) Cf. Temkin, *op. cit.*, p. 130.

86) Cf. *Forms of Prayer* . . . Vol. IV. 4th edition. London, 1890, p. 9.

87) *Forms of Prayer* . . . Vol. I. London, 1841, p. ix.

88) *Forms of Prayer* . . . Vol. I. 6th edition. Oxford University Press, 1931, p. v.

89) *Op. cit.*, p. 5.

90) *Prayers for the Pilgrim Festivals.* New edition. The Reform Synagogues of Great Britain. 1965, p. 10.

91) *Op. cit.*, p. 9.

92) Cf. Birnbaum, *op. cit.*, pp. 609–613.

93) *Prayers for the Pilgrim Festivals,* pp. 34f.

94) *Forms of Prayer* ..., Vol. I. London, 1841, pp. 15f., and throughout the liturgy of the West London Synagogue.

95) Bruno Italiener, "The Mussaf-Kedushah," in *HUCA,* Vol. XXVI (1955), pp. 413–424.

96) Italiener, *op. cit.*, p. 423.

97) *Ibid.*

98) *Prayers for the Pilgrim Festivals,* p. 64.

99) *Forms of Prayer for Jewish Worship. First Supplement to Volume I. Evening Prayers.* Edited by the Assembly of Ministers of The Association of Synagogues in Great Britain. 1952, p. 10.

100) *Forms of Prayer* ..., Vol. II. London, 1842, p. 50.

101) *Prayers for the Pilgrim Festivals,* p. 38. For a more detailed analysis of this edition of the prayerbook, cf. Jakob J. Petuchowski, "New Trends in the Liturgy of British Reform Judaism," in *Judaism,* Fall 1966.

102) Cf. Philipson, *op. cit.*, pp. 544–558; and W. Gunther Plaut, *The Growth of Reform Judaism.* New York, WUPJ, 1965, pp. 65–67.

103) Cf. Claude G. Montefiore, "Liberal Judaism in England," in *International Conference of Liberal Jews.* London, 1926, pp. 59–65.

104) Cf. Philipson, *op. cit.*, pp. 551–555.

105) Cf. Birnbaum, *op. cit.*, pp. 17f.

106) Cf. *op. cit.*, p. 353.

107) Cf. *op. cit.*, p. 359.

108) Cf. *op. cit.*, p. 439.

109) Cf. *op. cit.*, p. 463.

110) Cf. *op. cit.*, p. 337.

111) Cf. *op. cit.*, p. 367.

112) *Sabbath Afternoon Services.* (London), Liberal Jewish Synagogue, n.d.

113) *Sabbath Morning Services.* London, Liberal Jewish Synagogue, 1916.

114) Cf. Birnbaum, *op. cit.*, p. 351.

115) *Sabbath Morning Services*, pp. 1–15.

116) See below, pp. 202–205.

117) *Prayer Book of the St. George's Settlement Synagogue.* London, 1929, p. 4.

118) Cf. *Liberal Jewish Prayer Book*, Vol. I. 1926, pp. 405f.; *Prayer Book of the St. George's Settlement Synagogue*, pp. 26f.; and Birnbaum, *op. cit.*, pp. 11–14.

119) The reader will bear in mind that we are here reproducing Rabbi Rayner's own description of his prayerbook. What is, and what is not, an "over-emphatically particularistic" phrase is often a matter of subjective judgment and interpretation. The editors' notion of what constitutes "over-emphatic particularism" is not always shared by this writer.

120) Cf. Philipson, *op. cit.*, pp. 559–562; and Plaut, *The Growth* etc., pp. 64f.

121) Cf. Philipson, *op. cit.*, p. 559.

122) Cf. Birnbaum, *op. cit.*, p. 15.

123) Cf. *op. cit.*, pp. 17ff.

124) Cf. *op. cit.*, p. 51.

125) Cf. *op. cit.*, pp. 331ff.

126) Cf. *op. cit.*, pp. 55ff.

127) Cf. *op. cit.*, p. 71.

128) Cf. *op. cit.*, pp. 71ff.

129) See below, pp. 236f.

130) Cf. Birnbaum, *op. cit.*, p. 197.

131) Cf. *op. cit.*, p. 545.

132) Cf. *op. cit.*, p. 657.

133) Cf. *op. cit.*, pp. 135ff.

134) Cf. *op. cit.*, pp. 243ff.

135) Cf. *op. cit.*, pp. 337–348.

136) Cf. *Rituel des Prières Journalières*. Paris, n.d. (1925), p. 49.

137) *Op. cit.*, p. 217.

138) Plaut, *The Growth* etc., p. 65.

139) See below, pp. 236 f.

140) *Rituel des Prières Journalières*. Paris, n.d. (1958), p. 115.

141) *Op. cit.*, pp. 224–226.

142) See below, pp. 237–239.

143) Compare *Seder Tobh Lehodoth*, Vol. I, pp. 27f. with *Einheitsgebetbuch*, Vol. I, p. 139.

143a) *Seder Tobh Lehodoth*, I, p. 40

144) *Seder Toḇh Lehodoth*, Vol. I, p. 64.

145) *Op. cit.*, pp. 66f.

146) *Op. cit.*, pp. 76f.

147) See below, pp. 141–146.

CHAPTER FIVE

1) Cf. David Philipson, *The Reform Movement in Judaism*. New York, Macmillan, 1907, pp. 33ff. And see below, in the chapter, "What They Said About Their Work," pp. 133 f.

2) This was, of course, an exaggeration. As is evident from *Die Deutsche Synagoge* (1817/18), the more important rubrics of the service continued to be recited in Hebrew.

3) The Berlin services, which contained no *Musaph*, included the *Musaph* version of the *Kedushah* in the *Shaḥarith* Service. The *Musaph* version of the

Kedushah is actually more elaborate. Later on, the Hamburg Temple Prayerbook, even though it did contain a revised version of the *Musaph* Service, continued that practice. Could it have been that the early Reformers were less disturbed by the more detailed angelology of the *Musaph* version of the *Kedushah* than they were by the fervent plea for God's speedy return to Zion, as voiced in the *Shaharith* version? Compare the two versions in Philip Birnbaum, ed., *Daily Prayer Book*. New York, Hebrew Publishing Co., 1949, pp. 351 and 393.

4) Cf. Deuteronomy 14: 1, as interpreted in b. *Yebamoth* 13b.

5) Cf. Proverbs 1: 8, as interpreted in b. *Berakhoth* 35b.

6) These "accusations" are quoted by Libermann in אור נגה, pp. 1f., by Aaron Choriner in נוגה הצדק, ed. Libermann, pp. 14f., and by David Caro, in ברית אמת, p. 21.

7) Cf. Jakob J. Petuchowski, "Karaite Tendencies in an Early Reform Haggadah," in HUCA, Vol. XXXI (1960), pp. 224–233; and see the literature listed there.

8) On the somewhat doubtful reputation of Libermann, see Graetz, *Geschichte* ..., Vol. XI², p. 393n, and *J. E.*, Vol. VIII, p. 80, s. v. "Liebermann (Libermann), Eliezer."

9) For a complete biography of this interesting rabbi, see Leopold Löw, *Gesammelte Schriften*, ed. Immanuel Löw. Vol. II, pp. 251–420. Szegedin, 1890.

10) Note that Choriner's "retraction" in אלה דברי הברית, p. 98, specifically mentions facts which had come to light only *after* he had given his opinion in נוגה הצדק !

11) Quoted in אור נגה, p. 3.

12) Quoted in אור נגה, p. 4, and by Choriner in נוגה הצדק, p. 16.

13) Quoted in אור נגה, p. 5, and by Choriner in נוגה הצדק, p. 17.

14) Ed. Margalioth, p. 384. In Wistinetzki's ed., ch. 11, p. 9. Quoted in אור נגה, p. 4.

15) Ed. Margalioth, p. 466. In Wistinetzki's ed., ch. 1590, p. 389. Quoted in אור נגה, p. 4, and by Choriner in נוגה הצדק, p. 16.

16) Quoted in אור נגה, p. 2.

17) Quoted in אור נגה, p. 13. The full text of this letter is now available in *Teshubhoth Harambam*, ed. J. Blau. Vol. II, pp. 473–476. Jerusalem, Mekize Nirdamim, 1960. We give a summary of the letter only. It should be noted, as the Orthodox were careful to point out already in 1819, that Maimonides is giving a temporary "emergency ruling" within a specific situation. He had no intention of abolishing the twofold recitation of the Eighteen Benedictions.

18) Cf. Moses Gaster, ed., *The Book of Prayer and Order of Service according to the Custom of the Spanish and Portuguese Jews.* Vol. I. Oxford University Press, 1949, p. 107.

19) אור נגה, p. 13.

20) *Op. cit.*, pp. 8f.

21) *Op. cit.*, pp. 23f.

22) נוגה הצדק, pp. 17f.

23) אלה דברי הברית, title page.

24) *Op. cit.*, p. ii. In addition to this passage and the other excerpts we are quoting from this work, the reader will find further quotations in W. Gunther Plaut, *The Rise of Reform Judaism.* New York, WUPJ, 1963, pp. 34–37.

25) אלה דברי הברית, p. 10.

26) *Op. cit.*, p. 44.

27) Cf. Gaster, *op. cit.*, p. 117.

28) אלה דברי הברית, p. 38.

29) *Op. cit.*, p. 98.

30) Cf. Löw, *op. cit.*

31) Abraham Loewenstamm, ספר צרור החיים, Amsterdam, 5580.

32) Loewenstamm, *op. cit.*, pp. 30a–33a.

33) Loewenstamm, *op. cit.*, p. 42a.

34) Loewenstamm, *op. cit.*, p. 52b.

35) For excerpts from this tract, see Plaut, *op. cit.*, pp. 37f.

36) On Caro, cf. *J. E.*, Vol. III, p. 582, s.v. "Caro, David," and Graetz, *op. cit.*, pp. 397f., Note 3.

37) David Caro, ברית אמת. Dessau, 1820, pp. 52f.

38) Graetz, *op. cit.*, pp. 396f.

39) Ludwig Philippson, in *Allgemeine Zeitung des Judenthums,* Vol. VIII (1844), pp. 461ff.

40) Abraham Geiger, "Unser Gottesdienst," in *Jüdische Zeitschrift für Wissenschaft und Leben,* Vol. VI (1868), p. 5. Geiger, by the way, did not call for the immediate banishment of Hebrew. In the same article, p. 8, he says that the

change to the vernacular "can only gradually be realized. Here, the way of compromise is the only correct one."

41) See above, in the chapter on "Independent Reform," pp. 55 f.

42) Abraham Geiger, *Nothwendigkeit und Mass einer Reform des jüdischen Gottesdienstes.* Breslau, 1861.

43) Israel Hildesheimer, *Die Geiger'sche Broschüre Nothwendigkeit und Maass einer Reform des jüdischen Gottesdienstes beurtheilt.* Mayence, 1861, pp. 13f.

44) *Forms of Prayer Used in the West London Synagogue of British Jews,* ed. D. W. Marks. Vol. I. London, 1841, Introduction.

45) See above, "Reform from Within," pp. 39–42.

46) *Denkschrift zur Begründung des von dem Grossherzoglich Badischen Oberrate der Israeliten herausgegebenen Gebetbuchentwurfs.* Karlsruhe, n.d.

47) J. Wohlgemuth, *Der badische Gebetbuchentwurf und die Denkschrift des Oberrats. Ein Brief an die Gesetzestreuen Badens.* Frankfort o. M., 1907, pp. 4f.

48) Wohlgemuth, *op. cit.*, p. 10.

49) David Hoffmann, *Zur Aufklärung über die badische Gebetbuchreform.* Frankfort o. M., n.d., p. 11.

50) Moritz Steckelmacher, *Widerlegung des Sendschreibens des Dr. D. Hoffmann.* Mannheim, n.d.

51) See above, "Reform from Within," pp. 39–42.

52) *Mishnah Aboth* 5: 17.

CHAPTER SIX

1) The signatories of this document are identified in Graetz, *Geschichte,* Vol. XI[2] (1900), pp. 290f. Berlin (i.e., Berliner), Kalkar (i.e., Kaller) and Steinhardt were rabbis. Fränkel was the director of the Jewish school in Dessau. Heinemann was Israel Jacobson's secretary. Merkel was a non-Jew who had the task of supervising the consistory on behalf of the government.

2) Cf. Abraham Z. Idelsohn, *Jewish Music in its Historical Development.* New York, Tudor Publishing Co., 1944, pp. 212ff.

3) Albert M. Hyamson, *The Sephardim of England.* London, Methuen, 1951, pp. 27f.

4) Hyamson, *op. cit.*, pp. 277ff.

5) About the constitution and function of the Ober-Kirchen-Behörde, see F. F.

Mayer, *Sammlung der württembergischen Gesetze in Betreff der Israeliten.* Tübingen, 1847, pp. 67–78.

6) The reference is to the custom, observed by repentant sinners, of having thirty-nine stripes administered to them in the synagogue after the afternoon service on Atonement Eve. This observance is understood as a "reminiscence" of the old punishment of *malquth,* rather than its proper implementation. See *Shulḥan 'Arukh Oraḥ Ḥayyim* 607: 6.

7) The reference is to the custom of beating willow branches to the ground while *hosha'na* prayers are chanted. See Hayyim Schauss, *The Jewish Festivals.* Cincinnati, UAHC, 1938, p. 195.

8) *Jewish Encyclopedia,* Vol. XII, p. 572.

9) Cf. *J. E.,* Vol. V, pp. 78f.

10) The reference is to leaving the arm bare after putting on the phylacteries. The observance itself has not been abolished.

11) See Note 6, above.

12) See Note 7, above.

13) What is prohibited here is not the required ritual circumambulation with the *lulabh,* but the disturbance caused by having the men bring their *lulabhim* to their wives for the latter to recite the appropriate benediction.

14. Cf. *Seder 'Abhodath Yisrael,* ed. S. Baer. Berlin, Schocken, 1937, pp. 133ff.

15) *Ibid.,* pp. 229–230.

16) *Ibid.,* pp. 230–231.

17) *Ibid.,* p. 233.

18) *Ibid.,* p. 367 for *lulabh* meditation, and cf. *Sepher Qerobhoth Hu Maḥzor,* ed. W. Heidenheim, Vol. I. Hannover, 5598, pp. 116f. for mystical *shofar* prayers.

19) Poetical inserts within the standard prayers.

20) Cf., for example, Baer, *op. cit.,* pp. 629–670.

21) *Ibid.,* pp. 671–680, and pp. 722–725.

22) Cf. Philip Birnbaum, ed., *Daily Prayer Book.* New York, Hebrew Publishing Co., 1949, pp. 647–654.

23) Cf. *Sepher Qerobhoth Hu Maḥzor,* ed. W. Heidenheim. Vol. IX. Hannover, 5599, pp. 139–155.

24) *Ibid.,* p. 155.

25) Cf. Baer, *op. cit.,* pp. 109–111. The sentence to be omitted reads: "Our Father, our King, avenge before our eyes the blood of Thy servants which has been shed."

26) Cf. Schauss, *op. cit.,* pp. 92f. and 194.

27) See Note 6, above.

28) See Note 7, above.

29) Cf. *J. E.,* Vol. III, pp. 244–246, art. "Blessing, Priestly."

30) The Memorial Service.

31) Chapter V of *Mishnah Zebaḥim,* dealing with the details of the sacrificial cult, included in the daily morning service. Cf. Birnbaum, *op. cit.,* pp. 37–41.

32) Introduction to the *Sifra,* containing the Thirteen Hermeneutic Rules, included in the daily morning service. Cf. Birnbaum, *op. cit.,* pp. 41–45.

33) "For slander let there be no hope, and may all wickedness perish instantly. May all of it be cut down soon. Do Thou speedily uproot, crush, cut down and humble arrogance, speedily in our days. Praised art Thou, O Lord, who breakest enmity and humblest arrogance." The "reform" consists in the use of "slander" in place of the (traditional) "slanderers," of "enmity" for "enemies," and "arrogance" for "the arrogant."

The text in Birnbaum, *op. cit.,* p. 87, already represents a modified version of the original.

34) "O God, look! Our glory has waned among the nations; they detest us like the impurity of a menstruating woman. How long shall Thy glory remain in captivity, and Thy splendor in the hand of the foe? Arouse Thy might and Thy zeal against Thine enemies, that they may be put to shame and crushed despite their power."

For the whole prayer, see Birnbaum, *op. cit.,* pp. 111–113.

35) Cf. Birnbaum, *op. cit.,* p. 383. The passage to be omitted calls on God to "avenge the blood of His servants which has been shed."

36) The *Synagogenordnung* was published without a date. We have found it bound together with the Mayence prayerbook which was published in 1853.

37) Cf. *J. E.,* Vol. II, p. 297.

38) See Note 31, above.

39) Chapter II of *Mishnah Shabbath,* dealing with the fuels suitable for the Sabbath light, included in the Sabbath Eve service. See Birnbaum, *op. cit.,* pp. 251–253.

40) Babylonian Talmud *Kerithoth* 6a, dealing with the composition of the incense, included in the Sabbath *musaph* service. See Birnbaum, *op. cit.,* p. 407.

41) "Praised art Thou, O Lord our God, Sovereign of the Universe, who hast not made me a heathen," "... who hast not made me a slave," "... who hast not made me a woman."
Cf. Birnbaum, *op. cit.*, pp. 15f.

42) "... who hast made me an Israelite." This version is found in the Italian rite, which, however, also retains the benedictions, "... who hast not made me a slave," and "... who hast not made me a woman."
See Samuel David Luzzatto, *Mabho leMaḥzor Bené Roma,* ed. E. D. Goldschmidt. Tel-Aviv, Dvir, 1966, p. 80.

43) "For slander let there be no hope, and let all wickedness vanish like smoke. And speedily humble arrogance. Praised art Thou, O Lord, who breakest enmity and humblest arrogance."
Cf. Note 33, above.

44) Cf. Birnbaum, *op. cit.*, pp. 111f. See also Note 34, above.

45) Cf. Birnbaum, *op. cit.*, pp. 113–115.

46) The *Taḥanun* prayer (called here *teḥinnah*), on account of its sorrowful mood, is omitted on joyous occasions of the Jewish calendar. See Birnbaum, *op. cit.*, p. 103. The Mayence *Synagogenordnung* now extends that provision to patriotic occasions.

47) Cf. Birnbaum, *op. cit.*, pp. 237–243.

48) Cf. Birnbaum, *op. cit.*, pp. 243–247.

49) Cf. Birnbaum, *op. cit.*, pp. 377–379.

50) Printed in *Gebete und Lieder für die Sabbate und Festtage nebst Synagogen- und Gebet-Ordnung für die Synagogen-Gemeinde Beuthen O.-S.* Beuthen, 1906.

51) *Allgemeine Zeitung des Judenthums,* Vol. I (1837), No. 7, pp. 25–26.

52) *Allgemeine Zeitung des Judenthums,* Vol. I (1837), Nos. 26 and 28, pp. 101–103, 110–111.

53) Probably David Ottensooser (1784–1858), who translated Isaiah, Jeremiah and Job. See *J. E.*, Vol. IX, p. 445.

54) Cf. *J. E.*, Vol. VI, p. 372, art. "Hess, Mendel."

55) Ismar Elbogen, *Der jüdische Gottesdienst in seiner geschichtlichen Entwicklung.*[4] Hildesheim, Georg Olms, 1962, p. 411.

56) David Philipson, *The Reform Movement in Judaism.* New York, Macmillan, 1907, p. 52.

57) *Ibid.*

58) See attacks mentioned by Hess in *Beilage zu der nochmals aufgelegten Nr. 1 des Israeliten des neunzehnten Jahrhunderts.* 1840, p. 1.

59) See the report in *Allgemeine Zeitung des Judenthums*, Vol. I, No. 7, pp. 25–26, quoted above.

60) *Beilage zu der nochmals aufgelegten Nr. 1 des Israeliten des neunzehnten Jahrhunderts*. 1840, p. 3.

61) See *J. E.*, Vol. VI, p. 372, art. "Hess, Mendel."

62) *Allgemeine Zeitung des Judenthums*, Vol. I (1837), No. 26, p. 101.

63) Cf. W. Gunther Plaut, *The Rise of Reform Judaism*. New York, WUPJ, 1963, p. 220.

CHAPTER SEVEN

1) *Gebete der Juden auf das ganze Jahr*. Berlin, 1786. Reprinted in Amsterdam, in 1807.

2) *Ueber die, durch die neue Organisation der Judenschaften in den Preussischen Staaten nothwendig gewordene, Umbildung 1. ihres Gottesdienstes in den Synagogen, 2. ihrer Unterrichts-Anstalten, und deren Lehrgegenstände, und 3. ihres Erziehungs-Wesens überhaupt.—Ein Wort zu seiner Zeit.*—Berlin, 1812.

3) David Philipson, *The Reform Movement in Judaism*. New York, Macmillan, 1907, pp. 33ff.

4) For the specific details of Jacobson's services in Berlin, cf. Simon Bernfeld, תולדות הריפורמציון הדתית בישראל. Cracow, 1900. Pp. 240–243.

5) Cf. Graetz, *Geschichte der Juden*. Vol. XI^2, p. 297, who writes that Frederick William III, in 1812, granted the Jews of Prussia the right, indeed the obligation, to be citizens of the cities, but not the recognition of being citizens of the State.

6) On the situation in Denmark, cf. *J. E.*, Vol. IV, pp. 522ff., art. "Denmark." It appears that the Danish government actually *compelled* the Jews to have sermons in Danish, and to institute Confirmation. However, there seems to be no reason to suppose that the regular worship service itself—apart from sermon and "catechization"—was conducted in Danish. On the other hand, from 1817 through 1821, there were weekly "edification hours" in Copenhagen, on Wednesdays (!), which were conducted in Danish by Isaac Noah Mannheimer. Cf. Paul Rieger's essay on "Die Bedeutung des Hamburger Tempels für die Geschichte des neuzeitlichen Judentums," in D. Leimdörfer, *Festschrift zum hundertjährigen Bestehen des Israelitischen Tempels in Hamburg*. Hamburg, 1918, p. 23n.

7) See below, pp. 341f.

8) W. Gunther Plaut, *The Rise of Reform Judaism*. New York, WUPJ, 1963, pp. 48–50.

9) Cf. *J. E.*, Vol. VIII, p. 264, art. "Maier, Joseph von."

10) *Israelitisches Gebet- und Andachtsbuch*, ed. Joseph Maier. Stuttgart, 1848.

11) Maier is paraphrasing, or quoting from memory, a statement in b. *Gittin* 59b, which reads *kol hatorah kullah nammé mippené darkhé shalom,* "The whole Torah, too, (was given) for the sake of the ways of peace."

12) Cf. Alexander Altmann, "Zur Frühgeschichte der jüdischen Predigt in Deutschland: Leopold Zunz als Prediger," in *Year Book of the Leo Baeck Institute,* Vol. VI. London, 1961, pp. 3–59. See particularly pp. 13–20. Also, *idem,* "The New Style of Jewish Preaching," in *Studies in Nineteenth-Century Jewish Intellectual History,* ed. Alexander Altmann. Harvard University Press, 1964, pp. 65–116. See particularly pp. 87ff.

13) See above, pp. 124–127.

14) Plaut, *op. cit.,* pp. 57–60.

15) *Gebete für die öffentliche Gottesverehrung in der Synagoge zu Mainz.* Frankfort o. M., 1853.

16) Cf. *J. E.,* Vol. II, p. 297, art. "Aub, Joseph."

17) See below, p. 223.

18) *Israelitisches Gebetbuch für die öffentliche und häusliche Andacht, zunächst für die israelitische Gemeinde in Mannheim,* ed. M. Präger. Mannheim, 1855.

19) Literally: "For according to the number of thy cities are thy gods."

20) There were 5,478 Jews in Mannheim, in 1900. See *J. E.,* Vol. VIII, p. 294, art. "Mannheim."

21) Letter from the late Swedish Chief Rabbi Dr. Kurt Wilhelm to this author, dated August 23rd, 1964. On Wolff, cf *J. E.,* Vol. XII, p. 553, art. "Wolff, Maurice."

22) Cf. *J. E.,* Vol. XI, p. 540, art. "Stein, Leopold."

23) *Die Reform des Judenthums,* No. 32, November 4, 1846, pp. 252–253.

24) Cf. *J. E.,* Vol. V, pp. 484–492, art. "Frankfort-on-the-Main."

25) The resolutions of the Conference of Rabbis, held in Frankfort o. M., in October 1857, which are based on Stein's plan, are printed in the *Homiletisch-liturgische Beilage* to Vol. VII (1857) of *Der Israelitische Volkslehrer,* ed. Leopold Stein, pp. 91–100.

26) Cf. Stein's statements on this theme in *Protokolle und Aktenstücke der zweiten Rabbiner-Versammlung.* Frankfort o. M., 1845, pp. 98–101.

27) *Mishnah Zebaḥim,* chapter 5. Cf. Philip Birnbaum, *Daily Prayer Book.* New York, Hebrew Publishing Company, 1949, pp. 37–41.

28) *Mishnah Shabbath,* chapter 2. Cf. Birnbaum, *op. cit.,* pp. 251–253.

29) Cf. Rachel Wischnitzer, *The Architecture of European Synagogues*. Philadelphia, Jewish Publication Society, 1964, p. 206. See also the illustrations on pp. 204f.

30) Apart from the publication of Geiger's liturgical principles in the *Denkschrift* (Frankfort o. M., 1869), the identical text is also found in the following:
(i) *Thesen für die am 29. d. in Leipzig zusammentretende Versammlung*. (Published without indication of place and date of publication.);
(ii) The same, published in Geiger's *Jüdische Zeitschrift für Wissenschaft und Leben*, Vol. VII (1869), pp. 162–164;
(iii) "Plan zu einem neuen Gebetbuch," in *op. cit.*, pp. 245–247;
(iv) Within the Preface to the 1870 edition of his prayerbook.

The theoretical considerations underlying this statement had already been voiced by Geiger in his Breslau days, in a pamphlet entitled *Nothwendigkeit und Mass einer Reform des jüdischen Gottesdienstes. Ein Wort zur Verständigung*. Breslau, 1860. (Second edition, 1861.) That pamphlet immediately called forth the fierce opposition of Israel (Azriel) Hildesheimer, then still rabbi in Eisenstadt, Hungary. (Hildesheimer and Geiger were destined to be contemporaries in Berlin ten years later; Geiger as a rabbi of the Jewish community, and Hildesheimer as the rabbi of a Separatist Orthodox congregation and founder of an Orthodox rabbinical seminary in Berlin.) The title of Hildesheimer's polemic was *Die Geiger'sche Broschüre Nothwendigkeit und Mass einer Reform des jüdischen Gottesdienstes. Beurtheilt von Dr. Israel Hildesheimer, Rabbiner zu Eisenstadt*. Mayence, 1861.

31) Geiger is referring to the liturgical treatments of the "Binding of Isaac" (Genesis 22), to which he had a particular aversion. But one of his critics, who otherwise approved of Geiger's liturgical reforms, A. Wiener of Oppeln, accused Geiger of not being thorough enough in eliminating such liturgical references. Cf. A. Weiner, *Der Oeffentliche Gottesdienst, ein Wort zur Beherzigung, gerichtet an denkende Israeliten*. Oppeln, 1873, pp. 21f.

32) "Im Einverständnisse mit der Gemeinde-Verwaltung in Frankfurt am Main."

33) M. Joël, *Zur Orientirung in der Cultusfrage*. Breslau, 1869.

34) "Etwas über Glauben und Beten. Zu Schutz und Trutz," in Geiger's *Jüdische Zeitschrift für Wissenschaft und Leben*, Vol. VII (Breslau, 1869), pp. 1–59.

35) M. Joël, *Zum Schutz gegen "Trutz."* Breslau, 1869.

36) Joël here refers to a footnote which reads:

> The minor changes of a passage in the benediction before the *Shema* is not an arbitrary one, but only the restoration of the original wording as found in the *Siddur* of R. Amram Gaon. Moreover, the expert knows that the passages referring to Israel's future in the benedictions before and after the *Shema* are later interpolations which were opposed by men like Saadia and Rashi. But, because they are truly edifying (like *or hadash,* for example), we have retained them without change, even though they do not altogether correspond to the original intent of those benedictions.

37) Cf. *J.E.*, Vol. VII, pp. 673–674,, art. "Leipsic," *Jüdisches Lexikon,* Vol. III, pp. 1035–1038, art. "Leipzig," and Philipson, *op. cit.*, pp. 49f.

38) *Deutsche Gebete und Gesänge beim Gottesdienste im israelitischen Gemeindetempel zu Leipzig.* Leipzig, 1865.

39) Cf. Birnbaum, *op. cit.*, p. 11 and Note. Birnbaum has also adopted the change made by Goldschmidt. Without that change, the text would read: "Behold, He is the eternal Lord; to every creature He teacheth His greatness and His sovereignty." With the change, the text reads: "Behold, He is the eternal Lord; and every creature declareth His greatness and His sovereignty." The latter version seems more in accord with Maimonides' original formulation of the creed.

40) Goldschmidt copied this from Joël's Preface. See above, Note 36. Neither Joël nor Goldschmidt tell their readers that, although Amram's text *begins* with the words they have adopted, Amram's text also *continues* with the words, "and lead us speedily upright to our land"—words omitted from the two prayerbooks under discussion here. Cf. *Seder Rabh Amram,* ed. Frumkin. Vol. I, p. 196.

41) Cf. Birnbaum, *op. cit.*, pp. 93–95. The unchanged version reads: "Bless us with the three-fold blessing in Thy Torah, which was written by Thy servant Moses." Goldschmidt's version reads: "Bless us with the three-fold blessing which was written in the Torah by Thy servant Moses." In the next point raised by Goldschmidt, referring to the same prayer, the changed reading introduced by Goldschmidt speaks about "the priests *of* Thy holy people," whereas the traditional version speaks about "the priests, Thy holy people." In view of the other changes introduced by Goldschmidt, which he does *not* mention in his Preface, those two were hardly worth the *apologia.*

42) Cf. Ludwig Philippson, *Neues Israelitisches Gebetbuch.* Berlin, 1864. This prayerbook contains the main Hebrew prayers in their unchanged traditional form, but provides them with an elaborate German paraphrase written from a distinct Reform point of view. Philippson had intended this prayerbook to be used while the modern worshipper was attending traditionalist services.

43) Stein is obviously confining his survey to Reform rituals written for the use of entire Jewish communities, rather than for separatist Reform groups. Otherwise he would also have had to mention the liturgy of the Berlin *Reformgemeinde,* which preceded Geiger's prayerbooks, and which was radically and consistently "Reform."

44) On the background and composition of the Danzig Jewish community, cf. Sam Echt, "Das jüdische Schul- und Erziehungswesen in Danzig," in *Bulletin des Leo Baeck Instituts,* Vol. VI, No. 24. Tel-Aviv, 1963, pp. 352ff.

45) Above, pp. 36ff.

46) Cf. Caesar Seligmann, "Hundertzwanzig Jahre Hamburger Tempel," in Bruno Italiener, *Festschrift zum hundertzwanzigjährigen Bestehen des israelitischen Tempels in Hamburg.* Hamburg, 1937, p. 12.

47) Above, pp. 39–42.

48) *Vorbemerkungen zu dem von dem Gr. Badischen Oberrat der Israeliten herausgegebenen Gebetbuch.* (Karlsruhe), n.d.

49) Cf. *Jüdisches Lexikon,* Vol. V, p. 359, art. "Seligmann, Caesar." Also *Year Book of the Leo Baeck Institute,* Vol. V. London, 1960, p. 346.

50) A. Z. Idelsohn, *Jewish Liturgy and its Development.* New York, Henry Holt, 1932, p. 300.

51) *Denkschrift zu dem im Auftrag der israel. Gemeinde in Frankfurt a. M. bearbeiteten neuen israelitischen Gebetbuch von Rabbiner Dr. C. Seligmann.* Frankfort o. M., 1912. 70 pp.

52) Seligmann confuses some of the dates here. Holdheim died in 1860. The reference in Levin is *not* to the prayerbook which Holdheim published. The latter is referred to by Levin on page 92, and is the prayerbook of 1848. It is the later prayerbook of 1885, published long after Holdheim's death, which Levin (p. 96) has in mind when he speaks of its more "traditional" form. Cf. Moritz Levin, *Die Reform des Judentums.* Berlin, 1895, pp. 91ff.

53) But the 1926 edition of Volume II, and the 1928 edition of Volume I, are obviously the result of a later acceptance of this particular "thesis," showing that Seligmann must have pursued the matter again after the appearance of the 1910 prayerbook.

54) The 1928 edition of Volume I *did* include special provisions for the second and eighth days of the festivals—an indication that those days were "still rooted in the hearts of the participants in the new worship service." In this connection we recall the report (see Note 23, above), dated 1846, that Leopold Stein, as rabbi of the Frankfort congregation, had abolished the second days of the festivals!

55) But cf. Vogelstein's edition of the prayerbook for Westphalia (1894), where Geiger's emended version of those prayers *was* followed.

56) While not using Geiger's formulation, Seligmann did not, after all, shun an "unaccustomed formulation." He substituted his own. See Vol. I, pp. 397f.

57) Cf. David Philipson, *op. cit.*, pp. 21f., and Graetz, *op. cit.*, p. 288.

58) בית יעקב—*Gebete für den Gottesdienst im "Tempel" der Jacobsonschule zu Seesen am Harz,* ed. A. Strauss. Seesen, 1911.

59) Cf. A. Z. Idelsohn, *Jewish Music.* New York, Henry Holt, 1929, pp. 235f.

60) See the reproduction of a page from Jacobson's hymnal in Idelsohn, *op. cit.*, p. 237.

61) See above, pp. 73ff.

62) *Liberal Jewish Prayer Book,* ed. Israel I. Mattuck. Vol. I. London, 1926, pp. 56–58.

63) *Op. cit.*, p. 183.

64) Included are poems by P. Sidney, Emily Brontë, A. H. Clough, Browning, Wordsworth, Shelley, Milton, Coleridge, Matthew Arnold, Keats, and others.

65) This presupposes a very broad interpretation of what is meant by the "form" of the traditional services, seeing that Mattuck, throughout, changes the position and sequence in which the traditional prayers he retains occur in the traditional liturgy itself.

66) *Sabbath Services*. Experimental edition. Selected from the Weekday and Sabbath Prayerbook to be published under the direction of The Ministers' Conference of the Union of Liberal and Progressive Synagogues. London, The Liberal Jewish Synagogue, 1964.

67) Cf. Erwin Rosenthal, "Ismar Elbogen and the New Jewish Learning," in *Year Book of the Leo Baeck Institute,* Vol. VIII. London, 1963, pp. 3–28.

68) Cf. *Jüdisches Lexikon,* Vol. V, pp. 1220f., art. "Vogelstein, Hermann."

69) Cf. Philipson, *op. cit.,* pp. 404ff.

70) The qualifying words, "in Baden," would seem to indicate that, outside of Baden, there *were* congregations which adopted this prayerbook. However, we have not come across any other evidence which would substantiate this surmise.

71) In certain contexts within the literature under discussion, the word "liturgy" (*Liturgie*) was used to describe, not the prayerbook as a whole, but the German prayers recited by the rabbi within the context of an otherwise Hebrew service, e.g., the prayer said before taking the Torah out of the Ark, the prayer for the government and the congregation, etc.

CHAPTER EIGHT

1) See the chapter on "Some Characteristics of Jewish Liturgy," above, pp. 22–30. For the text of the Eighteen Benedictions, cf. Philip Birnbaum, ed., *Daily Prayer Book.* New York, Hebrew Publishing Co., 1949, pp. 81–95.

2) Cf. Birnbaum, *op. cit.,* p. 91.

3) *Ibid.,* p. 93.

4) The following substitute *ge-ullah* for *go-el:* Geiger (1870); Leipzig (1876); Stein (1882); Vogelstein/Westphalia (1894); Seligmann (1910); Mattuck (1926); Seligmann (1928); Liberal and Progressive Synagogues/England (1967).

5) For full bibliographical description of the prayerbooks mentioned in this chapter, see the listing on pp. 1–21.

6) *Liberal Jewish Prayer Book,* ed. Israel I. Mattuck. Vol. I. London, 1926, pp. if.

7) Except to the editors of the 1967 prayerbook of the Union of Liberal and Progressive Synagogues in England, who were disturbed by the possible angelological implications of the word *qedoshim,* and who changed the text accordingly.

8) Cf. *Israelitisches Gebetbuch,* ed. Caesar Seligmann. Vol. I. Frankfort o. M., 1910, pp. 69f.

9) Maier, who omits Benedictions 14 and 15 altogether, achieves a total of 18 Benedictions by breaking up the Benediction for the judges into two.

10) Note Geiger's combination of Benedictions 14 and 15 into one. They were one in the early Palestinian rite, though the concluding eulogy there, unlike Geiger's, made mention of both David and Jerusalem. See Elbogen, *Der jüdische Gottesdienst in seiner geschichtlichen Entwicklung.*[4] Hildesheim, Georg Olms, 1962, pp. 52ff.

11) The accompanying German translation, however, makes it quite clear that the "choosing" is understood to have been in the past only: ". . . der Du einst Jerusalem erwählt hast."

12) This seems to be a conflate version of both the traditional text, which names David as the "servant," and of the version printed in Göteborg, in 1858, which identified the "servant" with the "Messiah" thereby making it possible to refer the object of the petition to Israel, the "messianic" people. The version given here, perhaps quite unintentionally, stresses the connection between messianism and the Davidic dynasty even more than does the traditional version.

13) Cf. Birnbaum, *op. cit.,* p. 627.

14) Cf. Rashi to b. *Berakhoth* 11b, s.v. *wa'abhodah.*

15) The substitution of *werinnath yisra-el* for *we-ishé yisra-el* calls to mind the attempt made in England by the Rev. Morris Joseph, in 1890, to substitute *weshiré yisra-el* ("and the songs of Israel") for *we-ishé yisra-el* ("and the fire-offerings of Israel"). Cf. David Philipson, *The Reform Movement in Judaism.* New York, Macmillan, 1907, pp. 538ff. Morris Joseph was an Orthodox minister at that time, but, on account of his refusal to pray for the restoration of animal sacrifices, he soon thereafter found himself barred by the Chief Rabbi, and became minister of the West London (Reform) Synagogue.

16) That particular version of the Benediction became the standard version in the American *Union Prayer Book.*

17) This is an adaptation of the traditional Sepharadi version of this Benediction, for which cf. Moses Gaster, ed., *The Book of Prayer and Order of Service according to the Custom of the Spanish and Portuguese Jews.* Vol. I. London, 1949, p. 34. The unemended Sepharadi version was taken over by the first edition of the *Forms of Prayer* of the West London Synagogue, 1841. The fourth edition, 1921, of the volume containing the "Prayers for the Festivals," (and perhaps already earlier editions and other volumes which we have been unable to consult) reads *uthephilloth yisra-el* ("and the prayers of Israel") instead of *we-ishé yisra-el* ("and the fire-offerings of Israel"). The sixth edition of Volume I, 1931, changing "who restorest Thy divine presence to Zion" into "who causest Thy divine presence to rest upon Zion," marks a further change in the realm of religious belief.

18) We have been able to consult the fourth edition, designated *"Für den Gebrauch der neuen Synagoge zu Königsberg i. Pr.,"* and published in Breslau, in 1896.

19) See the Preface to the Leipzig prayerbook, above pp. 176–178.

20) *Forms of Prayer used in the West London Synagogue of British Jews,* ed. D. W. Marks. Vol. I. London, 1841, p. ix.

21) *Forms of Prayer for Jewish Worship. First Supplement to Volume I. Evening Prayers.* Edited by the Ministers of the Association of Synagogues in Great Britain. 1952.

22) Cf. *Forms of Prayer for Jewish Worship,* edited for the use of their own and allied congregations by the Ministers of the West London Synagogue of British Jews. Volume I. 6th edition, 1931. Pp. 1–2; 11–13.

23) This volume appeared without a date of publication—as did all the other prayerbooks of the Union Libérale Israélite. For determining the date of this and the other volumes published in Paris, I am indebted to my friend, Rabbin André Zaoui, the present rabbi of the Union Libérale Israélite.

24) *Des Ailes à la Terre.* Paris, (1913), pp. 85–89.

25) *Rituel des Prières Journalières.* Paris, (1925), pp. 61–72.

26) *Ibid.,* p. 127.

27) *Ibid.,* p. 64.

28) *Ibid.,* pp. 358–359.

29) *Rituel des Prières Journalières.* Paris, (1958), pp. 191–207.

30) Cf., for example, *Gebeden en Gezangen voor de Godsdienstoefeningen op den Grooten Verzoendag.* Amsterdam, Verbond van Liberaal-Religieuse Joden in Nederland, 1934. See pp. 34–35.

31) Cf. *Gebeden voor Vrijdagavond en Sjabbat.* Amsterdam, Den Haag, Verbond van Liberaal Religieuse Joden, n.d. See pp. 12–13.

32) Published by Solomon Schechter in *J.Q.R.,* Vol. X (1898), pp. 656ff.

33) In a private communication to the author, dated June 10, 1965.

34) *Gebetbuch für den Freitagabend,* ed. Eugen J. Messinger and Lothar Rothschild. Vereinigung für Religiös-Liberales Judentum in der Schweiz, 1965. See p. 13.

35) Cf. Lothar Rothschild, "Ergänzender Hinweis," in *Tradition und Erneuerung,* No. 21 (May, 1966), pp. 348–350.

CHAPTER NINE

1) Cf. Ismar Elbogen, *Der jüdische Gottesdienst in seiner geschichtlichen Entwicklung.*[4] Hildesheim, Georg Olms, 1962, pp. 115–117. For the traditional texts, see Philip Birnbaum, *Daily Prayer Book.* New York, Hebrew Publishing Company, 1949, pp. 391–403 (for Sabbath), and pp. 609–625 (for festivals).

2) Cf. *Forms of Prayer Used in the West London Synagogue of British Jews,* ed. D. W. Marks. Vol. I. London, 1841, pp. 74–75. *Musaph* is abbreviated in this liturgy, but the abbreviations affect the first three and last three benedictions only, and not the part in which the petition for the restoration of the sacrificial cult is voiced.

3) See above, pp. 148f.

4) See above, pp. 196f.

5) Cf. Simon Bernfeld, תולדות הריפורמציון הדתית בישראל. Cracow, 1900, p. 242.

6) *Die Deutsche Synagoge,* Vol. I. Berlin, 1817, pp. 78–98 (*Musaph* for New Year), and pp. 198–227 (*Musaph* for the Day of Atonement).

7) *Protocolle der ersten Rabbiner-Versammlung.* Brunswick, 1844, pp. 45f. and 103.

8) *Op. cit.,* p. 62.

9) *Protokolle und Aktenstücke der zweiten Rabbiner-Versammlung.* Frankfort o. M., pp. 285–318.

10) *Op. cit.,* p. 314.

11) *Op. cit.,* pp. 106–124.

12) Cf. *J.E.,* Vol. I, p. 193, art. "Adler, Abraham Jacob."

13) *Protokolle und Aktenstücke der zweiten Rabbiner-Versammlung,* p. 382. The statement is there ascribed to S. Adler. But this is obviously a mistake—in the light of the cross-reference to page 111, and to what *A.* Adler said there, and in view of the specific mention of *A.* Adler's authorship of this statement in the footnote on page iii.

14) *Op. cit.,* pp. 123f.

15) *Op. cit.,* p. 172.

16) Leopold Stein, *Plan des neuen Gebetbuches für die öffentliche Gottesverehrung der Israeliten.* n.d. This leaflet was printed without indication of date or place of publication. The Hebrew Union College Library owns a copy

(Adler Collection, No. 351). Our identification of the leaflet, which must have appeared between 1845 and 1846, is based on the references made to it (with matching pagination and paragraphs) in *Protokolle der dritten Versammlung deutscher Rabbiner . . . Breslau, 13.–24. Juli, 1846*. Breslau, 1847, pp. 31ff.

17) *Plan des neuen Gebetbuches etc.*, pp. 11f.

18) *Protokolle der dritten Versammlung deutscher Rabbiner*, pp. 31–35.

19) *Op. cit.*, p. 34.

20) *Op. cit.*, p. 35.

21) *Op. cit.*, p. 36.

22) *Homiletisch-liturgische Beilage* to Vol. VII (1857) of Stein's *Der Israelitische Volkslehrer*, pp. 91–100.

23) Cf. Birnbaum, *op. cit.*, p. 395.

24) Cf. Birnbaum, *op. cit.*, p. 613.

25) Cf. Birnbaum, *op. cit.*, p. 621.

26) See above, pp. 148f.

27) Geiger is aided here by the ambiguity of the word *musaph*, which can mean both the "additional sacrifice" and the "additional (prayer) service." By omitting the word *wenaqribh* from the traditional prayer, Geiger makes it clear that he is referring to the "additional (prayer) service" only; but, both stylistically and grammatically, the resultant phrase is somewhat clumsy.

28) See Note 22, above. The *Musaph* text is on page 99.

29) Cf. Eliezer ben Yehudah, *Thesaurus*, Vol. XIV, p. 6878, note 2.

30) See above, pp.. 176–178.

31) This form, derived from a different root, although not accepted by the current Ashkenazi rite, was used by the twelfth-century French scholar, Abraham ben Nathan (Hayarḥi). Cf. Baer, *'Abhodath Yisra-el*, pp. 238ff.

32) In the accompanying German version there is no mention of Temple or sacrifice at all, but a separate meditation of a religious and historical nature is devoted to each festival.

33) See Note 32, above.

34) The complete traditional text is also given, but in small print and without translation.

35) See Note 22, above.

CHAPTER TEN

1) Cf. Jakob J. Petuchowski, "Karaite Tendencies in an Early Reform Haggadah," in *HUCA*, Vol. XXXI (1960), pp. 223–249.

2) Cf. W. Gunther Plaut, *The Rise of Reform Judaism*. New York, 1963, pp. 112–124; and Jakob J. Petuchowski, "Manuals and Catechisms of the Jewish Religion in the Early Period of Emancipation," in *Studies in Nineteenth-Century Jewish Intellectual History*, ed. Alexander Altmann. Harvard University Press, 1964, pp. 47–64.

3) Cf. Jakob J. Petuchowski, "The Magnification of Chanukah," in *Commentary*, January 1960, pp. 38–43.

4) Cf. Jakob J. Petuchowski, *The Theology of Haham David Nieto*. New York, 1954, pp. 69ff.

5) סדר התפלות כמנהג הקראים. Vol. II. Cairo, 5695, p. 210.

6) *Op. cit.*, Vol. I. Cairo, 5706, p. 43.

7) *Minhag America*, (Cincinnati, 1857), Part I, pp. 112 and 113 in the Hebrew section.

8) סדר העבודה–*Ordnung der öffentlichen Andacht*, ed. S. J. Fränkel and M. J. Bresselau. Hamburg, 1819.

9) Abraham Geiger, *Der Hamburger Tempelstreit, eine Zeitfrage*. Breslau, 1842, pp. 78–80.

10) סדר עבודת ה'–*Gebetbuch nach dem Ritus der israelitischen Gemeinde in Aachen*. Aachen, 5613.

11) סדר תפלה דבר יום ביומו–*Israelitisches Gebetbuch*. Breslau, 1854.

12) סדר תפלה דבר יום ביומו–*Israelitisches Gebetbuch*. Vol. I. Berlin, 1870, pp. 95, 138, and 139; and cf. page 184 for the *lulabh*.

13) סדר תפלה–*Israelitisches Gebetbuch*. Vol. I. Berlin, 1872, pp. 133, 178, and 179; and cf. pp. 232f. for the *lulabh*.

14) סדר העבודה–*Bönbok*, Vol. II, Sabbath and Festivals. Göteborg, 1858, p. 69.

15) Private communication from the late Chief Rabbi Dr. Kurt Wilhelm, Stockholm, dated August 23, 1964.

16) סדר העבודה–*Gebetbuch für Israelitische Gemeinden*, Vol. I. Frankfort o. M., 1860.

17) סדר תפלות כל השנה—*Gebetbuch für den öffentlichen Gottesdienst.* 3 volumes. Berlin, 1866.

18) עבודה שבלב—*Der Gottesdienst des Herzens,* ed. M. Levin. Vol. I. Nuremberg, 1874.

19) סדר העבודה—*Israelitisches Gebetbuch,* ed. A. M. Goldschmidt. Vol. I. Leipzig, 1876.

20) סדר תפלות כל השנה—*Gebetbuch für die neue Synagoge in Berlin.* Vol. I. Berlin, 1881.

21) סדר העבודה—*Gebetbuch für israelitische Gemeinden.* Vol. I. Mannheim, 1882.

22) Leopold Stein, "Bericht über das, für die neue Hauptsynagoge zu Frankfurt am Main anzufertigende neue Gebetbuch," in *Der Israelitische Volkslehrer,* Vol. V, pp. 165–195. Frankfort o. M., 1855.

23) *Op. cit.,* p. 177.

24) *Israelitisches Gebetbuch.* Glogau, 1892(?), p. 204.

25) *Op. cit.,* p. 286.

26) *Op. cit.,* p. 288.

27) *Op. cit.,* p. 204.

28) סדר תפלה—*Israelitisches Gebetbuch,* ed. Vogelstein. Vol. I. Verband der Synagogen-Gemeinden Westfalens, 1894.

29) *Gebetbuch* herausgegeben von dem Grossherzoglich Badischen Oberrat der Israeliten. Printed as manuscript. Karlsruhe, n.d. (1905).

30) סדר תפלות כל השנה-*Gebetbuch der jüdischen Gemeinde zu Braunschweig.* Vol. I. Brunswick, 1906.

31) תפלת ישראל-*Bönbok for den offentliga Gudstjensten inom Mosaiska Församlingen i Stockholm.* Second edition. Rödelheim, 1907.

32) *Israelitisches Gebetbuch,* ed. C. Seligmann. Vol. I. Frankfort o. M., 1910.

33) תפלות כל השנה—*Rituel des Prières Journalières.* Paris, Union Libérale Israélite, n.d. (1925).

34) תפלות לכל השנה-*Gebetbuch für das ganze Jahr* bearbeitet im Auftrag des Liberalen Kultus-Ausschusses des Preussischen Landesverbandes jüdischer Gemeinden. Vol. I. Frankfort o. M., 1929.

35) סדר התפלות—*Forms of Prayer for Jewish Worship* edited for the Use of their Own and Allied Congregations by the Ministers of the West London Synagogue of British Jews. Vol. I. 6th edition. Oxford University Press, 1931.

36) תפלה לעדת ישורון—*Gebete für die öffentliche Gottesverehrung in der Synagoge zu Mainz*. Frankfort o. M., 1853. About the reasons for identifying the editor of this prayerbook with Joseph Aub, see our treatment of the Prayerbook Introductions, p. 147.

37) Morris Joseph, *Judaism as Creed and Life*. 2nd edition. London, Routledge, 1910, pp. 26ff. A somewhat similar point of view had already been expressed by Heinemann Vogelstein, in the Preface to his 1894 edition of the prayerbook. He wrote (page v): "We want to be truthful in everything we say, and most particularly so when, in prayer, we turn to the God of Truth. But I do not believe that I have offended against the principle of truthfulness by retaining, in their old form, the benedictions before the performance of commandments ordained by the scribes: before the recitation of the *Hallel* Psalms, before the kindling of the Hanukkah lights, and before the reading from the Book of Esther. Especially from the liberal point of view, which recognizes the evolution in religious matters, it did not seem right to me to designate as 'commanded by God' only those provisions which are contained in the Torah, while withholding this designation from the ordinances of the teachers of Israel who were filled with the spirit of God." But this *apologia* notwithstanding, Vogelstein retained the traditional form of the *Hebrew* benedictions only, while, as we have noted, completely departing from any idea of 'divine commandment' in his German paraphrases.

38) Israel Abrahams, *The Union and the Festivals*. Papers for Jewish People, No. XI. Revised edition. London, Jewish Religious Union, 1915.

39) *Op. cit.*, pp. 2–4.

40) *Liberal Jewish Prayer Book*, ed. Israel I. Mattuck. Vol. I. London, Liberal Jewish Synagogue, 1926.

41) סדר טוב להודות—*Gebeden voor Sjabbat en Feestdagen*. Verbond van Liberaal Religieuse Joden in Nederland, 1964.

42) מחזור לשלש רגלים—*Prayers for the Pilgrim Festivals*. Edited by the Assembly of Ministers of the Reform Synagogues of Great Britain. Amsterdam, 1965.

43) סדר התפלות—*Forms of Prayer Used in the West London Synagogue of British Jews*, ed. D. W. Marks. Vol. II. London, 1842, p. 50.

CHAPTER ELEVEN

1) David Friedländer, *Ueber die, durch die neue Organisation der Judenschaften der Preussischen Staaten nothwendig gewordene, Umbildung 1. ihres Gottesdienstes in den Synagogen, 2. ihrer Unterrichts-Anstalten, und deren Lehrgegenstände, und 3. ihres Erziehungs-Wesens überhaupt.—Ein Wort zu seiner Zeit.* (Published anonymously.) Berlin, 1812, pp. 16f.

2) *Ibid.*, pp. 33f.

3) *Israelitisches Gebetbuch*, ed. Abraham Geiger. Breslau, 1854, p. vi.

4) *Israelitisches Gebetbuch . . . mit Benutzung des bislang eingeführt gewesenen Rabbiner Dr. Geiger'schen Buches,* ed. M. Joël. Part I. Berlin, 1872.

5) M. Joël, *Zur Orientirung in der Cultusfrage.* Breslau, 1869.

6) Joël, *op. cit.,* p. 24.

7) "Etwas über Glauben und Beten. Zu Schutz und Trutz," in Geiger's *Jüdische Zeitschrift für Wissenschaft und Leben.* Vol. VII. Breslau, 1869, pp. 1–59. Pages 52–54 contain Geiger's critique of Joël's stand on Jerusalem.

8) M. Joël, *Zum Schutz gegen "Trutz."* Breslau, 1869.

9) *Israelitisches Gebetbuch,* ed. Abraham Geiger. Part I. Berlin, 1870.

10) *Gebetbuch für Israelitische Gemeinden,* ed. Leopold Stein. Part I. Mannheim, 1882.

11) Stein, *op. cit.,* p. iii.

12) *Forms of Prayer Used in the West London Synagogue of British Jews,* ed. D. W. Marks. Vol. I. London, 1841, p. 13.

13) *Ibid.,* p. 17.

14) For the "Biblicist" character of that congregation and its liturgy, cf. Jakob J. Petuchowski, "Karaite Tendencies in an Early Reform Haggadah," in *HUCA,* Vol. XXXI (1960), pp. 223–249.

15) This prayer was printed on gummed paper for insertion into the 1931 edition. The same prayer, with minor verbal changes, occurs, both in Hebrew and in English, in *Prayers for the Pilgrim Festivals.* New edition. Edited by the Assembly of Ministers of the Reform Synagogues of Great Britain. 1965. Page 58.

16) *Prayer Book for Jewish Worship throughout the year.* Revised edition . . . by Rabbi Jakob J. Kokotek. Part II. London, 1962.

17) *Ibid.,* p. 591.

18) *Seder. Tobh Lehodoth. Gebeden voor Sjabbat en Feestdagen ten gebruike in de Liberaal-Joodse Gemeenten in Nederland.* Vol. I. 1964. Pp. 76f.

19) סידור התפילות לשבת. מהדורה זמנית. ירושלים, החוגים ליהדות מתקדמת, תשכ"ב, דף 30.

20) Cf. Jakob J. Petuchowski, "Reform Prayer Out of Zion," in *C.C.A.R. Journal,* April 1963, pp. 31–37.

21) *Sabbath Prayer Book.* Third printing. New York, The Jewish Reconstructionist Foundation, 1953, pp. 164–166.

22) See pp. 214–239, above.

23) *Israelitisches Gebetbuch für die öffentliche Andacht . . .* , ed. A. M. Goldschmidt. Part I. Leipzig, 1876.

24) See I. Elbogen, *Der jüdische Gottesdienst,* pp. 19f., about the evolution of this particular benediction.

25) *Seder Rav Amram,* ed. Frumkin. Vol. I, p. 192.

26) *Ibid.,* p. 196.

27) *Siddur R. Saạdja Gaon,* ed. Davidson, Assaf, and Joel. Jerusalem, Mekize Nirdamim, 1941, p. 14.

28) *The Book of Prayer and Order of Service according to the Custom of the Spanish and Portuguese Jews,* ed. Moses Gaster. Vol. I. London, 1949, p. 28.

29) *Tikhlal Shibhath Tziyon,* ed. Joseph Kapaḥ. Vol. I. Jerusalem, Eshkol, 5712, p. 22.

30) *Daily Prayer Book,* ed. Philip Birnbaum. New York, Hebrew Publishing Co., 1949, p. 75.

31) *Seder Tephilloth Keminhag Italiani,* ed. D. Camerini. Torino, 1912, p. 60.

32) For full bibliographical details of the prayerbooks used here, see the listing on pp. 1–21, above.

33) Cf. Birnbaum, *op. cit.,* pp. 361ff.

34) Cf. Elbogen, *op. cit.,* p. 199.

35) Cf. Abraham Rosenfeld, ed., *The Authorized Kinoth for the Ninth of Ab.* London, 1965, p. 176.

36) The same sentiment was expressed in American Reform Judaism by David Einhorn, in *Olath Tamid—Book of Prayers for Jewish Congregations,* tr. Emil G. G. Hirsch. 1896, pp. 141–147. Further examples of European Ninth of Abh prayers can be found in W. Gunther Plaut, *The Growth of Reform Judaism.* New York, WUPJ, 1965, pp. 302–304.

37) Cf. Rosenfeld, *op. cit.,* pp. 36–37.

38) *Ibid.,* p. 37.

39) *Ibid.,* p. 38.

40) *Ibid.,* p. 39.

41) *Ibid.,* pp. 152–153.

42) *Ibid.,* pp. 161–162.

43) *Ibid.,* p. 176.

44) *Ibid.*, p. 177.

45) *Ibid.*, pp. 178–179.

46) *Ibid.*, p. 179.

47) Friedlaender, *op. cit.*, pp. 33f.

CHAPTER TWELVE

1) Cf. Philip Birnbaum, *Daily Prayer Book*. New York, Hebrew Publishing Company, 1949, pp. 135–137.

2) Cf. Joseph Heinemann, *Prayer in the Period of the Tanna'im and the Amora'im* (Hebrew). Jerusalem, Magnes Press, 1964, pp. 173–175.

3) Cf. Philip Birnbaum, *High Holyday Prayer Book*. New York, Hebrew Publishing Company, 1951, pp. 333–335.

4) Cf. Ismar Elbogen, *Der jüdische Gottesdienst in seiner geschichtlichen Entwicklung.*[4] *Hildesheim,* Georg Olms, 1962, p. 80.

5) Cf. Leo Baeck, "Das Reich des Allmächtigen," in *Festgabe für Claude G. Montefiore*. Berlin, Philo Verlag, 1928, pp. 7–10.

6) Cf. the version of the "Adoration" in the American *Union Prayer Book,* Newly Revised, Vol. I, pp. 71f.

7) *Sabbath and Festival Prayer Book*. The Rabbinical Assembly of America and the United Synagogue of America. 1947. Page 37.

8) Cf. *J.E.*, Vol. I, pp. 336–338, art. "*'Alenu.*"

9) *The Book of Prayer and Order of Service according to the Custom of the Spanish and Portuguese Jews,* ed. Moses Gaster. Volume I, Oxford University Press, 1949, pp. 57f. Actually, Gaster, in his translation, shows his own apologetic tendency by rendering the Hebrew participles into the past tense, viz.: "who worshipped . . . , and made supplication. . . ."

10) See above, pp. 223–225.

11) Cf. Jakob J. Petuchowski, *"Alenu,"* in *The Synagogue Review,* London, January 1951, pp. 141f.

12) Joseph L. Saalschütz, *Das Gebetbuch der Synagoge*. Königsberg, 1858, pp. 35f.

13) Thus in the Fourth Service, where it is used as a concluding prayer. The Ninth Service actually *begins* with an English version of the *'Alenu.* There, the relevant clause reads: ". . . Who chose His people Israel to make known to all mankind His righteousness and Unity." Cf. *Liberal Jewish Prayer Book,* ed. Israel I. Mattuck. London, 1926. Vol. I, pages 103 and 183.

CHAPTER THIRTEEN

1) *Mishnah Berakhoth* 4: 4.

2) B. *Berakhoth* 29b.

3) See, for example, the fourth edition, 1921, p. 70.

4) Cf. *Prayers for the Pilgrim Festivals*. New edition. Edited by The Assembly of Ministers of The Reform Synagogues of Great Britain. 1965. Pages 60f. and ii.

5) Cf. A. Wiener, *Der Oeffentliche Gottesdienst, ein Wort zur Beherzigung*. Oppeln, 1873, p. 11.

6) Cf. Philip Birnbaum, *Daily Prayer Book*. New York, Hebrew Publishing Company, 1949, p. 15.

7) Cf. Birnbaum, *op. cit.*, p. 383.

8) Cf. Birnbaum, *op. cit.*, p. 13.

9) Cf. *The Traditional Prayer Book*, ed. David de Sola Pool. New York, Behrman House, 1960, p. 635. But note how, in his English "translation" on page 636, Pool has glossed over the specific folkloristic reference to the messianic fulfilment!

10) This should be compared with the standard translations of the Bible; Deuteronomy 6: 4–9, and 11: 13–21.

11) See Birnbaum, *op. cit.*, pp. 82–86 for the literal translation of those prayers.

CHAPTER FOURTEEN

1) Cf. David de Sola Pool, *The Old Jewish-Aramaic Prayer, the Kaddish*. Leipzig, Rudolf Haupt, 1909.

2) Cf. Elbogen, *Der jüdische Gottesdienst*, pp. 95ff.

3) Philip Birnbaum, *Daily Prayer Book*. New York, Hebrew Publishing Company, 1949, pp. 737–739.

4) Birnbaum, *op. cit.*, p. 137.

5) *Ordnung der öffentlichen Andacht etc.* Hamburg, 1819, pp. 22–25.

6) *Mishnah Sanhedrin* 10:1, quoting Isaiah 60:21.

7) B. *Berakhoth* 17a, quoting Ecclesiastes 7:1, with minor deviations from the Talmudic wording.

8) *Mishnah Aboth* 2:16, with minor omissions and changes.

9) For the text, see *The Book of Prayer and Order of Service according to the Custom of the Spanish and Portuguese Jews,* ed. Moses Gaster. Vol. I. Oxford University Press, 1949, pp. 200–203, 205–206.

10) Birnbaum, *op. cit.*, p. 737.

11) Birnbaum, *op. cit.*, pp. 45–47.

12) *Gebetbuch der israelitischen Gemeinde in Aachen.* Aachen, 1853, pp. 199f.

13) *Israelitisches Gebet- und Andachtsbuch,* ed. Maier. Stuttgart, 1848, pp. 29–31.

14) *Israelitisches Gebetbuch,* ed. Geiger. Breslau, 1854, pp. 233ff.

15) *Gebetbuch etc., ed.* Stein. Frankfort o. M., 1860, pp. 52–54.

16) *Israelitisches Gebetbuch etc.* Hamburg, 1868, pp. 44–47.

17) *Israelitisches Gebetbuch,* ed. Geiger. Berlin, 1870, pp. 69f.

18) *Gebetbuch für die neue Synagoge in Berlin.* Vol. I. Berlin, 1881, p. 275.

19) *Op. cit.*, p. 101, etc.

20) *Gebetbuch für israelitische Gemeinden,* ed. Stein. Mannheim, 1882, p. 39.

21) *Israelitisches Gebetbuch,* ed. Vogelstein. Vol. I. Westphalia, 1894, pp. 106–109.

22) *Israelitisches Gebetbuch,* ed. Seligmann. Vol. I. Frankfort o. M., 1910, pp. 350–353, and 411–414.

23) Cf. A. Hyman, אוצר דברי חכמים ופתגמיהם. Third printing. Tel-Aviv, Dvir, 1955, p. 271.

24) Solomon B. Freehof, "Hazkarath Neshamoth," in *Hebrew Union College Annual,* Vol. XXXVI (1965), pp. 179–189.

25) Birnbaum, *op. cit.*, p. 605.

26) Birnbaum, *loc. cit.*

27) Birnbaum, *op. cit.*, p. 607.

28) Joseph H. Hertz, ed., *The Authorised Daily Prayer Book.* Revised edition. New York, Bloch, 1948, p. 1107.

29) Max Joseph, art. "Haskarat Neschamot," in *Jüdisches Lexikon,* Vol. II, pp. 1450–1452.

30) *Ordnung der öffentlichen Andacht etc.* Hamburg, 1819, pp. 279–288.

31) A. Wiener, *Der Oeffentliche Gottesdienst, ein Wort zur Beherzigung*. Oppeln, 1873, p. 14.

32) Max Joseph, *op. cit.*, p. 1452.

CHAPTER FIFTEEN

1) Cf. *Maḥzor Matteh Levi,* Part I, New York, Jerusalem Book Store, 1950, p. 1.

2) Elbogen, *Der jüdische Gottesdienst,*[4] Hildesheim, 1962, pp. 153f.

3) Elbogen, *loc. cit.*

4) See *J. E.*, Vol. IX, pp. 367–368, art. "Oath More Judaico."

5) Cf. A. Z. Idelsohn, *Jewish Music*. New York, Tudor Publishing Co., 1944, pp. 159f.

6) *Protocolle der ersten Rabbiner-Versammlung*. Brunswick, 1844, pp. 33–42.

7) *Op. cit.*, pp. 41f.

8) Joseph Aub, *Die Eingangsfeier des Versöhnungstages*. Mayence, 1863, pp. 15f.

9) Kurt Wilhelm, "The Jewish Community in the Post-Emancipation Period," in *Year Book of the Leo Baeck Institute,* Vol. II. London, 1957, p. 64.

10) Communicated by Rabbi Dr. Immanuel Jakobovits, in a letter to the author, dated May 23rd, 1963.

11) Leo Trepp, *Die Landesgemeinde der Juden in Oldenburg*. Oldenburg, 1965, p. 45.

12) On Stein, cf. *J. E.*, Vol. XI, p. 540.

13) For an English translation of the complete anthem, see Einhorn's *Olath Tamid,* tr. Emil G. Ḥirsch. 1913, pp. 64–66.

14) Leopold Stein, *Ḥizzuq Habayith*. Erlangen, 1840, pp. 81f.

15) See Lion Wolff, *Universal-Agende für jüdische Kultusbeamte*. Second ed. Berlin, 1891, pp. 332–335.

16) *Deutsche Gebete und Gesänge beim Gottesdienste im Israelitischen Gemeindetempel* zu Leipzig. 1865, p. 12.

17) This text appeared in *Israelitische Wochen-Schrift,* Vol. II, pp. 301f. (Breslau, 1871), with a Hannover dateline, and the following introduction: "The *Kol Nidré* formula newly introduced here last year might be of sufficient interest

to the readers of the *Wochenschrift* for it to be imparted to them." The Breslau *Wochenschrift* represented the point of view of German Conservative Judaism. Note that there is no editorial comment, positive or negative, accompanying this Hannover report.

18) Cf. *J. E.*, Vol. VIII, p. 527, art. "Meyer, Samuel."

19) Cf. D. Leimdörfer, *Festschrift zum hundertjährigen Bestehen des Israelitischen Tempels in Hamburg*. Hamburg, 1918, p. 62.

20) Cf. Philip Birnbaum, *Daily Prayer Book*. New York, Hebrew Publishing Company, 1949, p. 89.

21) *Gebete und Lieder für die Sabbate und Festtage nebst Synagogen- und Gebet-Ordnung für die Synagogen-Gemeinde Beuthen O.-S.* Beuthen, 1906.

EPILOGUE

1) Cf. A. Z. Idelsohn, *Jewish Liturgy and its Development*. New York, Henry Holt, 1932, pp. 47–55.

2) *Shulḥan 'Arukh, Orah Ḥayyim* 1: 4.

3) About Löwengard, see *J. E.*, Vol. VIII, p. 194, s. v. "Löwengard, Max." But note the deviating details in Tanzer, *Geschichte der Juden in Württemberg*. 1937, p. 74.

4) The literal translation of this verse is, "Praise waiteth for Thee." But the words, when taken out of context, lend themselves to the translation quoted by Löwengard. Cf. b. *'Erubhin* 19a.

5) M. Löwengard, *Auch einige Worte über das neue Gebetbuch im Hamburger Tempel*. Tübingen, 1842, pp. 21f.

6) Hermann Vogelstein, "Der gegenwärtige Stand des religiösen Liberalismus in Deutschland," in *First Conference of the World Union for Liberal Judaism*. Berlin, 1928, pp. 29f.

Bibliography

(a) PRAYERBOOKS

(European Liberal and Reform Prayerbooks are listed in the chapter, "Chronological Bibliography.")

Baeck, Leo, ed., *Feldgebetbuch für die jüdischen Mannschaften des Heeres.* Berlin, H. Itzkowski, 1914.
Baer, Seligmann, ed., *Seder 'Abhodath Yisrael.* Berlin, Schocken, 5697.
Birnbaum, Philip, ed., *Daily Prayer Book.* New York, Hebrew Publishing Co., 1949.
Birnbaum, Philip, ed., *High Holiday Prayer Book.* New York, Hebrew Publishing Co., 1951.
Einhorn, David, *Olath Tamid—Book of Prayers for Jewish Congregations.* Transl. Emil G. Hirsch. 1896.
Friedländer, David, *Gebete der Juden auf das ganze Jahr.* Berlin, 1786.
Gaster, Moses, ed., *The Book of Prayer and Order of Service According to the Custom of the Spanish and Portuguese Jews.* Vol. I (1901). Oxford University Press, 1949.
Heidenhem, Wolf, ed., *Sepher Qerobhoth hu Mahzor.* 9 vols. Hannover, 5598/99.
Hertz, Joseph H., ed., *The Authorized Daily Prayer Book.* Revised edition. New York, Bloch, 1948.
Mahzor Matteh Levi. Part I, New York, Jerusalem Book Store, 1950.
Mannheimer, I. N. ed., *Gebete der Israeliten,* 2nd edition. Vienna, 1843.
Pool, David de Sola, ed., *The Traditional Prayer Book for Sabbath and Festivals.* New York, Behrman House, 1960.
Rosenfeld, Abraham, ed., *The Authorized Kinoth for the Ninth of Ab.* London, 1965.
Sabbath and Festival Prayer Book. The Rabbinical Assembly of America and the United Synagogue of America. 1947.
Sabbath Prayer Book. Third printing. New York, The Jewish Reconstructionist Foundation, 1953.
Seder Hatephilloth Keminhag Hakera-im. Vol. I, Cairo, 5706. Vol. II, Cairo, 5695.
Seder Rabh 'Amram Hashalem, ed. Frumkin, 2 vols. Jerusalem, 5672.
Seder Tephilloth Keminhag Italiani, ed. D. Camerini, Torino, 1912.
Siddur R. Saadia Gaon, ed. I. Davidson, S. Assaf, B. I. Joel. Jerusalem, Mekize Nirdamim, 1941.
Tikhlal Shibhath Tziyon, ed. Joseph Kapaḥ. Vol. I. Jerusalem, 5712.
The Union Prayerbook for Jewish Worship. Newly revised edition. Central Conference of American Rabbis, Vol. I (Cincinnati, 1948), Vol. II (New York, 1957).
Wise, Isaac M., ed., *Minhag America.* Vol. I. Cincinnati, 1857.
Wolff, Lion, ed., *Universal-Agende für jüdische Kultusbeamte,* 2nd edition. Berlin, 1891.

(a) PERIODICALS

Allgemeine Zeitung des Judenthums, ed. Ludwig Philippson, Vol. 1. Leipzig, 1837.
Allgemeine Zeitung des Judenthums, ed. Ludwig Philippson. Vol. VIII. Leipzig, 1844.
Allgemeine Zeitung des Judenthums, ed. Ludwig Philippson. Vol. XLVIII. Leipzig, 1884.
Allgemeine Zeitung des Judentums, ed. G. Karpeles. Vol. LXXI. Berlin, 1907.
Der Israelit. Vol. 48. Frankfort o.M., 1907.
Der Israelit des neunzehnten Jahrhunderts, ed. Mendel Hess. Vol. III. Herzfeld, 1842.
Der Israelitische Volkslehrer, ed. Leopold Stein. Vol. V. Frankfort o.M., 1855.
Der Israelitische Volkslehrer, ed. Leopold Stein. Vol. VII. Frankfort o.M., 1857.
Die Israelitische Wochenschrift. Vol. II. Breslau, 1871.
The Jewish Quarterly Review. Vol. X. London, 1898.
Jüdische Zeitschrift für Wissenschaft und Leben, ed. Abraham Geiger. Vol. VI. Breslau, 1868.
Jüdische Zeitschrift für Wissenschaft und Leben, ed. Abraham Geiger. Vol. VII. Breslau, 1869.
Liberales Judentum, ed. C. Seligmann. Vol. II. Frankfort o.M., 1910.
Literaturblatt des Orients, ed. Julius Fürst. Leipzig, 1842.
Der Orient, ed. Julius Fürst. Vol. III. Leipzig, 1842.
Die Reform des Judenthums, ed. A. Adler and H. Wagner. No. 32, Mannheim, Nov. 4, 1846.

(c) LITERATURE

Abrahams, Israel, *A Companion to the Authorized Daily Prayerbook.* New revised edition. New York, Hermon Press, 1966.
Abrahams, Israel, *The Union and the Festivals.* Papers for Jewish People, No. XI. Revised edition. London, Jewish Religious Union, 1915.
Altmann, Alexander, ed., *Studies in Nineteenth-Century Jewish Intellectual History.* Cambridge, Mass., Harvard University Press, 1964.
Altmann, Alexander, "Zur Frühgeschichte der jüdischen Predigt in Deutschland: Leopold Zunz als Prediger," in *Year Book of the Leo Baeck Institute,* Vol. VI. London, East & West Library, 1961, pp. 3–59.
Arnold, Stephen A., *Ideas of Immortality in American Reform Ritual.* (Unpublished M.A. Thesis in the Hebrew Union College Library.) 1961.
Aub, Joseph, *Die Eingangsfeier des Versöhnungstages.* Mainz, 1863.
Baden. *Vorbemerkungen zu dem von dem Gr. Badischen Oberrat der Israeliten herausgegebenen Gebetbuche.* n.d. (1905), 15 pp. [Inserted in some, but not all, copies of the prayerbook.]
Baeck, Leo, "Das Reich des Allmächtigen," in *Festgabe für Claude G. Montefiore.* Berlin, Philo Verlag, 1928, pp. 7–10.
Berliner, A., *Das Gebetbuch des Dr. Vogelstein beurtheilt.* Berlin, 1894.
Berliner, Abraham, כתבים נבחרים. Vol. I. Jerusalem, Mosad Harav Kook, 1945.
Bernfeld, Simon, דור חכם. Warsaw, Tushiyah, 1896.
Bernfeld, Simon, תולדות הריפורמציון הדתית בישראל. Cracow, 1900.
Birkenfeld. *Gottesdienstliche Anordnungen für die Israeliten des Fürstenthums Birkenfeld.* Birkenfeld, 1843.

(Blatt, Marcus), *Zur Einführung der Gebetbücher der neuen Synagoge in Berlin im israelitischen Gotteshause zu Troppau.* Berlin, 1884.
Breslauer, Walter, "Der Verband der Deutschen Juden," in *Bulletin des Leo Baeck Instituts,* No. 28. Tel-Aviv, 1964, p. 345ff.
Bresselau, M. J., חרב נוקמת נקם ברית. Hamburg, 1819.
(Caro, David), ברית אמת. Dessau, 1820.
Dembitz, Lewis N., *Jewish Services in Synagogue and Home.* Philadelphia, Jewish Publication Society, 1898.
Echt, Sam, "Das jüdische Schul-und Erziehungswesen in Danzig," in *Bulletin des Leo Baeck Instituts,* Vol. VI, No. 24. pp. 352ff. Tel-Aviv, 1963.
Elbogen, Ismar, *Der jüdische Gottesdienst in seiner geschichtlichen Entwicklung.* 4th Edition. Hildesheim, Georg Olms, 1962.
First Conference of the World Union for Liberal Judaism Berlin, 1928. London, 1928.
Fränkel, Seckel I., *Schutzschrift des zu Hamburg erschienenen Israelitischen Gebetbuchs.* Hamburg, 1819.
Frankfort o.M. *Synagogen-Ordnung für die Synagoge der Israelitischen Religionsgesellschaft in Frankfurt a.M.* Frankfort o.M., 1874.
Frankfurter, Naphtali, *Stillstand und Fortschritt.* Hamburg, 1841.
Freehof, Solomon B., "Hazkarath Neshamoth," in *HUCA,* Vol. XXXVI (1965), pp. 179–189.
Freehof, Solomon B., "Reform Judaism and Prayer," in *Reform Judaism—Essays by Hebrew Union College Alumni.* Cincinnati, H.U.C. Press, 1949.
Friedland, N., *Zur Geschichte des Tempels der Jacobsonschule.* Seesen, 1910.
Friedländer, David, *Über die, durch die neue Organisation der Judenschaften der Preussischen Staaten nothwendig gewordene, Umbildung 1. ihres Gottesdienstes in den Synagogen, 2. ihrer Unterrichts-Anstalten, und deren Lehrgegenstände, und 3. ihres Erziehungs-Wesens überhaupt.—Ein Wort zu seiner Zeit.* Berlin, 1812. (Published anonymously.)
Geiger, Abraham, *Denkschrift.* Frankfort, 1869.
Geiger, Abraham, *Etwas über Glauben und Beten—Zu Schutz und Trutz.* Breslau, 1869.
Geiger, Abraham, *Der Hamburger Tempelstreit, eine Zeitfrage.* Breslau, 1842.
Geiger, Abraham, *Leon da Modena.* Breslau, 1856.
Geiger, Abraham, *Nachgelassene Schriften,* ed. Ludwig Geiger, Vol. I. Berlin, 1875.
Geiger, Abraham, *Nothwendigkeit und Mass einer Reform des jüdischen Gottesdienstes.* Breslau, Julius Hainauer, 1861.
Geiger, Abraham, *Plan zu einem neuen Gebetbuche.* Breslau, 1870.
Geiger, Abraham, *Thesen für die am 29. d. in Leipzig zusammentretende Versammlung* (1869.)
Geiger, Ludwig, *Geschichte der Juden in Berlin.* 2 vols. Berlin, 1871.
Geiger, Solomon Zalman, דברי קהלת. Frankfort o.M., 1862.
Goldberg, P. Selvin, *Karaite Liturgy and its Relation to Synagogue Worship.* Manchester University Press, 1957.
(Graanboom) Aaron Moses Isaac ben Abraham, *Sepher Melitz Yosher,* Amsterdam, 5569.
Graetz, Heinrich, *Geschichte der Juden.* Vol. XI. 2nd edition revised by M. Brann. Leipzig, 1900.
Greenwald, L., לתולדות הריפורמציאן הדתית בגרמניא ובאונגריא. Columbus, Ohio, 5708.
Güdemann, M., *Jerusalem, die Opfer und die Orgel.* Vienna, 1871.
Hamburg Beth Din, ed. אלה דברי הברית. Altona, 1819.

Hamburg Temple, *Theologische Gutachten über das Gebetbuch nach dem Gebrauche des Neuen Israelitischen Tempelvereins in Hamburg.* (ed. N. Frankfurter.) Hamburg, 1842.

Harkavy, A., ed. לקוטי קדמוניות, Vol. II. St. Petersburg, 1903.

(Heilpern, S.M.), תשובות באנשי און, האלדהיים וריעיו. Frankfort o. M., 1844.

Heinemann, Joseph, *Prayer in the Period of the Tanna'im and the Amora'im.* (Hebrew.) Jerusalem, Magnes Press, 1964.

Heinemann, Joseph, תפילות ישראל ותולדותיהן. Jerusalem, Hebrew University, 5726.

Heschel, Abraham J., *Man's Quest for God.* New York, Scribner's, 1954.

Hildesheimer, Israel, *Die Geiger'sche Broschüre Nothwendigkeit und Maass einer Reform des jüdischen Gottesdienstes. Beurteilt.* Mainz, 1861.

Hoffmann, David, *Zur Aufklärung über die badische Gebetbuchreform.* Frankfort o.M., n.d.

Holdheim, Samuel, *Geschichte der Entstehung und Entwicklung der jüdischen Reformgemeinde in Berlin.* Berlin, Julius Springer, 1857.

Holdheim, Samuel, *Über das Gebetbuch nach dem Gebrauche des neuen Israelitischen Tempelvereins zu Hamburg. Ein Votum.* Hamburg, Berendsohn, 1841.

Holdheim, Samuel, *Verketzerung und Gewissensfreiheit. Ein zweites Votum in dem Hamburger Tempelstreit.* Schwerin, 1842.

Hyamson, Albert M., *The Sephardim of England.* London, Methuen, 1951.

Hyman, A., אוצר דברי חכמים ופתגמיהם. 3rd printing, Tel-Aviv, Dvir, 1955.

Idelsohn, A. Z., *Jewish Liturgy and Its Development.* New York, Henry Holt, 1932.

Idelsohn, A. Z., *Jewish Music in Its Historical Development.* New York, Henry Holt, 1929.

International Conference of Liberal Jews. London, 1926.

Italiener, Bruno, ed., *Festschrift zum hundertzwanzigjährigen Bestehen des Israelitischen Tempels in Hamburg, 1817–1937.* Hamburg, 1937.

Italiener, Bruno, "The Mussaf—Kedushah," in *HUCA,* Vol. XXVI (1955), pp. 413–424.

Jelski, Julius, *Der Gottesdienst.* Berlin, Poppelauer, 1906.

Jewish Encyclopedia, ed. Isidore Singer, New York, Funk & Wagnalls, 1901–1905. 12 vols.

Jöel, M., *Zur Orientierung in der Cultusfrage.* Breslau, 1869.

Jöel, M., *Zum Schutz gegen "Trutz."* Breslau, 1869.

Joseph, Morris, *Judaism as Creed and Life.* 2nd Edition. London, Routledge, 1910.

Jüdisches Lexikon, ed. G. Herlitz and B. Kirschner. Berlin, Jüdischer Verlag, 1927–1930. 5 vols.

Karl, Zvi, מחקרים בתולדות התפלה. Tel-Aviv, Twersky, 1950.

Leo Baeck Institute, *Year Book V.* London, East and West Library, 1960.

Leimdörfer, D., ed., *Festschrift zum hundertjährigen Bestehen des Israelitischen Tempels in Hamburg.* Hamburg, 1918.

Levin, Moritz, *Die Reform des Judentums.* Festschrift zur Feier des fünfzigjährigen Bestehens der jüdischen Reform-Gemeinde in Berlin. Berlin, 1895.

Lewertoff, A., ed., 50 *Gutachten über das neue "westfälische Gebetbuch" von Rabbiner Dr. Vogelstein.* Höxter a/W., 1895.

Lewin, Adolf, *Geschichte der badischen Juden seit der Regierung Karl Friedrichs* (1738–1909). Karlsruhe, 1909.

Libermann, Eliezer, אור נגה. Dessau, 1818.

Libermann, Eliezer, ed., ספר נוגה הצדק. Dessau, 1818.

Loewengard, M., *Auch einige Worte über das neue Gebetbuch im Hamburger Tempel*. Tübingen, 1842.

Loewenstamm, Abraham, ספר צרור החיים. Amsterdam, 5580.

Löw, Leopold, *Gesammelte Schriften,* ed. Immanuel Löw. Vol. II. Szegedin, 1890.

Löw, Leopold, *Gesammelte Schriften,* ed. Immanuel Löw. Vol. V. Szegedin, 1900.

Luzzatto, Samuel David, מבוא למחזור בני רומא, ed. E.D. Goldschmidt, Tel-Aviv, Devir, 1966.

Maimonides, *Mishneh Torah*. New York, Hotza-ath Rambam, 5716. 5 vols.

Maline, Edward M., *Controversies over the Hamburg Temple Prayer Book*. (Unpublished M.A. thesis in the Hebrew Union College Library) 1963.

Mayence. *Synagogenordnung*. Mayence, (1853?)

Mayer, F.F., *Sammlung der würtembergischen Gesetze in Betreff der Israeliten*. Tübingen, 1847.

Mecklenburg-Schwerin. Der israelitische Oberrath von Mecklenburg-Schwerin, *Den öffentlichen Cultus betreffende Differenzpunkte zwischen den verschiedenen religiösen Partheien*. Schwerin, 1850.

Mishnayoth. Berlin, Schocken, 5697. 2 vols.

Montefiore, Claude G., "Liberal Judaism in England," in *International Conference of Liberal Jews*. London, 1926, pp. 59–65.

Petuchowski, Jakob J., "Alenu," in *The Synagogue Review*. London, January 1951, pp. 141f.

Petuchowski, Jakob J., "Karaite Tendencies in an Early Reform Haggadah." in *HUCA,* Vol. XXXI (1960), pp. 223–49.

Petuchowski, Jakob J., "The Magnification of Chanukah," in *Commentary,* January 1960, pp. 38–43.

Petuchowski, Jakob J., "New Trends in the Liturgy of British Reform Judaism," in *Judaism,* Fall 1966.

Petuchowski, Jakob J., "Reform Prayer out of Zion," in *CCAR Journal,* April 1963, pp. 31–37.

Petuchowski, Jakob J., "Die Sprache des Herzens," in *Tradition und Erneuerung* (St. Gallen, Switzerland), No. 21, May 1966, pp. 342–347.

Petuchowski, Jakob J., *The Theology of Haham David Nieto*. New York, Bloch, 1954.

Petuchowski, Jakob J., „קבע וכוונה בתולדות התפילה בישראל" in *Prozdor* (Tel-Aviv), No. 9/10, April 1965, pp. 27–32.

Philipson, David, *The Reform Movement in Judaism*. New York, Macmillan, 1907.

Philipson, David, *The Reform Movement in Judaism* (New & Revised Edition). New York, Macmillan, 1931.

Philippson, Ludwig, "Geschichte der deutschen Rabbinerversammlungen," in *Allgemeine Zeitung des Judenthums*. Vol. XLVIII. 1884.

Plaut, W. Gunther, *The Growth of Reform Judaism*. New York, World Union for Progressive Judaism, 1965.

Plaut, W. Gunther, *The Rise of Reform Judaism*. New York, World Union for Progressive Judaism, 1963.

Pool, David de Sola, *The Old Jewish-Aramaic Prayer, the Kaddish*. Leipzig, 1909.

Protocolle der ersten Rabbiner-Versammlung. Brunswick, 1844.

Protokolle und Aktenstücke der zweiten Rabbiner-Versammlung. Frankfort o.M., 1845.

Protokolle der dritten Versammlung deutscher Rabbiner, abgehalten zu Breslau, vom 13. bis 24 Juli 1846. Breslau, 1847.
Referate über die der ersten israelitischen Synode zu Leipzig überreichten Anträge. Berlin, 1871.
Reggio, Isaac S., ed., בחינת הקבלה. Gorizia, 1852.
Ritter, Immanuel Heinrich, *Die jüdische Reformgemeinde zu Berlin und die Verwirklichung der jüdischen Reformideen innerhalb derselben*. Ed. S. Samuel. Berlin, Emil Apolant, 1902.
Ritter, Immanuel Heinrich, *Samuel Holdheim. Sein Leben und seine Werke*. Berlin, 1865.
Rivkin, Ellis, *Leon Da Modena and the Kol Sakhal*. Cincinnati, HUC Press, 1952.
Rosenthal, Erwin, "Ismar Elbogen and the New Jewish Learning," in *Year Book of the Leo Baeck Institute*. Vol. VIII. London, 1963, pp. 3–28.
Rothschild, Lothar, "Ergänzender Hinweis," in *Tradition und Erneuerung* (St. Gallen, Switzerland), No. 21. May 1966, pp. 348–350.
Rothschild, Lothar, *Im Strom der Zeit—Hundert Jahre Israelitische Gemeinde St. Gallen*. St. Gallen, 1963.
Saalschütz, J.L., *Hauptprincipien bei Entwerfung einer zeitgemässen Liturgie für den Israelitischen Gottesdienst*. Königsberg, 1845.
Salomon, Gotthold, *Kurzgefasste Geschichte des Neuen Israelitischen Tempels in Hamburg*. Hamburg, 1844.
Salomon, Gotthold, *Das Neue Gebetbuch und seine Verketzerung*. Hamburg, 1841.
Salomon, Gotthold, *Sendschreiben an den Herrn Dr. Z. Frankel*. Hamburg, 1842.
Schauss, Hayyim, *The Jewish Festivals*. Cincinnati, UAHC, 1938.
Schlesinger, Samuel, et al., eds., *Zulässigkeit und Dringlichkeit der Synagogen-Reformen*. Vienna, 1845
Schreiber, Emanuel, *Reformed Judaism and Its Pioneers*. Spokane, Washington, 1892.
Schwab, Hermann, *The History of Orthodox Jewry in Germany*, London, The Mitre Press, n.d.
Second Conference of the World Union for Progressive Judaism, London, 1930. London, 1930.
Seligmann, Caesar, *Denkschrift zu dem im Auftrag der israelitischen Gemeinde in Frankfurt, a.M. bearbeiteten neuen israelitischen Gebetbuch*. Frankfort o.M., 1912.
Seligmann, Caesar, *Geschichte der Jüdischen Reformbewegung*. Frankfort o.M., 1922.
Seligmann, Caesar, "Zum hundertjährigen Geburtstag Abraham Geigers," in *Liberales Judentum*, Vol. II (1910), pp. 97–104.
Selinger, Max, *Samuel Holdheim: Theologian of Early Reform Judaism*. (Unpublished D.H.L. thesis in the H.U.C. Library) 1962.
Sepher Ḥasidim, ed. Margalioth. Jerusalem, Mosad Harav Kook, 5717.
Sepher Ḥasidim, ed. Wistinetski. Frankfort o.M., Wahrmann, 1924.
Shulḥan 'Arukh. New York, Otzar Halacha, 1959/61. 10 vols.
Silberman, Lou H. *American Impact—Judaism in the United States in the Nineteenth Century*. Syracuse University, the B.G. Rudolph Lectures in Judaic Studies, 1964.
Sinasohn, Max, *Adass Jisroel Berlin*. Jerusalem, 1966.
(M. Steckelmacher?) *Denkschrift zur Begründung des von dem Grossherzoglich Badischen Oberrate der Israeliten herausgegebenen Gebetbuchentwurfs*. Karlsruhe, n.d.

Steckelmacher, Moritz *Widerlegung des Sendschreibens des Dr. D. Hoffmann . . .* Mannheim, Mannheimer Vereinsdruckerei, n.d.
Stein, Leopold, "Bericht über das, für die neue Hauptsynagoge zu Frankfurt am Main anzufertigende neue Gebetbuch," in *Der Israelitische Volkslehrer*, Frankfort o.M., 1855, Vol. V, pp. 165–195.
Stein, Leopold, *Plan des neuen Gebetbuches für die öffentliche Gottesverehrung der Israeliten*. n.d.
Stern, Heinrich, "Die Entwicklung des Deutschen Liberalen Judentums," in *International Conference of Liberal Jews*. London, 1926, p. 46.
Talmud Babli. Vilna, Romm, 1895/1897. 18 vols.
Temkin, Sefton D., *The Liturgy of the West London Synagogue of British Jews*. (Unpublished Ph.D. "Minor" thesis in the H.U.C. Library.) 1963.
Trepp, Leo, *Die Landesgemeinde der Juden in Oldenburg*. Oldenburg, 1965.
Verhandlungen der ersten israelitischen Synode zu Leipzig vom 29. Juni bis 4. Juli 1869. Berlin, 1869.
Verhandlungen der zweiten israelitischen Synode zu Augsburg vom 11. bis 17. Juli 1871. Berlin, 1873.
Weizenbaum, Joseph S., *An Analysis of Nogah Tsedek*. (Unpublished D.H.L. thesis in the H.U.C. Library.) 1962.
Westphalia. *Bekanntmachung wegen besserer Einrichtung des Gottesdiensts in den Synagogen des Königreichs Westphalen*. Cassel, 1810.
Westphalia. *Gutachtensammlung, das Vogelstein'sche Gebetbuch betreffend*, herausgegeben vom Ausschuss des Verbandes der Synagogen-Gemeinden Westfalens. 1896.
Wiener, A., *Der Oeffentliche Gottesdienst, ein Wort zur Beherzigung gerichtet an denkende Israeliten, gewidmet der künftigen israelitischen Synode*. Oppeln, 1873.
Wiener, Max, *Abraham Geiger and Liberal Judaism*. Philadelphia, J.P.S., 1962.
Wilhelm, Kurt, "The Jewish Community in the Post-Emancipation Period," in *Year Book of the Leo Baeck Institute*. Vol. II. London, 1957. pp. 47ff.
Wischnitzer, Rachel, *The Architecture of European Synagogues*. Philadelphia, Jewish Publication Society, 1964.
Wohlgemuth, J., *Der badische Gebetbuchentwurf und die Denkschrift des Oberrats. Ein Brief an die Gesetzestreuen Badens*. Frankfort o.M., 1907.
Wolff, A.A., *Die Stimmen der ältesten glaubwürdigsten Rabbinen über die Pijutim*. Leipzig, 1857.
Wolff, Henrik, "Liberal Judaism in Sweden," in *International Conference of Liberal Jews*. London, 1926, pp. 68–70.
World Union for Progressive Judaism. *Second Conference*. London, 1930.
World Union for Progressive Judaism, *Report of the Third Conference*. London, 1934.
Württemberg. *Gottesdienst-Ordnung für die Synagogen des Königreichs Württemberg. Unter höchster Genehmigung festgesetzt von der Königlich israelitischen Ober-Kirchen-Behörde*. Stuttgart, 1838.
Zunz, Leopold, *Gesammelte Schriften*, Vol. II. Berlin, 1876.

Index

I. INDEX OF NAMES

II. INDEX OF HEBREW PRAYERS

III. SUBJECT INDEX